IN RELIEF OF GORDON

General Garnet J. Wolseley

IN RELIEF OF GORDON

Wolseley, Garnet

LORD WOLSELEY'S CAMPAIGN JOURNAL OF

The Khartoum Relief Expedition 1884-1885

EDITED BY

ADRIAN PRESTON

RUTHERFORD · MADISON · TEANECK
FAIRLEIGH DICKINSON UNIVERSITY PRESS

IN RELIEF OF GORDON. © Introduction and Notes,
Adrian Preston 1967. First American edition
published 1970 by Associated University Presses, Inc.,
Cranbury, New Jersey 08512

Library of Congress Catalogue Card Number: 79-92562

SBN: 8386 7572 7

Printed in the United States of America

To my parents
WILLIAM AND LILIAN PRESTON
who have been a constant source
of wisdom and inspiration

and to my daughter
HEATHER ELIZABETH

Contents

Preface ix
Introduction xiii
Journal 3
Bibliographical note 239
Notes 241
Index 261

Illustrations

General Garnet J. Wolseley (frontispiece) (*Public Archives of Canada*)

Between pages 116–117
General Gordon (*Public Archives of Canada*)
The Wells at Handoub: Lancers watering their horses.
Lord Wolseley inspecting the garrison at Otao.
Royal Engineers clearing the railway of burning sleepers near Suakim.
The Nile at Assuan, with the encampments of British troops.
Pulling through the rapids near Owli Island.
The march through the desert to Gubat.
The 'Square' at the battle of Abu Kru, fought by Sir Charles Wilson.
Lieutenant Stuart-Wortley bringing the news of the fall of Khartoum to the camp at Metemmah.
Sir Charles Wilson interrogating the last messenger from Khartoum.
Wilson's steamer rounding the bend of Tuti Island to find that Khartoum had fallen.
Lord Charles Beresford directing a cattle raid from one of Gordon's steamers.
Redoubt held by the Australians.
Consulting guides during Stewart's march from Korti to Jakdul.
Lord Wolseley's headquarters at Korti.

Map (facing page 3) The Sudan

Preface

This edition of Wolseley's campaign journal of the Khartoum Relief Expedition is the result of a few leisure hours set aside while working towards a Ph.D. under Professor Michael Howard in the Department of War Studies, London.

The genesis of this work is not perhaps without interest as an example of historical detective-work. In 1963, I returned to England after a long absence abroad dissatisfied with the peacetime prospects of the Canadian Army and the professional's attitude toward the study of war. Four years' tough tutelage under Professor G. F. G. Stanley at R.M.C., and another year under the singular direction of Colonel C. P. Stacey, Official Historian of the Canadian Army, then at the University of Toronto, inculcated a deep interest in military history.

I had two main projects in mind: a study of British military thought from 1853 to 1914; or a study of Wolseley as a reformer, 1871–1900. From undertaking the former I was easily dissuaded by the discovery that Professor J. Luvaas was on the point of publishing a book identical in object but wider in scope. I then began seriously to research upon Wolseley and the question of reform in the British Army; but after three months digging it became clear to me that not much could be made of this until such time as a comprehensive study of British military policy from 1871 to 1900, analogous to Marder's naval policy series, had been written. This I determined, on New Year's Day, 1964, to write. By New Year's Day, 1965, after much adventure, long scooter-rides and heavy correspondence, I had completed the research for the first volume, and immediately began to compose—a task that was to bedevil my thoughts for exactly another year, and result in a Ph.D.

My brief incursions into Wolseley's private correspondence—at Hove and at the R.U.S.I.—had convinced me that he was not altogether an attractive person. Moreover, the vast bulk of his demi-official correspondence and campaign journals appeared to have been lost or destroyed as a result of a family dispute. The Hove Collection contained only autograph specimens and Wolseley's early family correspondence from 1852 to 1871 which, while invaluable for a study of the young Wolseley, contained but a handful of letters dealing with the most vital period of his career. The War Office Collection concentrated, but merely duplicated, what was scattered elsewhere throughout the Public Record Office. There seemed little point in wasting more time on Wolseley and Reform; and I concentrated thereafter upon the wider problem of British military policy. When I had made considerable progress, however, I was blessed with a windfall, admittedly unexpected but not entirely useful for my immediate purposes: the Historical Manuscripts Commission and Public Record Office had at my prodding succeeded in unearthing Wolseley's few remaining, hitherto unpublished, campaign diaries.

Now Wolseley's earliest journals recording his experiences in Burma, the Crimea, India and China had either been lost in shipwreck or destroyed in warehouse fire. After his marriage, however, Wolseley took the precaution of despatching them in weekly bundles (or as the exigencies of the postal service permitted) to his wife who preserved them in brown canvas pouches marked according to campaign. As the contemporary, day-to-day accounts by one of the ablest and most controversial generals and colonial administrators of the mid-Victorian Empire, they are invaluable sources of historical evidence. Unfortunately, their quality is uneven and there are serious and unaccountable gaps. The Ashanti and Cyprus journals are incomplete; the journal of operations in Egypt, 1882, is altogether missing. The diaries of the Zulu War and the Khartoum Relief Expedition alone are complete: they are also the most revealing.

It was Wolseley's invariable habit through life to rise between 4 and 5 a.m., despatching his official and private correspondence and bringing his diaries up to date. For the most part these were compiled on foolscap-size sheets of blue War Office minute paper; and the writing necessarily took place under all conceivable active-service conditions. Nevertheless, Wolseley wrote freely and without correction. He concealed no military secrets from his wife; a common but dangerous practice among our generals that shows no signs of diminishing. Judging from the pencilled marginalia, occasional excisions and heavy over-writing, it would appear that Wolseley intended publishing these journals, in part or in whole, as a sequel to the *Story of a Soldier's Life* which, in fact, ends where the journals begin. Extracts were also later incorporated by Maurice and Arthur in their *Life of Lord Wolseley*.

Although Wolseley may have been reticent and generous of praise in public life, his diaries spare no criticism. Rivals and colleagues alike are treated in the same indiscriminate fashion. Most illuminating of all are Wolseley's harsh comments upon his closest Ring companions which go far to dispel the illusion of their legendary corporateness. Wood emerges as a vain and deceitful intriguer; Brackenbury, able, shifty and unscrupulous; Butler, exuberant but pontifical; Buller, uncertain of himself and in need of close supervision. Hamley, Sir Andrew Clarke, Admiral Lord John Hay, Sir Frederick Stephenson and Sir Charles Wilson, who had opposed the 'river' route or elsewhere questioned Wolseley's generalship, are given short shrift; and were unjustly slighted in the belated *Official History*. The war correspondents, the Cabinet and the Horse Guards receive the same unsalutory treatment. Thus, the image that Wolseley's diaries evokes—a slightly pompous, cynical and uncharitable general, unsure of himself probably for the first time in his life yet still managing to retain a sense of sour humour—contradicts legend, and complements the more idealistic sketch that Professor Lehman has recently drawn.

All historians should possess a diploma in advanced criminology; their lists of acknowledgements might then possibly be shorter. I wish to record my sense of indebtedness to the Historical Manuscripts Commission, in particular Mr. Alan Bell, who inadvertently pointed the way to the diaries and has shown me many kindnesses. The Secretary of the Public Record Office allowed me fully to transcribe the diaries before they were properly registered and publicly shelved; and has given me permission to publish Wolseley's correspondence to Buller. To Jack Dove, Borough

Archivist and Curator at Hove, and his assistant, Mr. Harry Parkinson, I render a special thanks. Research for the introduction involved long early rides from London to Hove on bitter November mornings. Often I arrived drenched, half-frozen and too stiff to write. I shall never forget the warmth of their Northern hospitality—the hot drinks, the massive meals, the strict guardianship of my privacy—that they unstintingly and characteristically afforded me, a total stranger. I have often prospered from the wise counsel of my colleague, Dr. Lucien Brault, who acted on my behalf, in his own time, to procure for me from the Public Archives of Canada copies of the photographs relating to the Canadian Nile Contingent. For permission to publish the photographs, I am indebted to the P.A.C. My brother Brian—draftsman, cartographer and teacher—kindly consented to find time in a busy schedule to draw the maps. I reserve my final remarks for one who has shared all with me for more than eight years, tramped and camped beside me in my travels or following the drum, and provided the strongest and best incentive to effort. Absolutely selfless, ambitious only for my career whatever it may be, cheerfully bearing my growing absorption in military affairs and the many inevitable separations which befell us, she above all has made this book possible.

A.W.P.

Purdy's Grove, Collins Bay.

Introduction

I

If anybody could be claimed as the embodiment of the mid-Victorian Army, it would undoubtedly be Sir Garnet Wolseley—self-advertising hero and reformer, victor of Tel-el-Kebir, friend of Gordon, and in his later days President of the Society for the Prevention of Bad Language. That he was the father of the modern British Army is a contention more difficult to support. That, given the opportunity of command in a war against a major European power, he would have proved himself one of the 'Great Captains' of history is to be doubted still further.

When Wolseley left Charing Cross Station for Cairo on 31 August 1884, he was embarking, although he did not know it, upon his last command. He was then fifty-one years old—not unduly advanced in age so far as British generals go—was occasionally forgetful, a Peer of the Realm, and convinced, as were many of his closest admirers, that he was the greatest commander his country had produced since Wellington. He was content to think that his most coveted ambitions and his most strenuous achievements were now behind him. Cough syrup and boot-polish manufacturers, as well as music-hall lyricists, who used his brand name to admonish the public, helped to perpetuate the legend of his enduring effectiveness. 'All Sir Garnet' became the universal tonic for every national ailment.

Yet the proud tower of this image was riven with cracks and controversy. His reputation as an Army Reformer was fatally committed to a system that was already breaking down and failing to respond adequately or promptly to the needs of Imperial defence. The Queen and the Duke of Cambridge were not alone in their suspicions that Wolseley, for all his talk about improving the national military condition, was a self-seeking, dangerous and irresponsible firebrand, a radical who would stoop to anything to usurp the military prerogatives of the Crown. Moreover, history has since shown that the various small wars and expeditions in which he held the chief command, though lacking nothing in his conduct of them, were yet not sufficiently important or exacting to distinguish him as a great commander or to contribute very materially to his country's safety or pre-eminence. Yet in August 1884, so confused, desperate and precarious was the Government's political position, so clamorous the demand to retrieve the honour of England's armies and to arrest her declining international prestige, so persistently did Wolseley's name ring at the mention of military adventure, that there could be no other choice.

For months past, since January, public attention has been riveted on the spectacle of Gordon's investment in Khartoum. Most historians and critics of this seige have concentrated almost exclusively upon the dramatic circumstances of Gordon's heroic defence rather than upon the nature of the expedition sent to relieve him and the soldier who conducted it. It has been largely assumed that Wolseley's failure to reach Khartoum in time was inherent in the Cabinet's prior dilatoriness and almost criminal procrastination. But this is by no means the whole story, for it presumes a soundness of conception, a thoroughness of preparation and a faultlessness of execution that were not at all evident in Wolseley's conduct of the campaign. Indeed, Wolseley's expedition has a greater significance than that of an abortive Homeric gesture towards perhaps the most eccentric and expendable of Britain's military geniuses. It was the crucial turning point in Wolseley's professional career and in the course of British defence policy alike. The last of a succession of mismanaged enterprises that had begun on the fields of Isandhlana, the Khartoum Relief Expedition foreshadowed all the deficiencies in training, administration and command that afflicted the British Army until the Boer War. It provided the final conclusive argument for those who sought the introduction of a General Staff and the creation of a Committee of Imperial Defence.

II

Wolseley was born at Golden Bridge House, near Dublin, on 4 June 1833—the same year as Gordon—the eldest of seven variously gifted children. As it was with his chief Indian rivals, Napier and Roberts, no public school guided Wolseley's early footsteps. Extravagance, the curse of most Irish families that have provided so much good British generalship, had impoverished his parents, and only a day-school in Dublin was within his mother's means to provide him with an education. But if Wolseley's own account of his boyhood is to be believed, he was an omnivorous reader, cramming his head with Hume's *History of England*, Alison's *History of Europe*, Caesar's *Commentaries* and Napier's *Peninsular War*, and 'devouring every work on the theory and practice of war' that he 'could beg, borrow or afford to buy'. Wolseley's father, penniless, irascible but proud, had sold out as a major but died before his son was seven years old. Nevertheless, the seed had been transplanted, and at the age of nineteen, in consideration of his father's somewhat unrequited services, Wolseley was given a commission in the infantry, which he could never have purchased for himself.

Wolseley was fortunate in his hour of joining the Army. After a long spell of peace and stagnation—excepting some Indian entanglements, dealt with, not always creditably, by local forces—wars emerged serious enough to engage the full strength of England, and give her considerable anxiety. Wolseley received his baptism of fire in some minor operations in Burma in 1852, during which he displayed conspicuous energy and gallantry, and was severely wounded. Recovering in time, he fought in the Crimea where he lost the sight of one eye before Sebastopol and where his service on the Staff, as a volunteer assistant engineer, brought him for the first time 'amongst all those in authority'. He was then, after experiencing a shipwreck and the loss of all his early diaries, busily engaged in the suppression of the Indian Mutiny, 'police duty,' he described it, 'and quite derogatory to a soldier's profession'; and finally saw less serious service in China on the Staff of Sir Hope Grant for whom he had a great admiration and to whom he was to dedicate his maiden literary venture, the *Narrative of the War in China*, a financial failure written over the Canadian winter 1861–2 when he was but twenty-eight.

This period of nine years brought to a close Wolseley's career of subordinate war service in a series of minor localised conflicts where there was at no time much possibility of failure or protracted warfare. Except for the Crimea, his experiences had been confined almost exclusively to Asiatic warfare—guerrilla and punitory expeditions. In future, he always took the field as the commander. It was without doubt a unique record of war service, accompanied by an equally distinguished record of promotion. Indeed, Wolseley had made the most of his opportunities. At twenty-seven, he was a major and prospective brevet-colonel, conscious that his career so far 'has been such a wonderful collection of fortunate circumstances' that he need never despair for future employment and advancement, and convinced that 'his destiny was war'. His extensive activities had brought him into contact with colleagues such as Evelyn Wood, Charles Gordon and Frederick Stephenson who would themselves attain positions of great authority or notoriety and were destined to meet again under more dramatic circumstances in 1884–5. He had been sufficiently perceptive to note that 'in future . . . the new arrangements for the Senior Department at Sandhurst or rather as it is now called the Staff College . . . will be the Grand Key to all good appointments and promotion,' and although he never passed through himself, the constitution of the Wolseley Ring shows how thoroughly he was prepared to advance the principle. Moreover, the Crimean War and the possibility three years later of Britain's involvement in the Austro-Italian War (1859) had kindled an unquenchable and ultimately unfulfilled desire—the dominant root of his ambition—to distinguish himself or die, in the fashion of Wolfe, Abercrombie and Moore, 'some day or other . . . winning a great victory, that will add great lustre to the renown and contribute to the security of our Empire, and that my name may be handed down to posterity in connection with that event'.

Wolseley left China forever in the winter of 1860, and although he struggled for ten years to acquire the Indian Command, never returned to fight or command in the East. From 1871 until the end of his active career in 1900, Wolseley's reputation as a General and colonial administrator was to hinge very much upon operations which—excepting the expedition to Cyprus which may nevertheless be considered an outwork of Suez—were conducted in some part of Africa. But his entrance into the arena of command, theorising and reform took place in North America.

Wolseley contributed almost a decade of service to the defence of Canada. Distinguished by his war honours, Wolseley was sent to Canada on the Staff of the detachment of the British Army quartered there, specially enlarged to deal with any emergencies that might arise from the American Civil War. Characteristically, Wolseley's mercurial imagination had envisaged the possibility of a major rupture with the Union States—an opportunity pregnant with infinite distinction—and it was with this in mind that he undertook his unofficial reconnaissance to the Confederate Headquarters in the autumn of 1862. By 1863, however, presumably because of the turning of the Union tide, the inescapability of Confederate defeat and the improbability of British intervention, Wolseley had lost all interest in the Civil War. His correspondence reflects the pinch of boredom, the consciousness of restrained ambitions and diminishing chances of experience and promotion the horror or prolonged stagnation in a colonial outpost, and extravagant dreams of European wars. Increasingly he becomes preoccupied with the ideas of marriage and foreign postings—to India, China or Japan. Nevertheless, the Fenian 'scares' that in the aftermath of the Civil War were to trouble Canadian-American border relations from 1865 to 1871 fortuitously provided him with his first agreeable opportunities of handling large formations of troops composed of elements of all arms. His successive appointments to the command of the Camps of Instruction and Observation at Thorold and Laprairie, and the brisk and enthusiastic discharge of his duties attracted the attention and respect of the Canadian authorities, earning him the command of the Red River Expedition in 1870, the logistical foundations of which had been theoretically and minutely foreshadowed in Wolseley's needlessly provocative but highly successful manual of small-war administration and tactics that was written intermittently between 1865 and 1869 as *The Soldier's hand Book in War*. The Red River Expedition, essentially, like the inglorious Nile Expedition, a professionally frustrating errand of peace not war, and involving the movement of 1,200 men 600 miles through a wilderness of rock, scrub and water, was Wolseley's first independent command and a cameo of logistical planning. Its bloodless success and the advertisement it received and continued to receive from the *Soldier's Pocket Book* (which in turn came to be popularly regarded as the recipe for unfailing and ubiquitous victory), left an indelible mark upon the few inflexible strategic concepts that Wolseley—impressionable, opportunist, and at the peak of his powers—possessed. Its unique character as a conflict rather against elements than men—the deceptive cheapness and ease of accomplishment, the improvisation of its logistic support, the reliance upon picked forces and the extensive use of inland river transport—decisively shaped the nature and conduct of Wolseley's operations in West Africa in 1873–4 and his projected plans for carrying war into Central Asia during the war-crisis with Russia from 1876 to 1880. Indeed, it would appear to have become a strategical fixation and —in the case of the Khartoum Relief Expedition, when conditions and circumstances were wholly different—an obsession that was to prove fatal, to Gordon and Wolseley alike.

Knighted for his services at Fort Garry, Wolseley was routinely posted after six months' leave to the War Office where the bulk of Cardwell's reform programme was already in its last stages of completion. It is usually young men who profit most from revolution and Wolseley, long effectually divorced from the mainstream of military thought and reconstruction that had been simmering since Herbert's day, rapidly became deeply involved in the obscure politics of reform agitation and soon became its self-appointed leader. Wolseley's reputation as an influential reformer—at Cardwell's elbow— has been grossly overrated. He was an agitator and publicist advancing opportune prospects of increased professional power and promotion rather than a thoughtful and constructive innovator genuinely disinterested in the national military condition. It is true that Wolseley, as many other junior colonels did, contributed an important share in sustaining the momentum of reform during the dying days of the Liberal administration; but his contribution—belated, out-of-touch, and inexperienced—was not that of initiative and could not have been permanent or decisive. Nevertheless, Wolseley's professional fortunes were from now onwards publicly committed to and identified with the Cardwellian system. In the most initimate sense, they became and remained interdependent, and the steady corrosion of the latter from political and other extraneous and irreducible influences that began to emasculate the system from the very start, was inescapably accompanied by Wolseley's decline and discredit, so strikingly manifested by the Khartoum Relief Expedition and the Boer War.

Wolseley emerged from the labours and intrigues of the Army revolution still a relatively obscure Colonel without social position or official support but nonetheless an object of uneasiness to the

Court and the Royal Duke, of virulent suspicion and distrust to the old school of officers, of interest to the younger and the public (who since the Crimea had watched a new kind of professionalism emerge in four major European wars), and with some claim to political gratitude. In 1872, he was offered the influential post of Military Secretary to Lord Northbrook, the Viceroy newly appointed upon Lord Mayo's assassination, but felt compelled to decline because of his wife's pregnancy. Again in 1873 and 1874 he turned down repeated offers of the Adjutant-Generalship of the Indian Armies and the newly created post of General Officer Commanding, Canadian Militia to secure what he believed to be a more important appointment—the command of the Ashanti campaign. Like that of the Red River Expedition, the object in view was not a serious or difficult military operation, the climate, strangeness of conditions, and necessity for economy being the most formidable obstacles. But again Wolseley had to improvise his instrument, foresee much that was difficult to calculate and organise efficiently his resources. This he did with characteristic zeal, efficiency and thoroughness. But the effect of his repeated success was to confirm the conceptual validity of the Red River strategy and to reassure Wolseley, in spite of altogether novel and unforseeable conditions, in the perpetuation of its use in the Sudan in 1884.

Perhaps the most interesting and undoubtedly the most controversial feature of this campaign was the birth of the Wolseley 'Ring'. The Queen's illogical refusal to permit the formal creation of a General Staff as the natural concomitant to abolition of purchase had provided fertile conditions for the creation and growth of that vicious 'ring' system—unofficial improvised general staffs for operational purposes, often rival, hostile and subversive of the ancient officer corps—that characterised the late Victorian British-Indian Armies in a way that results detrimental to efficiency and esprit de corps were bound to follow. 'The idea that any promiscuous group of officers who will work in tolerable harmony can form a staff', wrote Wolseley's most trenchant critic, Colonel G. S. Clarke, 'is opposed to the whole teaching of modern war.' It is perhaps incontrovertible that Wolseley's youthful lieutenants possessed more than their share of brains, courage and energy, that their willing subordination in the pursuit of glory and promotion ensured a captive harmony, and that performing as a composite whole they constituted an engine of extraordinary and diverse force adapted to a wide range of uses. But it is open to question whether some of them did not attain positions beyond their capacity, whether other and better men could not have been produced by some other system than that of a selected band earning all the current military distinction, and whether this—or indeed any—staff organisation whose efficacy is dependent upon a closed and intact membership, foregone harmonious relations and patent favouritism is fitted to cope with the demands of modern warfare, especially when those conditions can no longer be maintained.

The Khartoum Relief Expedition ruthlessly exposed all the vicious practices, abuses and weaknesses to which this unique staff system, so consistently advanced by Wolseley in the blind interests of self-advancement, was susceptible, although its full demise—and by implication that of Wolseley—was concealed and delayed until the Boer War by the passionate debates evoked by Gordon's fate and the few indestructible fibres remaining of the Wolseley mystique. The dispute over the Nile route as opposed to the Suakim–Berber railway strikingly showed how the ascendancy of one particular ring, in total ignorance of local topographical, geographical, logistical and military conditions and in defiance of a formidable array of technical opinion—intelligence, naval and engineering—could distort the impartiality of its strategic advice upon which the politicians relied, and upon which the successful prosecution of its subsequent operations depended. The shabby treatment accorded to Sir John Glover in Ashanti, Lord Chelmsford in Zululand, Sir Edward Hamley in Egypt and finally to Sir Charles Wilson in the Sudan revealed the vindictiveness of which the 'Ring' was capable when its views were opposed or its reputation questioned. By 1884, the 'Ring' itself was riven with dissensions and intestine disputes, or otherwise fatally weakened by the loss of some of its members. Colonel Robert Home had died in 1879 from typhoid fever contracted while serving as British Commissioner on the Bulgarian Frontier Delimitation Commission. Major-General Sir George Pomeroy Colley had been killed in 1881 at Majuba Hill after committing certain irretrievable tactical errors. By 1882, Wolseley's chief lieutenants, Buller, Brackenbury, Wood and Butler, had attained sufficient rank which not only made it difficult to justify their employment as a group in a small colonial expedition but also ensured a degree of awkward fractiousness and sullen non-co-operation that, as the succession struggle at the Duke of Cambridge's resignation later showed, developed to challenge Wolseley's own hitherto unchallengeable position. Finally, a rampant favouritism had caused Wolseley's staff system to become intolerably overgrown and unwieldy with superfluous special-service officers, such as Colonel Stanley Clarke, whose professional qualifications were questionable but whose claims Wolseley's snobbery could not disregard. All these things were to contribute to the failure to extricate Gordon from Khartoum.

Wolseley returned from Ashanti a seemingly indispensable national hero, fortified by a prestige and popularity that now overshadowed Napier's, commanding the public and official support that was required to sustain reform agitation in the face of royal obstructionism, and with revived preoccupations about capturing the Indian Command now that Disraeli's inauguration of an aggressive imperial policy and the reopening of the 'defence of India' question made war with Russia seem more than an imminent probability. But in the space of five crucial years, events were to show that although he was mooted in early 1876 as a likely successor to General Sir Patrick MacDougall as Head of the Intelligence Department, although in October 1876 he was seconded to the India Office as Military Member of the Home Council ostensibly to advise on Indian strategy and defence policy, although in that capacity he submitted numerous unsolicited memoranda on Indian army reform and grand strategy, and although both Lord Lytton, the Viceroy and Colley, his Military Secretary worked unsparingly to get Wolseley to India as supreme Frontier Commissioner or Commander-in-Chief, Wolseley singularly failed to exert much material influence upon the definition of a realistic War Office or Cabinet policy concerning the defence of India—partly because of his ignorance of Indian conditions but primarily because his ebullient militarism was suspect and inconsistent with the combustible state of international affairs—and he was compelled to accept a succession of pseudo-political appointments to Natal in 1875, Cyprus in 1878 and Zululand in 1879, which, while earning him much distinction as a colonial administrator, and enabling him to advance the interests of the Ring, did nothing to enhance his military reputation or to facilitate his chances of the supreme command in a major European war. Indeed, for once, the Queen, the Cabinet and the Horse Guards were at one in their reluctance to entrust such a command to one 'so celebrated and notorious'. The special defensive nature of the operations contemplated in Europe called for an engineer Commander-in-Chief designate such as the Inspector-General of Fortifications, Sir Lintorn Simmons or the former Commander-in-Chief of India, Lord Napier, and Wolseley was relegated to a Divisional Command or Chief of Staff. As for India, the recommendations of Lytton and the Simla Commission to remove the Commander-in-Chief from the Supreme Council, abolish the Presidential Armies and institute a General Staff, combined with Wolseley's somewhat indiscreet and irregular methods in advertising his claim to the Indian Command, filled the Duke of Cambridge and the Indian High Command—Sir Frederick Haines, Commander-in-Chief, and Sir Edwin Johnson, Military Member—with implacable alarm, and they detected in the silent congregation of 'Wolseley' men seeking Afghan service 'a great *plot*, for Wolseley to be put at the head of the Indian Armies worked by Colley, when he would be surrounded by Greaves, Baker, Baker Russell, all his *own men*, and the Governor General being in the hands of Colley ... dangerous, most ambitious, full of theories of his own ... whatever those may be ... and the representative and Apostle of those of his bosum friend Sir Garnet Wolseley ... and then the Indian Armies would be destroyed and upset in all their old traditions and details as he has done in our own Army by his introduction of all the new fangled notions and ideas, which we are now suffering from to such a deplorable extent. ...' The Duke of Cambridge would no longer hold himself responsible for the military condition of the Empire if Wolseley became Commander-in-Chief in India.

Exploiting the full weight of the Queen's position, Stanley's feebleness of character, Cranbrook's reluctance to engage in controversy, the Cabinet's absorption in election affairs, and the Liberal Government's aversion to an aggressive military policy in India, the Duke of Cambridge managed to prolong Wolseley's appointment in South Africa until such time as a compromise solution could be worked out: the cautious Sir Donald Stewart or Sir Neville Chamberlain rather than Wolseley would replace Haines as Commander-in-Chief; Wolseley would be kept in England as Quarter-Master-General; while Colley would be removed from India to replace Wolseley in South Africa. In this way, wrote the Duke of Cambridge, 'we should then get rid of several awkward susceptibilities which otherwise would probably give trouble'.

Wolseley's failure markedly to influence the course of British military policy during the Eastern crisis and his inability, in spite of all efforts, to succeed to the Indian command signified the real beginnings of his decline. Within months Colley—the ablest of the Ring—was unaccountably defeated at Majuba, and Wood became the instrument of what amounted to an ignominious surrender. In India, the competitive and potentially hostile counterweight of an Indian school of reform had unexpectedly arisen centred on Roberts and growing out of the Second Afghan War and the Simla Commission. The appointment of the Airey Commission symbolised the doubts cast upon the war effectiveness of the Cardwellian system. In Whitehall, the death of Disraeli and the insanity of Cardwell deprived Wolseley of his chief political supporters at a time when he was the object of intense Gladstonian suspicion and distrust for his part in the acquisition of Cyprus and the pacification of Zululand. At the Horse Guards and at Court, Wolseley's virtually continuous employment for five years by a Prime Minister who deliberately refused to consult his Commander-in-Chief about any aspects of military policy; his steady public flogging of the reform horse; his irregular attempts to influence military policy through the Press and unsolicited memoranda; his sinister creation of a school of special-service officers and his ambitious inveigling to obtain the Indian Command—all seemed to constitute a direct challenge to the Duke of Cambridge's authority and prestige, and a concerted effort to usurp the military prerogatives of the Crown.

Against the gathering hostility of such men and events, Wolseley fought desperately to eliminate the precariousness of his position and to prove the worth of the reformed system to which he was committed. His great opportunity now seemed at hand—the suppression of Arabi Pasha's rebellion against the Khedive of Egypt. This campaign culminating in the brilliant little action of Tel-el-Kebir, memorably distinguished by the night march in battle formation—a manoeuvre almost unprecedented and seldom copied—proved the meridian of Wolseley's operational experience, and a refreshing contrast to the patchwork of muddling confusion and reverses that overtook the Nile campaign two years later. It was not a severe task; but the conditions were novel, the British army untried and inexperienced, and time and economy—always Gladstone's ransom for honours—were important factors. Nevertheless, the image of total victory was marred by a damaging literary feud with Hamley and G. S. Clarke over the role of the Second Division. With the forthcoming long-coveted peerage and his final acclamation as a great commander, Wolseley seemed to have achieved all his material ambitions; attainments which, shortly followed by the death of his mother, robbed him in some degree of purpose and direction and spoiled his good sense and discretion. In the sequel to the Egyptian campaign, the effort to extricate Gordon from the Sudan, Wolseley was to prove less happy in the result.

III

To the new Liberal Government which had been returned after a violent anti-annexationist campaign and was disentangling itself with unblushing haste from the coils of the Armenian Convention and the Zulu, Afghan and Boer Wars, the need to underwrite the Egyptian Exchequer with a naval bombardment, a punitory expedition and a military occupation that could hardly be described as philanthropic, nor considered to have the virtues of a crusade, posed a moral paradox that it could never persuade itself to resolve and was at root responsible for the shifty evasions and fatal procrastinations that led infallibly to Gordon's death. For, on the morrow of Tel-el-Kebir, Gladstone's problem, however reluctantly he might admit it, was how best to encourage the growth of a stable government and economy in Egypt consistent with Liberal principles yet at the same time ensure the protection of the Suez Canal and curb the intrusion of French and Turkish influence and a return to the anarchic and bankrupt conditions he wished to prevent. The inescapable requirements of Indian defence were fundamental to any definition of Egyptian policy; for that country, as a virtually autonomous Ottoman dominion, represented a powerful Moslem community astride a communications-link strategically vital to British-Indian interests. Russian armed diversions in Central Asia, by disturbing Moslem sentiment and locking up British forces in India and along the North-West Frontier to prevent the explosion or contagion of a second Great Mutiny when they might be needed elsewhere, had always embarrassed Britain's Near Eastern diplomacy; and the Russian occupation of Merv coincident with Wolseley's suppression of the Egyptian rebellion conformed to an ancient pattern. Who could tell when Islamic insurrections in Egypt would encourage fresh Russian aggressions towards India, or these in turn spark dangers to the Suez Canal; and how, short of a massive increase in military establishment and expenditure and the total military occupations of Egypt and Afghanistan, which in the circumstances was unthinkable, could one prevent it. The early disasters of the Zulu, Afghan and Boer Wars had alarmingly revealed one of the great weaknesses of Cardwell's reforms; that until short-service had provided an effective Reserve, the British military establishment, especially in the event of successive or simultaneous frontier wars, would be dangerously and perhaps fatally over-extended. Britain could not hope to defend India if she were in any way committed to the territorial occupation and military defence of Egypt and the Sudan—which financially as well as politically would be altogether unacceptable. Gladstone's answer was to withdraw the British occupation forces under General Sir Frederick Stephenson. raise and train an Egyptian Army under Sir Evelyn Wood, its first Sirdar; organise the Gendarmerie under Colonel Valentine Baker and give the direction of Egyptian administration to an experienced Indian financial expert, with some pretensions as a military reformer and strategist, Major Evelyn Baring.

Even as this policy was maturing, an obscure but saintly shipwright had declared himself the Mahdi and proclaimed a Holy War which threatened to engulf not only the Nile Valley, but Egypt proper, Tripoli, Tunis, Algeria, Arabia and even India itself. Alarmed at the Viceroy's intelligence that Russian intransigence over the delicate Afghan Boundary Commission negotiations had stiffened as a result of the Mahdist revolt, the Government steadfastly pursued a policy of disentanglement and disinvolvement in Sudan affairs, dissociated themselves from the consequences of Hicks' expedition, and refused to entertain Baring's plea that Khartoum be considered an outwork of Egyptian defences. But the massacre of Hicks' ill-found and ill-directed army in Kordofan in November 1883 showed that the Mahdi was no ghostly prophet and raised the whole question of the future security of Egypt and its garrisons in the Sudan in a manner which the Government could, and the public would no longer ignore. It has been well said that the Gordon escapade was doomed from the start because it offered only choices between bad alternatives. The Sudan could be reconquered by foreign troops; but with complications along the Afghan border, crusading warfare of this sort, culminating in another Tel-el-Kebir—or another

Hicks' disaster—was an unpalatable and impolitic proposition; the Indian Government would almost certainly refuse to slacken its military hold on India by providing large expeditionary forces for any lengthy period or to bring its Native Armies into contact with a hostile Moslem fanaticism; while the dilatory Turks, even if prepared or able to finance and conduct such a campaign— which was unlikely, would not improbably arrive too late. The Sudan and Egyptian garrisons could simply be abandoned to their fate; but beside the obvious humanitarian objections, there was no way of telling how far Mahdism would spread, or what its effects would be upon India. Finally—and this was the policy firmly adopted by the Cabinet on 13 December—the garrisons in the Sudan would be evacuated, and steps taken to defend Egypt proper and the ports on the Red Sea against Mahdist incursions.

In the circumstances, it is difficult to see what other policy could have been devised. Yet no one bothered to explore its deep practical implications. Evacuation, as Baring, Stephenson and Wolseley warned, implied prolonged military occupation of Egypt with all that that entailed for Cardwell's reforms and Indian defence. More importantly, the actual evacuation process was totally ignored. This vital and elementary question—how to evacuate scattered and isolated garrisons, already closely invested by fanatical and victorious armies, from a million square miles of desert, barren of water, roads and railways, and seething with insurrection—was not asked, much less answered: instead a different question was raised—by whom?

On 22 December 1884, Baring had advised the Government that it would be necessary 'to send an English officer of high authority', perhaps Sir Charles Wilson, Chief of Staff to the Army of Occupation, to Khartoum, 'with full powers to withdraw all the garrisons in the Sudan' and arrange as best he could for its future government. But in the press campaign mounted by the *Pall Mall Gazette* in early January, one magic name swept all other claimants from the field: Major-General C. G. Gordon, a former Governor-General of the Sudan, already something of a national legend as a successful administrator of primitive peoples and a brilliant commander of irregular troops, whose reputation for wayward genius and whose unaccountable intuitions were not unknown to Whitehall. In an ill-hour for Gordon and themselves, Gladstone and his colleagues allowed themselves to be persuaded that somehow or other, Gordon, equipped only with his personality, his reputation and unlimited drafts upon the bankrupt exchequer at Cairo, could, alone and unsupported, pacify an immense and chaotic province and obviate the possible humiliations, certain dangers and unnecessary expense of sending a military expedition. A little reflection might have brought them—and him—to realise that he, like Wolseley afterwards, was singularly ill-equipped to conduct a retreat. But he accepted the task—momentous as it was and the later source of much ambiguous interpretation and wilful evasion—and set off carrying the Foreign Office's vague instructions to *report* on the military situation in the Sudan and the 'best mode' of effecting evacuation; orders which shortly received Baring's and the Cabinet's (though not Gladstone's) executive sanction. Accompanied by a single calvary officer, Lieutenant-Colonel J. D. H. Stewart, Gordon reached Khartoum on 14 February 1884.

In the Eastern Sudan, the situation was rapidly deteriorating. On 5 November 1883—the same day of the Hicks' disaster—a large Egyptian force, accompanied by Commander Moncrieff, the British Consul at Suakim, was annihilated at El Teb by the Mahdist Osman Digma. Again, on 4 February 1884, Baker's gendarmerie suffered decisive losses. On 12 February, in the declared interests of Egyptian defence, a force under Sir Gerald Graham, Herbert Stewart and Redvers Buller was sent to retrieve the situation at Suakim and inflicted two bloody reverses upon the Arabs at El Teb on 29 February, and Tamai on 13 March. But this did nothing to alleviate the encroaching investment of Khartoum or to stem the northward tide of insurrection. In April, communications with Sennar—the granary of Khartoum—were severed. On 26 May after a short and feeble resistance, the Mahdists captured Berber on the Nile, thus cutting Khartoum off completely and making it much more difficult to send help by the desert route connecting Suakim with Berber. The siege of Khartoum had begun.

Concern for Gordon's safety soon became widespread in England. Demands in Parliament and the press for a relief expedition were vigorously endorsed in private by Baring, Wolseley, the Queen and some members of the Cabinet. But the intelligence picture concerning the degree of danger to Khartoum and Gordon's capacity for holding out was not at all clear—at least not sufficiently to warrant the mounting of a large-scale relief force. Moreover, if Gladstone could convince himself that Gordon should be disowned for disobeying instructions, he was equally suspicious of Wolseley's motives for urging military preparations. Only when Lord Hartington, the Secretary of State for War, threatened resignation at the end of July, did Gladstone finally give way. On 5 August, Parliament authorised a vote of £300,000 'to undertake operations for the relief of General Gordon, should they become necessary, and to make certain preparations in respect thereof'. But even at this late hour, Cabinet policy suffered from an invertebrate lack of definitiveness. Stephenson's instructions to prepare to send a brigade to Dongola were founded on the conviction that Gordon could still evacuate the garrisons if he chose and the prime object of this meagre force was 'to afford the means of obtaining full and accurate information as to the position and intentions of General Gordon'. Such a demonstration would probably 'be sufficient to strengthen his position, and to secure the co-operation of the tribes which have not joined the movement of the Mahdi, to such an extent as to enable General Gordon to secure the principal object of his mission'. Thus precious, perhaps irretrievable, months had passed. All now depended on the quality and conduct of the military plans, preparations and operations that followed; things which themselves suffered from imprecise definition and were deprived of the time-cushion so essential to absorb all the minor frictions, accidents and errors of judgement and calculation, inherent in the conduct of all campaigns and such as actually took place with fatal cumulative effect. To all this Wolseley's contribution was decisive.

IV

As early as 8 April, Wolseley had, at Lord Hartington's request, produced a plan of operations which, he secretly hoped, by repeating on a vastly increased scale his earliest triumph—the Red River Expedition—would forever silence his detractors, recapture the disintegrating harmony and reputation of the Ring and confirm his title as a great captain. It would be 'the biggest operation the English Army has *ever* undertaken', possessing an almost Homeric quality. The most important question to be settled was that of the route to be followed, and on this Wolseley had no reservations. 'I would propose', he wrote, 'to send all the dismounted portion of the force up the Nile to Khartum in boats, as we sent the little expeditionary force from Lake Superior to Fort

Garry on the Red River in 1870. That force had to traverse a desert region, destitute of supplies, for a distance of 600 miles, taking provisions with it for three months in boats. . . . . . Remembering the great superiority of river over land transport, the ease with which stores of all sorts are carried in boats, the great distance, comparatively speaking, that can be traversed daily in boats, and the vast saving that there would be in expense, I have no hesitation whatever in saying that the river route from Wady Halfa to Khartum is infinitely preferable to any other.'

This opinion did not pass unchallenged. The military and political authorities on the spot in Cairo—Sir Gerald Graham, Sir Frederick Stephenson, Sir Evelyn Wood and Sir Evelyn Baring—unanimously ruled the Nile route impracticable and 'quite unsuited for the purpose intended' because of its great length, the vast amount of animal transport and forage required and the problems presented by the Cataracts. They favoured the Suakim–Berber desert route because it was shorter, because Suakim possessed greater facilities than Cairo for assembling an expeditionary force, and because the nearby presence of a war-fleet would offer great moral comfort to the withdrawing troops and garrisons. Colonel J. C. Ardagh of the War Office Intelligence Department, in a memorandum discussing no less than seven routes, arrived at identical conclusions, although the D.A.Q.M.G., Colonel J. F. Maurice, Wolseley's lifelong friend and amanuensis, dissented on the grounds that the fall of Berber rendered any further inland movement impossible. Admiral Cooper Key and Captain Hall of the Admiralty Intelligence Department, after a detailed examination into the navigability of the Nile beyond the Second Cataract, deprecated 'any joint expedition of the army and navy along the Nile' and dissociated the Admiralty from 'any responsibility for the advance of an expedition up the Nile in boats'—but they withheld judgement until the local naval authorities, Captain Molyneux, Commander Hammill and Vice-Admiral Lord John Hay, Commander-in-Chief, Mediterranean, had submitted their first-hand reports concerning the navigability of the Cataracts and the feasibility of the operation as a whole. Undoubtedly, Wolseley's most formidable critics and the most persistent advocates of the Suakim–Berber route were the Royal Engineers, notably the Inspector-General of Fortifications, Sir Andrew Clarke, and his more gifted protege and namesake, Major George Sydenham Clarke, whose exhaustive report on the bombardment of Alexandria had earned him instant recognition as a profound and practical military thinker. In a series of concisely written and closely argued letters to the *Times*, Major Clarke maintained that the Nile expedition, like most other English expeditions of the past, would be a costly and particularly unremunerative affair, suffering from 'a terrible want' of finality and popularity, and unable to achieve any permanent result or at least a result which bore any decent proportion to the expenditure. But whether an expedition were sent or not, he claimed that if the Sudan question were fairly faced, it would have to be admitted that 'some hold on the Sudan must be maintained by England'—and this could best be done through the instrumentality of a railway from Suakim to Berber.

The present dread of becoming involved in the affairs of the Eastern Sudan, he believed, was due solely to the vast distances. But when the railway was made, Berber would be within twelve hours of English ships and as easy of access as Cairo. England would have a permanent hold on Khartoum, the heart of the Sudan, without the smallest necessity for the permanent establishment of a European garrison there. The mere accessibility of Khartoum would give the Governor of the Sudan, whoever he might be, a power which the Mahdi could never possess. A Suakim–Berber railway, no less than the great frontier rail systems in India, America and Canada, would become an immense pacifying and stabilising influence, and the slave trade would die a natural death. But if Wolseley's policy were adopted, its results could be foretold with tolerable certainty. 'We shall have a costly expedition, relieve Khartoum, hold the lines of communication until the garrison has been withdrawn, and retire, having done absolutely nothing towards the final solution of the question of the Sudan. The Mahdi, or some other religious adventurer, will form a Mohammedan state, Egypt will be in a state of chronic ferment and will ultimately be invaded. Military operations which may again require us to go to Khartoum will then be inevitable.'

In June, when the Government were yet unconvinced of the seriousness of Gordon's plight and of the necessity for a relief expedition, these views by so competent an authority gained a momentary if unaccountable ascendency—and on the 14th of that month, Stephenson was instructed to begin preparations for the construction of the Suakim–Berber railway. It was at this stage that Lord Hartington, mindful of the assurances he had given during the debate on the Vote of Censure on 12 May that there would be a relief expedition in the autumn, threatened resignation if his pledges were not honoured, thereby reviving the feud over the 'routes'.

On 3 August, Vice-Admiral Lord John Hay submitted his considered opinion to the Admiralty. Commander Hammill's investigations had conclusively shown that small boats could neither be poled, tracked, hauled or rowed along the unchartered reaches of the Upper Nile. Wolseley's proposal had been clearly made in the mistaken belief that 'the features and circumstances of the Nile... are very similar to those presented to the Red River Expedition'. This outlandish affront to Wolseley's strategic insight was fiercely rebutted by a committee of three of his Red River companions, Major-Generals Sir John McNiell and Sir Redvers Buller and Colonel W. F. Butler, which, after consulting all the evidence at hand, concluded that 'the Nile will be found the easiest, the safest, and immensely the cheapest line of advance to adopt'. As for the total dissimilarity of conditions and circumstances between the Red River Expedition and the proposed Nile Expedition, they advanced the incredibly naïve assumption that, although they had never seen the Nile above Cairo, 'water is water, and rock is rock, whether they lie in America or Africa, and the conditions which they can assume towards each other are much the same all the world over'.

This remarkable view, advanced in chosen defiance of the collective recorded protests of the highest military, naval, intelligence and engineering authorities both in Whitehall and at the seat of operations, and in fatal disregard of the uniqueness of every military campaign and the novelty of its conditions, carried the day. Once committed to the relief expedition, the Government were naturally more impressed with the positive assurances of safety, ease and cheapness of Wolseley and his Red River colleagues than with the somewhat negative promises of failure advanced by the sailors and engineers. Moreover, the fall of Berber and the reluctance of the Indian Government to finance and construct the railway from Suakim had removed two of the essential pre-requisites that had earlier made the Suakim–Berber route appear both acceptable and practicable. Such a scheme would have committed the Government to an extension of responsibilities which, on second thoughts, they did not relish. Finally, it would have been difficult to override the convictions of the

General who was also the commander most likely to conduct the relief expedition.

Nevertheless, as the *Official History of the Royal Engineers in Egypt and the Sudan* forcibly declares, Wolseley 'based his calculations on his experience of river transport under very different conditions in Canada'. He had never seen the cataracts of the Nile beyond the bounds of Egypt, nor ever encountered a Dervish. 'The climate, the nature of the enemy, the size of the force, the urgency of the situation—all were different. Experience gained on the Red River was no sure guide for operations on the Nile.' While it may have tolerably sufficed to moved a mere brigade to Dongola, as originally planned, it was bound to prove disastrous when the relief force was materially strengthened. Most important of all, the decision to move by river involved the procurement of special boats and boatmen—arrangements which further delayed the departure of the expedition. After a final vain protest, Stephenson was superseded by Wolseley in the chief command in Egypt, ostensibly to prepare for an expedition but in fact to conduct it. It is at this point that the *Journal* begins. Lord Hartington, at Wolseley's connivance, informed Stephenson on 26 August that it would be unjust to him to ask him to direct an operation which he considered impracticable. 'The fateful die was cast,' wrote the official historian of the Royal Engineers, 'Gordon was already doomed.'

v

It might be well at this point to say something in more detail of the nature of the task that confronted Wolseley on his arrival at Cairo on 9 September 1884. Wolseley's object was to concentrate by mid-December at or near Korti—within striking distance of Khartoum yet untouched by revolt—a balanced fighting force, carrying with them not only supplies for themselves but also for the inhabitants and garrison of Khartoum, whom it was his mission to bring away. A considerable proportion of this force, notably the 2,500-man Camel Corps, was to be mounted, to make a dash across the desert in the event of unforseeable delays along the Nile or Gordon's known position becoming unendurably critical. In some respects, Wolseley's task was no less momentous or forlorn than Gordon's had been. What military prospects had existed a year ago had now depreciated or altogether disappeared, while Wolseley, although not prone to disobey orders, was no more inclined or suited than Gordon to conduct a retreat. It was Wolseley's great hope that the mere appearance of his force would overawe the Mahdi's followers, causing them to disintegrate, and allowing of Gordon's relief by a small flying column of camels. Events were to show, however, that Wolseley's hopes—and therefore his plans and preparations—were based on a facile appreciation of the militant fanatic strength of the Mahdist movement, and that had the Mahdi chosen to block his path, Wolseley, far from relieving Gordon, would have suffered a defeat as humiliating and complete as that which had overtaken Hicks.

It is evident that the campaign presented administrative difficulties of a unique and perhaps insurmountable kind, and that the outcome of any tactical operations that might subsequently arise would largely depend on how these difficulties were met. It is also evident that the Nile Expedition foreshadowed all the fatal inadequacies of the system of 'personal' command which proved so patently disastrous in the Boer War. The improvisation which might succeed on a small scale was dangerous when applied to such a campaign as that now under preparation. The vast distances involved simply meant that Wolseley could not be everywhere at once.

From Alexandria to the Second Cataract, however, the line of communication presented no difficulty. The railway and Thomas Cook's steamboat flotilla provided adequate transportation. But beyond that point it was necessary to consult Commander Hammill's report as to the nature of the four cataracts intervening between Wady Halfa and Khartoum. These were not single falls as the word might suggest but extensive ranges of rapids, in some cases several miles long. Moreover, between the cataracts dignified by number, there were numerous lesser but often equally obstructive ones, which above the Third Cataract were completely uncharted, and which gave the River Column so much trouble. It was Wolseley's intention to march the mounted force by land along the banks of the Nile. To negotiate the rapids and otherwise convey the infantry force, special boats—modified man-of-war whalers, hastily chosen, belatedly ordered, but rapidly built—were to be used, manned by West African kroomen and Canadian boatmen who bore no resemblance to the original voyageurs (who had, in fact, died out) and who were for the most part inexperienced lumbermen, lawyers and businessmen under the command of a Toronto alderman.

Undoubtedly, food was the greatest single problem. The whole force had to advance by a single line of communication, and the distant region where it was to operate possessed no resources for the support of an army. The official historian later went to considerable lengths 'to explain what was the great difficulty in the way of a successful campaign'. 'The Nile expedition', he wrote, 'was a campaign less against man than against nature and against time. Had British soldiers and Egyptian camels been able to subsist on sand and occasional water, or had the desert produced beef and biscuit, the army might, in spite of its late start, have reached Khartoum in November. But as things were, the rate of progress of the army was dependent on the rate of progress of its supplies.' This difficulty assumed unexpectedly severe proportions when it became clear that the fighting component of the relief force required a logistical support base twice its own size, that the creation of the Camel Corps in October had added 2,500 men 'who could not do a stroke of work towards carrying their own food to the fighting base' at Korti, and that the growing probability of an inescapable confrontation with the Mahdi necessitated the strengthening of the strike force from 5,000 to 8,000 men.

In view of all these factors, it is not surprising that Wolseley's plans for concentrating at Korti should have suffered a succession of exasperating delays. Buller's negligence to check coaling arrangements with Thomas Cook and Sons resulted on a complete stoppage of steamer movement between Assuan and Wady Halfa from 28 October to 10 November, when a new and less favourable contract was signed. Such a 'bizarre incident' reflected adversely upon Wolseley and Buller alike and upon the staff system they represented. 'With a properly organised Quarter-Master-Generals Branch of the modern type,' notes an intelligent critic of the campaign, 'such a happening would have been impossible.... The eighteenth century had a long twilight in the British service.'

Fresh news from Gordon dated 4 November that 'we can hold out 40 days with ease, after that it will be difficult' caused Wolseley to intensify rather than alter his plans for a methodical concentration of demonstrated power. It persuaded him of the 'almost impossibility of relief without fighting' and he determined to assemble 9,500 troops at Korti (a more advanced post than Dongola)—a force, he confidently assured Gordon, 'strong enough to wipe Mahommed Ahmed and all his followers off the face of the earth'. This unfortunate decision to strengthen the strike force produced further unforeseeable difficulties. The overloading of whalers with extra men and rations made the job of navigating the cataracts at once slower and more dangerous—a task that was in no way simplified by the rival methods and conflicting jurisdictions of Butler and Beresford, and indeed exacerbated by the amateurish inexperience of the voyageurs, and the falling of the Nile. Similarly, the overburdening of the camels diminished their stamina and slowed their pace.

Thus, in spite of some resourceful inducements to hasten the march of his armies, by 15 December Wolseley was far behind schedule. He himself, with Sir Charles Wilson, did not reach Korti until 16 December. By Christmas Day the Camel Corps had all congregated, but the bulk of the army, precariously straggling across a wasteland of desert, rock and cataract, was not expected to be concentrated until 22 January—barely four days before Khartoum fell.

It might be well at this point to unfold the gradual development of Wolseley's operational plans. We have seen that in October he had created a considerable mounted force in readiness to move direct across the desert to Khartoum should this prove necessary. On 11 December, he received intelligence of the Mahdi's 'intention of starving-out Khartoum'. 'God grant its garrison may be able to hold out until I can get there,' he confided to his *Journal*, 'if necessary we must then go out and attack this swaggering false prophet no matter how small my force may be. Until he is driven off no food can be brought into the place. . . . If I can only reach Shendy safely with 1,500 men on camels and with 30 days' provisions for then, I think I could tickle up the Mahdi. . . . I believe with 1,500 such men as I can dispose of, once arrived at Khartoum I could raise the siege and perhaps finish the whole business.' Between 24 and 27 December, Wolseley worked with Buller and Stewart on plans for dividing such force as had already collected at Korti. One column, which came to be known as the River Column under the command of General Earle, was to follow the Nile around its great eastern bend past Abu Hamed and Berber to reach Shendy on 1 February. The other force, known to history as the Desert Column under the command of Colonel Stewart, was to strike directly across the Bayuda Desert to Metemmah (opposite Shendy on the Nile) by 7 January. Wolseley hoped that this movement could be completed in a single operation, enabling him 'to push on to Khartoum without halting'. Nothing so disconcerted 'barbarous people as rapidity of movement', while the double line of advance would perplex the Mahdi and give him a 'still more exaggerated notion of our power and strength' than he presently possessed. To move by stages would simply 'give the Mahdi time to arrange his plans'. As he conceived it, the desert march was 'a great leap in the dark . . . the beginning of the first scene in the last act of this Khartoum drama'. He planned to accompany Stewart. 'If I can,' he wrote in his *Journal*, 'I shall avoid fighting until I reach Khartoum and will attack the Mahdi's position D.V. the day after I can ferry my troops across the White Nile to the neighbourhood of Omdurman.'

From the start, ill-luck dogged the enterprise, perhaps inevitably. The Secretary of State for War, mindful of Wolseley's capacity for indiscretion and his eagerness to attack the Mahdi, forbade the Commander-in-Chief to move his headquarters beyond Korti, compelling Wolseley to do what he had never done before—direct rather than command the decisive operations of his armies. Furthermore, a shortage of animal transport, a serious oversight in staff-work, meant that Stewart had first to establish an intermediate supply depot at Jakdul before pushing on to Metemmah, thus diminishing his chances of speed and surprise—the two qualities upon which the success of his operation depended. Finally, on 30 December, the day Stewart set out for Jakdul, Wolseley's messenger returned from Khartoum bearing a 'scrap of paper . . . the size of a postage stamp with Gordon's Arabic seal on one side and on the other "Khartoum, all right—14-12-84. C. G. Gordon."' But he also brought 'a long rambling message which I cannot depend on, saying that I am to come very quickly, that I must have a large force as the enemy is very numerous etc. He adds Khartoum can only be taken by starvation and that food is scarce. Altogether this is most unsatisfactory and unsettles my plans without giving me any information that is worth having.' The effect of this information was fatally to upset the balance of Wolseley's plans. 'Gordon's message', he telegraphed Baring, 'compels measures that will postpone my arrival at Khartoum. He warns me not to leave Berber in my rear, so I must move by water and take it before I march on Khartoum. Meanwhile I shall have established post at Metemmah, by men and stores sent across the desert. I shall be able to communicate with Gordon by steam, learn exact position, and, if he is in *extremis* before infantry arrive by river, to push forward by camel corps to help him at all hazards.' All intention of forcing his way into Khartoum had been abandoned, and there now devolved upon him the distasteful task of co-ordinating the movements of two widely separated columns, both susceptible to imminent defeat in detail.

Stewart's double journey and the great concentration of force at Jakdul had served to betray Wolseley's intentions to the Mahdi's forces. On 17 January, the Desert Column was intercepted by some 10,000 of the Mahdi's best troops who had occupied the vital wells at Abu Klea. Breaking through the unsteady ranks of the Heavy Cavalry Regiment, the Dervishes suffered 1,100 casualties before being compelled to retire. But it was a Pyrrhic and indecisive victory. Besides losing one of his ablest lieutenants, Colonel Fred Burnaby, Wolseley had received casualties and a tactical rebuff that were psychologically unacceptable in irregular warfare. Next day and all through the following night, the Desert Column continued its advance to the Nile, only to find the way contested by a further Mahdist force. While hastily erecting defences, Stewart received a wound that was to prove mortal and the command devolved upon Sir Charles Wilson. At Abu Kru, on the afternoon of 19 January, Wilson threw back a second desperate Mahdist charge and occupied Gubat, a little north of Metemmah. On the 21st, while preparing to attack Metemmah, contact was made with Gordon's steamers. Thus, in the space of two days, Wolseley's armies had fought as many actions, with the 'irreparable loss' of Stewart and Burnaby, two of the ablest of the Ring. The recovery of such remnants of Wolseley's prestige and of the Army's professional pride as remained now lay in the hands of a non-Ringer, Sir Charles Wilson, a political general who had never held a field command, and Buller was at once ordered to proceed to Metemmah and assume command of the Desert Column. Wolseley himself had suffered a severe psychological blow, disturbing his balance and discretion, from which he never entirely recovered. Stewart's return messengers had been misled by guides, perhaps intentionally, and for a full week until 28 January, Wolseley was kept ignorant of the whereabouts and operations of the Desert Column. 'This suspense,' he wrote, 'this longing for news, drives the blood from my heart.' He smoked and prayed incessantly, frustrated by his powerlessness. Leading storming parties, he confided to his *Journal*, was 'child's play compared with the strain which a General situated as I have been for some days past, has to undergo'. To be 'squatted down . . . unable to do anything to aid or help forward the end and objects aimed at, is not only galling to the pride, but simply heart-rending:

'In these operations I am so "fine-drawn" as regards the margin I have to allow for untoward events, that any serious repulse would be most inconvenient if not dangerous. The number of my troops is uncomfortably approaching the danger point. When therefore I am left a whole week without news of what is going on, or what had taken place after a hard fought fight such as that on the 17th instant, the tension on all vital parts of the bodily system becomes almost intolerable.'

Meanwhile, Wilson was drawing back the curtains for the last act in the Gordon tragedy. The story is well-known. Wolseley had specified that after capturing Metemmah, Wilson and Beresford were to push on by steamer to Khartoum to establish contact with Gordon. The need for extreme haste was evident, but Wilson nonetheless planned and moved with great caution. Both men and camels were thoroughly exhausted by the actions of 17 and 19 January. It has been suggested that Beresford, incapacitated by boils but anxious not to miss such an historic adventure, made the most of rumours of approaching Mahdists, and induced Wilson to waste time in making reconnaissances to the south and to the north, and in overhauling his boilers in anticipation of heavy fire from the banks of the Nile. Not until 24 January did the *Bordein* and *Tell Hawein* carrying but a handful of Sudanese and red-coated British troops finally set out for Khartoum.

Inescapable misfortune attended the operation. The *Bordein* struck a rock and ran aground on a sandbank. These accidents caused long delays. Eventually, on the 28th, Wilson, pushing southward through a storm of cross-fire, rounded the south-western point of Tuti Island, which lies at the approaches to Khartoum. The town had fallen. The little steamers turned forlornly back and ran, not without further incident, for safety. 'Never was a garrison so nearly rescued,' wrote Kitchener in his Official Report, 'never was a commander so sincerely lamented.'

VI

In England, the news of the fall of Khartoum and the death of Gordon was greeted with widespread horror and indignation. Wolseley himself, who hoped against hope that Gordon might somehow have survived as he had done so often before and who had for three days delayed divulging the news to his troops while he sought more authentic corroborative evidence as to Gordon's known fate, was consumed with a spirit of sacrificial vengeance. Henceforward he was to conclude practically every entry in his *Journal* with a vicious splenetic diatribe against the political criminality, hypocrisy and self-seeking of Gladstone, for refusing to recognise Gordon's true plight until it was too late. The initials G.O.M. served as a bitter lifelong reminder that he was also the 'Murderer of Gordon'. But it was Sir Charles Wilson who suffered the scapegoat's disgrace. The Ring were unanimous in their condemnation that Wilson had so cheaply thrown away all their toils, battles, losses and exhaustion and indeed the honour of the Army when success was just within grasp. Criticism then and now has identified the two days that separated triumph from disaster with the similar delay in Wilson's departure from Gubat. But that is by no means the whole issue. His was the last of many detentions that had multiplied with deadly cumulative effect and that were directly attributable to Wolseley's own false strategic outlook and the outmoded staff instrument that he represented, his tendency to confuse favouritism with efficiency, his negligence when President of the Confidential Mobilisation Committee to make adequate preparations or foresee likely obstacles, and above all, to his declining powers. Too much has been made of Wilson's alleged lack of field command experience, for his response to the chaotic and disintegrating situation surrounding Stewart's death was magnificent and courageous, and his handling of the action at Abu Kru showed a methodical and masterly appreciation of difficulties that Wolseley's desperate optimism was prone to overlook. As Wilson himself pointed out, had he left Gubat on 22 January he still could not have reached Khartoum in time. And it may be a matter of some doubt whether his handful of troops could at this stage have made much impression upon the Mahdi's confident hosts, poised as they were around the emaciated town. All along Wolseley had maintained a naïve complacency about the enemy, and only when Khartoum had fallen did he fully realise the stark strategic realities of his position. The Mahdi, vastly superior in numbers, now in possession of the key to the Sudan with its guns and resources, and fortified by all the prestige of victory, finally earned Wolseley's grudging admission that he was rapidly constituting himself into a 'great Military Power', and could now operate in concentrated fashion with all the security and freedom conferred by a firm and popular base. Wolseley, on the other hand, was conscious of the extreme vulnerability of his army, thinly strung out 1,400 miles from its base without hope of close immediate support. His two tattered columns, demoralised by two indecisive battles and the failure of their mission, and deprived (or about to be) of their original commanders, were still widely separated, groping forward in largely unknown country and dangerously exposed to defeat in detail. The Commander-in-Chief, almost pathetically distraught because failure had cast an indelible slur upon a stainless professional record and had given joy to his enemies and ammunition to those of the system he represented, simply did not know what to do. He halted his distant columns and wired his government for instructions.

Wolseley's own views concerning future military policy in the Sudan were oddly ambivalent. Privately and deeply conscious of his invidious strategic position ('With Khartoum in the Mahdi's hands, my present force is totally inadequate to meet him except under very advantageous circumstances'), he inveighed against any policy which might leave British soldiers to grill in the Sudanese sun in expectation of an autumn campaign against Khartoum. On the other hand, his outraged professional pride moved him to advocate an immediate forward policy; the capture of Berber, the destruction of Mahdist power at Suakim, and the reinforcement of his own army. The Government, mindful of the possible repercussions of the Mahdi's success upon Moslem feeling throughout India, and upon Russian obstructionism and opportunism along the North-West Frontier, at first temporised and tried to postpone a difficult decision that would commit large numbers of troops to an expensive guerrilla war, the end of which could not be foreseen. The unabated fury of public feeling and the precariousness of the Government's position, however, was such that only evidence of a strong forward policy to retrieve the disaster could satisfy the wounded pride of Parliament and the nation. Moreover, to concentrate and withdraw Wolseley's widely scattered army in the face of a triumphant enemy, through difficult country, would be in itself a hazardous military operation —though Wolseley's operational and logistic planning from the start should have been predicated on this assumption. Even if it succeeded, the impression created on watchful, critical foreign powers, such as Russia, of a British Army retreating tamely before the threat of the Mahdi would be ridiculous, leaving them equally free to embarrass British diplomacy as if she were embroiled in a great Sudanese war. Contrary to all arguments of high policy and common sense, therefore, the Government determined that 'the power of the Mahdi at Khartoum must be overthrown'. They endorsed Wolseley's military recommendations and requirements and left it to him to decide 'the military measures best calculated to attain this object'.

Overjoyed at the prospect of avenging Gordon, Wolseley at once urged his columns forward to combine for an attack on Berber as a prelude to the autumn campaign against Khartoum. But it was soon discovered that neither of the columns were in fit condition to march or fight. When Buller arrived at Gubat to supersede Wilson, he found that the abortive dash across the desert had reduced the Desert Column to a debilitated and broken condition. Only twelve days' supplies remained. Reconnaissance had shown that Metemmah was a strongly defensible town garrisoned by 2,000 troops capable of desperate resistance. Beresford's steamers were not of the slightest use for offensive purposes. Reliable reports indicated that reinforcements of 3,000 to 4,000 men, well armed with captured artillery, were on their way from Khartoum, while there were rumours that the Mahdi had ordered an army of 50,000, now freed from the siege, to march north. In these circumstances, Buller was reminded of Wolseley's earlier instructions of 5 February not to allow himself to be invested at Gubat and to withdraw at least to Abu Klea if the situation demanded. The evacuation was well under way, and he himself was already at Abu Klea, when he received Wolseley's subsequent orders to attack Metemmah and march on to Berber. But the march from Gubat had so fully revealed the complete collapse of his means of transport that he could not regard these orders as realistic or practicable. The camels were in a thoroughly emaciated condition, and the long marches across a stony desert had completely worn out the boots of his troops, many of whom were almost barefoot. Dispatches were sent to Wolseley at Korti informing him of this predicament.

Meanwhile, similar difficulties attended the progress of the River Column. The passage of the Monassir cataracts had proved slower and more difficult than expected. General Earle had been killed in a vigorous action fought near Kirbekan, the command devolving upon Major-General Henry Brackenbury who, like

Wilson, had had no previous operational command experience. Thirty per cent of the soldiers' biscuit had been discovered to be inedible. To Wolseley's instructions that the River Column prepare for a combined attack on Berber, Brackenbury sent a depressing reply. His rations were insufficient, and the unknown conditions of the cataracts made it impossible for him to fix any definite date for a junction with Buller.

These unfavourable reports from his two columns reached Wolseley almost simultaneously. It was clear that all hope of capturing Berber before the hot season had vanished and that the only alternative was to withdraw both columns and concentrate them in summer quarters between Dongola and Merawi where they could be refitted and reinforced for operations against Khartoum in the autumn. On 20 February orders were Issued accordingly, and by mid-March Wolseley's armies had iimped painfully back to the safety of Korti.

In the meantime, the Government had taken stock of its position and the sobering situation along the Indo-Afghan frontier. It had barely survived the Vote of Censure, but the storm of hostile opinion had since died down and its Sudanese policy now appeared inconsistent and prodigal in the extreme. Both Lord Kimberley, the Secretary of State for India, and Lord Dufferin, the Viceroy, were deeply alarmed at evidence that Britain's entanglement in the Khartoum imbroglio had strengthened the influence of the Russian military party over the Tsar, and that the recently aggressively high-handed conduct of the Russian Government was such as to make the Afghan border negotiations assume 'a very angry form' and lead to 'serious estrangement' between the two Governments. The Indian High Command had been quietly instructed to draw up plans to prevent Herat falling to a Russian *coup de main*, and otherwise to prepare to defend India against a Russian invasion. Wolseley's dispatch of 6 March, therefore, describing in dark terms the metamorphosis of military power that had taken place in the Sudan with the Mahdi's capture of Khartoum, the formidable resources and widespread fanatic religious support now at his command, and the vast military reinforcements —twelve battalions of infantry, four strong squadrons of cavalry and two batteries of horse artillery—that would be required to wage a successful autumn campaign, seemed to point to the distasteful prospect of two costly and prolonged imperial wars being fought simultaneously on distant and unrelated fronts. The

Penjdeh crisis in April brought the issue to a head, although there could have been no doubt which way the decision would go. Most commentators upon the Gordon Relief Campaign have suggested that Gladstone deliberately manufactured or exaggerated the seriousness of the Penjdeh incident as the most expedient method of reneging upon his responsibilities and extracting his armies from further embroilment in the Sudan, thereby depriving Wolseley of the chance to remove the slur of failure from his reputation. But a study of the correspondence of Kimberley, Dufferin and Gladstone shows this charge to be unfounded. The imperatives of high policy, military weakness and common sense alike demanded that Indian defence be given pre-eminence over military vengeance in the Sudan. 'Obviously we could not afford to burn our candles at both ends,' wrote Kimberley on 17 April. Four days later, it was announced in the House of Commons that it was not intended to undertake any further offensive operations in the Sudan, or to advance to Khartoum. The long retreat began. Wolseley himself reached London on 13 July, suffering from acute diarrhoea. 'The horrid fashionable world came to meet me at the station', he wrote, 'and so ends my unsuccessful expedition for the relief of Khartoum.'

VII

The failure to relieve Khartoum broke Wolseley physically, morally and professionally. He had suffered on the Nile what amounted to a military defeat that he feared he would be given no chance to redress. Although it retained an astonishing degree of its vitality until the Boer War, the fabulous mystique of the Ring had been dealt an irreparable blow. Wolseley suspected that Khartoum would be his last command, that he would not be granted his cherished opportunity of dying or distinguishing himself in a great war against a European military power. Excepting the inarticulate Buller, he alone of all the principal participants failed to publish, by design or otherwise, then or later, his account of the Gordon escapade. His subsequent career, in spite of the nominal importance of his successive appointments, was one steady process of disillusionment and decline, the long slow denouement of his active career that Professor Lehman has rightly called 'the epilogue'.

Wolseley's detractors and opponents were at last given heart and ammunition at a time when the legendary Ring was riven with dissensions that are the inescapable concomitant of failure. The Russian crisis and the rash of imperial small-wars that followed had produced a new breed of defence critics and analysts, such as G. S. Clarke, Spenser Wilkinson and Sir Charles Dilke, whose interest in improving the national military condition was genuinely independent of party politics and personal prospects. Clarke in particular detected in the Zulu, Afghan, Boer and Khartoum disasters sufficient evidence of the pernicious effects that Wolseley's promiscuous staff system had had upon the training, administration and command of the British Army, and emphasised its many weaknesses and limitations for the waging of modern war. Through his work on the Colonial Defence Committee and as Secretary of the Hartington Commission, his critical reviews of the *Official Histories,* and his many trenchant articles in *The Times*, he undertook a subtle, indirect but corrosive campaign discrediting the system of 'personal' command and preparing the conditions for the introduction of War Office reform that followed the Boer War. For him, the conflict of interests between Indian and Egyptian defence at the time of the Penjdeh incident had illuminated the chief weakness of Cardwell's reforms in failing to provide for the contingency of simultaneous or successive imperial wars. Moreover, the haphazard and irresponsible manner in which Gladstone's Cabinet had approached 'great questions of Imperial policy' had convinced him of the need for a 'Council of Imperial Defence' under the Prime Minister, with four associated representatives from the Admiralty and War Office whose job would be 'to bring the Cabinet face to face with professional opinion'. 'Had such a Council existed in 1884', wrote Clarke, 'General Gordon might have been saved.'

WOLSELEY JOURNAL

The Sudan 1884-5

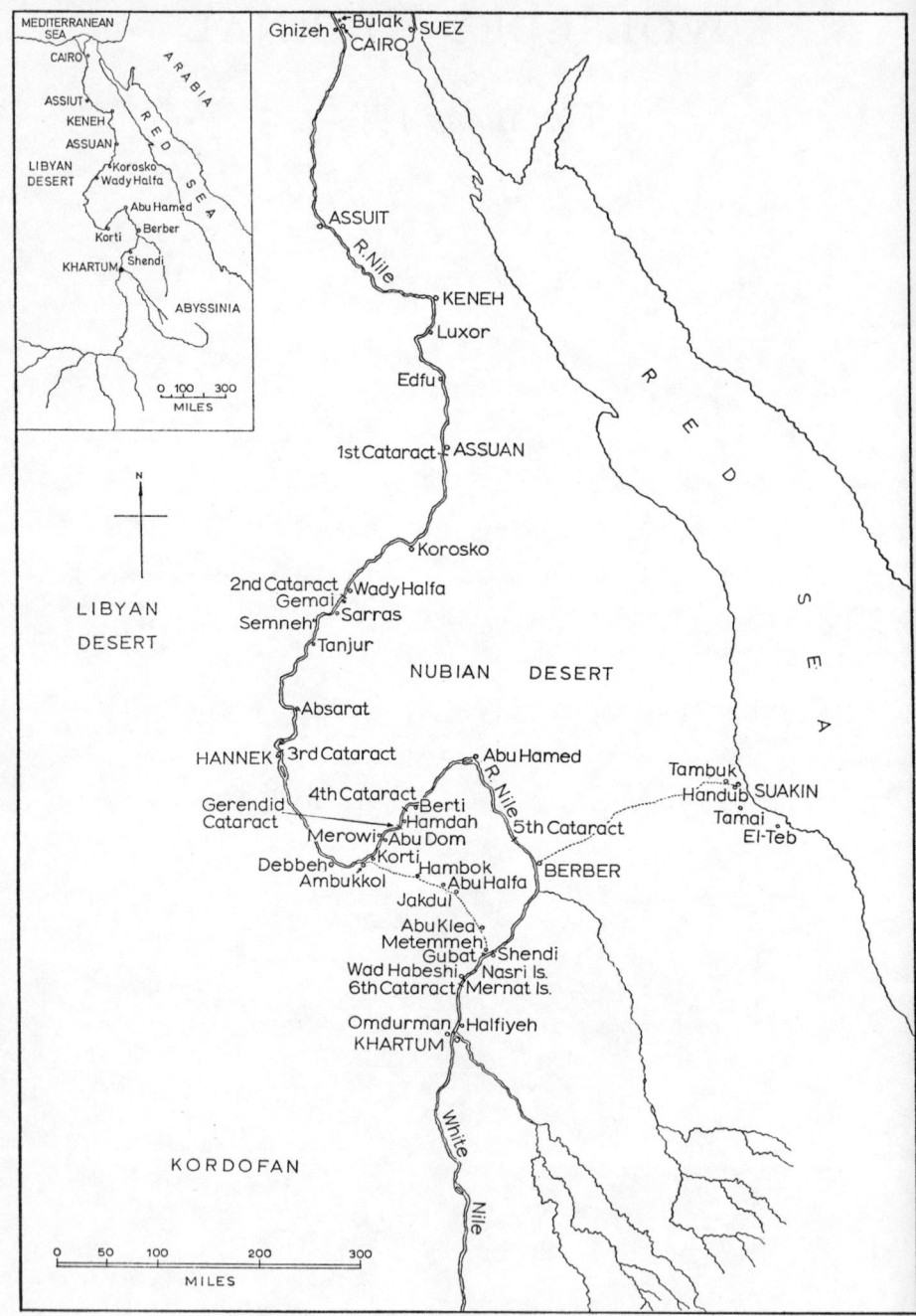

The Sudan

August 1884

Friday 22nd August 1884

Went to the War Office as usual, having walked as far as Devonshire House with Reggy Brett.[1] En route we naturally talked only of the expedition up the Nile for which we are now making preparations. He deplored the fact that the Govt. had not determined upon sending me to Egypt to direct matters there. He said that Ld. Hartington[2] was nervous, as he could see that the divergence of opinion between Stephenson[3] & his home advisers was so great that, this working at cross purposes could lead only to a break down or a failure: it was not fair on Stephenson to ask him to carry out a scheme which he declared to be impracticable, and it was not just to me who had devised it, and on whose responsibility Hartington had adopted it, to hand over its execution to men like Dormer[4] & Stephenson who had so emphatically pronounced against it, and who believed that if *Khartoum* was to be relieved, the Suakim-Berber line should be followed. In his telegrams of the last few days Stephenson has shown the greatest confusion of ideas & want of plan: they are worth studying as specimens of confused English and as an illustration of the misfortune of having men of small mental calibre in positions where the power of taking in all the phases of your position both as it exists and will be further on when influenced by change of season, high or low Nile for example or by easily forseen [*sic*] eventualities—such as the end of Gordon's ammunition having been reached—where the grasp of thought required for the solution of such problems is absent. Stephenson is in many ways the very best man for *Cairo* as long as no complicated propositions —military or political—have to be disentangled. His manners are perfect, and he is in every relation of life a high-minded English Gentleman: he is a very good linguist & thoroughly understands dealing with foreigners. At this moment I believe he is the only man in *Cairo* who is universally popular. He has had a difficult card to play with Evelyn Wood—the vainest but by no means the ablest of men. He is as cunning as a first-class female diplomatist and he himself, and his family who flatter him in a manner that is enough to turn most men's heads, mistakes this sharp cunning that he possesses to a very remarkable degree, for real sound judgement and native inborn genius. Here I may state, my opinion of him in a short sentence, that under a cleverly assumed outward semblance of frankness and openness, he has a depth of cunning that I could not have believed it possible for any brave man—such as he most undoubtedly is—to possess. He will always be a good third or fourth senior General in any Army or military operation. In such a position, under a strong hand, he will do admirably: his vanity must be flattered in many little ways by the commander, but his intrigues with Newspaper correspondents & his popularity-hunting propensities must be kept in check: as second-in-command he would be intolerable for this is certain he never could run straight in such a position or be true to any Chief. He would intrigue to oust his Chief, to dènigrer him in the estimation of his army & to undermine his reputation with the public and the Govt. of the day, through & by means of the press. Newspaper correspondents are easily taken in by a man of his temperment & disposition especially as he lays himself out to please and curry favor with them. He is one of those who believe the press to be all-powerful with the British Public, and he has consequently made newspaper worship the culte [*sic*] of his life. As second-in-command to most men, he would for these reasons be intolerable: he thinks of & cares only for one person in this world, namely for himself: his country and the public interests are of secondary consideration. Study his conduct at Lang's Nek[5] when he made peace with the Boers because Genrl. Roberts had been ordered to take command over his head. Well to wind up my opinion of him, he has not the brains or the disposition or the coolness or the firmness of purpose to enable him to take command in any war. If he is ever so entrusted as I dare say he will be, I know he will fail to do anything great: although the foolish newspaper correspondents may at the time be taken in by him, he will not be able to take in posterity by whom he will be found out and rated as a very second-rate general and an unpatriotic & selfish public servant, whose two most remarkable traits were extreme vanity & unbounded self-seeking.

After this long digression I may go on to say that Brett told me it was most unfortunate in his opinion that I had not been sent to Egypt to carry out all the arrangements for the coming Expedition, and was then going to Devonshire House to advise Hartington to insist upon my being so sent. He asked me what I thought of this. I replied, I fully concurred, & that were I the ruler here, I should certainly have sent myself to Egypt for this expedition, but that clearly it was not for me, I could not in fact tender such advice myself, and that moreover, I could not imagine this Govt. adopting any such heroic policy in this matter.

Brett went into Devonshire House & I proceeded to the War Office. At about 2 p.m. he came into my room to say that Hartington wished to see me: that he had telegraphed to Gladstone, Granville,[6] & Northbrook[7] saying that as the Military Authorities in *Cairo* and us at home were at cross purposes he wished to send me there as the plan he had resolved to follow in the event of an expedition being sent to relieve Gordon was my creation. He did not think it fair to Stephenson to ask him to carry out a plan he did not believe in. That he considered my presence in Egypt would be most likely to enable us to avoid sending any expedition at all and to secure its success should that operation be forced upon us. He said that he had been acting with me for months past on the most confidential terms & that I thoroughly understood the policy of the Govt. on this Soudan affair. That my assuming command in Egypt did not necessarily mean my going myself in command of an expedition if one were decided upon.

I saw Hartington who repeated this to me & said that very likely he would have to ask me to go out to Egypt. I said I was ready to go whenever he wished. Months ago, when the construction of a Railway from *Suakim* to *Berber* was contemplated, I had written to Hartington to say that if that operation were determined upon, I hoped he would remember how glad I should [be] to command it. Quite lately when things seemed to be going all wrong in Egypt he said 'What do you think of going out yourself to put these matters right.' I answered that of course I should be very glad to go if I were asked but that I had every confidence in Buller,[8] whom I had then recommended should command the Gordon relieving force.

I may here state that I had a regular turn up with H.R.H. of Cambridge on this command subject. In his opinion, the senior must always be the best man for any command, therefore Earle[9] should be selected. His ideas upon war are childish in the extreme, clever man as he is upon all ordinary routine matters. He thinks that the man who can command well at a field day is capable of commanding in war. Of war he litterally [*sic*] and actually knows nothing. He was at the Alma & at Inkerman, but he lost his head upon both those occasions & I fancy forgets all their incidents, for he never refers to them, and after Inkerman he went off his head altogether and retired at once but forever from all the excitement of War's alarms. Then again Buller is a young man who has received all his steps for service in the field and is a very young General, having been promoted over the heads of any number of other Colonels. This makes him unpalatable to the Duke who opposed his being made a General officer after Graham's campaign at *Suakim*. A compromise was effected at last proposed by me, Earle to command the expedition & Buller to be his Chief of the Staff. I feel somewhat culpable for having made this proposal, for had I remained firm, I must have carried my point. After this, Buller, when sent for, had a long inning with the Duke at which, he told me he said, 'Well sir, I think I quite understand the position, the Authorities in Egypt condemn and are strongly opposed to the proposed boat expedition, and I am being sent out to act as Wet-nurse to Earle.'

Earle is an old friend of mine, and I like him & appreciate him very much. I should be very glad to do him a good turn if possible but I feel I am a wretch to have consented to an arrangement which does this, but which in my heart I feel is not the best for the public service. I should like to have sent Earle under Buller, giving the latter local rank as Lt. Genrl. for that purpose. Earle is a very good officer, and he should be tried in command of troops under fire & if he showed an aptitude as a leader of men, then upon another occasion he might be made first man. I strongly object however to entrusting any independent command to an untried unproved man as long as [I] have available one who has proved himself in the field to be a capable General. Besides my own opinion—it is only an opinion—is, that good an officer as Earle undoubtedly is, he will never rise to the position of commander. He has not it in him to influence troops or to inspire them with any enthusiasm.... He never would have got to Fort Garry[10] in the allotted time for he never could have got the work out of the men employed that I did. I may venture upon this piece of vanity and this self-glorification in my own private journal. And so it will be with this Nile expedition: it will be a soldiers' campaign & unless the leader is able to get their all out of the men engaged & they give it willingly & manfully, Earle will break his men's hearts and the result of the expedition will be—to say the least—unsatisfactory.

Brackenbury[11] dined with us and we went to see *Twelfth Night*— Irving as usual Irving, dropping his jaw & raising his eyebrows to make that grimace which is so familiar, so sickening to all those who frequent the Lycaeum theatre.

Saturday 23rd August 1884

Before I left Hill St. for the War Office, I received a note from Hartington saying that Gladstone concurred in the proposal of sending me to Egypt. I was astonished, for although I thought matters by and by would force him to send me out, I did not think he would have the necessary design of character to make up his mind quickly, especially as he has not yet allowed his mind to dwell upon the necessity of sending any expedition at all to relieve Gordon. He thinks, or at least he says so, that Gordon can come away from *Khartoum* whenever he likes, and that he has received all the Government messages & despatches but won't answer them as he is determined to have nothing more to do with a Cabinet to whom 'he has left the indelible disgrace &c. &c.'

This shows the chemistry of Gladstone's mind. We all know that, even assuming for argument's sake that Gordon's actions are influenced by such childish motives, there is with him in *Khartoum* a *Times* correspondent to whom it is all important to get messages to his employers, and yet not one line has come from him as yet. To the military, the commonplace mind, this is the clearest proof that *Khartoum* is most closely besieged, those inside being completely cut off from the outside world, and unable to communicate with it in any way. It is said, the note sent by Gordon that was received by the Mudir of Dongola, was little larger than a postage stamp. Mr. Gladstone's idea is, that if an expedition be sent to *Khartoum*, Gordon will refuse to leave that place.

During the course of the day, Hartington heard from Granville saying he fully entered into his colleague's difficulties and therefore gave his concurrence to the proposal to send me out. He did so evidently with no light heart, for he said that military enterprise was the most fascinating and absorbing of human passions, and that under its influence I should be sure to bring about an expedition when I was in Egypt. He added, what did Hartington mean to do when I left, who was to advise him on military subjects? Had he anyone else to rely on? When Hartington read me this letter, he said, but when you get to Egypt we shall wash our hands entirely of all responsibility regarding any expedition or other military operation in that country: on you will rest all such responsibility and we shall only have to comply with your demands upon us. He then discussed the question as to who should take up my work when I left. He is to ask Stephenson to stay on in *Cairo* to command under me in Lower Egypt, but if he asks to be relieved, he will bring him home to be Q.M.G., Herbert[12] acting for me in my absence.

Hartington wrote to the Queen giving his reasons at length for my appointment, and sent a copy to the Duke of Cambridge—poor old man he will be furious. I am very useful to him, but at the same time he must feel that I overshadow him at the War Office & that it is my views and not his which prevail there. He has sufficient power often to thwart my most reasonable proposals for reform, but he can initiate nothing on reactionary lines as long as I am Adjt. Genrl. Now with Herbert and Stephenson he will once more be Lord again in what he regards as his own house, and I dread the initiation of some backward policy during my absence. However I cannot be in [two] places at the one time, and must only rely upon Sir R. Thompson[13] to prevent dangerous measures being adopted during my absence. Mr. Gladstone is very anxious that the announcement of my appointment should be made with great caution: he dreads my departure for Egypt interpreted as the determination on the part of the Govt. to send an Expedtn. It is any such operation that he dreads—as well indeed he may, for owing to the extreme folly with which he has conducted our affairs in Egypt, the despatch of such an Expedition now has been rendered doubly difficult. In April last I begged of them to prepare for this expedition which it was clear to me then—as it was to most ordinary men—we should be forced to send to *Khartoum*. If even a dull soldier had governed our policy in Egypt for the last year, no expedtn. would now be on the *tapis* & we should not be in the difficult and unbecoming position in which we now find ourselves on the Nile. These Ministers, of Gladstone's stamp, think they have nothing to learn from soldiers, & that they are much more capable of governing a foreign and even an Eastern country than the best of soldiers. Our present position in Egypt is the result, and similar conduct will always bring about similar results, but no Government by politicians is fit for rough weather, especially beyond our own shores.

Loo & I went to stay with the Alfred Austins[14] near Ashford, until Monday—Herbert Stewart travelled down in the train with us. Lovely warm weather.

Sunday 24th August 84

Was up at 5 a.m. & wrote until breakfast. Played lawntennis all the afternoon, Hothfield[15] & his soldier brother being at the party. A really hot day: everything in the neighbourhood burnt up from want of rain.

Monday 25th August 1884

We returned early to London. The Queen will not yet say Yes to my appointment. She is in communication with 'George', who is doing all he can to prevent my going out. Hartington is at Bolton Abbey. The Duke was to have gone to Dunrobbin today, to which place I sent my letter on Saturday. He went to Edinburgh instead, from whence he telegraphs his useless appeals against my going to Egypt.

Tuesday 26th August

I write this so long after the event that I forget the exact dates, but I think we dined with Lady Burdett-Coutts[16] at Holly Lodge & when at dinner received the notice that the Queen had given her consent. The mode of announcing the fact in tomorrow's papers had been settled in the War Office during the afternoon, also the telegram to poor Stephenson, for whom I feel the deepest sympathy in this matter.

Wednesday 27th August

Entries for the following days, pages 14, 15 and 16 of the Journal, are missing.

September 1884

Tuesday 9th September 1884 On board H.M. *Iris*.

We had timed our rate of speed so as to reach our moorings in Alexandria Harbour by noon, which was duly accomplished. In approaching the entrance we steamed through four of our very finest Ironclads at anchor outside. We found one Ironclad inside with the Admiral flying his flag on the despatch boat *Helicon,* now on its 'last legs'. Bands playing and usual salutes in honor of Lord Northbrook who flies a flag as 'High Commissioner'. A number of boats came round us, sight-seeing and a crowd of people—most of them idlers—to welcome us to this infortunate country of the Pharohs [*sic*]. Arranged to leave for *Cairo* by special train at 3.30 p.m. Crowds in the streets to see the latest development of the uncertain English policy. Col. Ashburnham[17] K.C.B. at the station. He commands for the present in *Alexandria*. An old Gentleman of the very old school, very Gentlemanlike and stupid: a very bad commanding officer, but of a sort which H.R.H. wishes to honor. The Duke told me before starting he is to be given a Staff appointment at home. Stephenson tells me he will be very glad to get rid of him, and would be grateful to H.R.H., if for regard to uselessness for all practical purposes H.R.H. would similarly reward some other of the Commdg. Offrs. who are here. The Duke thinks Ashburnham a first-rate officer, in which view dear old Whitmore[18] fully concurs. The latter was never any use as an officer on service himself and is partial to men of his own mental & military calibre. Stephenson, Dormer & Buller came on board to meet us.

The first named has become a real old man. He is such a Gentleman in every sense so honest, straightforward, and anxious to do right to the utmost of his capacity, that I hate the idea of superceding him. Buller tells me that when he received Hartington's telegram informing him of my appointment he determined to resign, but before telegraphing to that effect received my letter written to him on the 21st or 22nd August before I was asked to come out, in which I told him that it was quite natural he should take the view he did regarding the impracticability of the smallboat scheme; that had I been in his place without the experience of the Red River Expedition, I feel sure I should have arrived at the same conclusion that he had done. Adding that this plan having now been definitely settled, I knew he would throw his heart & soul into it as earnestly as if he had invented it himself. This letter so rubbed him down the right way, that he resolved to stay on, and I am very glad he has done so. However the position is a disagreeable one for both of us: he is so much older as an officer than I am, and commanded as a Lt. Colonel the troops on board H.M.S. *Transit* in which I sailed as merely a captain commdg. a company in the year 1857. He was always very slow and never very clear in his ideas, but he is sensible and very safe, and such a universal favorite, that all who surround him, feel a pleasure in serving him.[19]

We reached *Cairo* at 8 p.m. The usual crowd to meet us. Drove in one of Khedive's carriages to the *Kasr el Noussa* the palace where the Duke of Connaught lived when in *Cairo* with me in 1882. It is a charming place with nice gardens round it. Buller came & dined with me: he gives an unpleasant account of the planless manner in which military matters are conducted here. Dormer, Stephenson's Chief of the Staff is no organizer and although a hard-working officer is not the man to carry out or arrange the details for such a complicated operation as that before me.

Lord J. Hay[20] who was as pompous as usual told me he had yesterday received a telegram from E. Wood saying the first steamer they had endeavoured to get up [the] second cataract had stuck & that Commdr. Hammil[21] reported it was unsafe to attempt to take her up higher. Wood did not concur in this view, & wished to incur the risk. Hay very properly said that at that distance he could not decide between them; those on the spot must do so, and the Navy, having stated their opinion professionally, must carry out the General's order. The only point that seemed to interest Hay was the question which he put to me 'whether I was commdr. in Chief or General Commdg. in Chief'. I had never thought of the point and do not care a farthing which I am—I want power, not its name.

10-9-84

I afterwards learnt he put the same question as regards my rank the day following to Swaine[22] when he arrived at *Alexandria*. This is a good index to the man's character, & yet they tell me he is a good officer. The weather here is charming—much cooler than it was in 1882. Thermometre in a room closed by day & open at night only ranges between 71° and 78°. This I subsequently verified with a registering thermometre. The Nile is low and they tell me it is not now to be expected to rise again to any extent that would help the crop of Indian corn upon which the mass of the population in Upper Egypt depends for food & subsistence. There are whole districts there which cannot be cultivated except the Nile runs beyond a certain point as the general level of the country is so high above the river. I presume that by and by this may be rectified by canals starting from the Nile above the Cataract at *Assuan*. In the meantime there will be a great diminution of revenue next year. Fricke[23] I think is somewhat impressed by the magnificence of having a palace provided for his accommodation.

Wednesday 10th September

Paid my respects to the Khedive in my old quarters in the Abdin Palace where he now lives, having quitted that in which he lived as Prince & then as Khedive when his mother died, to whom he was very much attached. His reception of me was not only cordial but affectionate: he spoke English; two years' association with our officers having renewed his acquaintance with that most manly and vigorous language which he told me he had learnt when very young. He is not in the least changed since I last saw him; not stouter or thinner. He told me he had fitted out & sent up the Nile for my use, one of his best Yachts. Nothing could be more gracious than he was. After leaving him I went to Evelyn Baring's[24] to have the question considered as to what is the smallest amount of troops that can be left in Egypt proper when an Expedition is sent up the Nile beyond the 2nd Cataract. Mr. Egerton,[25] Lord Northbrook, Evelyn Baring and Genrl. Stephenson, and the two head police officers of *Cairo*—both English—were present. I propounded the proposition, and asked if 1½ Battns. of Infry. & one Garrison Battery were sufficient for *Alexandria* & for *Cairo* 3 Battns. of Infry., the Batteries of Horse & Field Artillery, one Garrison Batty. and 1 squadron of Cavalry would suffice. All said yes. The Khedive returned my visit at 11.30 a.m., when I again thanked him for all his kindness and hospitality. Then I had visits from Nubah Pasha & the other Ministers—Nubah, very Turkish in features, a cunning old fox who is striving to run with the hare and hunt with the hounds. Dormer came to lunch bringing answers to a series of questions I have put to him. He is [a?] very Piano and thinks he ought to be employed. I impressed upon him the fact that I should have only one Infantry Brigade & could not find employment for more than one Majr. General. I wrote to Wood & telegraphed to him the substance of my letter asking him to become the General of Communications, explaining to him that under the circumstances it was the best post I could give him. Of course he thinks he ought to be Commdr. in Chief for a vainer man God never created. My plan of operations may be briefly stated thus. In Lower Egypt under Stephenson, 4½ Battns. of Infry., 1 Squadn. of Cavalry, one Horse one Field & two Garrison Batteries Rl. Artillery. Between *Assiout* (the southern terminus of Rl. Rd.) and *Hannek,* Wood's Native Army & one Battn. British. From *Hannek* to *Berber* (inclusive) five Battns. of British, and for the fighting force to relieve Gordon 5 British Battns., 3 squadrons XIXth Hussars, one Camel Battn. (6 guns) R.A.: 2 Guns of Native Battery, 400 Mounted Infry. (on camels), the Native mounted Infry. (on camels), and a Camel Corps to be specially raised in England by taking 40 men from each Regt. of Cavalry at home—Household Cavalry included, from each Battaln. of Foot Guards, & from the two Battns. of Rifle Brigade at home—also 100 men from the Rl. Marines at *Suakim*. This will give a Corps of 1200 first-class men.

Of course H.R.H. will combat this proposal tooth & nail, but I shall be firm and must trust to Hartington to support me & overcome all such obstruction. In my despatch asking for these men I have asked for two more Battns. from Malta.

Wardrop[26] & I drove in the evening to see Wauchope[27] Rl.

Highlanders. He looks thin & far from well but is as stout-hearted as if he had never been ill for one moment.

Thursday—11th Septr.

Working hard at calculations about stores & provisions for the expedition. Dined with Evelyn Baring, Stewart, Maurice,[28] Harrison,[29] Ld. C. Beresford[30] and Swaine arrived here last evening, also St. Leger Herbert.[31] They have just scraped through before the Quarantine for ships coming from Trieste was imposed. Brackenbury & others who will arrive by next week's steamer will have to do 5 days' quarantine on arrival at *Alexandria*. Serve master Brackenbury right for not coming by first ship he could as Stewart and others did. The climate delightful.

Friday 12th Septr.

At work all day. Begin to see some daylight through the job I have before me. I can afford to say in this my private journal that if I had not come out there would have been little chance of relieving *Khartoum* this winter. if enemy does not funk when the news of our arrival at *Debbeh* reaches those who are now besieging Gordon.

Saturday 13th Sept.

This day two years ago, God blessed me with a great success:[32] may he similarly bless me in this new undertaking. The Khedive has sent me a splendid riding Camel, beautifully caparisoned. It is from his own stables: the price of such an animal here ranges from £120 to £200. Before the days of telegraph or postal steamers on the Nile they were common in Egypt: now they are rare in these parts. A very gracious telegram from the Queen in remembrance of this anniversary. I had a very nice letter from Stephenson in answer to one I wrote him asking him to stay on here until this Nile expedition had been brought to an end. Of course he naturally feels most deeply the fact of being superceded. It is the heaviest blow a man can receive. Canrobert[33] had to live through it in the Crimea, and very possibly the keenness of the pain may yet be in store for me. May Almighty God deliver me from it however. In this present instance I can compare Stephenson's conduct with that of other men whom I have superceded on various occasions & I am bound to admire it. He is a far better soldier from every point of view than Chelmsford:[34] he is by no means clever, but he has more brains than that very silly noble lord and when I contrast the airs and graces he, Chelmsford, gave himself when I tried to be amiable to him in South Africa in 1879, I am struck with the superiority of Stephenson's character.

The bazaar rumor here is, that *Khartoum* has for a long time been in the possession of the rebels by whom Gordon is said to have been hanged. These bazaar rumors which in India in 1857-8 & 59 were almost always true as to the main facts, the events, such for instance as the fall of *Delhi*—are here it appears invariably unreliable.

14th September—Sunday

At present we are living very well, all our meals coming from Shepherd's Hotel.[35] A cup of tea at 6 a.m.: breakfast at 11 a.m., tea at 5 p.m. & dinner at 7.30 p.m. I have no horses of my own so I ride those of a small escort of the 19th Hussars which I keep with me at the *Kasr el Noussa*. Being freely interpreted I believe that means the Palace of Victory. I hope the omen is a good one. Took a pleasant ride in the evening.

Monday 15 Septr.

Rode to the Citadel in the morning. In returning I found Ld. Northbrook & Stephenson & a large staff going there to see the men at their posts as if it was being attacked. Upon returning I drove to the Canal to see an experiment tried of one or two camels harnessed to track a boat. It was most successful, and I hope by arranging 1000 of our baggage camels with this gear, to help our boats forward a great deal. Drove out in the evening to return visits which above all things I detest most. Had a very interesting conversation with Riaz Pasha whom I presume will be the next Prime Minister if Nubar is turned out as I should be inclined to recommend. Yesterday I received the news of three men being drowned in 2nd Cataract. I hate men dying so. How much better to die nobly fighting with all one's nerves strung up & full of that sentiment of loyalty to Queen and of patriotism which fills me with a sort of pride in myself when I am being shot at and fighting for my country.

My living here costs me £20 a day besides my own wine & my pay is only half of that—very pleasant this! What stuff it is asking a General Officer in the field to live on such a stipend. However when I leave *Cairo* I shall come down to camp fare and live on less than half that amount. Received telegrams announcing that my proposal to extend Halfa Rl. Rd. was approved & that 1100 men from Foot Guards & Cavalry at home would leave England about 25th inst. I shall be curious to hear how H.R.H. viewed my proposal.

Tuesday—16th Septr.

Rode to *Abasseyba* and inspected ponies from Russia. They are for the present a failure. Very foolish of Stephenson to have imported them. Dined with Dormer & his party—music afterwards.

Wednesday 17th Septr.

Inspected the Black Watch at 7 a.m. at *Kasr el Nile* Barracks: they looked very well: made them a little speech & praised their behaviour in Suakim campaign. Rode in the evening to Ghizereh Islands where I saw a very good game of polo played. Dined with Stephenson, Nubar, and Andul Khadir there. Curious telegrams from Gordon in *Khartoum*, announcing his intention of sending Stewart[36] to *Berber* to take it, hold it for a fortnight & then burn it: Stewart to go on to *Dongola* with Egyptian troops. He again asks for Tebelu to succeed him & recommends Sultan sending Turkish troops to hold Soudan.[37] This will cause Mr. Gladstone to believe that no expedition to *Khartoum* is necessary—why send troops to Gordon if he can come out when he likes? Brackenbury & Webber[38] arrived.

Thursday 18th Septr.

Inspected the Gordon Highlanders in Citadel at 7 a.m. A splendid Battn. Drove in the afternoon with Mr. Beaman[39] to the Bazaar & bought carpets, etc. Dined with the Khedive in my old quarters in the Abdin Palace. Fireworks afterwards. More telegrams from Gordon.[40]

Friday 19th Septr.

Inspected the Cameron Highlanders at Abdin Barracks, afterwards the 1st Berkshire at *Kasr el Nile*. In the evening paid visits & had a dinner party at home. Gordon inundates us with telegrams without giving us any satisfactory intelligence.[41]

Saturday 20th Septr.

Inspected the troops at *Abessiyeh* at 6.30 a.m. All well turned out: the Rl. Irish from India a very *varmint*-looking lot all truly Irish in appearance. Then rode to Evelyn Baring's & had a long talk with him, Ld. Northbrook and Sir C. Wilson[42] who arrived yesterday evening, (with A. Creagh,[43] Childers[44] & Adye.[45]) A telegram had arrived early from Mudir of Dongola saying that the siege of *Khartoum* had been raised & most of the tribes were making their submission.[46] This was at once made public here. I thought Northbrook talked very sillily, Baring listening to him, with respect but apparently attaching no importance to his views. I said that I thought I should go up the Nile as soon as possible & proposed to start this day week. This was agreed to—Wilson to start next Tuesday. I telegraphed to Gordon asking him for information as to the strength & composition of his Garrison, supplies &c and whether report of siege being raised was true—If so, for what purpose he wanted British troops at *Khartoum*, adding I could be at *Debbeh* with respectable British force early in December.[47]

I am extremely put out with Haliburton[48] the Director of Stores & Transport: it was laid down in his presence by our Mobilisation Committee that all boat supplies should reach Egypt a fortnight before the boats. I expect the first batch of boats in *Alexandria* on the 23, 24th and 25th inst. & yet not an ounce of boat provisions has yet arrived.

Telegraphed to Hartington that I should not most probably require the services of the two Battns. I had asked for from Malta but that when I had consulted with Ld. Northbrook tomorrow I should let him know definitively.

Had a dinner party at home, Northbrook, E. Baring & others dined here. Thermometre in my room ranges from a minimum of 68° at night to 78° by day (only ten degrees of range).

Sunday 21st Septr.

Had a long conference with Northbrook & E. Baring. Settled the instructions I am to receive. They will go home by tomorrow's post, & the Govt. will telegraph their approval or any alterations they wish to have made in them. Telegraphed to Hartington that I should not require the two Battns. from Malta, but might possibly ask for them by & bye if affairs altered for the worse. I shall most probably leave this on Saturday next the 27th instant for *Wady Halfa*. Took a pleasant ride in the evening. It is now tolerably certain that the siege of *Khartoum* has been raised. Had a large dinner party at home. Wrote letters all day for English mail which leaves *Cairo* tomorrow evening. The Hd. Qtrs. of Sussex Regt. reached *Dongola* last evening having left *Sarras* in Native Boats on 8th instant. It has only two months' provisions with it, so I must soon send it more groceries & flour—possibly they can obtain plenty of fresh bread & meat locally.

Monday 22nd Septr. 1884

As was to be expected, I received a telegram from Hartington asking if the despatch of the Camel Corps from England might also be delayed as well as the two Battns. from Malta. I have answered certainly not. Lord Northbrook left for *Alexandria*; I saw him before he left, and discussed matters with him. A telegram[49] from Kitchener saying he had just returned from *Merawi* and wanted to take all the Mudir's troops with him and to start for *Berber*. I have replied[50] that he must remain at *Debbeh* where the telegraph ends as I want to have a reliable agent there until I can get troops to that place and until Sir C. Wilson who leaves *Cairo* tomorrow reaches *Dongola*. Paid a visit to Sheriff Pascha [*sic*] who takes a very gloomy view of his country and of its future. Had a dinner party at home. Met Mr. Barère[51] today.

Tuesday—23rd—Septr.

Had a pleasant ride in the evening.

Wednesday—24th Septr.

Paid a number of visits in the afternoon, to the Princess Rozalie amongst others.

Thursday 25th Septr.

Started a little after 5 a.m. on horseback for the Pyramids where I breakfasted: rode home and dressed for dejeuner at the Abdin Palace with the Khedive at noon. Called on E. Baring who showed me telegrams[52] from Granville approving of my having full powers in the Soudan. Gordon has been told by telegram[53] that he is not to burn *Berber* & that his authority in Soudan is restricted & that he is to obey my orders.

I am to be armed with a firman from Khedive which I am to hold in reserve using it only in case that Gordon refuses to obey me—which I do not for a moment think is possible.[54] The firman revokes Gordon's powers & gives them or at least most of them to me.

The Khedive was most anxious to learn what our policy was to be when I reached Soudan. I could only say that nothing definite has as yet been settled. Butler[55] arrived in great spirits. I recommended Baring to ask Ld. Granville to allow me to make the Mudir of Dongola a K.C.M.G. when I reached that place & it has been approved that I am to do so if I think it expedient.[56] I have borrowed Buller's decorations for that purpose.

Friday 26th Septr.

Inspected Lt. Col. Lloyd's[57] mule battery of Mountain Guns (200 lb. guns). The turn out very creditable considering it has only had this mule equipment for a few days in possession. Writing hard for the mail. Dined with Nubar Pasha.

Saturday 27th Septr.

It was this morning & not yesterday that I inspected the mule Battery in the Citadel. Took an affectionate leave of the Khedive & then had long conversations with Baring and Northbrook about what is to be done with *Khartoum*.

Saturday 27th Septr. continued

I told everyone I did not like being 'seen off' but still there was a goodly crowd at the station to say good bye. We started at 8.30 p.m. by special train.

Sunday 28th Septr.

Reached *Sint* at 6.30 a.m. after a very dusty journey. Found

Maurice in great form: piles of camel saddles, grain bags, fire wood, and all the usual signs of military operations in every direction round the Rl. Rd. sidings and river's banks. The arrangements for lading ships very bad as the line ends at right angles to the river & the rights of private property prevent a siding being run up along the bank. Our rowing boats from England are also being packed away in barges, Messrs. Cook doing all the work for us. The early mornings are simply delicious now: I have never felt any air so exquisite, so enjoyable and yet so fresh. I feel as if I could do anything in such a climate. We did not succeed in getting under weigh before 8 a.m. The Steamer is named the *Ferooz* and is the largest of the Khedive's Yachts for the river. She is clean & comfortable: a paddler. She has a Captain & Lieutenant in smart naval uniform who greeted me on going on board. The Lieut. understands some French but the Captain speaks nothing but Arabic. To show me he understood a little English, when I shook hands with him on making his aquaintance he grinned from ear to ear & said 'Good bye, Good bye'. We steamed gaily along all day against a current of about 3 miles an hour getting over the ground at the rate of about $7\frac{1}{2}$ miles an hour, & moored alongside a floating stage at *Girgeh* about 8 p.m. the distance run being nearly 100 miles. . . .

I forgot to mention that when discussing our political position with Evelyn Baring yesterday, apropos of the jealousy & hatred of France towards us at this moment, that he told me he had said to Northbrook when in England your policy must be dictated by your naval strength: if your fleet is not in perfect order and fully & certainly able and in every unmistakable way able to destroy as well as to cope with that of France, you should sing small, and not attempt to bluster or force your policy down Johny Crapeaud's throat. Lord N. replied our navy would if required be fully equal to the occasion. Baring had told me this before and I replied that I hoped Northbrook was right, but that every good officer in our Navy told a different story. Yesterday Baring said that owing to my remarks on the subject he had again pressed Northbrook on the subject & had received from him the most positive assurance that our naval superiority & preparedness were undoubted, that we might remember this in all our diplomatic dealings with that swaggering, impolite and vainglorious nation. God grant this may be the case: I cannot forget Le Boeuf's answer to Napoleon III when asked as to the preparedness of the French Army for War in

1870. I know that all Northbrook's professional advisers do not think this, and party politicians who are civilians, easily persuade themselves that Army & Navy is in the best condition when the very reverse is known to the best men who belong to those professions....

Monday 29th September

Started about 4.30 a.m. & reached *Keneh* about 1 p.m. passing on the way the *Black Watch* in two steamers, towing four large iron barges, lashed together two & two. It is curious to see the number of rock tombs dug into nearly all of the precipitous sides of the cliffs we go by. It appears the ancients never buried their dead on the side of the river where their towns stood. Whenever you see any great number of these rock sepulchres, you may assume that a town or large city existed in by-gone ages on the opposite bank. *Keneh* is on the right bank, but we landed on the opposite side of the river to visit the temples & ruins of *Denderah* the home of Cleopatra. The great temple which still exists there was finished by her & it was there she received by night in its gloomy & mysterious chambers the ambassadors & envoys of all the sovereigns who sent to pay her court. Close by her majestic temple is that of the god *Tiphou* the god of evil to whom she offered her prayers. There is also a triumphal arch standing. When the French were here at the end of the last century, there was nothing to be seen here but some great mounds of earth: all these remains have been excavated since then. We had some iced soda water in the cool chambers of the temple: smoked a cigar whilst the Mudir—a squinting Turk—looked on. We started [&] returned to the river riding the inevitable donkey as usual. The telegraph station is on the left bank opposite *Keneh*, and before I started on our visit to the ruins I had left a Corporal of R.E. to telegraph to *Cairo* for any messages that might be waiting me there. I found a long one from *Suakim* saying that 5 letters had been received from Gordon, the two latest being dated the 30th & 31st July.[58] In these he describes some of the fights they have had with the rebels round *Khartoum* in one [of] which Stewart was wounded but was then quite recovered. He said he had spent some hundreds of thousands of pounds, & was in want of more money—had expended 500,000 rounds of S.A.A.: that the people would not let him leave unless he brought away with him the women & families of the employees even if he wished to do so. He said any abandonment of the Province of Senaar would be fatal to Egypt, and that nothing could be done until British troops arrived: their best route would be the left bank of the Nile as far as *Berber*. This is the route I have always recommended. Our wretched creatures whom we term a Ministry have now got a straight declaration from Gordon: he has been most consistent all through, although they have endeavoured to throw blame upon him and to make him appear ridiculous in the eyes of our people. He is so infinitely superior to every man in our Cabinet both as a patriot and as a high-minded man of honor that I hope our people may be able to distinguish between the dross of party politicians and the honest pure metal of which he is made. The only exception I would make is Lord Hartington. He has been bred and educated by Granville in the Whig faith but is far more of an Englishman than his master and is more of a patriot than a party politician. I think he is right not to break with his party just now: such a move would injure his power of usefulness in the future and would not break up the faction that is now bringing our once great & proud Empire to the level of Holland. Northbrook wishes to do right, but he is a strong party *official* & not a statesman: he is weak, with the impetuosity and obstinacy of all weak men & has no talent, little real ability although considerable administrative experience. My earnest hope is that Gladstone may be turned ignominiously out of office soon on account of his utter failure in Egypt and that when the Conservatives come in they may take up this Egyptian muddle in a patriotic way & deal with it on purely patriotic grounds. I think it great folly—the worst of ignorant, cowardly folly—to force Egypt to give up the Eastern Soudan. I would administer it by an English Governor for Egypt, and I believe it would pay all its expenses in five years and secure peace to Egypt. If it is evacuated without any stable Government being established, there will be no peace for Egypt, and more military expeditions will be entailed upon us with all their costliness.

Rec'd a telegram[59] from Baring saying as I expected he could not approve of the terms of the Khedive's letter to Gordon of which I am the bearer & would ask Nubar to have another one written & sent to me in place of it. The Black Watch reached *Keneh* at 5 p.m. having started from *Assiout* last Wednesday the 24th inst. They will not reach *Assouan* before the

5th or 6th proxo. It is slow work, a steamer taking two heavy barges.

Tuesday 30th September

Started before daybreak, and reached *Luxor* at 10 a.m. Visited *Karnak* which ruins Ferguson[60] the great writer on architecture says are the most wonderful in the world. We preferred going forward so as to reach *Assouan* quickly to going over the ruins of *Thebes* on the opposite bank. I should have liked to have examined the two Colossi which I could plainly see standing in the plain opposite, but as regards the other ruins generally I confess that I cannot work myself up into anything like a deep interest in the ruins of this country. They refer to a period of which I know nothing and of which even the most learned in the subject know little: I became worne [*sic*] out in contemplating their hieroglyphics, one set being apparently exactly a repetition of the other. To me York Minster or Litchfield Cathedral appeals more & more the more I see of Upper Egypt: the monuments of those great churches are those of men whom I seem to have known personally and the history they seem to breath, is the history I know, and of a time I enjoy to dwell upon. When I am told such or such a monolith was erected by Ramses the IIId of the 18th dynasty it is gibberish to me: it recalls nothing I take any interest in or care to investigate. This plain of Thebes is a fine one, but it is very restricted, and I cannot understand how it was that so small a country as Egypt must always have been, could ever have afforded to construct such vast piles of useless buildings in honour of an obscene and senseless and idolatrous religion. It must have been a country with a royal family who assumed priestly if not sacred pretensions with perhaps a very small nobility whilst the Army and the rest of the population were slaves both in mind & in body. It fell easily a prey to foreign nations: it had not the real strength or vitality to defend itself, & foreigners have ruled here ever since and will do so till the end of time as has been foretold in our Bible. I am thus far very agreeably surprised with the scenery on the Nile. I expected to find it very monotonous, but have not done so as yet. This life on the Nile is delicious idleness: today is a little warmer than is pleasant when in the sun but in another month the climate will be superb. No wonder men & women worn out by dissipation or hard work find relief on its waters. If one were an idler, one might dream away a winter here most enjoyably: but working not dreaming is my lot and very fortunately my lot in life, and I am here to serve England, not to lie on my back and think of imaginary pleasures. We halted for the night at *Edfu*.

October 1884

Wednesday 1st October

Off before daybreak & reached *Assuan* about 2 p.m. I am told it is much hotter here than at *Halfa*. The heat is much less here now than it was a fortnight ago. Coming here we passed one place where the River narrowed considerably between cliffs of rock in some of which were curiously cut tombs. Then the remains of a fine temple on a rocky eminence on the right bank dedicated I believe to the worship of the Crocodile.

We ran along side the right bank, near where the dahabeyeh was moored in which Grenfell[61] lives. Captain Boardman R.N.,[62] and several Colonels boarded us at once. I just caught the post boat as it was starting with the mails for England, so I hope my letter of today to Loo[63] & my Journal up to yesterday may be at *Cairo* in time for this week's mail for home. In the evening rode through the camps: never has there been a dustier site found: I am sure the men will suffer from opthalmia if I have to leave them there long. The town is much better built and cleaner than those we have hitherto passed to the north of this, and I am told they are also much cleaner inside. Indeed the first thing which struck me as we arrived today, was the increased cleanliness of all classes here: even the small boys had a smarter appearance and most of them had clean clothes on: the type of feature is somewhat different and I am told the language is very different, so much so, that few of our interpreters can understand this dialect. We may now be said to be in Nubia, where the people are certainly more manly than the miserable Fellaheen of Lower Egypt. It must be remembered that whenever Egypt pushed conquering armies into Nubia and the Soudan they were composed of foreigners not Fellaheen. The only really Fellaheen Army that ever faced the men of the Soudan was that under poor Colonel Hicks and its fate does not encourage one to repeat the experiment. I don't think I have mentioned that in my conversations with Cheriff Pasha—who was Prime Minister when Hicks' army was destroyed—he took the greatest trouble to impress upon me that Hicks was confident of success & was told not to attack unless he felt certain of victory. That neither he— Cheriff, nor the Khedive were responsible for Hicks' operations for which Hicks alone was to blame. This is a very hot place, and two months ago the heat must have been very trying to the English Officers stationed here: it is always hotter, I am told, than *Wady Halfa*, which is 233 miles further south (2° further South) [Marginal note in pencil 'something wrong here'] and well within the tropics.

Thursday 2d October. 84

Inspected the garrison: The 2/Cornwall, 2/Essex, and one Battn. the Regt. of Cavalry, two Batteries of Camel Guns, Mounted Infry. & a small Camel Corps of the Egyptian Army. The dust was so terrible that when the troops were marching past one could barely see them. I then saw the Camel Guns come into action & the men of the Camel Corps dismount and advance on foot. I then went by rail to *Phila* where I went over the ruins whilst the *Ferooz* was coming up the rapids which she did easily and safely a few hundred men being stationed at the worst point to haul her through where she could not use her paddles. Started at 2 p.m. having two dahabeezehs in tow—what a diabolical word to spell is this infernal Nile boat. Above *Assuan* the river assumes an entirely different aspect: bare rocky hills come close down to the river covered with loose boulders reminding one of the hills and kopps of Sikukuni's country.[64] Here and there narrow patches of cultivation and a few houses with now & then little villages, but palm trees on both banks sometimes in great numbers. The French who had pursued the Mamlooks [sic] to *Assuan* in 1799, after Napoleon's victory near Cairo—which he called the battle of the Pyramids—halted here for some time under General Desaix, Genrl. Davoust being also with them. Of course they wrote up their names like the ordinary vulgar tourist, but they also recorded the Lat. & Long. which I presume is quite accurate, as the French Army was then accompanied by many savants who gave to the world under the directions of its greatest son, the first—and perhaps even up to date the best and most learned account of this strange land of slavery & idolatry. Their calculations may therefore be assumed to be accurate, so I record them Lat. N. 24°–3′–45″–Long. E. (from Paris) 30°–16′–22″. As I looked at that inscription amidst a mass of ruins many of which were built by the Caesars, I thought of that great strange man who at the beginning of this century struck terror into every civilised nation all of whom were only saved by the courage of the English people and skill of an English Admiral and of an English General, directed by the far-seeing grasp of a real English Statesman. It was here as it was in Europe, the visions, the great dreams of conquest and universal Empire entertained by that Giant amongst the Pigmies of the earth were dashed to pieces by British courage, & he slunk back to Paris a wiser and a sadder man with an intensified hatred of that island Nation which was eventually to send him to that little dot of land in mid-ocean which was to be his prison & his grave. I confess that this record of Napoleon, here on the very frontier line of Egypt, afforded me more interest than all these 'cartouches' of wretched ox & cat worshipping Pharoahs of whom the little we know, cannot allow us either to admire or to respect. As I dwelt with pride upon the recollection of what England under great statesmen had done for Europe, I bent my head with a feeling of degradation when I compared the England which Mr. Gladstone has demoralized and ruined, with what it was in its glorious days when it shone forth as the first champion of liberty. Oh, how are the mighty fallen!

We brought up for the night on the left or western bank a short distance beyond a little ruined temple and at the entrance of a very narrow gorge called *Bab-el-Kalabsheh* (bab means gate) through which the pilot said he could only take us in broad daylight. The flies today have been a real plague—they attack you even in a strong wind which in most countries protects you against their annoyance. As the sun goes down however they retire apparently to regain strength for their work next day.

Friday 3rd October 1884

We did not get under weigh until about 5 a.m. so as to have good, clear daylight for the rocky gorge before us. The river narrowed to under 400 yards, so the rush of water must have been great, yet its surface was unrippled: it must be very deep at such points—as yet we have seen nothing that our boats need dread. Yesterday's cataract is a plaything. The total fall of water is now about 17 feet.... My Aneroid shows 300 ft. as the difference between *Cairo* and the river as we are nearing *Korosko,* and my registering thermometre shows the same in my cabin as it did in my room in the *Kasr el Nousa* namely 68° the minimum & 78° the maxm. Adye has been attacked by opthalmia: the fact is he is not fit for this work and as soon as we begin a real rough life he will cave in and either die or I shall have to take care of him when I have other things to do than look after weakly young men. If he gets to *Khartoum* he will never come back I feel assured. Yet his father will never listen to the idea that he is not as strong as other young fellows of the same age—Old Adye is himself as hard as nails and cannot realize anyone not being as tough as he is, much less his own son. We ran on until past 8 p.m.

Saturday 4th October

I do not intend smoking until the 1st of next month. [(Marginal note. A vow I made. It was in accordance with a similar vow to God made subsequently at *Korti*, that I gave up smoking for ever. It was the greatest of my creature comforts & to punish myself I gave it up forever. I have never broken that vow since: 6-5-1904).] Got under weigh at daybreak and reached *Korosko* at 8.30 a.m. Maj. Rundle R.A.[65] in command there: he has one other English officer with him Captn. Shakespear[66] of the Marines: 2 Companies of Egyptian Infry. No news: amongst the telegrams[67] I received was one from Central News saying *Times* announced I had been recalled & asking if it were true. The rumor here is that Stewart bombarded *Berber* killed several people and then retired. It is said there are no troops at *Abu Hamed* or *Berber,* & that everyone lives in dread of Gordon's attacks. I asked Rundle what the people thought of Gordon & if they often talked of him. He said oh yes, they have the utmost respect for him, they never know what he is going to do; he makes a man a pasha one day, degrades him perhaps the next and will flog him the day following: in the same way he gives rewards of money. Then as a camel traveller he is looked upon as a prodigy. He can even tire out the Bedouin & can get more out of a camel than other men. In fact he is wise enough to know that in dealing with an Eastern people you must do so upon Eastern lines & in accordance with Eastern ideas. The truly British notion of thinking that what is good enough for an Englishman must be equally suitable to all the world—nothing is more repulsive to the Eastern mind than our cold logical system & practice of justice. It is the exact reverse of an Eastern's notions on the subject. To him, everything must be personal, & the ruler more or less in the position of a father, the head of a family.

Hussein Pacha Khalifa formerly Governor of *Berber* who held out as long as he could has a son, Sala, who is now the principal man at *Korusco*. He is a nice-looking, well-bred and intelligent fellow. He has about 79 brothers & sisters, so his father must be what Artemus Ward called, a very extensively married man. We took in coal at *Korosco* & then steamed away, at about 10 a.m. going on until about 9 p.m. when we halted for the night. A complete eclipse of the moon.

Sunday 5th October 1884

I am annoyed at the Intelligence Dept. Almanac of which I have a proof copy given me before I left London. Well in the first place no other copies have been sent out here, and then again, no allusion whatever is made in it to the complete eclipse of the moon last night. This is monstrous: an eclipse of the sun may be in store for us just the very day that I might want to have his brightest rays for some military operation. Altogether I cannot say that the work done for war purposes of late in the Intelligence Dept. has been at all good. The book on Egypt was a poor & yet a bulky affair, and the recent red book on the Soudan is wretched. On the whole Murray[68] is quite as good upon many important points. The work seems as if turned out by men who have no practical knowledge of campaigning or of its requirements. . . .

Reached *Angash* (the northern end of *Wady Halfa* Rl. Road) about noon. There found telegrams[69] from Kitchener telling us that Gordon had carried out his programme about *Berber*. Some three or four steamers had reached that place and bombarded it.

Then Stewart and the European Consuls proceeded down the river in a steamer and two boats, the other steamers returning to *Khartoum* and setting fire to *Berber* as they passed it. Stewart's steamer seems to have got safely through all but the very last Cataract where within one day's camel journey of *Meravi*, the steamer stuck on a rock. All the neighbouring people bolted at first, but then came back: the Sheikh went on board and peace was established—he was given a sword & dress of honor, promised to provide camels & to be their guide. When the camels arrived the party went on shore & were set upon and murdered. This villain took the steamer & killed everyone except four. The news requires confirmation but it is too circumstantial I am afraid not to be true. Poor Stewart, his loss just at this moment is a national one. A fine chivalrous fellow to die at the hands of a murderer! May that murderer fall into my hands.

I rode with Earle and Wood about the camp in the evening. I like this place much better than *Assuan*. Wood, Earle & a large party dined with me on board the *Ferooz*. Wood's vanity and self-seeking and belittlement of everyone but himself would be positively disgusting if one did not view it from the ridiculous side, and laugh at it & him instead of being angry over it. He is now anxious to make everyone believe that Earle is a fool & an old woman, this because he, Wood, is his junior & therefore Earle being in his way, must be got rid of. When I look back and remember my estimate of Wood's character as it was presented to me ten years ago & for many years subsequently, I begin to think I can be no judge of character, for Wood's cunning completely took me in, & I must have more than once done men wrong in valuing them in accordance with Wood's reports to me. He himself I have always known as one who is no judge whatever of men; the greatest goose can stand well with him if he only flatters him enough. Now one would think that a man so open to flattery as he is, would not believe in its power with others, but on the contrary, he is just like a woman whose one idea is that all men can be won over by flattery. He lays it on very thick. I believe I know when men & women are flattering me, and to me the most unpleasant sensation is the feeling that I am having compliments paid to me. *Very often* they try to flatter me by quoting the *Soldier's Pocket-book* as one might quote the Bible. When this is 'tried on', every fibre of my body bristles inwardly with rage against the individual who thus insults me. Wood at dinner last night was all on this track and very annoying it was. I know he is furious at my coming here but yet he would try to persuade me he is delighted to see me. Everything with him is a personal matter: he is a good soldier but he has every bad quality that women have. All this ridiculous Egyptian Army has been worked by him for purposes of self-glorification. Sir Henry Norman[70] was to have had the organization of it, and I have long felt how much better he would have done it. His object would have been the public service; Wood's sole object has been Wood.

Here we are in difficulty with our short railway. Baring & Vincent[71] in the interest of economy withdrew the engines from here and dismantled the line & now we have not only to submit to the expense of bringing all these things back here again, *up* the river, but what is much worse we have our progress seriously delayed by having to devote our steamers & river transport—which is very limited—to the conveyance of this Rl. Rd. material when it is all so much wanted for the conveyance of stores.

6th October: Monday

Shifted our quarters to a camp on the bank, alongside of which I have a dahabeeyeh moored in which I mean to sleep for the present, having my meals ashore. Buller adopts the same plan. Earle also lives in one, but Wood having come here first has appropriated a fine building for his mess & sitting room. I believe he sleeps from preference in an Indian tent.

Monday 6th October

Shifted into camp below the other camps. I am not sure it is a good move as now the water comes to us somewhat fouled, we being down stream. On the other hand our camp is more conveniently situated than it would have been above and we are now to windward of everyone. In these camps there are great numbers of scorpions. Why should we have venomous things of this sort? Visited the hospital in the evening: one man died today of enteric fever: 59 patients all doing well. Two nuses here. I dined with Wood: his compliments are repulsive. I wonder if he pays them to everyone he wishes to help Wood, or does he think me an especial idiot made to be fooled by flattery? He says he intends leaving the Egyptian Army and wants to get either Genrl.

Bulwer's[72] or Elkington's[73] places at the Horse Guards. Farewell to all harmony whenever he gets in there, for we should have nothing but intrigues on his & his sister, Mrs. Steel's part in the interest, not of any scheme or policy, but simply in Wood's interests. Besides I do not think he would fill either place well. My Aneroid 29° 90′—at *Cairo* it stood at 30° 20′.

Tuesday 7th October

Rode with Earle, Wood, Buller &c. &c. [to] the 'great gate', of this near Cataract, about 14 miles off. Started at 2 p.m. & got back about 6.30 p.m. We went at a good pace over level ground. I was disgusted with nearly all the boats I saw in the rapids today. They were of the very ricketiest nature with sails in ribands. The sailors under Commandr. Hammil are working very well. We passed in going out a company of the Egyptian Army on the march & it was disgraceful. No attempt whatever at keeping any formation, the men straggling all over the country. It was hot work riding fast & the flies were vexatious to suicide point almost. I find I have that nasty smell from my body which I always imagine it and clothes have in very hot countries. Fricke my butler I can now scent a long way off. This is a disagreeable idea, but what can one do? Sit still and do nothing? Yes & what would then become of the expedition?

Wednesday 8th October 1884

Inspected the I/South Stafford & the Mounted Infry. here early in the morning. Have heard nothing further in any definite shape yet as to poor Stewart's fate. He may possibly be still alive. Kitchener[74] is raving to be off in pursuit of something or somebody, but I don't like these aimless expeditions before arrangements are made for following up success. Otherwise any success you can gain is of very little use, and any failure—although it may only be partial—is more or less fatal. The Vakeel of the Mudir of Dongola is here, having arrived some time ago with some laborers to work in hauling boats through the cataracts. I sent for him today & had a talk with him about the Cataracts between *Murowi & Aboo Hamid*. He knows that District well, as he has lived there for years as Vakeel at *Berber*. He also knows the desert route from *Merawi* to *Berber*. He had come down in a Nugger from

Berber to *Dongola* at very high Nile without any difficulty or ever striking any rock. He is the first man I have ever spoken to who has done so. He says there are seven cataracts between *Aboo Hamid* & *Merawi* but that none of them are as bad as the *Halfa* cataract. He said he had heard a rumor in the bazaars that Stewart had been attacked & asked me for news. I asked him if a steamer could come down those 7 cataracts at any time of the year, he said certainly not & that a nugger could not do so now. This makes it difficult to believe in the story of Stewart and his party having come down near to *Merawi* in a steamer. The story of his having done so is told so circumstantially that it is hard to disbelieve it, and yet this Vakeel's evidence would apparently show it to be impossible for Stewart having ever got into the position described in that story. I am afraid it is too true in its main features, although I eagerly grasp at any straw that holds out any prospect of its being a bazaar concoction only.

In the evening I rode with Zorab Bey to the range of hills which bound the Nile valley on the east. There you can see how the desert sand has been formed by the disintegration of these sandstone hills during the last 4000 years. The extreme heat by day & great change of temperature at night has gone on splitting off great flakes from the exposed surface of all these rocks for centuries: in fact we here see exactly the same process which goes on in Canada with the granite there which disintegrates very freely by the alternate action of extreme heat & extreme cold upon all exposed surfaces, the frost after rain had filled up cracks & cranies, bursting rocks asunder as if by the force of wedges. As I looked north, south, east & west from the top of this range of hills, what a dreary prospect on all sides, the Nile forming the only one bright spot in the landscape. We could see the masts of our boats and our tents which together with the few palm & gum trees and the patches of green dhoura formed a strange contrast to all the surrounding desolation. The Camel Corps & the Voyageurs have reached *Alexandria*. Today Messrs. Cockburn,[75] Cameron,[76] Burleigh[77] & some other correspondent (Scudamore[78] I think) sent home a joint telegram saying that owing to the manner in which the censorship was exercised over their messages, & the delay in sending them forward it was quite useless their continuing to send any. I have asked these 'high-toned Gentlemen' to state particulars & let me know which of their messages have been delayed & in what injurious manner they have been altered by the military censor. The fact is they have little or nothing to send home and they wish to account for the meagerness [*sic*] of their messages. As long as they were with Evelyn Wood they received ample information of all that was going on, he being prepared to go any lengths with them as long as they praised him & made much of him in their telegrams. It was through him that most of our cypher messages became known.

Thursday 9th October 84

In few if any of my campaigning journals have I given any description of the clothes I wore, so I shall here state what I wear daily—flannel shirt, linen or a sort of mole-skin, khaki-colored breeches and untanned boots: during the day I wear a sort of Norfolk jacket of same material as my breeches, a good Kummerbund and a huge solar topee on my head. When the sun goes down I put on trousers and Norfolk jacket of serge—the latter being scarlet, being in fact the identical one I wore in the 1882 campaign. It is very necessary to have a padded protection to the backbone when exposed to the sun. Blue goggle spectacles are indispensable both to protect the eyes against dust, glare & flies. I remained in my boat writing all day as the post for England closes tomorrow early & I shall be away early. In the evening I took a trip a couple or three miles up the river in the little steam wherry Ld. John Hay had supplied me with. Telegram from Butler at *Assuan* saying the first lot of our 'whalers' (as we now call them officially) were rowed, tracked & poled up to the 1st Cataract safely yesterday. This will be strange news for Lord John Hay who wound up his pompous report upon the proposal to use whalers for this expedition by stating they could neither be tracked, rowed or poled up the Nile.

Friday 10th October

Started about 5.30 a.m. by rail for *Sarras*. There we mounted Egyptian cavalry horses & rode out along the line perhaps six or eight miles, & had a good view of how a branch could easily be run from the line down to the river to the head of the *Senneh* cataract. Over & over again I asked this question of Stephenson before I left England & was always told the same thing, it was impossible. That *'blathering'*, inaccurate Irishman Frazer[79] [*sic*] who is Wood's chief Staff Officer, repeated over & over to me that this could not be done. I ought to have insisted upon someone being sent to examine the ground accurately between the *Semneh* cataract and the railway, Had I done so, this line might now have been in working order and all our difficulties about this troublesome cataract be at an end. Now all I can do is to lay down rails & complete the line beyond *Sarras* for 17 miles, from whence an 11 miles' march down hill will take us to the top of the *Ambigole* cataract. How very annoying all this is. Wood has been here six weeks and has never found this out. In fact he relies upon that braying fellow Frazer.

Breakfasted at *Sarras* & got back to my dahabeeah about 2.30 p.m. This armed steamer *Nasif-el-Kheir* has reached *Dongola,* and I hope that Wilson may be there tonight or tomorrow. I have ordered him on in her to *Merawi* to enquire about facts of Stewart's steamer said to have been lost near there. What a thirsty country this is to be sure. When I eat frizzled ham for breakfast I feel as if nothing can quench my thirst all day. I shall give up eating salt or sugared things for this reason. What surprises me most here, is the small number of boats on the river above *Assuan*. We passed very few coming here, and there is only a small number at this place. Above *Hannek* where I had been led to believe there were hundreds of them, there are it is said only 60 some say 80. This shows to my mind that the trade between the Soudan & Egypt is really small. Of course the absence of forests, indeed I may say of any timber that could be used for boat building, accounts in a measure for the fewness of the craft on the river. The rumor now is, that Stewart was not in the steamer that was captured by the enemy near *Barkal-en-Nurri* that the party were under the command of the Greek Consul. I cannot believe this, for I don't think a Greek capable of attempting to run those seven cataracts in a steamer! it would be a wild exploit requiring the nerve of a Britisher, at least of someone more gifted with pluck than the contemptible modern Greek, the most wretched of all European races if one can flatter him with the idea that he is really the product of Europe's soil.

Saturday 11th October 1884

There was quite a storm in the night, and there have been clouds in the sky ever since, still it was warm in the afternoon. Sir C.

Wilson reached *Dongola*. Lord Northbrook has gone north. I hope he will soon let me have his steamer back, as I cannot afford to lend a steamer even to a 1st Lord of the Admiralty. We are horribly pressed for steam power on land and water. I went out for my first ride on a dromedary in the evening. We call all the riding camels dromedaries, in distinction to the camel which carries a load at a walking pace. They have both only one hump and are really the same animal but distinguished one from the other as the race horse is from his 1st cousin that draws a cart. I hate camels, they are so stupid: they begin to howl the moment you put a saddle on them and they smell abominably although not nearly so badly in this country as in India.

Every day makes me realize the difficulties I have before me if we must go in fighting condition to *Khartoum* by the Nile valley. Those who constitute the troops, think only of the excitement they may have in fighting with a brave enemy, but I have to think of & prepare for a far greater difficulty than the fighting part of this affair, namely the feeding of the men, horses & camels to be employed. Our time is so short that we cannot easily collect all the grain & chopped straw we require at *Dongola* or *Debbeh*.

Sunday 12 October. Wady Halfa

Divine service in the South Staffordshire Regt. A very hot day. English post of the 26th September arrived but no letters from *Loo*. In the evening I went out for a ride on my camel. During dinner—we dine at 7 p.m.—we had some heavy drops of rain and a heavy wind with a great deal of lightening and some very distant and very faint thunder. After this storm, as it was a storm for this country, the temperature became very oppressive. When I went to bed there were heavy thunder clouds about.

Monday 13th October 1884

A very trying night, extremely hot & no air: when it did blow the dust covered up everything. There was some rain during the night. This is most unusual here: is puzzling even to that omnipresent & misleading old fellow '*the oldest inhabitant*'. Rode early in the morning. Found Duncan[80] dressing when I routed him to enquire about light balls which I want to take with me if I have to fight to protect me against night attacks. I am also bringing up two miles of light wire to form entanglements[81] to protect our bivouacs at night. Rode into the hills to the east of the camp & saw the South Stafford manoevring through them. Telegram from *Suakim* says Chermside's[82] most reliable messenger just returned from *Berber*. He had started from *Suakim* on the 30th Septr. & had reached *Berber* on 6th October when he found three steamers bombarding town, which he was afraid to enter on account of the soldiers who were on the top of the houses firing. Now if this be accurate information it cannot be true that Stewart was murdered in the steamer near *Barkal-en-Nurri*. Those murdered upon that occasion must have been murdered about the 1st instant, and if the steamers were still bombarding *Berber* on the 6th we may assume that Stewart was with them; at least we may hope so with some appearance of certainty. At 3.30 p.m. the most violent storm came on from the North, blowing such clouds of sand from the desert on the left bank that we could not see that side of the river for some time. The reach of the river where we are moored rises [runs?] N.E. and S.W.: quite a heavy sea ran for some time. I hope it may clear the atmosphere which has been very oppressive for the last 48 hours. Rode my camel in the evening. During dinner another violent dust storm blowing this time from the South which covered us with mud. Some straggling rain. We were nearly blown from our moorings out into mid-stream, and until our Reis and his jabbering crew succeeded in furling our awning we lay over so much to leeward that the idea of turning bottom upwards flashed innocently through one's brain, and the suggestion that such a catastrophe would be followed by the loss of all one's campaigning kit did not serve to make the discomforts of the moment any lighter. After violent struggles with napkins & table cloth, we reached the saloon, each man saving a wine glass, tumbler, plate or mustard pot. There our table was respread, each and all of us begrimed with mud. During the night another and I am told a still more violent storm, but as I slept steadily through it I only realized the fact at daybreak when I found myself lying on a sort of sandbank, with a sandbag for a pillow.

Tuesday 14th October 1884

My cabin as I looked round it when I woke was a filthy place—my flannel shirt which I had taken off before going to bed covered with clay as well as everything else in the place. I breakfasted early and started at 9 a.m. on horseback for the 'Great Gate' called the [blank space] which is just 14 miles from my camp. En route I halted at the spot *el Gamai* where our boats (whalers) are towed up to by the steamers bringing them here. A number of these whalers—the first that have reached *Halfa*—arrived this morning towed by three steamers. Found Lord C. Beresford hard at work, getting the whalers & their gear into order. Then went on to the 'Gate' and saw a nugger hauled by main force through it: the arrangements were very good: everything proceeded with the utmost regularity. In riding home I dispensed with my helmet using a forage cap only, the sky was so overcast with clouds that exercise was very enjoyable. The latest news here is that it was not a steamer but a nugger that was wrecked in the cataract near *Merawi*. My hope that Stewart is still alive grows stronger. I never had much reliance on Kitchener's reports but this story about Stewart was told with so much circumstance about it that it was calculated to deceive most men when coming from an English Officer who is supposed to know the native character well besides the language. Those '*who know the country*' are put out by the vagary of nature sending us rain at this season.

Wednesday 15th October

Remained in my cabin all day. Heavy clouds threatening rain but a very stormy sky. In the evening went to see the Egyptn. Artillery practice with the 9 centr. Krupp at a target on other side of river, range nearly 2000 yds. common shell—practice very good. Heavy sandstorm with showers of rain. The two nurses from the Hospital and the Priest—that excellent man father Brindle—dined with me. I was to have sent the steam pinnace for them, but it blew too hard and it was too dark, so they came on foot, escorted by the Priest, Childers & Arthur. It is always pleasant to see an Englishwoman. She is so much cleaner & less stuffy than the women of other nations, and it is especially agreeable to find them in an out of the way place like this bent on usefulness and good works, not gadding about as nine out of ten always are, bent solely & exclusively on amusement, either passive or active according to the energy or laziness of their natural disposition. I am sorry to say there are thousands of Englishmen quite as bad as their sisters, who think of nothing from morning to night but of what they can do to afford them pleasure: to pass their time pleasantly is their only object in life, and oh, what a despicable object such is!! They have less excuse than women, for their physical strength is greater: they could plough or clip hedges or even break stones if they have not brains for any more spiritual work. If ever I become a rich man I shall build a monument to Manual Labor—it is noble to work, and the noblest work is productive labor, that which man gives to the soil. And yet in these days of puny men with big heads, big stomachs and little fibre, back-bone or animal courage, it has become the fashion to look upon the communist shoemaker of Northampton or the Manchester spinner or Birmingham screw & nail maker as men occupied at a higher work in a loftier calling than the tiller of the soil. The Gentlemen of England are much to blame for this inasmuch as the wages paid to the field laborer has been a shame & a disgrace to all landowners. In order to keep up high rents to enable the landed proprietor to send his wife & daughters to London for the Season & to Paris in the Autumn, it was necessary to keep down the labourers' wages to the lowest possible rate. Generations of badly-paid men develop bad citizens. The Landlord & the farmer divided the spoil of the land between them, whilst the poor devil who tilled the ground was fain to live upon the crumbs that fell from the rich man's table. I hope to see the day when every man who works in the field will receive a wage that will enable him with thrift to feed, maintain & bring up a family of healthy children.

Thursday 16th October

Went out riding in the morning and on a camel in the evening. A sultry day: wrote letters & at last received my English post of the 26th September. No news of any importance: the usual cry, don't fight if you can help it & spend the smallest possible amount of money. A foolish letter from the Duke deploring that he felt bound in this instance to give way about allowing volunteers from so many Regts. & Battns.: declaring it to be ruinous to the Army, to esprit de Corps and all that usual bosh to which I have listened for years. I believe he would prefer us to fail as long as we adhered to the old traditions in preference to success arrived at in defiance of all those cherished ideas of his childhood. I don't intend arguing the point with him. He is too old to take in new ideas about a subject—war—of which he is most profoundly ignorant. He says he hopes I may never ask him to repeat this process. If ever and whenever I have either to command or to arrange for the organization of a little army to be commanded by another when it is [a] question of fighting an irregular or a barbarous enemy such as the Boers or the Arabs for example where every man is either a crack shot or a born warrior, I shall never cease to press the Govt. to do as they have now done in selecting a small number of the best men from every Corps in England. The only other alternative will be to send out five times the number of soldiers required & then on the spot when away from the power of H.R.H. to select one-fifth of each Regt. or Battn. for the actual fighting work and leave the remaining 4/5ths behind to guard the Line of Communication &c. &c. &c. As I have often said before, an English General under existing conditions when detailed for any military operation has to begin his campaign by fighting the Duke of Cambridge.

Friday 17 October

Rode in the morning. In-doors all day writing a paper for the guidance of officers doing duty with Camel Corps.[83] A violent dust storm from the South about 3.30. Had to shut up every crevice & still could not keep the fine dust out.

Saturday, 18th October 84

Started by train at 6.30 a.m. for *Sarras* & rode from thence to the *Semneh* Cataract. Saw some nuggers being taken up. It is a trifling obstacle compared with the Great Gate (*Bab-el-Kebir*). The railway is to join the river some few miles above the cataracts, & Majr. Clarke R.E.[84] who is superintending the work promises me it will be finished about the first week if not the first day of November. Got back to *Sarras* in time to start for *Halfa* by the train arranged to return at 3 p.m. When we reached the crossing place at *Gemai* which is about half way between *Sarras & Halfa,* the idiot of a sapper who was driving the Engine allowed the fire plug to burn out, so there we were stuck. Very fortunately a telegraph station was opened there yesterday so we announced our unfortunate condition to *Halfa*, and another Engine was sent out to fetch us in. We got back about 9 p.m. having had rather a long day of it. It is a foolish thing to depend upon the British sapper to drive an Engine

—we want a Volunteer Corps composed of Engine drivers, plate layers and other Rl.Rd. servants, who for a strong retaining fee during peace, will be always ready to serve abroad in case of war. I find that being out all day in the sun if you make any exertion such for instance, as riding at a canter or a gallop over rough ground, makes me fearfully thirsty. The fact is my life in London and my age of 51 has not improved my powers of bearing fatigue. I strive to conceal it from myself, but the fat I have put on during the last few years has rendered me unfit for violent exercise during the midday & afternoon sun in the tropics. Today I really felt as if the Nile could not satisfy my thirst. I attribute a good [deal] of this to the fact that since I have been tormented by sneezing fits, one of my nostrils has become so choked up, that when I am going fast, I have to keep my mouth open to breathe through & consequently my throat inhaling the hot air becomes parched and greedy for water.

I have remarked a very curious phenomenum here lately during some of the sandstorms, in the shape of a rainbow. Upon several occasions, when I don't believe there was a drop of rain in the whirl of sand as it approached one, I saw a lovely rainbow. I was immensely surprised today to see the damage done to the Rl.Road and to the patches of dourrah which one ought to term the 'crops', by the rain lately fallen here. Today there were large patches of water at places still remaining, and the railway had been washed away at places. 'The oldest inhabitant' is astonished: this freak of nature has thrown out the calculations & prognostications of that old liar & of his first cousin Sir Samuel Baker.[85] 'The man who knows the country well' is generally a dangerous guide to the military leader. It is very amusing to me to read in the papers now the sad stories and prophicies [*sic*] about this campaign if I may so style it. Even Sir A. Clarke[86] who is of the Colonial politician, Childers'[87] class in life, who did all he could to induce me to take him as Chief of the Staff, has lately submitted a paper to the Govt. saying there is only one possible way of getting to *Khartoum* & that is by *Suakim*; that the Railway from thence to *Berber* could be laid at the rate of 30 miles per week &c. &c. whilst the Nile route has already proved a failure & if persisted in must be a disaster. I **never** had any opinion of Clarke's views, but I did not think he was goose enough to have written such a paper, the most foolish illogical & unmilitary production I have ever read. Thank heaven he is not with me here! ....

Sunday 19th October

Attended church parade: and rode a camel in the evening. Butler arrived very fit & dined with me.[88] He is afraid to run any risks with the boats at first as the croakers who always object to novelties would be down on the expedition worse than ever. It is amusing to see how everything that I ever put my hand to is at once decried by all the croakers of all the clubs. In my little wars I generally hit upon some novel expedient, and it frightens many: the foolish don't understand it, and my enemies hope it may ruin me. This is now the case here with my boats and Camel Corps.

Strong wind from the North which brings up my boats with stores. It somewhat backs up the river so that between it and the recent rain the Nile has risen for the last two days. The English mail arrived, but as usual my War Office Bag not with it. They tell me the river here becomes quite clear when it falls very low. . . . It would appear that Lupton Beh [*Bey*][89] had arrived in *Khartoum* with two steamers. Mr. Power's[90] journal published in the *Times* of the 29th shows what a hopelessly cowardly race this falaheen is: & yet men like Wood pretend to believe in them.

Monday 20th October 1884

A pleasant ride in the early morning into the hills which form the eastern side of the Nile valley—traced some wild animals home to a cave, most probably a hyena. There are I am told a good number of these brutes about at night. It appears they establish one particular spot as their public privy, and go there exclusively. The ferret at home does the same. The air this morning was delightful, a very strong breeze blowing from the North sending all my boats up the river at a slashing pace. I hope it will last as long as we are bound south & that on our return we may find a balmy wind from the equator to help us as we drift steadily down stream to *Khartoum Cairo*. I wrote *Khartoum* by mistake as that place is always foremost in my thoughts at present. I think of my friend Charlie Gordon shut up there with a cowardly lot of Egyptian soldiers, enemies on all sides of him and his own Govt. at home anxious to decry & discredit him; to damn him with faint praise, & to sneer at his actions. Our Cabinet is composed of men without one manly instinct amongst them: to a lot of place-hunters Gordon is a standing reproach: his unselfishness, his courage, his truth. You cannot be a party-politician & place-hunter and possess these qualities. If God gave them to you as a child, you must rid yourself of them if you wish to rule mobs of Birmingham roughs. News from Wilson from *Ambukol*. He had been to *Dugiyet* at foot of *Gerendid* cataract, and could not find out much about the reported murders. It was after all a small steam launch that was wrecked & it is quite certain that all, except perhaps a few slaves on board were treacherously murdered. This, joined to the fact that Gordon told us some time ago that he intended Stewart to leave *Khartoum* & proceed to *Dongola*, leaves little hope that Stewart is still alive.

Had a pleasant ride on my camel in the evening: I gave £30 for him & when I leave, expect to get perhaps 30 shillings for him. Stewart's murder will annoy Gladstone & Co. as it is a stern denial of Mr. G.'s repeated assertions that Gordon was not really shut up in *Khartoum* and could come away whenever he wished.

Tuesday 21st October

Rode in the early morning to the Egyptian camp at *Khor Moussa Pasha*, where our 'whalers' are taken to by steamers as they reach *Halfa*. It is a pretty spot. Met Evelyn Wood, also Beresford & Brackenbury the two latter on camels who were off for a happy day at the Great Gate. The air quite refreshing: the distance is about seven miles from my camp which is far down stream, and yet the exertion of cantering there and back was not a whit more than what it would have been in England. When I first got up this morning, it was positively cold. Strong North wind blowing all day. My post bag from England still missing. A serious telegram[91] from Baring, saying that both he & Northbrook thought I ought not to hesitate to dismiss Wilson if I found he did not get on well with Mudir. It was so essential to keep on good terms & to work with him. The Khedive hates Wilson as do also all H.H.'s entourage: I have no doubt the Mudir has been informed of this, and loses no opportunity in abusing Wilson to please Tewfik.

Wednesday 22nd October

Was glad to get into my blanket sack last night: it was positively cold when I went out riding this morning at 6.30 a.m. We play a rubber of shilling whist every evening now after dinner. Rode some distance into the hills this morning: what a wilderness! not a blade of grass, not a shrub nor anything green. Here in the plain between the hills & the river, there is every here & there that large-leafed shrub full of poisonous white juice like milk and bearing large green fruit as big as apples: it is called the 'Tree of the desert', at least that is the only name I have ever been able to extract from any of the natives for it. In these hills however not one of these shrubs is to be seen anywhere. Here and there on the tops of peaks are Arab graves, evidently of Sheiks or important men, marked by cairns. I telegraphed[92] to Baring telling him my proposal to Northbrook in a letter I wrote him on 19th instant & saying that if my proposal were approved, I would at once go to *Dongola* to broach the matter to the Mudir, although I had not intended leaving this until the 10th November. Had a pleasant camel ride in the evening. Until yesterday I wore both morning & evening when riding a cotton jacket, but now I wear woolen serge, the temperature has changed so much for the better. When waiting as at present for stores to accumulate in sufficient quantities to admit of an advance, the General & his Chief of the Staff have really very little to do. Whatever is done, is carried out by the General of Communications, and even he has not very much to occupy him when once his arrangements & his plan has been perfected. I have always remarked that active-minded men holding important Staff posts at such a time are apt to fret from an idea that they were not sufficiently employed. There are many men who are Generals or in high positions, who think that unless they themselves are constantly busy, looking into matters themselves that others have been detailed to do, they are not properly discharging their duties. They are easily appalled [*sic*] by idleness, although no amount of hard work would affect them: in fact they consider themselves invented for hard work and unless they have it, are apt to think something is wrong either with themselves or the system under which they are working. All through life I have endeavoured to work on the opposite principle: having served my time in all sorts of positions on the Staff I know from experience what a bore it is to have the man who is your immediate superior doing your work & leaving you idle. Those men always break down in the long run, and in the meantime the work is not as well done as it would be by the man whose function it was to do it, and he, poor devil, is deprived of the opportunity of fitting himself for higher duties & therefore the public service suffers. It is a very stupid thing in any position in life to keep a dog & bark yourself. When I began work with Sir R. Buller as my Chief of the Staff I explained this to him, telling him I would never interfere with him: that he must keep me constantly, hourly if necessary, informed of all he was doing: that I would give him the general outline of the policy to follow & that he should be responsible to me for carrying it out: that I was always ready to give him advice and help him & support him, but that I had no intention of attempting to be my own Chief of the Staff.⁹³

Thursday 23rd October

A little out of sorts so did not go out this morning. I am in trouble about coal. Before I came here everything done by Dormer seems to have been arranged by him with Mr. Cook by means of private agreement or conversation. I had talked this coal question over in England with Mr. Cook himself & arranged before any expedition had been determined upon that he was to lay in a large stock of coal, 10,000 tons as well as I remember, & that in order to secure himself against loss in the event of there being no expedition, he was to write me an official letter saying what he was doing & that in the event of no expedition coming off, he would hold our Govt. indebted to him to the extent of £30,000 which was about the amount he would then be out of pocket. This he did, & I sent on the letter to the Secty. of State with a minute saying I considered Mr. Cook's request a fair one. I was then given to understand that he was under some contract with our people in *Cairo* to supply coal all along the river as far as *Halfa* at a fixed rate. It now turns out that Dormer had no written agreement with him & the result is, we have no coal either here, or *Korosko* or *Assuan*. We have had to stop the despatch of steamers from *Assuan*. The delay will be only temporary but still it is very provoking. In the evening I went up the river in the steam launch a long way, very close to the *Khor* [space left [*Moussa*?]] Pasha camp. The scenery very pretty. In the evening I received an answer from Baring⁹⁴ to my proposal about making the Dongola Mudir a ruling Prince over *Khartoum* &c.—Northbrook & Nubar have discussed my proposal & practically approved of it. They talk of the finances & the advisability of giving a smaller subsidy. All stuff: unless they can set up some strong Government at *Khartoum* the defence of Egypt will cost them many hundred thousands a year. However, practically my general lines have been accepted, and I am left to carry out the details on those lines. I shall leave this on Monday night or evening. and start from *Sarras* on Tuesday morning at dawn for a seven-days' journey on camels through the desert to *Dongola*. Fricke & my camp will start by boat with Adye on Sunday and, if they have luck, they should reach that place on Wednesday the 5th or Thursday the 6th November, we reaching on Monday the 3rd. I ought not therefore to be longer than two or three days without my baggage & camp.

Friday 24th October 1884

Had a pleasant ride up the river & in returning paid Wood a visit to see how he is, as he has been suffering from his eyes: he has a disease called—I think—conjunctivitis. I don't know how it is spelt, but it is the next thing to opthalmia. I discussed my journey with him. Steamer arrived & left again in a couple of hours taking my post bag for England with it. Camel ride in the evening. Very cross letter from Butler about the Naval management of our boats.[95] I know it is very bad and have no opinion whatever of Commandr. Hammill's skill or organizing powers, but yet unless I go through the usual humbug of praising the Navy & all their work I am looked upon as jealous of that great service. I have now served in many campaigns where they have taken some part, and I have always found them a nuisance: their officers have no control over them in action and in rivers with boat work they are all adrift.

Saturday 25th October

Left by 7.30 a.m. train for Ṣailor's camp where our horses met us. Rode to the *Bab-el-Kebir* where Butler is now encamped.[96] Found he had early in the morning got one of our whalers through the *Bab* with a small party of natives before the sailors appeared on the scene: he was in the seventh heaven of delight. Hammill with all his sailors & swarms of natives employed all morning in rigging up their heavy gear for taking the whalers through according to their notions. They are right good fellows at sea, and could I have no doubt haul an ironclad up a hill, but they have as much idea of working boats in rapid water as my big boot has. Having worked for hours at these preparations they began about 1 p.m. trying to get a boat up & a pretty mess they made of it. The boat having shipped some water was at last got up but I thought she must have been wrecked, so badly was the affair conducted. I then interviewed Koko the Sheik of the cataract who had taken up boat for Butler early in the morning and made a contract with him to take up 20 boats per diem for 25 piastres each & for 30 piastres for every boat over 20 taken up any one day. The Navy to bring the whalers up to the foot of *Bab*.

Beresford in meantime goes on portaging about 15 or 20 boats with Egyptian soldiers every day. I did not get back to my camp until sundown. Returning I saw a Nubian funeral: all the men squatted round the grave to which the body had been carried on a charpoy, all the women squatted huddled together about twenty yards off, wailing in a low tone. I was told these people always have their grave yards in the desert & never in cultivateable[*sic*] land. This is not so here as I have ridden through many burial places near *Halfa* where they are in the midst of cultivated & irrigated land: the desert is certainly the rule. All graves placed North and South, and each covered neatly over with pebbles having a big stone at head & foot & actually with water in it, which I believe is kept full for forty days by the deceased's friends.

Sunday, 26th October 1886 [*4?*]

Maurice arrived. The coal question which has been disturbing my mind lately looks better today. Attended church parade at 7.30 a.m. Fricke, Adye & all my camp started for *Dongola* (via *Sarras* by rail). I hope they may get there in 10 days, if so they will not be long behind me....

Went on a camel to *Khor Moussa* Pasha to see the Canadian Voyageurs who are encamped there,[97] having arrived this afternoon in about 40 whalers towed by the *Ferooz*. A rough-looking lot, but I hope I shall get plenty of work out of them. They won't funk this river at all events. I often wonder who was the clever fellow who first styled the rapids of the Nile 'cataracts'. If Messrs. Cook had been in existence then I should have said it was started by the firm to increase the number of tourists and add zest to the desire to come here. The idle Englishman who had seen Niagara would say, 'Oh I'l [l] go and see the cataracts of the Nile.' Poor devil, when he arrived he would be shown a very muddy, ugly river gurgling through hideous rocks after the fashion of an insignificant rapid. No, the cataracts are a swindle. Just heard that the Armed Steamer *Gluzah** manned by R.N. has gone down in the Tanjoor Rapid. To get her up has cost a large sum of money & the energy of all the Naval authorities & seamen on the Nile.

Monday 27th October

Rode to the Voyageur camp. A lovely morning for a canter. Had a telegram[98] from Hartington asking if I could dispense with [the] Battn. of Rl. Scots from the West Indies in order to send it to the Cape if reinforcements were required there. I replied Yes on the understanding I reduced Garrison of Lower Egypt from $4\frac{1}{2}$ to $3\frac{1}{2}$ Battalions: I added if Stephenson thought this too little the Navy should station some ships at *Alexandria*. Stephenson has telegraphed home against proposal. In my telegram[99] I recommended a Mounted Infantry Corps to be raised from our Cavalry as far more effective for Cape work than twice its numbers if supplied by whole Regts. The Duke will be furious, but I want to teach him that the Army exists for the use and service of the Nation, not as a plaything for him to amuse himself with in Hyde Park or Aldershot. Writing of him who is so fat reminds me that I have never seen even a stout man since I left Lower Egypt, and there even they are rare and only to be found amongst the richer classes of people.

Strong northerly wind still blowing, which brings our laden native boats up well: it is curious to see these same boats when emptied, drifting down with the current, but against the wind, they turn & walze about in a seemingly idiotic fashion. Of course our returning steamers tow as many of them as possible. My camp today wears a deserted aspect. I sent off Spenser Childers this morning to have all arrangements ready at *Sarras* tomorrow for my early start from there. I shall now close this, as it will be some time before I can send home any portion of my diary. Dined with Evelyn Wood. Buller away all day returned when I was at dinner & I think he had had a little too much liquor on board for he entered into a noisy altercation with Wood as to the proposed Rl.Rd. extension.[100]

**Gizeh?* see page 51

Tuesday 28th October

Started a little after 6 a.m. by train for *Sarras* where we arrived at 9 a.m. and breakfasted with Colonel Harrison as well as the flies would allow us. We there mounted our camels which had been sent two days before with the 100 mounted Infantry I had arranged to go with me. This detachment had started early in the morning to go by a different route, more direct, as I wanted rather to hug the river as much as I could in order to see the rapids and the various depots established or being established along the line of advance.

We left *Sarras* with a small escort of Mounted Infry. on camels at 10.10 a.m., under young Sherston[101] of the Rifle Brigade, my party consisted of Swaine, Mill. Secty. Wardrop, Creagh, Childers, Zohrab Bey — A.'s D.C.,

Dr. Pratt,[102] and Capt. Maxwell[103] of the Black Watch who looks after my camp. We carry *tentes d'abri* with us and a very limited amount of baggage, the rest of my things having been sent on with Adye A.D.C. on Sunday, Fricke & other servants being with him.

The day was warm and the latter part of the journey very stony and hilly. Reached *Ambigol* at 5.10 p.m.; seven hours' journey including a halt of quarter of an hour. The baggage did not come up until 8.30 p.m. It was a long day as I had shaved a little after 4 a.m. and I was glad to lie down and sleep, sleep as only those can appreciate who have marched all day in the sun over a sandy desert, broken here and there with hills of loose stones the collected heat of which seemed to scorch the face as when you open the door of a furnace and look in. We found the two nuggers containing Adye and all our worldly goods, including those of Generals Earle and Buller and my little steam launch struggling to get up the *Ambigol* cataract under sail. The wind was not strong enough for their wretchedly small sails, so I saw them with regret make for the bank below the Rapid at sunset. The distance we marched today from *Sarras*, I should say, was something over 30 miles.

Wednesday 29th October

Left *Ambigol* at 6.40 a.m., and reached *Akasheh* at 2.20 p.m.

having gone round by Tanjour to see the S.S. *Gizeh* which is hopelessly wrecked there. The baggage arrived at 4 p.m. Distance marched by baggage which came straight about 25 miles. Today before I reached the Tanjour rapid we passed the picket boat manned by R.N. which patrols between *Ambigol* and *Akashah*. The officer who commanded the *Gizeh* when she was lost was on board. Passed Lieut. Montgomery[104] on a camel going down to wreck of *Gizeh* for some oil.

Thursday, 30th October 1884

Left *Akasheh* at 6.15 a.m. & reached *Sarkamatto* at 9.15 a.m. This is where Wood·is forming a large depot of stores which is practically at *Dal* rapids. Here I found a Detachment of Egyptian Army encamped under a young English officer. Lieut. Montgomery R.N., whom I had passed yesterday on the road, had returned here during the night: his Picket boat is lying here. There is no difficulty in obtaining grain & camel fodder everywhere. Started from *Sarkamatto* at 10.45 a.m. & reached *Magrakheh* at 1.20 p.m. The baggage had started from *Sarkamatto* at 5 a.m. & went direct, reaching *Magrakheh* at 12.45 p.m. Here we founded [sic] the Mounted Infantry under Captain Fetherstonehaugh.[105] They moved forward at 5 p.m. to get over the 40 miles of desert to *Absarah* during the night & early morning. We started from *Magrakheh* at 7 p.m. with a bright moon & marched into the desert until 9.40 p.m. when we encamped. The baggage which had started at 6 p.m. came up at 10 p.m. which at the rate of $2\frac{1}{2}$ miles an hour told us we were 10 miles on our road and would only have about 30 miles to do the following day. This camping in the desert did not impress me in any way. Possibly if I had been alone it might have done so. This is the first night we have camped far from the river. The camel goes better during the cool of the night than during the heat of the sun. Our Guide is a funny old Sheik from *Dongola*: he rides a white camel that moves remarkably well. He carries a long sword fastened amongst his various bundles of clothes, dates &c. &c. to his saddle. He especially dislikes any of the officers going in front of him which they often do, the track being well marked by the numbers travelling over it, especially of late. We daily meet numbers of labourers going to *Halfa* who are sent there by the Mudir to relieve those who have been working under us at the rapids for the last six weeks. At

Dal we have opened a telegraph office, so I had telegrams today at *Sarkamatto* & sent off replies. Unfortunately, the line—which follows the left bank all the way—is there some three or four miles from the river, so the office is at *Dal*, a little lower down where the line of wire nearly touches the river.

Friday 31st October 1884

Started at 6.15 a.m. and reached *Absarab* on the Nile at 1.25 p.m. having halted en route for about 15 minutes. The baggage having left at 6 a.m., arrived at 4 p.m. Distance done, under 30 miles. Found the Mounted Infy. encamped on arrival. They had lost a Corporal of the Transport Compy. during their night march. He rejoined them in the middle of the day quite off his head, partly from the funk of having lost himself in the dark & partly from the sun. This points to the necessity of having signal rockets with columns marching in the desert at night, to be fired say every one or two hours, so that all stragglers should know in what direction to proceed. It also impresses upon me the advisability of instructing our soldiers in the use of the compass and in a knowledge of the North Star and Southern Cross. Officers who wished to give lectures to their men in places where it was difficult to amuse them might do so on these subjects.

We encamped on a high sand bank overhanging the river, and when it came on to blow we had a *'bad time'* of it. Soon after leaving *Ambigole* I remarked that all women go about naked to the waist and the little girl children entirely naked, those of about nine or ten having however a fringe round their waists. In every field of Dhurra (millet) there is a little raised stage, generally a charpoy mounted on poles which enables the woman who is perched on it to overlook the whole field of corn. From this point of vantage she not only shouts to keep the birds off as is done in India, in Egypt and amongst the Zulus &c. &c. but she freely plies the birds with stones from a sling which these women use with considerable effect. I suppose the race have been slingers since the days of Moses.

Our pace on these riding camels is a slow jog trot averaging from 4 to 5 miles an hour according to the nature of the ground. The camel will do long distances if not pressed beyond that pace. The camel sweats at the first joint of his neck behind his head which is his most sensitive spot; a blow from a stick on that spot will bring him to the ground and probably kill him. Our old Guide assured me that before leaving *Sarras* he had seen a camel killed thus by an Egyptian soldier who struck it there with his fist. At this cold!!! season these camels only drink once every two days. Our camel saddles are well-designed, but abominably made—many of them break after a few days with their full marching-order equipment on. They were made in the Arsenal at *Cairo*. Months ago, long before I knew I was coming here, I pressed Stephenson to have camel saddles made in India but he assured us by telegraph he could have them well made in Egypt, and this is the result.

November 1884

Saturday 1st November

Started from *Absarab* at 6.15 a.m. & reached the *Kaibar* rapid at 1 p.m. The baggage had started at 4.45 a.m. & reached camp at *Kaibar* at 3.45 p.m. We encamped in a grove of palm trees on the bank of the river. As I was sitting under a tree thinking, and waiting for the baggage to arrive, I remarked there was something of a very dark bluish-green color sitting on a rock about 250 yds. from the bank in the river, the upper edge of which was serrated in one part & which looked to me very like a crocodile. I had heard so much of crocodiles & had seen nothing of them as yet that my first idea was, I must be mistaken, more especially as I had been told these brutes never frequented the cataracts. I got my glass and looking through it at once realised there was a crocodile in front of me. I collected the few rifles we had, and each all being leveled at him I gave the word & bang went four bullets at the monster. One I think hit him: the other three missed him, but in half a minute he had plunged backwards into the river, coming to the surface in a minute afterwards and once again when he had gone down stream about 100 yds. We were all delighted to have at last seen one of these far-famed enemies of man. Distance marched today about 28 miles.

Sunday 2nd November

Left *Kaibar* at 6.15 a.m. & reached *Abu Zetmeh* 12.15 p.m. The baggage started at 4.30 a.m. & arrived at 1.30 p.m. I have always given the time taken by the baggage because it gives the best estimate of the distance marched, the pace of the loaded baggage camel being $2\frac{1}{2}$ miles an hour; sometimes a little more. Distance today was I should say however about 25 miles. Just before the sun rose this morning whilst going through a mild form of ablution, one of our party announced another crocodile, this time on a rock under 100 yards off and entirely different in color from our friend of yesterday, being of a light yellowish green. The same process was gone through and again we flattered ourselves that one bullet had taken effect. Before we had gone two miles, a third crocodile was discovered on a bank in the river about 800 yds. off who was also honored by a volley. I was astonished to find two of the rifles of the four men I had with me were jammed & the breech action would not work owing to the sand which had got into it. This I must guard against by a careful inspection & cleaning of all arms twice a day. It is also necessary to have the barrel covered with hide where the left hand holds it, as in this country a few minutes quick firing, would otherwise render it unserviceable.

Last night my Doctor, Surgeon Major Pratt was stung by a scorpion & his arm is very much swollen today & he has suffered severely although making light of the pain. During the day's march we saw a Gazelle, the first I have seen. We saw some Sand Grouse also, and killed a brownish yellow snake about 30 inches long which I don't believe was a dangerous one, judging from the roundness of his head: I believe he was a harmless rock snake.

I forgot to mention in my yesterday's diary an amusing scene with our Guide the Sheik. He had informed Zohrab Bey early in the morning that we should during that day's march pass by the grave of a celebrated Fakir where it was customary for the Guide to descend, say a prayer, put his hankerchief on the ground in order that all gentlemen of the party might give him some buckshish in it. Accordingly when we reached the holy spot yesterday, the Sheik duly descended and we all did so. He produced a red cotton pocket handkerchief, put it on the sand and kept it in position—as it was blowing fresh at the time—by means of a stone on each corner, whilst he put an English sovereign in the centre, St. George & the Dragon side up. We each threw in a few piastres, & at last Spenser Childers added two large English pennies. He in the meantime had drawn his sword and danced howling round the hankerchief. When he saw how small was his 'collection' he was furious: picked up his sovereign & his hankerchief leaving our money on the desert. I at once gave it to a native groom who was present: this made him still more angry for he had evidently intended trousering the two or three shillings a little later on. He said it was the invariable custom for every man of any importance to give his guide a sovereign at this place. I told him we were not travelling for pleasure, were not tourists and had no intention of giving any buckshish until our journey was over. Spenser Childers added 'We English intend abolishing all these customs.' Subsequent enquiries made me believe the whole thing had been invented by this wily Sheik who thought he could bleed us easily. He was a garrulous old man, and seemed to know & to be respected by every soul he met on the road. He was given dates at every village which he distributed to those of the party that liked them. I ate quantities and came to the conclusion that if I had only to provide for myself on such a journey I would only take tea, sugar, dates & biscuit with me & would then avoid all the bother of mess baggage, cooking pots &c. &c. As it was we had champaigne every day. I am looking forward with something like pleasure when all our wine & liquor will be finished and when we shall have only tea to drink. I have announced that I don't mean to buy any more when the present stock is at an end.

Abu Fetmeh is a Sheik's tomb on a high mound just above the *Hannek* rapids: there is no village there: we are laying in supplies there and also at a village below the rapids. There I found the S.S. *Nassif Kheir* awaiting me. Her crew comes from the Navy, her commander being Lieut. Poor R.N.[106] There has been a mistake in the telegrams I sent to *Dongola*, for it appears that I am expected there tonight. The Mudir had left *Dongola* this morning in his steamer to come and meet me.

It was very pleasant getting into even the very untidy cabin of this steamer and having a good tub and wash all over: I was dirty but not with dirty dirt, as sand, although very penetrating, does not make you black or muddy. I had shaved most days during the journey but to save time in the morning I had always slept in my clothes even in my boots, so a good wash all over and clean things were very welcome. From the news which Sir C. Wilson—who came in steamer to meet me—brought me, there can now be no longer any hope that poor Stewart is alive. Such is life—I wish he had died in battle in place of being murdered like an Irish landlord by a cowardly skulking reptile such as this country and Ireland produces in large numbers. My news from Buller is disheartening. I had left him some questions to telegraph answers to, as to the time when I can be in fighting trim with all my Force in the neighbourhood of *Debbeh* and it appears there is no chance now of the Army being concentrated there before Xmas. I had calculated upon being at *Berber* by that date. If I have to advance upon *Khartoum* by the Nile, I cannot be there before the 15th Feby. so that it must be well into the hot weather before this little Army can be back again at *Cairo* to embark for England. Alas. Alas!! This is a cruel disappointment to me but, the steamers have broken down all along the line, and our coal difficulties have been serious. I shall therefore be all the more urgent in my endeavours to settle matters for the future Government of *Khartoum* without going higher up the Nile than I shall have to do in order to punish the Monasir tribe for poor Stewart's murder. If I can only catch that villain who treacherously murdered him, he shall hang high for it, but whether or not I shall destroy every shakieh along the river where his tribe cultivate their crops & if I can will kill all the oxen that work their shakiehs.

Monday 3rd November

Under weigh a little after 6 a.m. in the steamer *Nassif Khea*. In about a couple of hours came up with the Mudir in his steamer. He had left *Dongola* yesterday expecting me to reach that place in the evening, so he must have had an unpleasant night of it, not being prepared to pass the night away from his house. He had a small field-piece on board which he blazed away from in my honor & then started up the river ahead of me, so as to be on shore to welcome me. I had arranged to arrive at *Dongola* at half past four p.m. having told Stewart to make as grand a military display as he could with the small number of men at his command.

A large crowd at the landing place and all the Mudir's Army presenting arms &c. &c. but I remarked the Mudir himself was not there, so I sent Zohrab to tell him he must come down to meet me. Zohrab says he thinks this was done in ignorance, but at any rate there is nothing like beginning well and having a clear understanding with Easterns. I am most anxious to get on well with him, & to be most civil and complimentary in every possible way to him, but he must begin by recognizing me as his Commdg. Officer.

The reception was very well done. The Mudir walked up with me to his Mudirate where I had the chief officers presented to me, and paid his Excellency many compliments. I then went to a house enclosed in a large garden which Stewart had secured. It is a curious house designed to have three large rooms of about 40′ × 20′ each, but unfortunately one room was never roofed over, so two only are habitable of which I occupy one & the other used as a general reception place: we dine on the landing or verandah in front, which is about 8′ above the surrounding garden. There are no glass windows & consequently the wind blows in clouds of dust which cover even this paper as I write. One great comfort in it is that although it has a desolate tumble-down appearance, there are no fleas or bugs in the melancholy-looking divan which goes round two sides of the room. There are no mosquitoes and comparatively few house flies. The white ants are the drawback to *Dongola*. They eat all woodwork but are death upon leather. If you leave your boots in the one spot without moving them for 24 hours, they will probably have eaten well into the soles. They are insatiable and of untireable energy. Strong wind blowing from the north which ought to bring our Nuggers & boats here in good style. Heard from *Dal* that Alleyne[107] who had left *Sarras* on the 30th October with six heavily-laden whalers manned chiefly by Canadian voyageurs had safely reached *Dal* today. At *Semneh*, he had lightened the boats a little before hauling them up the rapid, but at no other rapid had he done so. In the open water the boats were sailed and rowed. This is good going against a big river. There can be now no doubt that poor Stewart was murdered by the *Monassir* tribe, as already reported. The latest news is that the Mahdi went to *Khartoum* where he summoned Gordon to surrender who told him he would if necessary hold the place for twelve years: the Mahdi is said to have gone south up the White Nile about a day's march & to have announced that he did not mean to fight for 60 days. If this be true I cannot help thinking that the crisis has come in the Mahdi's career. If he started from *Abeid* to take *Khartoum* & if he fails to do so, any little prestige that still clings to him will disappear. Already many who were at first inclined to throw in their lot with him say he cannot be the real prophet as he never goes into action but stays miles away in the rear telling his beads whilst others fight. If he were the real Mahdi he would go in front & lead his army.

Tuesday 4th November

The Mudir paid me a visit of ceremony at 8 a.m. which I returned at 5 p.m. when the Khedive's firman was read by the Emaum, and I then gave the Mudir the K.C.M.G. fastening the decoration round his neck. He was evidently very much pleased & gratified. The Native troops marched past very fairly & the ceremony ended with a salute from the Mudir's Artillery. The Mudir is surrounded by a lot of Turks & Bashi Bazouks who oppress the people in every way. He himself is said to be above bribery & corruption and his holy character and reputation raises him above such imputations. He cannot do everything himself & he must rely upon these villainous Turks about him: I doubt very much even if I dare punish many of these Turks. As an example of their villainy he sent down a small party of his Bashi Bazouks to *Abu Fatmeh* where we were collecting supplies & forming a depot. The first night they were there they ravished several women and carried off several young married women who escaped the following day. The next evening a small gang of these brutes obtained leave from their officers to be absent from camp. They made a sudden descent upon the houses where the escaped women lived; the women were not there, so they seized the husbands, brought them to their own camp and went through a mock Court-martial on them, the sentence being death. On the husbands swearing on the Koran they would if allowed their freedom send their wives at once into camp, they were set at liberty. Is it therefore any wonder these people should be ready to welcome the Mahdi or any other man who promised them deliverance from such cruelties, such oppression. At this moment I believe the Mahdi as a Mahdi is '*played out*': the people begin to remember that the Mahdi must come from Arabia & not be greedy of women & gain as this Mahmond Ahmed is. Besides they say, if he were the Mahdi he would expose himself to danger and go into action, but this Mahmond Ahmed always remains miles in the rear when we are fighting for him. But this Mahmond Ahmed has been successful and his cause seems to be theirs & his success it seems to them would free them from what they term the hated Turks. Under that term is comprised all Egyptians & those like us who ride with the Pashas.

After the tomasha I rode round the camp and town with Stewart. Never have I seen any place in better order: nothing seems to have been forgotten, markets opened, police established, a redoubt thrown up, the defensive requirements of the position attended to, all sanitary precautions adopted, the hospital in good order &c. &c.

Wednesday 5th November

Had a sham fight at 6.30 a.m. between the Camel Corps here and the Sussex Battalion which was amusing and well done. The Camel Corps here under Maj. Gough[108] has been better trained than that under Barrow at *Halfa*.

Mudir came to see me in the afternoon: we had a long conversation upon position of affairs in Soudan. In accordance with his advice I shall not send Mounted Infantry to *Ambukol* until arrival here of I/South Stafford Regt. which leaves by wings from *Sarras* tomorrow & following day in our whalers. He thinks the arrival of a small force at *Ambukol* might be a risk & would certainly have no moral effect. I have arranged with him to send one of Mahmond Ahmed's relations to see him & impress upon him the folly of continuing his pretensions to be the Mahdi & with a message to say that if he will now accept peace, I shall gladly give it to him & recognize him as Sultan of Khordofan on condition he gave me up the European & Egyptian prisoners in his possession. He also promised to obtain a messenger who would take in a letter from me to Gordon. He is a curious-looking man of the crablike species. He is Circassian by birth having come when very young to Egypt as a slave boy. He is intelligent, has a good face on which is written either extreme ill-health or starvation from asceticism. He seems to have no inside: his legs are twisted together, the rounded knees closely pressed one against the other whilst his toes are turned in as he sits as if he were deformed. If you can imagine Lord Carnarvon turned Fakir, & dressed in a long black reach-me-down patelot with a native shirt & no shirt color [collar?], a Fez on head, black shiny alpacka-like trousers, and a pair of thin patent-leather but curiously designed French boots with elastic sides on, such is my Mudir of *Dongola*. All—high & low—fear him. He is an absolute sovereign, and although feared is respected for his victories and revered for his religious fervancy. He omits no law of Mahomed. He won't drink coffee or smoke tobacco & he prays the five times a day ordered in the Koran and makes his entourage do likewise. He is a man I cannot help admiring notwithstanding his mesquine appearance and his want of physique. His force of character impresses me & his earnest faith in the religion he professes. This faith gives him the highest and truest courage. They say that in action he is always in front and takes up [a] handful of sand and throws it towards the enemy which demoralizes them. A man with this earnest firm faith in God—who after all is the God we profess to worship—is certain to succeed, for God will bless him: the great creator who watches over the affairs of men must delight in men of this stamp and although he is not a believing Christian through the misfortune of his education, I hope to meet him & men like him in heaven and would prefer to associate with them to having anything to do with many of the villians who swarm through the world as nominal Christians but whose touch is contamination. Who, for instance, could stay in heaven if Bishop Nelson, Lord Nelson's brother, were allowed in there; and yet he was an English bishop.

The climate is very pleasant here: I have two blankets over me towards daybreak. Strong winds from the North which ought to send our boats and Nuggers along at a spanking pace. Plenty of sheep to be had here: also corn and flour. Altogether this *Ordeh* or *Dongola* is a flourishing place.

Thursday 6th November 1884

Rode early in the morning and had a charming gallop on some real green turf which extends in a narrow strip for some miles near this. I was seedy most of the day having a touch of my old fever hanging over me. Received my English mail bag of the 17th October, the Duke furious because I have recommended Brackenbury to be Depty. Adjt. Genrl. He forgets I strive to employ only the best men and I don't care whether they be My Lord Tom Noddy or Mr. Jones as long as I believe them to be the best men for the Public Service. H.R.H. would prefer nonentities belonging to his own club, men socially agreeable to him, and to his own set.

Friday 7th November

The Mahdi's power seems very much on the wane. News today says that all the Khababish have now left him, & that Hussein Pasha Khalifa had returned to *Berber* where he had been badly received by the Mahdi's Emir & that he had retired amongst the Bishareen in consequence & was possibly making his way to *Cairo*. I wish he would go into Rundle at *Korosko*, who by the bye is reported to have gone as far as within sight of *Abu Hamed*. When Mahmond Ahmed attacked *Omdurman*, he is said to have lost severely. The political prospect looks brighter & if I could only get forward a few thousand men to *Debbeh* at once I might save a great deal of cost & trouble.

Saturday 8th November

Adye & Fricke arrived today with all my baggage & camp equipment. Fricke laid up with a bad hand. He got a thorn into it, & although the thorn was pulled up, the wound festered and an angry boil was set up: these Nile boils are well known to all European travellers here. This is a bad country to be wounded in, as nothing seems to heal. If I have a fight, I shall send all my wounded to *Cairo* as quickly as possible. Had an interview with the cousin of Mahmond Akmeh [sic] (the Mahdi) whom the Mudir has selected to send into that worthy's camp: I gave him a note written in German from myself to Slaten [sic] Bey,[109] telling him he had better tell his friend the false Prophet that everyone now laughed at his sacred pretensions & that if he were wise in time he would ask me for peace & I would then recognize him as Sultan of Khordofan on condition that he gave me up all European & Egyptian prisoners in his possession. The messenger gets $200 for the trip & I have promised him a good buckshish provided he brings me back an answer from Slaten Bey, & that if he be murdered, I will do what I can for his children who reside in a village near this. The Mahdi has several times written to him begging him to join his camp & some of these letters he intends to carry with him so that if taken prisoner on the road he will say he is going to join his kinsmen & as a proof will point to these letters of invitation.

My note to Slaten Bey was written on a piece of paper about $3'' \times 2''$ and folded up small. He means to place it between some verses of the Koran which in common with all these people he carries as an amulet in a little leather case fastened to his arm above the elbow. The true Arab came out in him, as he kept constantly during my conversation, recurring to the $200 the Mudir had promised him, which he said was entirely inadequate even for his expenses. He takes one slave servant and a Guide with him & means to start from the other side of the river & to go by the desert route to *Merawi*: he will thus avoid all the riverine villages in most of which he is well known.

The Mahdi's Commander in Chief is named *Abu Angah*.

I dined in the evening with the Mudir who gave us an excellent dinner, except the water which came out of the skin with which it was strongly flavored and was neither cold nor clear. This is strange, for in Turkey the people are most particular to have clear filtered water, but here in Nubia, no attention is paid to it & they are quite contented to drink it as it comes out of the Nile. We have no flies here and were it not for the clouds of dust that blow into this wretched room which I inhabit, life would be pleasant here.

I went round the Hospital this morning which I found in a most satisfactory state, 36 of Sussex, 18 of Mounted Infry. & 2 sailors R.N.—56 in all, of whom 6 are venereal cases, and many are boils, sore hands, feet &c. There are 6 enteric cases all doing well —2 smallpox—very slight—7 diarrhoea & dysentry, mostly slight & all doing well—one man with epileptic fits. Since the troops arrived there have been 5 deaths. The men even in hospital look very healthy. This place swarms with small birds of all sorts. I see a good many wild geese & sand grouse about, some of whom I hope may shortly be in our Kitchen Pot.

Sunday—9th November. Dongola

Divine service in camp 7.30 a.m. The Rev'd Mr. O'Neal arrived yesterday & officiated: many of the passing Arabs coming in from their villages with supplies, stopped to watch our proceedings which seemed to interest and amuse them. Had a good long gallop afterwards before breakfast. My pocket barometer shows a difference of 300 ft. between this place & *Halfa*. Had a long camel ride in the evening. Telegram[110] from Buller to say he is going to *Assuan* to see how matters are going on there as the transport of troops is extremely slow. Sent Mudir a present from myself of a sporting 12-bore gun with an affectionate letter which has pleased him very much.

Monday 10th November 1884

Started about 6.15 a.m. on camels to try and get some sand grouse: there are quantities of them but they are so wild there is no getting near them in the open desert. Firing into the 'brown' of a pack at 70 or 80 yds. on the chance of a stray shot taking effect, is poor sport. We saw nothing else in the way of grouse, but the party brought home six couple for the pot. Strong Northerly wind. Fricke seedy with a band [*sic*] hand and a swollen face. Stafford Regt. passed *Semneh* yesterday & today. Progress forward very slow. Had a good gallop in the evening and on my way back went to see the camels of the Compy. of Mounted Infry. which reached the opposite bank of the river this morning, coming over in nuggers.

Tuesday 11th November

I have often remarked when on outlying piquet in the field when a Subaltern or a Captain that as day broke each country, each District almost, each race of people had its or their own distinctive waking noise. . . . Daybreak always parades before me many curious scenes in my past life, and I feel pass through me even the very sensations which influenced my body & the same ideas pass through my brain which upon those occasioned [*sic*] worked upon my mind & possibly influenced my conduct at the time. If I were to be an idle man in old age I would write a great deal about those times, for I think I could relate much that would interest most soldiers, & that might be of great use to young men beginning a military life as I did in 1852 without one friend or even acquaintance in the Army.[111]

Had a good gallop over the desert and found the Mounted Infry. out drilling under Gough. I then went to where the Sussex Regt. were drilling & was very much pleased with it. Rode again in the evening for a couple of hours.

Heard from Buller.[112] He leaves today for *Halfa*. I cannot fathom the mystery of all the delays that are taking place. I have resolved upon running back to *Halfa*—a long run of over 230 miles but I cannot help it. Something is wrong & I must examine into it myself. This is a horrid bore.

Wednesday 12th November

Sent for Stewart when it was daylight & told him I intended going to *Halfa*. The English post is due here tomorrow so I shall wait to get my letters & then start going down river in steam launch as far as *Abu Fatme*[*h*], & if possible as far as *Kaibar*. I sent on Arthur today with my camels to the latter place which I must manage to reach tomorrow evening. If the camels hold out well I should get to *Sarras* on Sunday evening or Monday morning. I mean to spend one whole day at *Halfa* & then return as quickly as possible to this place, to be in time to push on to *Ambukol* with Stafford Regt. when it arrives here. During the day received a more hopeful telegram from Buller[113] from *Assuan*: he has adopted my advice, & is pushing on troops from there in whalers. Arthur crossed the river here early with my camels & goes straight to *Kaibar*. I have ordered camels from *Halfa* to meet me on Saturday at *Akasha*, so that my own camels will really only have two long days' marches. Reuter announces that Franchise Bill passed 3rd reading without a division. Now comes the crisis. Will the Lords be firm? Shall I find upon my return home that I have no longer a voice in the legislature!!!? Hoorah!! What a farce the whole business is: the wheel of democracy turns at present gaily. Some one day or other when it has dragged England through the mire, we shall have an awakening. If I could only live until then! but that is impossible & I have no sons to hang the spawn of men like Mr. Bright, Chamberlain & Co. The eggs here are excellent which is much more important as a fact.

Thursday 13th November 1884

Left *Dongola* at 7.25 a.m. in steam launch—Lt. [blank space] R.N. for *Abu-Fatmeh*, en route for *Halfa*. I had with me Zohrab Bey & Wardrop, a guide & a native servant of Zohrab's—no one else. We ran down the river at a good pace & reached *Abu-Fatmeh* at 11.10 a.m. where I found the camels of Mounted Infantry I had sent down yesterday. In an hour we were packed and off on camels into the desert. I visited the little hospital before I started. Reached *Kaibar* at 5.25 p.m. where I found Arthur Creagh with my own camels. Here I met General Earle on his way to *Dongola*. Started on my own camel again at 6 p.m. & rode on into the dark until 8.40 p.m. when we halted for the night at the straggling village of *Agettary*. Lovely day, not too hot—night very cold especially towards daybreak. Sleeping in the open air delightful as long as one scrapes a good hollow to fit one's hip.

Friday—14th Novr

Left *Agettary* at 6.30 a.m. The sun rises now about 6.23 a.m.: reached *Absarat* at 10.15 a.m., having passed Major Barrow[114] & the last detachment of Mounted Infry. on its march to *Dongola*. Started again at 2.30 p.m. having fed our camels and halted in desert at 6.45 p.m. having led our camels since 6 p.m. in the dark. A very cold night with strong Northerly wind from which we obtained good protection by having our camel saddles put up on end at our heads.

Saturday 15th November

Started at 7 a.m. & reached *Magrakeh* at 1.55 p.m.; fed camels & started again at 2.40 p.m. & reached *Sarkamatta* at 5 p.m. Maurice who commanded there rode out to meet me. We dined with him. Saw Henderson[115] who is better & out of danger, but who will not again be of any use this campaign. Started again at 7 p.m. & reached *Akasheh* at 11.40 p.m. the Guide having lost his way in the dark more than once. We slept in the large E.P. tent of Captain Cole[116] of the Egyptian Army who is in charge of the post.

Sunday 16th November

Started at 7 a.m. & after at least 54 miles of desert reached *Sarras* at 9.30 p.m. The Guide lost his way several times in the dark as we neared *Sarras* so that the last four or five miles was fearful work on tired—very tired camels. I had a 'snack' with Col. Harrison who commands at *Sarras* whilst steam was being got up in locomotive & then left at 10 p.m. for *Halfa* which I reached half an hour after midnight. Slept in my cabin on board the diabeeyah I lived in when I was at *Halfa*.

Monday 17th November

Busy all day with Buller & Brackenbury on military matters.[117]

The coal question had never been looked into by Buller who *assumed* that Dormer had made all the necessary arrangements before he, Buller, had arrived in the country. Dormer it seems had made very few arrangements & those few were not very good. However Buller is of course to blame for not having made certain that all was right on this most vital point. All *was wrong* hence the delay. I blame myself too, for although I trust Buller fully, I should not have relied upon my trust in him on such a vital question, & ought personally to have gone into it. In dealing with a Chief of the Staff in whom one has every confidence I feel too much inclined, I know, to give him a free hand. I know from my own personal experience when I was a staff officer, how inconvenient and difficult it was to serve a General who wished to command, & to be his own Staff officer at the same time. At the beginning I told Buller I looked to him for all details which I left unreservedly in his hands & that I had no intention of keeping a dog and barking myself. The result has been in this one respect unfortunate.[118] However, the difficulty is now over, but instead of having the Army, concentrated at *Debbeh-Ambukol* about the middle of December it cannot possibly be so until the 7th or 10th January. At last I have had a letter from Gordon:[119] it is dated 4th instant and acknowledges receipt of my letter of 20th Septr. but adds he cannot read it as he sent his cypher code away with Stewart who left *Khartoum* on 10th Septr. That any man could have been so idiotic is to me a puzzle. If, as he says, he did not consider it safe to keep cypher any longer in *Khartoum* why not have burnt it? I have sent in any number of copies of this letter which must now be with Mahdi & it is extremely provoking that when at last I do get a copy in, the answer I receive is, he cannot make it out having no longer any cypher. I sent him another letter today which was telegraphed to Kitchener at *Debbeh*. Of course my letter goes in clear, and I send him cypher page from the *Soldier's Pocket Book* telling him to use either of the two cyphers described there, the Christian name of his mother's father being the key for one, and the number of 'Cash' in a stated number of 'Taels', with the day of the month on which he himself was born added thereto as the key to the other. If my letter reaches the Mahdi, I don't think that either he or his *'Chief of the Staff'* are likely to make out either of these keys. I have also told him the date I should have my Army concentrated at *Debbeh-Ambukol* by telling him it will be so many days from this year's anniversary of his being made a Major General, a date that no one but himself is likely to know. I hope thus to correct the mistake he has made in sending away his cypher with poor Stewart. Dined early & started at 8 p.m. by train, reaching *Sarras* at 10 p.m., where we transferred ourselves & saddlebags to a trolly [*sic*], on which we started at 10.30 p.m. & went out to end of extension—about 7 miles—which we reached at midnight and halted for the night in the desert.

Tuesday 18th November

Started at 6 a.m. & reached *Akesheh* at 7 p.m. Pushed on again at 8.15 p.m. on ponies & reached *Sarkamatto* quarter of an hour after midnight—a long day of over 18 hours.

Wednesday 19th November

Left *Sarkamatto* on ponies & mules at 8 a.m. & reached *Magrakeh* at 9.30 a.m. Took an hour arranging ourselves & effects on camels. Started at 10.30 a.m. & reached *Absarab* at 8.30 p.m. Passed en route in the desert the first lot of the Guards' Camel Corps about 120 men under a fellow called Rowley,[120] who struck me as being of little use—I believe he plays cricket well. Glad to know he can do something well for soldiering does not seem to be his forte. When leaving these Guards I trotted my camel very quickly through their lines of camels: I had only one foot in the stirrup, the other leg being crossed carelessly over in front as if I were sitting on a side saddle. When the brute got to the end of the lines, he stopped suddenly & wheeled round, throwing me heavily on the very hard stony desert there: my hands were full, as I had a long whip, a horse tail fly whisk & my large pith hat in them, so I could not catch either spike of the saddle. It was a merciful providence that saved me from a very serious accident. I fell on my right hip; if I had fallen on my left hip, my sword hilt would have broken some of my bones: if my head, I might have broken my neck, & if on my shoulder, I must have smashed my collar bone. I picked myself up at once as the men were looking at me and mounted again & went off at a brilliant pace for miles into the desert, feeling however all the time as if my hip joint had been pulverised & every rib on my right side broken & driven into my lungs. When we halted for the night I was a cripple & could barely stand, but had to be helped along. I never had a nearer shave of a very disagreeable accident, but God ruled it otherwise & I subsequently found I had broken no bones, although I could not draw a long breath without pain for some days. I write this from notes made in a pocket book during the journey.

Thursday 20th November

Started from *Absarab* at 7.30 a.m. I was very stiff & uncomfortable & suffered much main [pain?] during the day from the jolting of the camel. Reached *Kaiber* at 1.10 p.m. & left again at 4 p.m. & marched into the desert until 6 p.m. & then halted for the night.

Friday 21st November

Off at 6.30 a.m. & reached *Abu Fatmeh* at 9.30 a.m. having lost at least half an hour on the way in amusing ourselves with firing at sand grouse with our revolvers. Left *Abu Fatmeh* in steam launch at 10.30 a.m. & reached my quarters in *Dongola* at 4.30 p.m. Few men have made the journey from *Dongola* to *Halfa* & back again in 8 days, 9 hours & five minutes, inclusive of one day spent at the latter place & half an hour squandered in the Desert trying to shoot sand grouse with revolvers. This camel travelling is not fatiguing and being so long as we generally were in the saddle & sleeping in the desert is a very healthy mode of life. And yet what a brute the camel is! The more I become acquainted with him the less I like him. He is a strange animal. He feeds mostly in the evening or at night: to feed him in the middle of the day does him apparently no good for that day. His strength today depends upon what he ate yesterday. You cannot revive him as you can a horse by a few hours' rest & plenty of good food & water. Complete rest for a day or two when he breaks down is absolutely necessary. In sleeping in the desert at this season the night & early mornings are very cold: I put on my overcoat & slept with two blankets over me each night. The poor devils of Natives who have no blankets & whose only clothing is their cotton clothes cannot sleep in the open from the cold during the winter & consequently are difficult to keep awake during the day. Sometimes it blew quite fresh from the north at night which added considerably to the cold. A camel saddle placed on end just behind your head is a good protection from wind & cold & enabled us to boil our kettle morning & evening over a spirit lamp which we found most useful. Travelling as quickly as I was, we had to eat *sur la ponce* or as best we could, but at daybreak, say 5.45 a.m. we always had some of that invaluable mixture known as Moor's Chocolate & Milk with some biscuit broken up in it, and sometimes a slice of preserved tongue or sardines fried over the spirit lamp. Wardrop did the cooking & excellently well he did it: when we halted for the night we had hot soup made from tinned soup or Liebeg or sometimes both together, prepared also over my lamp arrangement. During the day we munched biscuit or dates & were always hungry & ready for any food we could pick up en route. The regulation camel saddle is much pleasanter to make a long journey in than that used here by the Natives. One can vary one's position on it in so many ways that you never feel stiff. The great drawback to our journey was having no moon, & consequently we always had to finish each day's march with one, two or three or more hours in the dark, where the camels could only go at a walking pace, which is very trying to the rider. The slow jog of my camel is $4\frac{1}{2}$ miles an hour but when going well 5 miles an hour. With a baggage camel to lead it is very difficult to keep up this pace—I mean a trotting camel carrying baggage, for of course the ordinary baggager would be of no use at all on such a fast journey. It was only by one of us keeping behind the le[a]d camel with a stout whip that we could keep up the pace. When we dispensed with a guide & had only the one native with us, we got on best. A large party can never go quickly. If you want to travel fast, don't take a man with you who is fond of eating & who is miserable unless he has his meals '*regular*'. The less you cook & the more you live on dates, biscuit & water the quicker you will travel. . . .

Saturday 22nd November

Very stiff & unable to walk without limping. Thank God, no bones broken. Indoors all day working hard. I find the climate here is warmer than when I left and consequently the flies have again become lively. Mudir has been impertinent to Wilson & sent impudent messages to Kitchener during my absence. Sent Zohrab Bey to him to say I would not allow this. Had a humble apology from him. He came to see me yesterday when I returned here. Unfortunately we have now 10 cases of smallpox in this camp. Earle has very properly moved the camp of the Sussex Regt. further up stream. This smallpox is evidently given to our men by the women they consort with here: one man died of it this evening. I am still strongly of opinion that the Mahdi is in a fix and far from happy. I intend offering reward for his capture—I think I shall offer £10,000....

Sunday 23rd November 1884

Attended divine service in Mounted Infantry Lines; the Sussex Regt. being in quarantine owing to smallpox had their service later. Went to telegraph office & had a conversation with Buller about supplies. He said he wished to push on to *Dal* and I approved of his doing so. Sent Herbert Stewart up river to select a camping ground for Mounted Infry. and Camel Corps as I want to get them away from this infected neighbourhood. He came back in the evening, and the result of his investigations is that I mean to push him on to *Khandak*, about 40 miles above this, there to collect all his mounted force. Zohrab Bey sounded Mudir today as to the possibility of his succeeding Gordon, but to succeed him as an independent Sultan, the position to be hereditary in his family &c. &c. &c. He enjoyed the prospect much, but could not give me the information I required most which was whether he would be strong enough to hold his own in such a position without the presence of our troops. Hassein Pasha Khalifa is the man I should prefer to set up if I could only catch hold of him to open negociations with him. He is however I fear with the Mahdi still. The man of the name of whom we heard lately as having gone N.E. from *Berber* was a nephew of his.

Monday 24th Novr.

I have telegraphed home about forming a small Naval Brigade asking that the officer to command may be selected by Lord Northbrook. I shall send two gardiners[121] with them and may possibly send them on camels across desert to *Shendy* from *Ambrukol* to man the guns in Gordon's 5 steamers there. Remained indoors all day as I am still very stiff.

Tuesday 25th November

A very desponding telegram from Buller.[122] He says Butler sends unfavourable reports as to progress of whalers & recommends reducing load in each by 1000 lbs. Having replied[123] that all these difficulties about supplies make it all the more important to push forward mounted troops with all speed to *Ambukol* so that I may influence neighbouring tribes. It is the hot weather coming on which terrifies me: had this wretched Mr. Gladstone only had the grasp of a Statesman he would have begun this business two or three months earlier and we might now have had in that case ample supplies here by this date for all the Force. May God grant me success: without his aid I can do nothing.

I walked up and down my wretched room today for a good two hours, at the end of which time I found I had been dreaming, plotting out a possible campaign for myself in which the Mahdi was to be fool enough to come to the vicinity of the Nile somewhere about *Debbeh* or *Ambukol* to attack me: that after three days' hard fighting I was to have a brilliant victory killing the Mahdi with my own sword in the final cavalry charge and I did not find out how ridiculous I was until I began to construct my telegram to the Queen to tell Her of our signal success—may this be an augury of what is to come. I still feel quite hot over with the excitement which in my imagination I felt as I headed this final & victorious charge.

The day has been very warm & the flies in consequence very annoying. Herbert Stewart & Staff left this morning in steam launch for *Handak* to make arrangements for his camp there. The Mounted Infantry Regt. 394 of all ranks under Majr. Gough started at 5 p.m. to make *Handak* in two marches. I went to see them off and they looked all that could be desired. Was however angry to find that every officer, I should say, had a pony or a horse led. I shall not allow them to go beyond *Handak* as I have no idea of their eating up provisions required for other purposes.

Wednesday 26th November

Had a good canter in the desert where I found the Sussex Regt. out drilling. Rode back by the hospital in which there are far more patients than pleases me: they are however mostly slight cases. Colonel Rowley with 121 men of Guards Corps arrived—crossed the river to see them—such a magnificent lot of real soldiers! The world could not produce finer. I felt a hundred per cent pluckier as I looked at them, for I felt that with a thousand of such men I could & would face 25000 of any men the Mahdi could bring into the field. I was worried to see them under so inexperienced and incompetent a man as Rowley whose ignorance of what his first duties are has resulted in his having one third of his camels with sore backs. I had a talk with Buller over the wire. Wood's system is something that no one understands. Told Earle of my difficulties & said I wished him to go to *Abu Fatmeh & Kaibar* to look Line of Communication matters up. He is one of those men who never thinks of self when the public service is concerned, so he starts tomorrow for *Abu Fatmeh* and *Kaibar* taking Verner[124] with him.

Thursday 27th November

English post arrived: a very interesting letter from Brett giving me plenty of political news. Today much warmer & the flies more annoying in consequence. We have had two or three cases lately of the Mudir's sentries at night attacking our officers & men. Have told the Mudir that he must stop this or our men will take the law into their own hands, and the result will be ill-blood between us. Dr. Pratt whom Brackenbury recommended to me as the best possible man to look after a mess has turned out the most abject failure in that respect, and that was all I wanted him for. Our food is filthy and there seems to be little order or regularity in the mess. Have telegraphed to Buller[125] telling him to move to *Sakrametto* [*Sarkamatto*?] whenever he thinks it best in the interest of the public service to do so. I have also told him to employ Colonels Blundell,[126] Stracey[127] & Burnaby[128] on the Line of Communications. The employment of the last-named will raise the devil's own row at Marlborough House.

Friday—28th November 1884

Last night I received intelligence that Lt. Eagar had shot himself. This morning I hear from Earle at *Abu Fatmeh* that he committed suicide on the 25th instant. This will be a sad blow to poor Mrs. Fortescue. When passing through *Kaibar* last week (on 20th inst.) he gave me a very good lunch there: he had a company of Egyptian troops & was Commandt. of that place. He was very cheerful but enquired anxiously about the post, & said he had not had his letters regularly. He seems to have shot himself just after the last post reached him. I suppose some woman is at the bottom of it.

Out riding at 6.30 a.m.: had a good gallop to the *Abu-Fatmeh* telegraph station which is about 4 miles off. We had not wire enough to run it in here, so we use the heliograph for the gap. I hope to have the necessary amount of wire in a few days when the R.E. arrive in their boats. In the afternoon went to the Mudiriate [*sic*] to give away the decorations sent here by the Khedive for a few of the Mudir's officers. There were some very amusing Arab war dances, and even with palm stalks for assagais and hide shields, a little smaller but shaped exactly similarly to the Zulu shields, were very clever in fighting one against the other, throwing their sham assagais with great force & accuracy & cleverly catching them on their shields. After I had given away the decorations, I bid Mudir good-bye & went to see the three companies of Sussex Regt. start from their camp for *Debbeh* under Lt. Col. Tolson[129] (an odd name). I became a little nervous about the safety of the large quantity of supplies I have collected and am still heaping up there: hence this move. A strong redoubt is to be constructed at *Debbeh*. These 3 companies went off in '*Nassikeyeh*' towing 3 nuggers: they should reach their destination some time on Monday. I shall be much happier in my mind when I hear of their safe arrival there. Telegram from *Kitchener* saying man who took Northbrook's letter has returned: he was taken prisoner near *Khartoum* & his letter given to Mahdi: he escaped after 4 days' imprisonment. Such is his story but how much is true & how much false, it is difficult to say. His story corroborates all the previous information we had as to the condition of things in the Mahdi's camp & confirms the story about 500 regulars having deserted Mahdi & gone over to Gordon. In the evening just as I was going to bed messenger from *Khartoum* arrived bringing a very old letter from Gordon, dated 9th September before Stewart left that place. I calculate the date of Stewart's departure to have been 10th Septr. This messenger went down with the steamers that accompanied Stewart, but went ashore at *Shendy* of which neighbourhood he is a native & where he remained some considerable time. There is nothing in the letter we did not know before.

Saturday 29th November

Telegram from Buller[130] saying he had reached *Abu Fatmeh* & was at end of wire. At once started on camel to talk with him: when half way out to our station which is four miles off, met Adye coming back with a message from Butler saying he had waited at end of wire from last night & as he could get no message from me & a fair breeze had started up he would be off at once for *Dongola* to see me. I was extremely angry, as I don't want him here where he can be of no use to public service & I do want him on river in rear to hurry forward whalers. I send my little steam cutter down to meet him & turn him back sending him a letter which he won't like. I have no idea of having my orders disobeyed by him or anyone else. I am now very hopeful of being able to do a great deal by negotiation & possibly ending the business without any serious fighting. The messenger who came in from *Shendy* with Gordon's letter goes back tomorrow with another copy of my letter of 17th inst. & one of Northbrook's letter to him which we know fell into the Mahdi's hands. Earle returned today: his visit to *Kaibar* &c. has I know done good. Herbert Stewart made a Brigdr. General.

Sunday 30th November

Had a long letter from Butler[131] which my steam pinnace brought back. I don't like its tone, but it is quite Butlerian: he is in his own opinion the only wise man out here and anything that has gone wrong has been occasioned because I did not consult him more, take him more into my confidence and follow his advice. I was being deceived by some of my oldest & most trusted officers who always crabbed this expedition & were—although he does not say so in exactly these words—determined it should be a failure. Formerly I consulted him & admitted him to my confidence— now I don't, & Buller is determined he is to be an outsider: & so on. The fact is Butler's talent is erratic:[132] it can neither work in any ordinary groove, nor work in harmony with the talents of other men in a team. This fact reduces his usefulness by one half. He is one of those men who imagine they have been and who are convinced they always are, in the right. He extends his vision to the future & will tell you when an event happens 'I warned you or someone else of this a year or some years ago.' He is an impulsive, talented Irishman, wanting in method, and who will never rise to the position in the Army he aspires to, & which, if he had more ballast, & more businesslike habits might be within his reach. All my old companions, men whom I brought on—E. Wood— Redvers Buller, Brack, Butler &c. are now reaching that age &

standing in the service when it is difficult to place them in a small Army in the field, and when there, each and all are so jealous one of the other, that the team is a difficult one to drive. The fact is, there are very few first-rate men, & it is only a first-rate man—such for instance as poor Colley was,—who can manage such a handfull. I have suspected a little captiousness more than once in my followers since I came this time to Egypt: Butler is the first upon whom my wrath has fallen, & I hope he may be the last.

Attended divine service in the Sussex camp, at 6.45 a.m. I do not gallop about much now as my hip on which I fell from my camel is stiff & hurts me if my horse jolts me at all. I issued today the following G.O.

General Order.

The first English boats with troops on board having now passed the Third Cataract, the following Special Order will be read at the head of every Regiment, Battalion, Battery and Detachment, on three successive days, and will be published in all Regimental, Corps, and Station Orders:

To the Soldiers and Sailors of the Nile Expedition.

The relief of General Gordon and his garrison, so long besieged in Khartoum, is the glorious mission that the Queen has entrusted to us.

It is an enterprise that will stir the heart of every soldier and sailor fortunate enough to have been selected to share in it, and the very magnitude of its difficulties only stimulates us to increased exertion.

We are all proud of General Gordon's gallant and self-sacrificing defence of Khartoum, which has added, if possible, to his already high reputation. He cannot hold out many months longer, and he now calls upon us to save his garrison. His heroism and his patriotism are household words wherever our language is spoken, and not only has his safety become a matter of National importance, but the knowledge that a brave comrade is in need of help urges us to push forward with redoubled energy. Neither he nor his garrison can be allowed to meet the sad fate which befell his gallant companion in arms, Colonel Stewart, who, when endeavouring to carry out an enterprise of unusual danger, was foully and treacherously murdered by his Captors. We can, and with God's help we will, save General Gordon from such a death.

The labour of working up this river is immense. To bear it uncomplainingly demands the highest soldierlike qualities—that contempt for danger and that determination to overcome difficulties which in previous campaigns have so distinguished all ranks of Her Majesty's Army and Navy.

The physical obstacles that impede our rapid progress are considerable, but who cares for them when it is remembered that General Gordon and his garrison are in danger?

Under God, their safety is now in your hands, and, come what may, we must save them.

It is needless to say more to British Soldiers and Sailors.
Head Quarters, Dongola
30th November 1884. (signed) Wolseley General
Commanding in Chief.

I wrote this in the morning & had Brackenbury to the end of the wire at *Halfa* & telegraphed it to him in the afternoon. It is a difficult thing for an Englishman to compose an order of this sort. For a Frenchman & perhaps all other foreigners, the task is easy: he can afford to be heroic & pompous in his expressions without being thought ridiculous. With us it is very different and I have no doubt the *Pall Mall Gazette* and *St. James Gazette* who are nothing if not cynical will find fault with my grammar and hold up my appeal to all that is good in the British soldier—and there is certainly plenty of good in him—to the ridicule of their readers. However that will concern me very little if I can but get to the heart of those under my command. The labor on the river in this climate is very great, and if I cannot infuse some heroic zeal into my men, this Army will be little better [than] a poor emaciated body without any spirit or soul in it. I also issued an order promising £100 to the Battaln. that made the best time between *Sarras* & *Debbeh*, and promised that the successful Battn. would have every consideration shown it by the honorable position it should occupy during our forward movements. I hope these orders may bear some fruit. When I was a young man, if any General had addressed an order like mine of today to any Army I was serving with, it would have made every nerve in my body tingle, & have sent the blood pounding through my veins, until I should have longed to have gone forth & fought the Mahdi by myself. But then I was always very impressionable which I owe to my Irish education and early Irish surroundings.

December 1884

Monday—1st December 1884

How my hope has been disappointed as to the time when I should have been in a position to do something. I expected to have been at *Ambukol* by this date with a force large enough to have walked through the Monassir Country with fire & sword. Had a pleasant ride but did not go very far or very fast as my hip still annoys me. Great quantities of land here that has been formerly cultivated now lying fallow, all, or certainly chiefly owing to aggressive taxation. The Mudir says he cannot make both ends meet because Gordon reduced all the taxes by one half. Each Shakeeyah used to pay £5 or £6—now only £2.10.0 is paid for each, and so on, by his orders.

Going through the desert here I saw one or two species of Euphorbia but although they were so common in parts of Zululand & South Africa I could not for the life of me remember the name until now. Hence this note apropos of nothing. Melons and water melons, cucumbers and vegetable marrow of sorts are very plentiful and cheap here. Since the Mounted Infantry moved forward & the Detachments of the Camel Corps move south also by the other bank without crossing here, the prices of everything has fallen here considerably.

Tuesday 2nd December 1884

Rode in the early morning. What poor creatures we are! I have had a violent tic in the back of my head and have been wretched today in consequence: may my enemy have a similar pain the day I have to fight him. In the evening crossed the river in my little steam launch and inspected the Hd. Qtrs. & 4 sections of Guards' Camel Corps. The Mudir went across & walked down the ranks with me. He said he was much pleased: the men were in red & looked very well and very healthy. They marched off en route for *Handak* when I had inspected them. The days are now much hotter than they were three weeks ago & the nights not so cold. It is this question of climate that oppresses me when I think of it. Heard from Buller from *Dal*. He wants more camels on that portage & between *Tanjour* & *Ambigol*. Bazaar rumor, the Mahdi is dead—never have I wished anyone dead before more earnestly than I now wish him carried off to his fathers. What an amount of anxiety his death would take off my shoulders! and how furious all these ambitious young officers would be if the bubble was to burst without fighting! It is however a solution to the question I desire with all my heart.

Wednesday 3rd December

Mr. Cook & Son arrived in a small diabeeyah: he tells me his bill against Govt. will not amount to more than about £120,000—I think this must be far under the amount. Hot day. There is a rough sort of gold and silver ornament made here which has a cachet of its own. I am buying a few silver bracelets for presents at home. Silver coinage is so scarce here that it is not easy to have work done in that material. The Medjidieh & the Maria Theresa & pillar dollars are really the only coins these people value: of course the Turkish and Egyptian small pieces of a few piastres each excepted. The sovereign is at a great discount & few Arabs here will take it. In all our agreements with camel men we have to promise to pay in silver dollars which is most perplexing as moving up large amounts of silver is very difficult, and even by sending, as we have done, to *Constantinople*, is very difficult to obtain even in *Cairo*. It takes a long time to make an inland people who have little trade with the outside world learn the value of gold coins. Years after our expedition to Abyssinia men of that country sold handfuls of sovereigns for a few silver dollars. A sharp Jew money changer here might make a fortune out of this expedition if he would coin & bring up here Medjidiehs and dollars. A cameleon (wrongly spelt? I am sure) has just scampered along the wall in front of where I write, chasing a little fellow which he failed to catch: they are common in these regions, and several live in the ceiling of the room in which I sleep, if room I may call it: there is a very well-written and amusing book called I think 'The inhabitants of my old pear tree' or something to that effect: if the writer stayed a few days in this room he might [write?] several volumes upon the manners, customs, and dispositions of the various birds, beasts, reptiles & insects which have nests & houses in the floors, walls & roof of this apartment. However I ought to be thankful, for there are neither fleas nor bugs here, so I sleep in peace. The first two boats of the Stafford Regt. arrived in the evening, having left *Sarras* on the 7th Novr. The Cook family dined with me.

Thursday 4th December

Had a good canter and then came back to find the English post of the 14th November arrived. Spenser Childers showed me a letter from his father in which he made use of the expression that they were living 'from week to week' not knowing what their fate as a Government was to be, or words to that effect. Several more whalers with Staffordshire on board passed here today. In the evening at 5 p.m. had a long talk for nearly two hours over the wires with Baring at *Cairo*. Am glad to find that generally he agrees with me in the policy I proposed for the Eastern Soudan. Chermside seems to have been leading him astray and he has under that influence been urging home Govt. to undertake an expedition with British troops to *Tokah*. I don't think the Cabinet will agree, but with a Govt. torn with internal dissensions & strong only in the weakness of the Tories, it is difficult to say what they will or not agree to. They have now consented to a very large augmentation of naval expenditure simply to keep themselves in office through the reputation they expect to gain by the 'Rule Britania [*sic*]' business. In my day no such contemptible lot have been in office; they bow before a leader who is no statesman & who is ruining the life of the Nation. May he suffer in the next world for having taught the Irish to steal and for having endeavoured to persuade the people of England that it was a righteous thing to be insulted and wronged as a nation. Cant and cowardice describe his proceedings since he has come into office. Unwisdom and unreadiness has marked our proceedings since he has been in office & 'Too late' describes every resolution his Cabinet has ever come it [to?].

Friday 5th December

When having a pleasant gallop this morning my horse put his foot on a rotten piece of ground into which he sunk to his knee and went down an almighty smasher. I stuck on him for some seconds and after a good slide along the ground he nearly recovered himself, but not completely and ended by rolling over. The ground was soft so thank God I was not hurt. Telegrams from Buller[133]— more delays in rear: it is enough to break my heart for nothing I can do will rectify the folly of the Govt. in postponing preparations so long: still I am quite confident of ultimate success, but I hate to think we shall have to pay many, many valuable lives lost from prolonging our operations into the hot weather for the folly and ignorance of Mr. Gladstone. And yet the foolish English people cheer him in Rl.Rd. stations ignorant of the fact that every soldier who dies on our return journey has been killed by the folly of the Minister whom they have for the time at least, seen fit to deify. Mr. Cook & Son came to say goodbye. They start tomorrow & hope to be in London before New Year's day—I wish I could be in *Khartoum* on that date!! .... One squadron of the 19th Hussars arrived here & go on tomorrow towards *Handak*. Had a 'kit inspection' and all my staff also and reduced my personal kit to the smallest limits. I mean to send all the superfluous articles to *Halfa* on some of those camels that go there to bring up loads. The Nile is very low now, much lower than is usual at this season of the year. The Mudir says that in the next 5 months i.e. to say 1st May it will fall 2 metres more—one metre in the first $3\frac{1}{2}$ months & one in the last $1\frac{1}{2}$ months. My aneroid stands here usually at $29\frac{1}{2}$ but sometimes rises one-tenth.

Saturday 6th December

Rode in the morning & evening as usual. One company of Sussex left for *Debbeh*. News received that confirms the story of Mahdi's attack on *Omdurman* about middle of November when he is said to have lost severely. After fight he told his followers that if they would go into the Nile it would dry up to let them across to take *Khartoum*. The 23rd Novbr. was the day fixed for the miracle. Some thousands rushed into the water with their spears &

many were drowned. The Ma[h]di then retreated due west about one day's journey having no one but some Dervishes with him. I don't believe all the details, but in the main the great features of this story are true: it is also confirmed that a considerable number of black troops deserted from the Mahdi to Gordon. Mahdi has now announced he would starve *Khartoum* out & has constructed a line of works completely across between the two Niles to prevent supplies coming in from the South.

Sunday 7th December 1884

Sent orders to Stewart to march to *Korti* (about 100 miles above *Handak*) on Thursday the 11th. Staffords to rendezvous at *Debbeh* and move forward on 13th inst. to same place to which place I mean to transfer all the stores I have collected at *Debbeh* as well as the Sussex Regt.

Church service in Sussex lines at 7 a.m. Angry telegram from Duke of Cambridge protesting against employment of officers on leave without his sanction. My answer tries to deprecate his wrath, but I give him a dig by pointing out that if these officers can be spared from their Regts. on leave, they can be spared to do useful work on our 1200 miles of communications. From the first day I came in contact with H.R.H. up to date he has always evinced the hatred towards me which is born of jealousy & begotten by spite. He is a Royal Prince and nothing more & that ought to content him. His Creator did not build him upon the lines on which soldiers can alone be constructed: to begin with, he lacks the first necessary quality of a soldier, namely physical courage, a peculiarity which his eldest son has unfortunately inherited. He is a dangerous man to ignore, and yet for one in my position, it is almost impossible to keep on cordial terms with him.

Monday 8th Decembr. 1884

Rode early as usual. Zohrab Bey having given the Mudir a broad hint that his steamer would be of great use to me in my journey to *Ambukol* has placed her at my disposal. My camels & spare horses marched this morning for *Handak*, from which place they will go on with Stewart up the river-bank.

Tuesday 9th Decembr. 1884

The first really cold morning. Decided last night upon starting on

Saturday next—13th inst.—for *Ambukol*. Hd. Qtrs. of 19th Hussars arrived. Very much amused by Barrow's account of the D.T. Correspondent, Mr. Burleigh. They met him at *Sarras* where of course he sponged upon them for a meal. He had a boat there and said he would join them again at *Semneh* the following evening. They started inwardly hoping they had got rid of him for ever as they did not think he would be able to reach & get over *Semneh* that day. They camped for the night above the cataract & to their astonishment in the evening Burleigh & his boat arrived & drew up near the bank where they were. Of course he again drew upon their hospitality: although he swaggered about living on 9 dates a day, he pitched into their food with a vengeance. He had carried away his rudder, & his mast, & his sailing gear was all in a bad way. He gaily asked Barrow if there were any Hussars who were sore from riding as he would be glad to take a few to *Dongola* in his boat—good natured man! he wanted them to pull him & his boat there. His crew consisted of a pilot, one boy & himself. Barrow & he parted. The following day I think it was that Burleigh with nothing on but a canvas pair of trousers was seen on the bank of the river scraping a hole deep enough to bury his pilot. His boat was wrecked, went down and he lost the few things he had with him, the pilot being drowned. As he covered up the pilot's body with sand he was heard to say 'I don't wish to say anything ill of the dead, but this was all his fault.' A day afterwards he appeared clothed again, having begged things I suppose of those whom he met. He is a real good beggarman. This begging talent is a very necessary one for the regular out-and-out newspaper correspondent and is one of several reasons why it is so difficult for a Gentleman to serve in that capacity where he is pitted against men who are not bound by certain generally accepted canons of honor. To rival Billy Russell or Forbes you must be utterly indifferent to truth and prepared to fawn upon those who will either give you a dinner or information & who will not scruple to bribe servants, telegraph & other clerks and to 'jump' a horse or pony when you require them. This man Mr. Burleigh begged sugar, tea & coffee &c. from the Qr. Mastr. 19th Hussars before starting on his journey which has ended so unfortunately for him. I am glad to say the Correspondents that are now here in *Dongola* are by far the nicest lot of fellows I have ever known in that capacity. Williams[134] who is I think for the Central News, Cameron for the *Standard*, Pearce[135] for the *Daily News*,

Pigott[136] for Reuter, Villiers[137] for the *Graphic* & little Melton Prior[138] for the *Illustrated*. I have not mentioned poor old Jack Colburn, the distinguished Lord Seaton's son, who dreams for a German Illustrated Paper—what a career his has been, and what opportunities thrown away! Here he is now a wreck, but still a Gentleman.

Wednesday 10th December

I often laugh as I look back a few pages over my journal before it goes to you, and think how you must yawn over it & hate having to read it. I always remember your description of how you endeavoured to read my Narrative of the China War and how you failed to get through more than a few pages of it. This diary is still duller, for anything that could possibly interest you, I put in my letters to you, & I [am] fully sensible of their monotonous dullness. A dozen things occur here daily out of any one of which you would make a capital and interesting and amusing letter. But although I love to be made laugh, and think I have a strong sense of the comic & ridiculous, yet for the life of me I cannot sit down to describe even the scenes that amuse me most. I become pond[e]rous and pompous and weary of the heaviness of my own descriptions. I cannot touch a subject lightly as you do, leaving your reader to supply details from his own imagination. I love poetry: I love to learn it, & when alone I frequently repeat long bits from Shakespear[e] or from Byron which I learnt as a boy, and do so to my own intense satisfaction admiring the beauty of lines as I repeat them, but still never was there a man more devoid of original poetic fancies than I am. I dream of heroic events, and I delight in lovely scenery with babbling brooks surrounded by many-colored woods, but I am afraid that all power of describing sentiment, or the lights and shades and little differences in color or intensity of human affections in all their tenderest aspects is wanting to me. I shall write a story some day & publish it as a second volume or appendix to the *Soldier's Pocket Book,* for its phrases would, I know, be similar to it in tone, and equally devoid of all that pathos without which life would be intolerable to educated Christians.

The Mudir who seems to have frequent communications with other worlds & to see visions, told Zohrab that he had had two visions one that the Nile was filled with salt water, which being interpreted means that its waters are covered by the English in their boats who have come across the ocean. The other was he saw me reclining and resting on the bank of the Nile after the fatigues of a great victory over our enemys [*sic*]. My own vision this day is that I shall be in *Khartoum* before the end of January. God grant it may be a true one. All the mounted troops 'cameled' today. Everyone belonging to this operating army at or passed *Halfa* except the Cameron Highlanders who are at *Korosko* where their presence is a standing menace to *Abu Hamed*. I am in hopes that when we occupy *Abu Hamed*, Rundell[139] may be able to organize some camel convoys of provisions to that place from *Korosko*. It has been blowing a strong wind all yesterday & today from the North which ought to send our boats along right royally. The dust here has been horrible. Today was pleasantly cool even at noon: the flies of little moment in consequence. Of all the dirtiest people in the world these are the nastiest & have the least excuse—...

11th December—Thursday

A really pleasantly cool day with a strong Northerly wind blowing. Post from home delivered at 8 a.m. Nothing new by it. I am heartily sick of the Franchise Bill and the compromise and everything about it. The compromise must have been a bitter pill for those rascally radicals, and anything that annoys them must be pleasant to all lovers of England as a great & powerful nation ready to fight for 'the right' all over the world & to defend Her Majesty's subjects no matter whether they be injured in Madagascar or Timbuctoo.

Earle has strained himself in some way unknown to himself & is I am sorry to say confined to his bed in consequence. If he is laid up several days it will be serious for he is the most businesslike & reliable man I have on the Line of Commns.—I wish he had been at its head instead of dear puzzle-headed Evelyn Wood. The Mahdi has now announced his intention of starving-out *Khartoum*. God grant its garrison may be able to hold out until I can get there. If necessary we must then go out and attack this swaggering false prophet no matter how small my force may be. Until he is driven off, no food can be brought into the place.

12th December—Friday

Rode to see Earle in the morning. Cold morning & fresh day. Men talk of the Mahdi's intention to attack me by night: I can scarcely believe he will get his poorly-clad followers to do much fighting in these cold nights.

13th December—Saturday

Bid a long farewell to *Dongola*, and never wish to land here again. I don't object to looking at it in my downward journey home if I return by this route, but it is not a place one could ever feel any attachment to. A large proportion of the servants in *Cairo* came from this place and the people of this neighbourhood are supposed to make the best servants in that city. I embarked at 9 a.m. in the Mudir's diabeeah which was to be towed by his steamer. En route to the quay, I paid him a visit & he accompanied me on board. I believe he is a little disappointed that I have not asked him to accompany me, but if I want him I can always send for him & dealing with Easterns of his nature one must pay no regard to their feelings on such points, but learn to throw them over when you don't want their services any longer just as they do one to the other. We had not been under weigh more than about an hour when the Reis said the diabeehah was leaking forward & we must stop to caulk her. This we did at the ruined village of [blank space] where there are the remains of a temple & apparently of copper smelting works—I am told that some good bronze statuettes have been dug up here, also some scarabei. We were soon caulked & embarked again, Sir C. Wilson having found a good stone hatchet. When ashore we saw the 4 sections of the Heavy Cav. Camel Corps on the march which had reached *Dongola* yesterday. They are under Byng[140] 1st Life Gds.: a splendid body of men. The Mudir said today was an especially lucky day for my start, and assured me that he did not believe I should meet with any opposition until we reached *Khartoum* itself: he said it was all clear to there. I wish I could believe this. I replied 'if so why should there be any difficulty in communicating with Gordon?' We ran on until nearly 7 p.m. and halted alongside the left bank for the night at a point about 12 miles from *Handak*. We passed the Head Qtrs. and about a couple of dozen whalers with South Staffordshire on board all sailing & rowing. Hard work but very healthy:

what condition these men will be in if I have to let them in at the Mahdi!! No men could be put through a better course of training for fighting.

Sunday 14th December 1884

Started about 5.30 a.m. & reached *Handak* at 8.30 a.m. Some good houses in the town, which is built on a rocky eminence overlooking the river pointing it out as a place where a village must have existed ever since this province was peopled. There is the ruin of an old castle abutting on the river in the centre of the village. We in the diabeeah left the steamer there to take in wood & call at the camp about 4 miles higher up & then to catch us as we were under sail. There I met Mr. Curtis the soi-disant Abdel-Kader. I asked him if he still had any of the letters which he brought out to deliver to Gordon; he said no, but said it in such a tone that it was evident he was lying. He said that the last news from the Mahdi's camp was that he has received large quantities of provisions down the valley of the White Nile & that cattle were so plentiful with him that cows were selling in his camp for less than one dollar. . . . As we passed the site of Stewart's camp at *Handak*, the 19th Hussars were ferrying across their horses in boats. The water of the river is perceptably clearer than it was when we were at *Halfa*: close in to shore you can see the bottom to a depth of about a foot. As yet we have seen very few wildfowl, although today is really cold in the shade the sun however being still warm. We pulled up for the night at Old *Dongola* on the right bank: it was very dark when we halted so we saw nothing of the town which is some distance from the river & the bank is there very high: at one time many years ago this was a place of considerable importance, but has withered & decayed under the hopeless rule of Egypt. The number of date trees has diminished considerably. The women as we pass their villages shout us their weird and curiously intoned welcome.

Monday—15th December

Under weigh at daybreak. Reached *Debbeh* at 12.20 p.m. Inspected the two forts there. The Bashi Bazouk garrison looked the greatest ruffians imaginable and I believe their enemies call to Heaven for redress. It is no wonder the Egyptian rule should be hated by this people or that they should be glad to rebel when they can, when the cruelties & injustice they receive from these bands of ruffians are remembered.

Hartington telegraphs[141] that public want official news of our operations. I must throw that news-devouring monster a sop now & then, but I shall tell them little until I can announce some good blow struck. If I can only reach *Shendy* safely with 1500 men on camels & with 30 days' provisions for them, I think I could tickle up the Mahdi. . . .

The Correspondents who had started in a sailing diabeeah just after we left *Dongola* & whom we had left far behind the first day, reached *Debbeh* a few hours before us, by sailing all through the night, having bribed their Reis to do so. I started from *Debbeh* at 2 p.m. Col. Tolson of the Sussex Regt. commands there: he has 5 companies of his Regt. with him, only 2 men being in Hospital. I mean to clear out all the stores we have collected there as soon as I can & leave the defence of the place to the Mudir's blackguards. I shall thus save a Battalion which I had originally designed as a garrison for these parts. We passed the 4 whalers that had started this morning from *Debbeh*, and as we did so—it was about 6.15 p.m.—the steamer grounded in a difficult channel. She only draws about $4\frac{1}{2}$ feet, & we draw about 3 ft. We had picked up the Nugger with Buller's stores on board, so we were soon in a sort of knot in the middle of the river. When we got loose we crawled along the bank a little, tracking and sailing until the wind died away altogether: in the meantime the steamer had got afloat again & hauled into the bank where it made fast for the night. Saw a large crocodile & our sportsmen expended a few rounds of ammunition without doing the brute any harm.

Tuesday 16th December

Under weigh about daybreak but wind so light we could make no way until the steamer picked us up about 6 a.m. Then as our course soon became N.E. with a strong wind ahead we made little progress, very often barely moving forward at all. The four whalers that halted about a mile astern of us on right bank—for I make all troops in whalers halt for the night always on that bank beyond *Debbeh*—very nearly caught us up, & held their own with us for a long time in the early morning. . . . Very cold morning: indeed in the shade it is cold now until noon. About noon passed

Lt. Montgomery's (R.N.) Picket running down stream at a furious pace. We were making such little way that I cast off the Nugger in which was my camp equipment &c. We reached *Korti* a little after 6 p.m. where I found Herbert Stewart established in a very pretty camp on left bank of river. The village is about 1000 yds. inland from the river: in fact it is in the desert. The camp is pitched on what was cultivated ground but Stewart bought the standing corn & all on the land for £100. This green forage is not dear at the price & will be good for the camels & horses. There is no news, except that Mahmond Ahmed sent to Osman Digma at *Suakim* asking for help to fight the English coming to attack him from *Dongola*. He consulted Sheiks and all said no, as they required their men in case of attack from English at *Suakim*. The Berber head man replied in similar strains. Great complaints everywhere as to the atrocities perpetrated by these accursed Bashi Bazouks. The wing of the South Stafford have left *Sarras* on the 5th Novembr. and reach *Dongola* on 5th December having been 24 days going. They dawdled however a good deal & I an in great hopes that the other troops may make the distance on an average of 22 days.

Wednesday 17th December

Telegraphed the Mudir I must keep his steamer here a few days to tow along this reach. Appointed Wardrop D.A.A.G. to Stewart's Brigade of Mounted troops. Remained in my diabeeah all day because my eyes have troubled me a little for the last few days: a feeling as if there was sand in them which is the first sign of 'conjunctivitis'—(I think this is the name of the first mild form of opthalmia). I bathed them frequently in very strong cold tea & felt better towards night. I did not have my camp pitched as I wished the ground to dry well first after the standing crops had been cut. The Sheik of the Sowarrab came in. Part of his tribe are with the Mahdi. Had him sounded as to how he could help us with camels in a march across the desert to *Matammeh* (on left bank of Nile opposite *Shendy* which is on right bank). He will take time to consider. Wilson who is a sanguine man believes he will supply about 300 camels.[142] By Christmas Day I shall have here the R.A. Camel Battery & between 1100 & 1200 of the Camel Corps & Detachments of Bearer Co. Moveable Hospl. & say 500 transport camels: my idea is to move with 1100 Camel Corps & 4 guns of

Camel Battery on evening of 28th instant in three marches to *Gakdul* wells, 100 miles from this & there to halt our day. To carry 30 days' supplies for men & 4 days' grain for camels. To march by night—full moon on 1st Janry. Three more night marches to take me to *Matemmeh*. Buller with remainder of Camel Corps to move on 6th Janry. in same way to same place. It is however quite possible I may not be able to move before the 1st Janry. In the meantime a force will be concentrating at *Hamdab* above *Gerendid* cataract under Earle for an advance into the Monassir country and upon *Abu Hamid*. However this is not a sound calculation to go on. It is the fact of the moon being full on the 1st Janry. that induces me to try & move so early as I should prefer waiting until I could move all the Camel Troops in two or three echelons across the desert for a concentrated march from thence to *Khartoum*. I believe that with 1500 such men as I can dispose of, once arrived at *Khartoum* I could raise the siege & perhaps finish the whole business. Rundle from *Korosko* is very hopeful about being able to send 80,000 rations across the desert from thence to *Abu Hamed* provided we occupy that place by the 1st February & to repeat the arrangement by the 25th February, the cost being £2000 for each trip. I have consented to the terms which I consider reasonable. 80,000 rations is food for 5000 men for 16 days. The transport of each ration would therefore cost 6d. —I shall however send groceries for 32 days with each convoy— the Arabs to have no protection from us; I calculate that it will require about 1000 camels to take that amount of stuff across the *Korosko* desert, calculating the ration roughly at 4 lbs. gross weight, the package being heavy.

I sent off a long letter to Gordon[143] during the night, mostly in cypher sending him the pages on cypher from the *Soldier's Pocket Book* and giving him the key thus—(a), to be the number of guns in the Battery of Rl. attack (Arty. ?] that was called after a friend of his: (b) to be the day of the month when C.G.C. was born—: (c) to be the number of letters in the name of the General who commanded in Shanghai in 1862. The key to be $a^2 \times b^2 \times c$. I don't think the Mahdi or any of his friends will be able to make that out. I have asked him a series of questions & begged him for an early answer.

Thursday 18th December

I interviewed the *Sowarrab* Sheik Mahomed el Kheir after he had signed an agreement to carry 250 loads from this to *Matammeh* at $10 per load. He is a nice-looking fellow, if he were not an Arab. I should have said it was the face of an honest man. Strange to say unlike any other Arab I have seen he is actually stout. Moved into camp; very glad to leave the Mudir's diabeeah where I was bitten badly every night by some insect, I know not what, & where there was a large colony of rats just behind my pillow. I rode in the evening and arranged with Stewart for the outposts. We have the most lovely sunsets here every evening, the coloring on the river as the sun goes down quite a dream of brightness and richness. The banks here are cultivated on both sides of the river and as you approach *Merawie* the depth of the corn fields goes on increasing. I was at first puzzled at finding the dourra crop quite one month behind that at *Halfa* and the country between *Dal* and *Dongola*, but I learn now that the lateness of the grain here is accidental and entirely owing to the unsettled condition of the country and not to any peculiarity of climate. As soon as the dourra is cut, they plant wheat which is fit for cutting in three months. As I write this in my tent about 9.30 p.m. the noise of the shakeeyah on the opposite bank is very strange: it goes on all night. I sent my steam pinnace across the river this morning to try & buy fowl &c. & was very much amused when Dr. Pratt came back in here & said that the Sheik of the village opposite was very much disturbed in his mind because one of our whalers had brought up alongside a sand bank in the river & pitched a tent there: he declared that all the men in it would be eaten by crocodiles. I sent it there to be in quarantine because one of its crew had been dropped at *Debbeh* ill, & the illness has since then develloped [*sic*] into smallpox. Here owing to the scarcity of trees & the hardness of the wood, one cannot afford to have those great camp fires which on the Red River expedition and in most campaigns make a camp or bivouac so pleasant and almost romantic. All the men here are still without tents as Stewart, in order to reduce the load to be carried by the camels, sent his *tentes d'abri* by water, and the nuggers carrying them have not yet arrived. The wind along this reach is always downstream, so unless the men in the boats can either row or have the energy to track, their progress is consequently very slow. News this evening from the Mahdi's camp tells us he has heard of the English army being at *Dongola*, a fact which I presume he has learnt from the man—his cousin—whom I sent from thence into his camp shortly after my arrival at *Dongola*. The common native idea is that for some reason of our own we pretend to have only a small army whilst our strength is very great: Arabs have no idea of numbers and when they see 1000 soldiers marching solidly in a body they believe it to be a force five times that strength. I am glad of this and hope it may have a soothing!! effect on the minds of the Mahdi's followers. . . .

Friday—19th December 1884

Rode out to see Stewart drill his two Regts. on camels. It was very satisfactory. He is a first-rate officer all round. . . . What curiously mysterious river is the Nile whose volume of water becomes greater the further up we go, certainly until the point where the *Atbarra* flows into it. We were told we should suffer from want of firewood: nothing has surprised me more than the quantity of wood to be had along the river from *Halfa* here. Then we were told that as the Nile went down & exposed the previously submerged banks, tracking would be impossible, as the men could not walk over the soft sand—all bunkum. It is always so before every fresh campaign: one is told hundreds of lies about the country & its inhabitants, and a certain set of croakers never tire of predicting all sorts of evils and misfortunes. The mosquitoes are said to be as large as wasps; every snake deadly & yards long: climate pestiferous, water undrinkable etc. Some ass, tired of England, has paid the Soudan a flying visit: he is not a man who observes anything perhaps beyond the substance & quantity of the food he obtained & about that perhaps he is somewhat vague, but he has no hesitation in laying down the law upon every topic connected with the Soudan because he has been a week here. Of course there are observers & observers. A week spent at any time in any country would be invaluable to the General who had even years after to plan a campaign in it: there is nothing like personal experience no matter how slight to give you an idea of a country; a little of it is worth all the information to be obtained in the Library of the Geographical Society. Nine men out of ten who travel are entirely incapable of giving you any useful military information about the countries they visit: but then nine men out of ten & ninety-nine women out of a hundred are simply fools.

In calculating the rate of progress made by troops so as to ascertain what troops I should have here by any named date I have allowed as follows. For camels from *Sarras* to *Dongola* 14 days.

From *Dongola* to *Korti*—7 days. For troops in boats from *Gemai* to *Dal,* 14 days; from *Dal* to *Dongola,* 10 days; & from *Dongola* to *Korti* 10 days. Mahamed el Kheir the *Sowarrab* sheik hopes to be able to persuade the *Huwawir* tribe to supply 250 camels to carry loads to *Metammeh* on same terms as he has agreed upon.

20th December—Saturday

Rode in the morning to *Ambukol* which is now mostly in ruins, but has evidently been at one time a large place: in centre of village is the remains of a considerable building which was the Palace when the district of *Ambukol* had a King, a condition of things that existed until Mahomed Ali conquered this country and turned out all the old reigning families. The Kashif of this district is now the son of the last king—how is Royalty fallen! On our way we passed over part of the ground where the Mudir's battle took place and those of the party who cared to moralize over the insignificance of man were able to enjoy their bent as their horses trod on the remains of the poor devils who fought and died for what they possibly believed to be right.

I went on to the camp on the river where the Mudir's ruffianly soldiers are stationed: they were taken by surprise by my visit but their little tom-toms were soon beating and the men falling in in response to that signal as I reached their parade ground. In the afternoon I went out to see some experiments with gun-cotton as a cutting down agency for trees. I am short of axes, so I shall use gun-cotton to cut down the hard acacie trees to make our yeribas with in the desert. Today has been very warm, as there has been no wind. All crossing of the Camel Corps at *Handak* delayed for two days owing to want of wind there. Hd. Qtrs. & 3 troops of 19th Hussars arrived here. Post for England left today at 5 p.m. It should reach home on 15th January by which date I hope to be in or near *Khartoum.* . . .

[Re Byrons poetry] How that poetry rings still in my ears much as I despise the man who wrote it, and how weak and puling is the verse of Tennyson and how dull and meaningless is that of Browning in comparison with that rush of intelligible sentiment which pervades Tara, the Corsair, the Bride of Abydro &c. &c. On one side we have the sickly meanderings of a schoolgirl or the jargon of a rymster [*sic*] who did not understand the words he strung together, and on the other all the pathos of a manly, though possibly an eccentric, genius. One is feminine, the other is male, one is weakly expressed, is without fibre & muscle, the vision of fair women, the foibles of the weaker sex, the other the strength, the vices & crimes if you will of manhood, but still vigorous, strong, bespeaking the courage peculiar to man. Better one hour of such manhood, even though it be criminal than a cycle of such bread & butter missishness. This is being written when I am alone with my thoughts before I go to sleep for the night. How I hate, loath and despise the effeminacy of those who decry prize fighting and turn up the whites of their eyes when duelling is mentioned.

Sunday—21st December

Divine service at 7.30 a.m. The Rev. Mr. O'Neil. Oh what a dreary useless sermon! He recounted all the glories of the Church. Now I am far more intelligent and infinitely better read than 9 out of every 10 of our men to whom he was preaching to & yet I know little of church history & never mean to read it. The church to which our Lord so frequently refers, is the body of believing Christians no matter what their denominations may be & not the narrow, exclusive & bigotted establishment of the English church only. No one who listened to him cared much for the church which he glorified and few cared for or understood the meaning of the great annual church festivals to which he referred with so much pride. What bunkum all this sort of preaching is. If our clergy men would only preach the pure doctrine which our Saviour taught leaving theology and church Government as subjects to be discussed in Universities, how much better would be the result. It is sermons like that of this morning that make our men shirk church parade whenever they can. And yet what infinite good a really good chaplain could do. Father Brindle amongst the Roman Catholics is invaluable: a man who never thinks of himself & whose heart & soul is in the high mission he has embarked upon. We want a few Protestant chaplains of his type who by their example, their manner, zeal, earnestness and rough eloquence could get hold of our soldiers' hearts & exercise a wholesome influence over their conduct. Good people at home spend large sums on missions to the heathen and earnest men are to be found who will risk everything in order that the Gospel may be preached in all corners of the uncivilized world. I wish their energies & their fortunes could be devoted to preaching it to our soldiers & sailors instead.

I forget whether I recorded the upsetting of the boat in which Mr. Williams of the Central News and Mr. Villiers of the *Graphic* were coming here from *Debbeh*. Everything in the boat worth having was lost and both were nearly drowned. This is the third boat belonging to correspondents that has come to grief. The *Illustrated News* man & Mr. Burleigh of the *Dy. Telegraph* both came to grief. In fact that is all the English boats made use of by the Gentlemen of the Press. The others have one diabeeah between three or four whilst others stick to terra firma. This is very amusing to me, because some of these wise people who think they can teach a soldier his trade, ridiculed the idea of our soldiers being able to manage our whalers. Our soldiers can now not only manage their boats but many could give these goose-quill fellows some good advice as to how to avoid upsetting their newspaper boats. What an ass Billy Russell[144] was to commit himself to the opinions he expressed in the *Army & Navy Gazette* against our boats & the boat scheme: it was something like his denunciation of my strategy in 1882.[145] I wonder if there is any man connected with the *Army & Navy Gazette* who knows the difference between Strategy & Tactics. Billy Russell does not certainly or he would not write the nonsense he does about war and the plans of campaigns. Because he has been a camp follower during several wars he and the other camp followers who write for the home press think they are justified in expressing opinions upon a science of which they are entirely ignorant. My groom follows me about in campaigns & he might just as well imagine that he were a soldier because he followed the Army. He is quite as much entitled as Mr. Cameron of the *Standard*, who always runs away if he by accident finds his body in any danger, to express an opinion upon the strategy or tactics employed. Our press is a monstrous humbug unbridled and uncurbed as it is. Who can gauge the amount of evil done by newspapers of the 'Reynolds Miscellany' class to our people? But because we have silly notions about liberty we do not think licence should be checked, & the propogation of infamous heresies, foul untruths and bestial immorality interfered with. However of all the absurd sides that our Press presents, none is so very ridiculous as that afforded by the newspaper correspondent. Some penny-a-liner is sent to an army by a newspaper, because he is believed to be a pushing fellow, with zeal & energy in him. He arrives: he does not know the difference between a Battalion & a Regt.: strategy & tactics are unknown subjects to him: perhaps he is a coward, as many of the Correspondents I have known in my life most certainly are; but yet after any fight or operation this creature will lay down the law on all military subjects without any hesitation, & many people at home will shake their heads when the name of any officer who has been condemned by them is mentioned. Dear me, how wrong the world is when governed upon so-called liberal principles. An oligarchy is the only safe Government to live under, except perhaps, an intelligent despotism....

Rode round the outlying pickets in the evening. This has been a pleasant cool day with agreeable breeze blowing all day.

Monday 22nd December 1884

Had a pleasant ride into the desert & then to the banks of the River a few miles above this. At 4 p.m. without telling even Herbert Stewart, I sounded the alarm & was satisfied with the quickness with which all ranks turned out & fell into their places. English post in. To my unutterable astonishment I hear on excellent authority that our proposals about Egypt now before the Powers mean the permanent occupation of the country & our gradual absorption of all power. Bismark agrees, so it matters little what the others think. This has taken me by surprise, for I thought if this Government had any fixed principle, one firm resolve on any subject, it was to withdraw from Egypt, whenever they could possibly do so. I shall be curious to hear whether any increase to our Army Establishments will be made in consequence. It will be to exceed the limit of all common sense, if they continue to hold Egypt with an Army establishment that had been fixed at about its present strength before we had a soldier in this country....

Tuesday 23rd December

Some of the Heavy Camel Regt. under Byng arrived today. Had a very good field day this morning & tested the courage of the camels when collected together by making the 19th Hussars charge cheering up to them as they lay down & charging past them: all were wonderfully steady. I have now been able to trace the line of communication between the Mahdi and his French & Egyptian friends in *Cairo*. It follows the *Korosko-Abu Ahmed* road & is carried on through the connivance of Hassain Khalifa's sons living there & near *Assuan*.

In all the little wars against barbarous people that I have been engaged in, we have always had a very numerous enemy to contend against who were in occupation of a very difficult country or a country so far away from the frontier that it was a very difficult matter to get at him. It is always difficult to get information in a country where money is no temptation to its people to betray it, and the cruelties of barbarous people not only to the spy but to all his family make men hesitate before they undertake to give the invader information. In Europe or in America of course money will provide the energetic man with any amount of information. In all these wars the obtaining of reliable news about the enemy's doings, numbers & whereabouts is most curiously difficult: German officers who have no acquaintance of any sort with military operations outside of Europe cannot realize how great this difficulty is. Even if an Arab or other Savage gives you information or rather tells you what you know under pressure or fear of punishment, he is so ignorant of time, distance or numbers that he often leaves you more bewildered than you were before you questioned him. Of course native rumors are important and generally contain some grains of truth in them but they are apt to frighten those whose nerves are not the strongest. One day I hear the Mahdi is surrounded by thousands of warriors longing to die for him: that he has plenty of supplies of all sorts, and is longing for my advance in order that he may destroy us all root & branch. The rumours and stories I hear seriously repeated by fairly sensible men very often here are to me simply ludicrous. In all my wild campaigns this has always been the case, and I have found and even now find it requires the exercise of a very calm judgement to hold an even tenor throughout. I confess that this time I broke down one day although no one near me could have guessed it, but in the fullness of a depressed heart, I wrote Loo a most lugubrious epistle which I have ever since regretted as I had no business to make her feel wretched because for the moment my courage failed me. It is better to err on the side of overgood spirits than ever to look, even for a moment, depressed. The more frequently I have command of troops in the field the more difficulties do I find to be inherent in and necessarily attached to the position: the more numerous do I find the qualities and qualifications required by the Commander. Amongst them the power of listening to alarming rumors, to predictions of impending disasters & the certainty of eventual failure & destruction without winking an eye or evincing the least sensibility, is by no means the least important.

What stuff I write when I deal with anything but events, but on service I think more than when I live at home surrounded by society. Here my dinner is over & my guests gone away always by 8.30 p.m. and I retire to my own tent. My eyes pain me too much to read, but I can scribble without taxing them much.

Wednesday 24th December 1884

Upon returning to camp this morning from my early ride, I found Buller & Brackenbury just arrived in a picket boat.[146] Told Buller my plans & that I wanted to get off the 1st Detachment across the desert to leave this on 2nd January, so as to reach *Shendy* on the 7th of that month, the date on which I told Gordon I should be there. Buller to come on with detachments and 2nd lot of Camel Corps about the 8th or 9th Janry. to the same place. Earle to leave this for his campaign up the river on the 7th or 8th Janry. with three Battns. and another following close in his rear. Other Battalions to halt here and at other places between this and *Abu Ahmed* which Earle is to reach on 1st Febry. the date when I hope with God's aid to be in *Khartoum*.[146a] I may be there some days earlier. If I can I shall avoid fighting until I reach *Khartoum* & will attack the Mahdi's position D.V. the day after I can ferry my troops across the White Nile to the neighbourhood of *Omdurman*. McCalmont[147] arrived, as cheery as usual, and with his camels in a better condition than any other man has brought his in.

Thursday 25th December—Xmas Day

Divine service in camp. Inspected the Cavalry Mounted Corps. Buller in great doubts as to the possibility of my being able to start for *Metemmeh* (*Shendy*) on the 2nd proxo. It is quite possible I may be obliged to postpone my move for one week. I don't want to get there to have to wait a long time for the remainder of my mounted troops. That would give the Mahdi time to arrange his plans. What I should really like best would be [to] move across the desert with the whole of my force in one body or in two echelons one behind the other at one day's interval. I should then be able to push on to *Khartoum* without halting. Nothing so disconcerts barbarous people as rapidity of movement. In the meantime I shall begin pushing troops up the river to *Hamdab*, just above the *Gerendid* cataract, so that the news of the Army's movement upon *Berber* may become generally known & believed in. The double line of advance will perplex the enemy and give him a still more exaggerated notion of our power & strength even than he has at this moment. It is very curious that in all wars but more especially in those undertaken against an uncivilized enemy, there is generally a sort of vague notion that all your movements & even intentions are well-known to the enemy. We are too prone to endow the savage with a power of collecting information and with the sagacity to understand its importance that as a broad general rule is entirely absent in all barbarous & uneducated people. We had a very good illustration of how utterly unfounded is this notion in 1882. Arabi had a host of desert Arabs as allies, who were supposed to be always prowling round our camps, and communications watching and reporting to him all our movements. The fact was he knew nothing of our intentions or of even what we were doing and was completely surprised by our attack on the 13th Septr. Generals unaccustomed to weigh all these things in their mind, who have never had to discount all these ideas when trying to form a sound view as to the enemy's strength, whereabouts, intentions, &c. &c. are apt to be unduly influenced by stories about the enemy's valour, fierceness, knowledge of what was going on in our camps. Young Staff Officers are prone to jump to conclusions on these points: older heads listen to these stories, consider them deliberately, but adopt the smallest grains of them with the utmost caution. The savage is generally totally incapable of estimating numbers, a power that is most essential if the movements of an enemy are to be watched to any purpose.

We had a good plum pudding for dinner & two very good fat wild geese. Their meat is very dark and rather strong but everyone pronounced it excellent. My party consisted of Buller—Brackenbury—McCalmont—Zohrab Bey—Arthur—Adye—Childers—Dr. Pratt & Swaine. We dined early in order to attend an open air concert at 7 p.m. at which the whole Camp were present: a little amusement goes a long way in a camp in the middle of Nubia. The stage consisted of biscuit boxes. We had large bonfires to light up the scene: Wardrop was the master of ceremonies.

Friday 26th December

Engaged with Buller & Stewart all day, off & on, in working out the details for the advance from this in two columns; one up the river, Earle in command with Brackenbury as Brigadr. General & 2nd in Command, the other under Stewart to *Shendy* & *Khartoum*. George[148] arrived in the evening looking very well and strong. I am making him Asst. Adjt. Genl. to accompany Hd. Qtrs. into *Khartoum*.

Saturday 27th December

Absolutely nothing to record. My thoughts bent on this desert march: it is a great leap in the dark. The Camel Battery arrived.

Sunday 28th December

The South Stafford under Col. Eyre[149] reembarked in their whalers—50 in number—the Battalion being 550 of all ranks, and started up river en route for *Hamdab*. Brackenbury follows tomorrow in the picket boat. The Camel Corps are pouring in daily. The 1st boat of the Cornwall Regt. arrived. The Sowarrab Chief has not turned up as he promised to do. There is some influence at work amongst these Arabs that I cannot fathom. They do not yet know apparently which side is going to win or the Mudir is not working loyally with us. I wrote to the Queen, the Prince of Wales & to the Duke of Cambridge: a good allowance of Royalties for one day.

Monday 29th December 1884

The English post due yesterday evening did not arrive until this afternoon, & as we had to send the outgoing mail away at noon we were unable to answer any of our letters, not however that it mattered much as we have a telegraph wire still connecting us with civilization. Brackenbury started in a picket boat for *Merawi*, & *Hamdab* there to establish a camp as a rendezvous for the force Earle is to operate up the river with.

Tuesday 30th Decembr.

Herbert Stewart started with all the available camels in camp for the *Gakdul* wells, having as a fighting body the Mounted Infry. and the Guards Regt. with him. I expect him to reach his destination on Friday 2nd proxo. He will halt the 3rd & probably leave during the night of the 3rd or morning of the 4th January & be back here on 6th or 7th—to rest the 8th, & I hope get off again with me at their head on the 9th or the 10th at latest. The march of all these men on camels looked most imposing. The natives must have thought it a large army. It is the beginning of the 1st scene in the last act of this Khartoum drama. May God bless this expedition, and grant that it be in every aspect a complete success. Late in the evening a telegram[150] from Vakil at *Merawi* to say that a messenger had just arrived from Gordon having left *Khartoum* 18 days ago. Then a telegram from Brackenbury[151] from the same place complaining of Vakil who had not fulfilled his promises about supplies and requesting permission to send him away & replace him by the Kashif. Have ordered Vakil to come here with Gordon's messenger tomorrow morning in picket boat—will give him a bit of my mind—telegraphed[152] to Mudir to come here without delay telling him I had reason to complain of Vakil.

Wednesday 31st December 1884

The last day of this year finds me surrounded by difficulties, the serious difficulty having been occasioned by the want of Statesmanship of Mr. Gladstone who would not prepare for this expedition in proper time. It is the health of my men that makes me uneasy, but to such a grand politician as Mr. Gladstone the health and comfort and lives of 10,000 of Her Majesty's soldiers is of little moment. On Xmas day the Khedive—who is not a Christian nor an Englishman sent me a very nice telegram wishing us all a merry Xmas. The Sect. of State for War & Commdr. in Chief did the same, but the Queen who telegraphs about trifles connected with Her own family all over the world has ignored us. She is generally so thoughtful on such points that I am surprised. I have now written to Her Majesty three times. The third time was only by the last home mail but I think she might have made one of Her Ladies-in-Waiting write me a few lines in acknowledgement of the two previous letters, or Ponsonby[153] might have said thank-you in Her name & Heaven knows it is no pleasure to me to write Her long letters. She may think Lady Wood a bore & presuming for having written frequently to Her, but my letters must interest Her & besides they are written because the Queen asked me when I said good-bye at Osborne to write to Her about our proceedings. Anxiously looking out for the picket boat from *Merawi* bringing Gordon's messenger, which a telegram had announced had started at 7 a.m. It arrived about [space left] p.m. bringing also the Vakil whom Brackenbury has managed to quarrel with without just cause in my opinion. [Marginal note: He is of a quarrelsome overbearing temperament. He fawns upon those in power & bullies his subordinates without any regard for their feelings. Indeed, I have looked upon him as '[not?] quite a Gentleman'. Neither has he the tact of the educated & experienced Gentleman. He thinks he is the ablest of diplomats, an amusing assumption according to the views of those who know him best. But, he is very able & will serve you with real interest and great ability as long as he thinks that doing so will be to his advantage. He has Greek blood in him & consequently does not know what real loyalty to any man—except to himself—can possibly mean or why it should be cultivated in man.]

The messenger is the man sent from *Dongola* on 29th October with a copy of my cypher letter of 20th Septr. & a long postpost [postscript?] of mine dated the 26th October also in cypher. He left *Khartoum* on the 14th December & the only scrap of paper he brings me is a thing the size of a postage stamp with Gordon's Arabic seal on one side and on the other 'Khartoum, all right—14-12-84 C. G. Gordon.' The messenger brings me a long rambling message which I cannot depend on, saying I am to come very quickly, that I must have a large force as the enemy is very numerous &c. &c. He adds *Khartoum* can only be taken by starvation & that food is scarce. Altogether this is most unsatisfactory, & unsettles my plans without giving me any information that is worth having. This fellow was five days in Mahdi's camp; he saw Mahmond Ahmed who lives in a tent like one of ours. I suppose it is one taken when Hicks was defeated. Slaten Bey is there in chains—Hussein Pasha Khalifa is there but is free. All the people with Mahdi have their families & their cattle with them: his army covers an immense space of country: there is much sickness in Mahdi's camp, but the people there have enough to eat.[154]

January 1885

1st January 1885

I went to bed with a heavy heart—Oh God how heavy! Rose at 4 a.m., roused Buller up & told him to halt the Squadn. of 19th Hussars that was to have marched at 7 a.m. to join Brackenbury at *Merawi* this morning. Went back to my tent and reconsidered my position with reference to Gordon's message. All along I have been counting on an expression which occurs more than once in Gordon's letters, that the whole attack upon *Khartoum* would collapse if he had a few hundred determined soldiers upon whom he could depend. I have been basing my calculations on this view of the position & had therefore determined upon forcing my way into *Khartoum* with about 1500 of the finest men in our or any other Army. Now this message from him tells me not to advance unless I am strong. I have therefore determined upon sending four Battalions to *Matemmeh* across the desert, one to be the garrison of that place, the other three to go on with the Camel Corps, 19th Hussars & 10 guns to *Khartoum*. I shall have to hold the wells at *Abu Llea, Gakdul* and *Hambok* as well as *Korti*. So including *Matemmeh* & *Korti* I shall have three Battalions on this desert line of commns. leaving only two Battalions & detachments of Cavy., Artillery & R.E. for operations up the river towards *Abu Ahmed*. This will be a safer plan of operation than that I had previously determined upon but it will take more time & prevent me perhaps from being in *Khartoum* as I had hoped to be with a fighting force on the 31st Jany., at latest. However, God is great, in Him is my trust & with his aid I shall yet be in *Khartoum* on or before that date. The new year has not opened brightly for me, but I don't believe things are nearly as bad as they look: Gordon's nerve cannot be as fresh and vigorous after all he has gone through during the last eight months as they were when he & I last met. No nerves could remain uninfluenced by the position in which he finds himself. This messenger says that Gordon during the day goes to the top of one of the two Palaces on each of which he has a gun: there he spends some time studying the enemy's position through his telescope. Then he sleeps—indeed he sleeps a great deal during the day, but is up all night going round the works & keeping everyone up to the mark. He says Gordon has 18,000 soldiers & besides them the population, men, women & children number 27,000. Gordon who is one of the very greatest smokers I have ever known, still has cigarettes as he offered the messenger one. I have been carrying about 500 for him as a present for some months now, and am delighted to learn that the gallant soul has at least this one earthly pleasure left him. . . . Gordon's messenger said he had seen when in *Khartoum* the enemy fire stone from their guns: this was in reply to my question as to how they were off for ammuintion: he said they still had a good supply of S.A. ammunition.

KORTI. *Friday 2nd January 1885*

Another morning's study of the problem before me, going carefully into distances and dates, and Buller's calculations of the several problems I have set him, has caused me to fix upon the following plan of campaign. As I originally intended, I shall move all the mounted troops & the Battery of R.A. & provisions for them to *Matammeh* & there create a post which I shall eventually garrison with a Battn. of Infry. This will enable me to communicate direct by steamer with Gordon & to arrange for our final advance upon *Khartoum* with him. At the same time Earle will advance up river & punish Monassir tribe & then on to *Abu Ahmed* where I hope he may receive supplies direct from *Korosko*. He will leave a Battn. or half a Battalion at *Abu Ahmed* & then move to attack *Berber* in which operation I hope some of Gordon's steamers may be able to assist, the Naval Brigade manning them. *Berber* taken and a Battn. left there as a garrison, Earle to move on with all haste with three Battalions, the Egyptian Camel Corps & Egyptian Camel Battery & a Squadron of XIXth Hussars to join me at *Matammeh*. The united force then to march for *Khartoum*. Of course our relief of Gordon will be thus greatly postponed, but this will enable me at any moment if Gordon sends to tell me he is *in extremis*, to push on with all the camel Regts. to *Khartoum*. The risk would perhaps be great, but no risk would be too great under those circumstances. I have today telegraphed to Baring in answer to a message from him of yesterday asking me about an expedition from *Suakim* that no such operation could be effected in time to help me at *Khartoum*, but that it would do much towards the final settlement of the country. As long as Osman Digma is at large the Eastern Soudan can never be tranquil. Baring asked me if I was confident of success: I replied yes, provided Gordon would hold out until my infantry going by river could reach *Khartoum*. He referred to the effect of a reverse—I replied that I assumed the greatest disaster would be the capture of Gordon & fall of *Khartoum*, & that I thought it would be greater than any possible danger to me & the mounted troops in an endeavour to save that place. I then added that I thought Govt. ought to give me an expression of opinion on this point—of course they won't: but at any rate I have asked for it, & my request is on record. I shall doubtless receive some enigmatical phrase concocted by Mr. Gladstone, worded so as to save himself but carefully avoiding the question I have put.[155]

I hear general complaints of the very faulty manner in which the biscuit in the boats has been packed, & nearly all the lime juice has been broken.

My father having been very unfortunate in the Army, having served 30 years & only a Major, did not wish any of his sons to be a soldier. He was a man deeply imbued with religious belief & had the firmest faith in the efficacy of Prayer, believing that the righteous man had only to ask God in faith for any blessing to receive it, unless it was asked in folly, when God in his wisdom would not allow such foolishness to prevail. That is the best description of the simple but fervent faith possessed by my father. I remember his teaching it to me and impressing it upon me by stories of Prayers having been answered and petitions granted. Of course however my chief knowledge of all this was from the subsequent teaching of my mother as I was only seven years old when my father died. The result of all this upon me, was to infuse & instill [*sic*] into me a (deeply)* religious (feeling)* as a child, and from

*Overwritten

my earliest recollections I announced my boyish intentions of entering the Church. I read the Bible & the Prayerbook a great deal and used to say when I was eight or nine years old—I think even earlier—that the text of my first sermon should be the last verse of the XXVIIth psalm. [Marginal note of later date. 'Wait on the Lord: be of good courage, & he shall strengthen thine heart: wait I say on the Lord!] Although I have never preached a sermon, this text has always had a sort of cabalistic effect upon me, and whenever at any period of my somewhat eventful career I have been brought up face to face with any serious difficulties I have always found myself repeating this verse, frequently doing so almost involuntarily & almost without knowing that I was doing so, at times. It has been in my mouth all today, hence this long digression from my narrative of ordinary events.

I still feel that I shall yet be in *Khartoum* before the end of the month.

Saturday 3rd January 1885

Earle left in a picket boat for *Hamdab* taking the Vakil with him who goes back I hope a wiser man. I gave him a carbine when he left as a present, but I fear the civil element here is against us. I wish I had removed the Mudir from the first.[156] I have instead tried to make a friend of him & I have not succeeded. He works behind my back against me. I have found out that the reason the Sowarrab & Hawawir Sheiks have not brought in their camels to help is that they have been told the Mudir does not like us & does not wish to hasten our progress. It is most difficult to fathom that curious man's mind or to ascertain what he is driving at. Wilson's notion has always been that he hates Gordon with the hatred that a Turk only can feel, & that to be revenged on Gordon, he would not care what the consequences should be either to himself or the Khedive or to all the world. Gordon ordered his removal from the Mudirate of Dongola but through Palace influence at *Cairo,* he was reinstated. I have ordered Zohrab to go to *Debbeh* tomorrow to meet him & tell him he must see the Sheiks I have mentioned & insist upon their supplying the camels promised. I have also telegraphed to Baring[157] asking him to see Khedive at once & make him telegraph personally to Mudir on this subject. If this fails, even at this late hour of the day I shall have to resort to a Coup d'Etat and arrest him & send him post-haste to *Cairo*. How difficulties crop up on all sides!

Sunday 4th January 1885

Divine service as usual. Zohrab Bey left in picket boat for *Debbeh* to meet Mudir who started from *Dongola* yesterday at 6 a.m. in his diabeeah; the steamer requiring repairs will follow shortly. Butler arrived more Irish than ever.[158] We have at last caught one of the Mahdi's spies sent out from *Berber* to *Assuan* where he was taken. We have not obtained any valuable information from him. . . .

Yesterday the Stafford Regt. *rowed* up the so-called cataract of *Gerendid,* and is now encamped at *Hamdab* where I mean it to remain until a sufficient force is collected there to move into Monassir country to settle our score with them for poor Stewart's murder. Anonymous telegram to me just received from London saying 'don't despise your enemy, go strong into desert'. Also from the Govt.[159] in answer to a question I put to them as to the propriety of my attempting to relief [*sic*] Gordon with an insufficient force in the event of his being *in extremis*. They say such a risk should not be encountered as any reverse to my Force would be a greater disaster than the fall of *Khartoum* & the capture of Gordon by the Mahdi. All these sort of messages strain one's nerves a little when 1300 miles from the sea & beyond all possibility of receiving assistance from without, looking to the time of the year at which we have arrived. The Mahdi's cousin, who went from *Dongola* into the enemy's camp, has returned & is today I hear at *Abu Gus*.

At 8 p.m. just as we had finished dinner, Lord Cockran[e][160] came into the straw hut where we were sitting. I need scarcely say I was delighted to see him. I had a newspaper correspondent at table so I took him into my tent and there learnt that he had left Stewart at the *Hambuk* wells, who would be in here tomorrow about noon. He brought letters & reports[161] from Stewart giving particulars of his march. He says he has left Guards Regt. at *Gakdul*[162] strongly fortified in an impregnable position with plenty of good water & all the supplies we sent out—about 50,000 rations. He picked up a few prisoners, some of them in the Mahdi's uniform: all this is very satisfactory. As usual, our movement was a complete surprise to the prisoners taken. [Not a man sick in his column.]*

*Pencilled in later

Monday 5th January. 85

English post of the 12th December arrived at 9 a.m. & ours for home left camp about noon. I rode out to meet Herbert Stewart's column which marched back in very good order. Charlie Beresford arrived.

Tuesday 6th Janry.

Half the Naval Brigade arrived. Another officer Maj. Inglefield of the Egyptian Army has committed suicide. He was off his head, poor fellow, apparently from exposure to the sun. I hope this may not become an epidemic in Wood's army of non-fighting soldiers. Visited the Hospital. [Marginal note added later: 'Telegraphed[163] to Baring in answer to one from him. Recommended all available ships of war should anchor off *Suakim* & often send firing parties & Marines ashore to practice. News, when it reaches *Khartoum*, might help us.']

Wednesday 7th Jany.

Colonel Stanley Clarke[164] started in command of a convoy of 1,000 camels for *Gakdul* towards sundown. Nothing could be worse managed: he had had the advantage of being with the previous convoy and seeing what a well-conducted convoy should be like & how it should be managed, but it was of no use to him. His heart was in Marlborough House or some Court circle. Any old woman who shines in such society would have done quite as well as he did. This is the first & it shall be the last time that he followed [*sic*] my fortunes. Yet I have no doubt he writes to the Prince of Wales and tells him that everything here is badly managed. It is just such fellows as these who always find fault the most. I am in great hopes that my message to the Mudir & the pressure I brought to bear on him through the Khedive will result in my securing the services of the Sowarrab & Hawawir Tribes as carriers across the desert to *Matammeh*. I have telegraphed today to the Govt.[165] asking if they wish to give me any new instructions, pointing out that if it is intended to hold Egypt for an indefinite period, a tranquilized Eastern Soudan is very essential to peace in Egypt. I also gave Baring an outline of my plans. . . .

Thursday 8th January

A very hot day: oh this dreadful tropical heat, how I dread the long sicklist which it foretells! This is the enemy I dread. Had a long telegram[166] from Hartington in answer to those I sent to Baring yesterday. In it he proposes to send to *Suakim* 2 strong Battns., one Regt. of Cavalry, Batty. of R.A. &c. &c. if necessary two Native Cavalry Regts. from India. They would only be meant as a demonstration, & would not be allowed to act offensively against Osman Digma. I had proposed to send the fleet to *Suakim* as a demonstration. It would answer all the purposes required if it were announced that an offensive movement on shore were intended, the Admiral alone being in the secret. But that is just the sort of assistance the Navy never will give us: it brings them no credit or promotion, & the Admirals in Whitehall are too strong on such points for the First Lord & he with his backing of Admirals is generally too strong for the Secretary of State for War who would have no backing on such a point from his Colleagues in the Cabinet. I thought my proposal might however have a chance as it would cost nothing to speak of. It could be effected at once, but because it is such a simple thing our wiseacres at home won't do it. Hartington winds up his telegram by asking if I wished him to send this force to *Suakim* & considered it would support my operations as apart from all other considerations. In saying this he referred to my having always reported that I did not require anyone to fight at *Suakim* for the purpose of helping me, but that a force sent there to crush Osman Digma would go far towards pacifying Eastern Soudan. The tone & tendency of all recent official telegrams has been to try and force me to say that this Suakim expedition would at least materially help me if I would not go so far as to say I actually thought it essential to my success, which they evidently thought they might induce me to say. Before I received Hartington's telegram I received one from Brett telling me that important cypher telegram was coming to me & that he hoped I would agree to proposal. My answer to him when I received the cypher message was, 'I don't want the 2000 extra men, but I should like 2000 umbrellas sent at once.' I hope this will let them see that I have neither lost my nerve nor am in a funk, but make light of the funk in which apparently they are all in. My answer[167] to Hartington was of course a serious one, impressing on them my confidence in success and that proposed demonstration would be absurd. That even if the force landed at *Suakim* were allowed to dispose of Osman Digma, the operation would still be an expensive luxury.

That I always hoped and still intended to send back a column over the Berber–Suakim route to deal with Mr. Osman Digma & open road. I said if I wanted an extra Battn. in Egypt I would ask for it for *Assouan*, that no amount of troops at *Halfa* even could be of any use to me if I were repulsed before *Khartoum*, & could not receive reinforcements via *Suakim* if misfortune overtook me. There is somebody frightening the Govt. about my expedition, & I cannot but think that Andrew Clarke, who does not understand the first elements of the science of war, has got hold of those who influence the *Pall Mall Gazette*. He wants this Suakim-Berber railway made for private reasons of his own, and hopes that if an expedition were sent to *Suakim*, the construction of the Railway would follow, and perhaps his employment in some military capacity on that route. I telegraphed again[168] in the evening to Hartington announcing departure of Stewart for *Matammeh* & the fact that Reuter's agent arrived here today from *Gakdul* with no escort beyond one native guide having left that place on 4th inst. This fact ought to quiet their alarmed nerves. By & by when I *do* get to *Khartoum*, these same alarmists will be the first to turn round & say this expedition has been a pic-nic badly carried out with little difficulties to encounter, & no enemy to contend with worthy of the steel of 'Generals of the old School' who have served under old-fashioned leaders, & who despise eratic [*sic*] leaders like me who do not conform to the Queen's regulations, who make cavalry fight as foot soldiers in square, & mount sailors on camels, & ask for umbrellas for the use of his soldiers. What can be expected from a man capable of such atrocities except defeat? & it must be evident to the mind of the meanest capacity that when he succeeds, his success is all luck or has been earned by other men. I can see in my mind's eye an article by Billy Russell, or some other equally well-informed man on war, in the *Army & Navy Gazette*, denouncing me as a miserable failure who knew nothing of his profession if I met with any check, and as simply one of those lucky fellows who always win without in any way deserving it, if I met with a great & complete success. One of the worst signs of democracy is that the people or any section of them should believe men of Billy Russell's class in society on subjects of which they can know nothing. However, I have done all I can to protect the Govt. against embarking in foolish military enterprises out here, and if they prefer to take the opinions of men who have had no experience as Military commanders in the field to mine, I cannot help it. I can only deplore that England is governed by men so unfitted to be at the helm.

I went out to see Stewart start for *Matemmeh*:[169] what a different spectacle from what I saw of the start last night under Clarke: one is a soldier, the other a courtier. Brackenbury came back from *Hamdab* to arrange matters about the force to advance up the Nile. He tells me he has just heard from Stephenson that at a recent very large party given by Barère the French Consul General, at which all the Cairo world were present, the only Consul General not invited was Baring & his wife. The position in Egypt between the two nations is as strained as it can be without war. If we were as strong at sea as we ought to be and could command the Mediterranean with our fleet, France would comport herself very differently towards us, and Germany would not dare to hoist her poor, miserable & modern flag on distant possessions which our Colonists want. But alas we are a fallen nation. We have given up great national objects & aspirations and settled down to the contemplation of party politics and caucus business. How are the mighty fallen from Pitt to Gladstone!

Latest information leads me to believe we shall have no fighting with Earle's column until *Berber* is reached & very probably even none there. I have for long thought the enemy's power was a great bubble that only required pricking with a stout bodkin—a pin would not be strong enough—to collapse entirely. The half of the Naval Brigade which has arrived here left with Stewart's column today under Ld. C. Beresford, a really first-rate man all round.[170] It was amusing to see these Blue Jackets mounted on camels, their Captain on a white donkey which he means to make drag his Gardiner gun if he has to take it into action on shore. He takes one Gardiner with him & when the other half of the Naval Brigade arrives, they will take another with them across the desert to *Matammeh*. I hope with these selected naval officers & seamen to be able to man some of Gordon's steamers with which I shall cooperate in attack on *Berber*, and use along the river between *Shendy* and *Khartoum*. This is certainly a strange episode in our Military history. It is the biggest operation the English Army has *ever* undertaken. I think those engaged in it, are now beginning to realise this fact, and to feel they have the honor of taking part in an operation the like of which has never been undertaken before. When Mahomed Ali's army mounted the Nile it was a slow operation, there being no intention even of returning that same year, and the possible enemy had no fire-arms. Besides to feed the same number of British soldiers that he employed is a very different matter from that of feeding Egyptians who can live on the produce of the country. Our hospital establishments and paraphernalia alone weigh tons and tons that have to be transported from the sea to this place, a distance by river of about 1400 miles. My pocket barometre registers 29°.43′ showing an altitude above the sea of 1420′.

Friday—9th January

Last night was entirely different from any other we have had here: it succeeded a very hot day, and was a warm night. Hitherto I have always slept under two blankets with comfort and felt very pleasantly cold towards daybreak, but last night one was ample & under it I perspired freely at first. Lately it has come on to blow freshly between 2 a.m. and 4 a.m., it being perfectly still & calm at sunrise. Brackenbury tells me there are quantities of crocodiles up the river towards *Hamdab*. Brett telegraphs[171] in answer to my chaffy message to him of yesterday, 'all right, contract with Briggs accordingly.' In my morning ride I met Primrose[172] on a camel bound for camp. He has avoided *Debbeh* and all stations where he could be reached by a telegram, for as he said he had been stopped ten days at *Dongola*, he was determined, that having escaped from that place, he was determined not to be caught again until he had reached *Korti*. Burnaby also arrived. He wears a coat lined with fur and except for a short spell during the hottest time of the day, wears a great woollen muffler round his throat. Everyone tells me he has been working very hard on the Line of Communications & has done excellent service. . . .

What an odd man is Buller. I should never again have him as Chief of the Staff. He always raises objections to every proposal, although in the end he comes round to it. He loves to build up imaginary difficulties with one hand to have the pleasure of demolishing them with the other. No one does right but himself: he thinks of everything. No one else ever makes any useful proposals; in fact all the world are fools & he alone is wise. He would make a much better fighting General than a Staff officer. I have given him head & perhaps done so a little too much as the tendency with him is in consequence to assume a little too much the role of General-in-Chief. He is not a patch all round in my opinion upon Herbert Stewart who would make a very first-rate Chief of the Staff: but then it would be extremely difficult to replace him as the leader of the advanced Guard of an Army. I always here, dread the idea of his breaking down or some stray bullet going through him. It would be most difficult to find a successor to him. Clarke would be ridiculous. Buller works hard and he is, all round, one of our best men, but he is better as an executive than as a Staff or Administrative Officer. He is too fond of argument.

Saturday 10th January

Burnaby with a convoy of about 100 camels started at 1.30 p.m. for *Gakdul*. He takes dourrah of which Stewart was very short when he started. The Mudir arrived in the evening. He promises a great deal and I think he will really do good service because he is feared by all classes. Backshesh has a certain influence with Arabs but it is as nothing in its power when compared with fear. Fear is the real lever to work with these people. He tells me that Sheik Salah of the Kababish is coming in at once, and that in a few days I shall have plenty of camels. He laughs at the idea of our meeting with any op[p]osition up the river.

Poor old Jack Colburn—the first Lord Seaton's son—dined with me this evening. All the other correspondents have gone on to *Gakdul*; he, who only represents some German Illustrated Paper, goes up the river with Earle's column. Although he has been a courier all his life, I pity the poor old fellow because he is a Gentleman forced to live amongst the commonest set of people who think they are Gentlemen. He gave us, in corroboration of the stories that are current in the camp, a sad account of the manners, customs and moral considerations of those with whom his lot is cast and amongst whom he lives. They call one another '"Cads", liars, cowards, &c. &c.' most freely. The day they all started, the vilest Billingsgate was bandied amongst them & when one threatened to hit another, the reply was if you lay a hand on me I will shoot you as I would a dog. This arose from one of these fellows having reminded the other of how he had run away at the fight of *Temai* near *Suakim* last year, a fact which all who were present know to be perfectly true. And yet these are the creatures that John Bull pays to supply him with news!!! Fellows, the best of whom are weak about their H's, who are mostly cowards and who do not in the least care how they lie as long as they can furnish their employees daily with a certain amount of sensational rumors reported by them to be facts. Everyone who has ever taken part in any of our campaigns since this accursed animal the Newspaper Correspondent was invented, knows in his heart what an unscrupulous lying set of vagabonds they are, but no one dare say so. If he did so, he might as well hang a mill-stone about his neck & drown himself as every scribbling rascal in England would be at once up in arms to defend his brother of the Goose-Quill & to denounce the soldier who dared to tell the truth and paint the view in their real & true colors.

The wind still blows daily from the North, and consequently all progress along the river from *Debbeh* to *Merawi* is very slow. We have not had a drop of rain since we left *Halfa,* nor have we had anything one could call a shower since I landed in Egypt.

Sunday—11th Janry.

The messenger who left this on the 18th December with a letter from me to Gordon returned here this morning. He was only one day in *Khartoum* & delivered my letter. Gordon gave him an answer & he had three other letters from Kasm el Moose and others. Unfortunately he was taken prisoner & the letters found. They were twisted into the halter of his camel. The enemy read the letters in Arabic, but could make nothing of Gordon's letter. They bound his arms behind him & beat him, stole all he had and then left him. He came back across the desert via *Bayuda* alone & on foot. There seems to be a fatality about my correspondence with Gordon—I can never get his answer to the questions I put to him.

No church service this morning as our parson is seedy, but I read my own prayers & had a good gallop instead, and remembering what a man he is, I feel I am better than if I had listened to a dull, meaningless sermon from him. Evelyn Wood arrived, his eyes looking very bad, and I think he is deafer than ever...

Monday 12th January 1885

Just for the moment we are badly off for dourra here, the crop of which is still unripe in this neighbourhood having been some six weeks—it is said—later than usual owing to the disturbed condition of the country. In another ten days we shall have plenty, but in the meantime we have difficulty in feeding our camels when marching quickly in the desert. I am buying large quantities of dates to have them for the refugees from *Khartoum*. There are no fowl in this part of the country & therefore no eggs are to be had, but our hospitals and indeed our camps generally are well supplied with milk and fresh butter. All the way down the line the hospitals have plenty of fresh milk. Last night quite warm: even at daybreak had only one blanket over me.

The messenger who came here yesterday from *Khartoum* was so frightened on arrival that he was dazed & stupid. By degrees he begins to remember a little that happened. He now says that he overheard his captors reading aloud the letter in Arabic which Kasm el Moose had given him, & he remembers that the letter said 'it is only necessary to send us 2000 men to finish the whole business'. This seems to have disturbed the minds of those who read it, for they at once sent off a messenger to the Mahdi with a copy, the captured camel affording the means of conveyance....

The Sowarrab & Hawawir Sheiks arrived yesterday evening and Buller & Zohrab talked the camel question over with them.[173] They had previously promised us lots of camels to carry loads to *Matammeh* at the rate of $10 the load; now they demand $30. After a great deal of bargaining I have agreed to pay them $15 a load to *Gakdul* on the Mudir's advice. His idea is that if they once begin to carry for us, others will soon follow their example and we can then make new terms. I don't realize or believe this, and distrust the Mudir as I distrust all these Sheiks. However a camel load is a camel load & they swear we shall have as a beginning 50 camels here in 5 days. What a people to deal with. They know they have us on the hip. I shall forever regret that I did not at first have the Mudir sent to *Cairo* & let him go from thence to *Mecca*. How my heart is weary of waiting here....

Second half of the Naval Brigade arrived. Just as I was lying down for the night Major Turner—who acts for Sir C. Wilson in his absence—brought me two telegrams from the *Merawi* direction saying the enemy were coming across the desert from *Berber* and with others coming down the river were to attack our camp at *Hamdab* during the night. I dismissed Turner with the remark that I did not credit the report though I wished most sincerely it was true.

Tuesday 13th January

Have contracted for 45 more camels from people at *Merawi*, to be here in 6 days. You never can get anything in this country 'today'. It is always 'next week'. When time presses this is most provoking, but then it is no use talking of time to men to whom tomorrow or next month is the same as today: time is not a marketable commodity in their world. Had a note from Earle who construed my letter to him advising against reconnaissances as a prohibition to him against raiding upon the enemy's camps in the desert. Have telegraphed to him to correct this and advising raid at once. A convoy of 100 laden camels left for *Gakdul*. . . .

We have now a large dockyard here where all the boats are being repainted and repaired. The Mudir is sending a messenger into Gordon so I have sent a letter with him, although I expect Wilson will be in *Khartoum* long before this messenger can reach that place. Primrose has made great improvements in this camp since he assumed command of it. Although unpopular, he is a good man and I shall endeavour to employ him actively the next time I command in the field. I wonder where & when that will be? Perhaps this is my last campaign: one thing is certain, as long as Mr. Gladstone is in office we are bound to have wars.

Wednesday 14th January

Rode about five miles into the desert on the *Gakdul* road. An army of 100,000 men might march over it in line. I wish the Mahdi would come here with his hosts and let us have it out there. Our spell of hot weather lasts still; laden camels suffer from it during the day & it is only on moonlight nights we can march by night. I am sure that 30 miles by night is not as severe upon a camel as 20 miles under a sun. The English post of the 19th Decembr. arrived in the afternoon: it was due here last Sunday evening. It brought us a letter from the Queen written in the nastiest tone. I have written to Her because She desired me to do so, and I endeavoured to make my letters as interesting as I could and was even mean enough to spice them with hits at Mr. Gladstone as I knew She hates him. But it is all to no purpose. I have an unhappy knack of freely expressing my opinions upon the one subject which I feel justified in speaking on with some authority, namely war and our Army as created for war. She, poor good

General Gordon

The Wells at Handoub: Lancers watering their horses
Lord Wolseley inspecting the garrison at Otao

Royal Engineers clearing the railway of burning sleepers near Suakim
The Nile at Assuan, with the encampments of British troops

Pulling through the rapids near Owli Island

The march through the desert to Gubat
The 'Square' at the battle of Abu Kru, fought by Sir Charles Wilson

Lieutenant Stuart-Wortley bringing the news of the fall of Khartoum to the camp at Metemmah
Sir Charles Wilson interrogating the last messenger from Khartoum

Wilson's steamer rounding the bend of Tuti Island to find that Khartoum had fallen

Lord Charles Beresford directing a cattle raid from one of Gordon's steamers

Redoubt held by the Australians
Consulting guides during Stewart's march from Korti to Jakdul

woman, knowing nothing of the subject and taking her news from the Duke of Cambridge who is certainly as ignorant as the Queen is on war & its art and science, won't have my views at any price, and is evidently offended at the frankness with which I express them. I have done my best, & have failed. I even shook hands with John Brown and grinned at him as if I did not see how drunk he was, but all to no purpose so as the children say 'I won't play any more.' I shall retain more self-respect in giving the Royalties up than if I tried to compromise with my conscience, and deal in Courtier-like language in all my dealings with them. This is amusing to me, for in my heart I know there is not a greater royalist in England than I am, & were the throne in danger would stand by it in my small way to the last whilst many of the perfumed Gentlemen who now live on Court incomes were making terms for their personal safety and emoluments with some President Chamberlain or Bradlaugh.

Thursday 15th January

On 7th inst. I telegraphed home saying that as I expected to be in direct communication by steamer from *Matammeh* with *Khartoum*, it was very necessary I should know if H.M. Govt. adhered rigidly to the instructions they had given me. I have just received my answer[174] which is, they see no reason for changing them but give me full discretion as to present military operations but I must not commit them to lengthened occupation of Soudan. I have today answered a message[175] received yesterday evening again urging sending troops to *Suakim*. Sir A. Clarke who assumes to himself the position of military adviser to the Govt.—he has never seen a shot fired—has been writing or instigating letters in the *Times* still harping on the Suakim–Berber route and decrying this expedition up the Nile. The man who writes these may be 'a military man' but he is no soldier, and he therefore very naturally falls into the great but very common error of estimating for the march of an Army, the length of a road by the number of miles it is long, and when two roads are available comparing them by a direct comparison of their respective lengths in miles. It is a very natural mistake for a man like Sir A. Clarke to fall into. In my next edition of the *Soldier's Pocket Book* I shall [make] the comparison between the Nile route and the Suakim route as an illustration of the fallacy of considering the shortest road in miles the best to select.[176] Napoleon said the strongest frontier a country could have is a desert.[177] Now for all practical purposes the 250 miles between *Suakim* and *Berber* is nothing but a howling desert. To have placed a fighting force of 5000 men at the latter place & to have fed it there would have required 50,000 camels. So that if the question is gone into minutely by one accustomed to arrange for the march of even small armies through hostile countries the operation would be put down as almost impossible, for where are 50,000 camels to be found? Because Sir S. Baker went over that route with 20 or 50 horses, he thinks any troops could be marched over it, and as he is not skilled in war it is but natural he should think so. The poor little princess who when told the people were in want of bread replied, 'why not give them bonbons then' and Sir A. Clarke are each on a level as regards knowledge of their respective subjects. Heard from our post at the *Howeiyat* wells up to the 12th instant: all going on well there. Stewart will not take *Matammeh* I fear until 17th instant, as he is short of dourra & has to graze his camels which takes time.

Friday 16th January

The Mudir, whenever he is put out, telegraphs to the Khedive begging of him to let him go to *Mecca*. He has done so recently several times. The day before yesterday he renewed his petition on the grounds that he understood that we did not trust him, or believe that he was doing his best to help us. He is a very vain man & wishes me and the Cairo Govt. to understand that everything is done by him or through his influence & that without him nothing can be done....

Kitchener returned at noon having left *Gakdul* on the 14th at 10 a.m.[178] He left Clarke's convoy last night at 2.30 a.m. at *Hambook*. It will be here tomorrow. He says the camels generally are looking tucked-up, food being scarce. He was not able to open any communications with the people near *Gakdul*. It is well I brought the Mudir here, for whether he be heart and soul with us or not, he is at least able to manage these people and to some extent makes them serve us. Stewart was to leave *Gakdul* for *Matammeh* at 2 p.m. the 14th instant, so he will not occupy that place until tomorrow, & I shall not know what he has accomplished until the 21st inst.

Saturday 17th January

Started at 6 a.m. on a camel for what we call the 'Twelve Mile Hill'. It is the first good landmark in the desert away from here on the *Gakdul* road. I met Clark[e]'s convoy coming in when near the hill. I felt as I stood on this landmark and looked out towards *Matammeh* that at that very time probably Stewart was hammer & tongs at it there with some Dervishes. It was a satisfaction to feel that I was 12 or 14 miles nearer the point of interest than I should have been in my tent in camp. I hope & trust Stewart may have a great success. Including all stoppages I was just $6\frac{1}{2}$ hours away. I should say the distance travelled was at least 26 miles and we stopped a good 20 minutes at the hill, 10 minutes to talk with Stanley Clarke and lost at least quarter of an hour in halts to allow Childers & Arthur & McCalmont to dismount at different times to fire fruitlessly at gazelle of which we saw what Mr. Lowell would call 'quite a number'.

I feel inclined to moon about doing nothing being anxious for news of Stewart. I wish I were with him, & if it were not for all the jealousies of those about me, I would have joined him with one A.D.C. I should have enjoyed 'the sport', & been on the spot to act in any way Stewart has not the power of doing. But if I were to start off now, I should have all these round me say that I had left them in the lurch or behind to do the dirty work whilst I careened about in front for my own amusement. I have just rec'd a letter from Stewart[179] in which he says that owing to the condition of his camels and in order to save them as much as possible, he did not intend occupying *Matammeh* until tomorrow Sunday, so, all my sympathy with him this morning when I thought he was attacking was thrown away. The Sowarab & Hawawir who had promised to supply 50 camels arrived here today with 70. This looks well. Saleh has reached *Debbeh*, and will come on here at once. If he throws in his lot with us it is all up with the Mahdi. Things go brightly now, but as is always the case out of Europe, I might almost say out of England, without any regard to time, & it is time that is my greatest difficulty. I might almost say my most serious enemy.

Sunday 18th January

Sent off Kitchener to *Debbeh* to meet Sheik Saleh, & conduct him here. No divine service as our clergyman is still on his back. At last these infernal Sowarrab & Hawawir have supplied a few camels. They had promised 50 & brought 88 and I am in great hopes that more will turn up every day to carry for us.[180]

Monday 19th Janry.

92 more camels sent off today. These Arabs are a funny lot: they begged for an English escort: even two men: they are all armed with spears & a few have old guns. I am sending a small escort to give the first few convoys confidence. The convoy question being settled they said they must have a Guide!! That was too much for a gentle Briton. I see that pestilential combination between a fool & a madman, Mr. Wilfred Blunt[181] wants to come here to settle the Soudan. If he comes without permission I shall deal with him & in a very summary fashion: if he comes with the permission of the Govt. I shall be in England earlier than I expected, for the day he comes on this theatre of operations with the sanction and under the protection of Mr. Gladstone's Cabinet, I shall make tracks for England & leave Gladstone, Blunt & Co. to settle this Soudan business. Saleh does not start from *Debbah* until tomorrow.

Tuesday 20th January

.... In the evening had a telegram from Earle[182] reporting that some 19th Hussars & the Egyptian Camel Corps under Major Flood had made the reconnaissances I had ordered along the road from *Hamdab* to *Berber*. They say they went 35 miles & were then 15 miles according to their Guide from *Bir Sariyeh* which was the point I intended them to go to. They returned without going there having really effected nothing. I am thoroughly disgusted. When Brackenbury was here last week I told him to make every preparation for surprising those wells, as I had heard they were held by the Monassir people who had many cattle and camels there. It was most desirable to pounce down upon them, as such an operation would have frightened all the desert people far & near and have spread consternation as far as *Berber* where the Mahdi's Emir is already in dread of being attacked by a direct march through the desert. I thought either Earle or Brackenbury would have gone with this raiding party, but they neither went nor organized the party that did go in a reasonable manner. Failure has been the result. This does not presage much for their future operations up the river. I am indeed disappointed. Today has been cool and pleasant. An English boy killed a mongoose here yesterday. Hartington has ordered on the 2nd Battn. Sussex Regt. to *Alexandria* to replace the Berkshire ordered to *Suakim*. Two guns Horse Artillery & about 90 of 19th Hussars also go there from *Cairo*. This is intended as a demonstration & the orders are they are not to attack Osman Digma but by showing themselves at *Suakim* to keep that worthy there & prevent him from moving on *Berber* when our troops approach that place by the Nile from *Abu Ahmed*. I am afraid Earle will not be able to move into the *Monassir* country until the 24th instant. The delay has been the company of Transport intended for Earle's column which only left this for *Hamdab* today.[183]

Wednesday 21st January 1885

. . . . Messengers arrived from Stewart.[184] They left him at *Abu Klea* wells on morning of 18th instant, so they have come in well, 150 miles in three days on the same camels all the way. Stewart had a real big fight on the 17th inst. A regular *El Teb* or *Tamai* over again: our loss has been heavy arising from the unsteadiness of the Heavy Camel Regt. which allowed the enemy to break into the square. Poor devils they have suffered for it, as out of 64 killed 35 belonged to that Regt. There were 9 officers killed & 9 wounded;[185] amongst the former poor Burnaby who was stabbed by a lance through the jugular. All the correspondents speak most highly of the manner in which our soldiers fought and also of the way in which Stewart handled his troops. He & his staff were for some minutes in great danger: I believe they were knocked down in melee and Stewart had his horse killed. His loss would have been irreparable, and I dread to think of his being killed in some of these early affairs. He intended pushing on to the Nile on the 18th instant, to occupy *Matammeh* if the enemy would not fight again, but if they were going to defend the place, he meant to cut in either above or below it, water his camels, form post for impedimenta and attack *Matammeh* on 19th instant. If the enemy makes a resistance it will be nothing like that of the 17th but it is most probable they will vacate it without fighting. They have two guns there, & one at *Shendy* on opposite bank. Kasm el Moose with three steamers is some distance up the river, but I hope he has heard the guns at *Abu Klea* & moves to or close to *Matammeh*. I am very sorry about this Heavy Cavry. Camel Regt. The men and officers were magnificent, but not being drilled as Infantry, they did not have that confidence in their rifles that an Infantry Regt. would have had. It is a dangerous experiment, using cavalry as foot soldiers under such a trial, but being picked men they ought to have done better. I confess I am somewhat disappointed in them. How delighted the Prince of Wales & the Duke of Cambridge will be that poor Burnaby is killed. His high military spirit, energy, zeal & remarkable personal courage were not sufficient in the eyes of those Royal tailors to cover up the fact that socially Burnaby was distasteful to them and their set. When once these August Personages pronounce a man to be a snob, no great services rendered to the Nation, to the people of England can cover up such an unpardonable sin. Theoretically and at a distance I am the most loyal worshipper of Royalty, because I know that without it we could not now be a great or a prosperous people, but if I had my wish, I would never again enter a house where I should be personally brought in contact with any of the Queen's sons or cousins, or indeed with the Queen herself either: & yet if required I would die for Her, and that is the most one human being can do for another in this world. I have lived my life in her service and a hard life it has been in many ways. I have had far more than I deserve done for me both by Conservative and by Liberal Governments, and the people of England have been generous in every way to me, but I can conscientiously say I have never had a word of cordial thanks from the Queen or from any of her Royal family. Because I do not kow-tow to them & to their wishes, I have long since been condemned as a dangerous man & as a snob. Thank heavens they are afraid of me, and I mean them to retain that feeling of respect for me.

 Today has been pleasant with an agreeable wind and a low temperature. Sheik Saleh came in today. He looks about 30 years of age: he is fat: eats a sheep all to himself every day and has a very cunning look about his face and an expression that I do not like. He is very black. I made Kitchener sound him when on the road here as to the possibility of his becoming the independent ruler of Kordofan, but he would not listen to such a proposition, whilst at the same time he intimated that the selection must be a man who was agreeable to the *Kabbabish* Tribe. He proposed an old fellow named Elias who is now living in the desert about two day[s'] journey from *Obeid*.

Thursday 22nd Janry. 1885

.... Telegram from the Queen congratulating &c. &c. Another from the Khedive much more cordial & sympathetic. I have been rather amused at a letter written by Sir C. Wilson to Swaine. This has been his first fight and it has evidently from his letter shaken his nerves a good bit. This has influenced his usefullness [*sic*] somewhat for he made an agreement with 4 Bashi Bazouks, a Corpl. of those worthies & a Guide to bring Stewart's despatches in here, promising the Corpl. £10 & each of the others £5 apiece if they reached my camp at 4 p.m. 23rd instant, each man to have a pound for every 4 hours before that time that the despatches arrived. The consequence is I have to pay about £110 for them. Well, although the bargain was a stupid one, the despatches are worth five times that amount. The Mudir's troops returned here this morning from *Keren*, in the Wady *Abu Gazalis* on the road from *Gakdul* to *Merawi* and about 15 or 16 miles from that place. It was there the *Merawi* people used to send their food for sale to the Mahdi's agents. These Bashi Bazouks of the Mudir pounced down on it and have carried off herds of goats, some camels, donkey and cattle & *they* say they killed 20 men, I suppose harmless villagers. However, it will do good in frightening the people here that if they send supplies to the enemy we shall punish them for doing so. The sufferers in this instance are the Hassineyahs who have never shown any disposition as yet to submit.

Friday 23rd January

.... To me today has been a quiet day of anxiety. I look forward to good news from Stewart before tomorrow evening. Earle is at last ready & moves forward tomorrow towards *Birti* which is only by river about 33 miles from *Hamdab*. May God grant him victory, but I don't expect the enemy will make any serious resistance until *Berber* is reached.[186] Reports from *Hamdab* say results of Stewart's victory have been great, that fugitives from the battle crossed to right bank of Nile & made for their own homes.

Saturday 24th Janry.

Rode out along road to *Gakdul* to see if any messenger was coming in the distance: it was quite 'Sister Anne, Sister Anne do you see anyone coming?' I am naturally most anxious to have news from Stewart who ought to have occupied *Matammeh* on the 19th instant. Earle started today from *Hamdab*, en route for *Abu Ahmed* which he should reach on 10th Febry. Rundell at *Korosko* is ready to despatch a large convoy from there to *Abu Ahmed* as soon as it is certain when we shall be there. Among our many difficulties here, the ignorance of the people as to the relative value of gold & silver is no small one. Our sovereigns command no respect here, whereas great, coarse Austrian dollars or Medjidics of doubtful quality of silver are looked upon as real money. A man who could bring here £100,000 in silver would make a good thing of it now in buying up all our sovereigns at a reduced price.

Sunday 25th January

Stewart having sent away the only Bashi Bazouks (5 in number) he had with him when he wrote to me on the 18th instant, must now send his reports by English camel men. Hence I presume the delay in hearing from him, for I imagine his camels will be all more or less knocked up by his recent operation. A holy man who lives in the village just above our camp says he left the Wady *Bishan* or *Bishara* on the Nile on Sunday evening the 18th inst. states he reached that place on Saturday & that *Angar* with 5000 men (800 having rifles) also arrived there that day by whom he was made prisoner but released when he showed them the Mahdi's pass. This party were on their way to *Berber* for which place they started on Sunday morning. [Marginal note: This story was I think accurate.]

The news of Stewart's victory had not yet reached Wady *Bishan* on Sunday. They were being sent by the Mahdi to *Berber* to depose Mahomed el Kheir, the Emir there, because he would not send the £40,000 which had been sent there for Gordon before the town fell into the possession of the rebels. The Emir said the townspeople would not allow him to send it as they said 'When the *Turks* come back, if we cannot produce this money, they won't ask Mahomed Ahmed for it, but they will make us pay it up.'

Now the question is, are these 5000 men likely to have reached

Matammeh before Stewart did? He must have occupied that place or at least taken up a position on the Nile near it on Monday the 19th inst. The 5000 men will have met the fugitives from *Abu Klea* on Sunday & they will halt to consider what they should do, so that even if they decided upon pushing on to *Matammeh*—which I think improbable—they will not have reached that place until Monday when Stewart will have been ready to receive them. However I think I shall hear from Stewart before the day is over.

Divine service at 7 a.m. Our Clergyman who has been in hospital lately is much improved in appearance by his illness, having lost a good deal of the superfluous fat and large stomach which had previously marred the proportions of his figure. Earle reached *Owli* Island yesterday afternoon, & Butler had reconnoitred the country some distance ahead without finding an enemy.

I sent Childers & Maxwell out to what we call 'Twelve Mile Hill' to wait for Stewart's messenger & come in on their galloping camels with his despatches. They returned when I was in the middle of dinner having seen no one on the road.

Monday 26th January

The English post of 2nd January arrived about 9 a.m. I also received a private telegram from Hartington expressing grave anxiety for news from Stewart. I have replied that I was hourly expecting news, but there were no grounds for anxiety. I shall be really anxious if I do not hear before nightfall, & yet I know how many small accidents may occur to prevent news coming in: the detachment carrying the despatches may very probably have lost their way: possibly they might be attacked. I know that Stewart is short of guides, but I feel that in this case, no news is good news, for I am sure that if he be alive he will feel how necessary it is to keep me informed of his proceedings, more especially if he had met with any repulse. However, although I argue this way to myself I confess the suspense is hard to bear: if I were on the spot myself I should feel no anxiety; & yet it is from no self-conceit that I am an abler soldier than Herbert Stewart, but in the midst of danger or difficulty, one is in high spirits: one's soul seems to arise to the position, & one laughs at danger which is palpable & present. Not so however when at a distance from such danger: one is apt to exaggerate the danger & to minimize the force one is able to bring against the danger to be encountered. As I wake in the morning about 4 or 5 a.m. my heart sinks—it is very cold at that hour—as I pass in review before me all the difficulties we have to encounter. But then, when the sun rises, & I have had a good gallop, I realize that no amount of the Mahdi's troops could withstand the smallest of our columns.* What poor creatures we are! There never yet was a philosopher who could remain unaffected by a really twisting pain in his stomach. I dined with Evelyn Wood who gave me champagne and an excellent dinner: I ate, drank and talked to drive away the care which knawed my inside all day. I am sure it is wrong, but whenever I meet Evelyn Wood now he reminds me of the disgraceful peace he made with the Boers in 1881. Talking to Spenser Childers today about this peace he told me that he had walked in Piccadilly with his father when this peace was proposed and he said he would resign if it were made. It was made however and he did not resign. So much for the influence of party over the righteous and honourable & patriotic instincts and resolves of public men now-a-days.

Tuesday 27th January

Rode to Beacon Hill to strain my eyes in the direction of *Gakdul*. Sent on Spenser Childers to 12 Miles Hill to spend the day there & come in at racing speed if a messenger from Stewart reached that point. The first Native convoy returned, or rather its English escort, for a camel having died yesterday, the camelmen halted for the day to eat it. The loads they carried were handed over with regularity at *Gakdul*. They only did about 20 miles a day as they grazed their camels daily. The escort left *Gakdul* on the 24th up to which date no messenger from Stewart had reached that place except those who came in here the 21st instant with news of the success on the 17th instant. This suspense, this longing for news drives the blood from my heart: Oh God have mercy on me. Good news in from Earle, who is making satisfactory progress up river. He has passed the fourth cataract called *Edermith* which is at the head of *Owli* Island & not at the bend of the river near *Birti* as shown on our maps. When he reaches a cataract he lands a Battalion below it, marches it to a selected position above cataract whilst cavalry reconnoitre about ten miles ahead and the second

*Editor's note: All the foregoing written almost illegibly, close & slanting, uneven, and full of corrections & overwritten words.

Battalion gets its boats up the cataract. When up, it takes the place of the Battalion that had been sent on ahead, which then marches back and takes its boats up the rapids. He thus keeps his force well in hand together. He expected cavalry to reconnoitre to *Birti* today—as yet everyone is running before him & it is doubtful if they will make a stand there.[187] If Stewart has only succeeded as well at *Matammeh* all will be well, but if he has been repulsed and has suffered very heavily the enemy will be so elated that our prospects will be darkened.

Wednesday 28th January

Woke a little after 3 a.m. & lit my candle and read the Psalms for the day, my mind running upon Stewart. Before it was 4 a.m., I heard the grunting of a camel which told me that some-one was dismounting from one of those ungainly beasts. In a few minutes heard voices & got up & found Captn. Pigott of the Mounted Infry. in Swaine's tent & learnt the news from him. He had left the Nile near *Matammeh* at 7 p.m. on 23rd inst. with a large convoy under the command of Regy Talbot: had marched with it until they had cleared the bush & then pushed on with his soldier servant & one native. Having reached the scene of action on 17th inst. found some of the enemy's cavalry about and their footmen evidently engaged in burying their dead. He returned to *Abu Klea* and found Talbot had arrived from whom he got eight more men & then started for *Gakdul*. Pushed on all night and the next day when he found guide had lost his way. He thus lost 24 hours, so that Talbot with his convoy had reached that place before him. He made his final start from *Gakdul* at 10.30 p.m., Monday 26th and did the 100 miles in here in 29 hours. He is a fine gallant fellow & has proved it on many occasions.

We have not taken *Matammeh* but have established ourselves on the Nile about two miles above that place. The fighting has been brisk but Pigott tells me the enemy did not fight with the same boldness they displayed on the 17th instant. Our losses have all been from rifle fire very well delivered. The action near *Matammeh* took place on the 19th instant, poor Herbert Stewart being wounded about 10.15 a.m. on that day. He has received a bullet somewhere in the lower part of his stomach which must be very dangerous. At any rate we lose his services for rest of campaign & that is at present a real national loss.[188] I told Buller at once he must go to *Matammeh* and assume command.[189] Our losses in killed & wounded have not been great. Poor St. Leger Herbert shot through head. A braver soul never lived. Cameron, the *Standard* Correspondent of whom I cannot say the same, also killed.

Wilson has proved a great failure as a soldier: he succeeded to command when Stewart was wounded. On 21st instant Wilson made a foolish reconnaissance of *Matammeh* moving his men about in square and then fell back, a line of conduct that of course has encouraged enemy.[190] During this silly operation four steamers arrived from up river, landed men & guns to cooperate in attack on village. On 22nd *Shendy* was reconnoitred by steamers but nothing of any importance took place. Enemy have one gun there & two or three in *Matammeh* but have little ammunition for them. Of the shells they fired, scarcely any burst. I am extremely sorry we have not taken *Matammeh* from which Buller will now have to turn them out. Wilson with two steamers & 20 men of Sussex started on 24th inst. for *Khartoum*.[191] Charlie Beresford is seedy but says he hopes in a few days to be all right again, & to clear out enemy from neighbouring villages with the two steamers and Naval Brigade. Thank God for all his mercies: the position looks once more bright again. I am pushing forward Rl. Irish at once, West Kent to follow as soon as possible. Talbot was to start today with large convoy for *Gabut*—the village we occupy near *Matammeh*—and when it reaches that place there will be plenty of provisions for everyone. God grant it may reach its destination in safety. The enemy has had a severe handling again, and they will think twice before they charge our men again.

Pleasant news in from Earle dated this morning:[192] he is at the *Kabb El Abd* cataract about 12 miles below *Birti*. It is one of the worst if not the worst in this part of the river. Colville who is on right bank with Mudir's troops reconnoitred *Birti* where he estimated enemy's force at about 1000. It is very doubtful if they will fight there. Two uncles of Suleiman who live in *Birti* have sent to say they mean to come in. The people are returning to their villages in rear of our troops as they advance which is a good sign. I have smoked four cigars today as a relief to the tension my soul and body & nerves have sustained for the last three days. Men talk of the strain sometimes experienced in great danger. Well I can speak of that from personal experience better than most men, but having led storming parties I can assert them to be child's play compared with the strain which a General situated as I have been for some days past, has to undergo. In a fight, one fights and everything one does has some visible effect: you feel you are doing good work, that you are contributing, no matter how humbly, towards the general result; individually you are of some consequence. But to be squatted down as I have been here, unable to do anything to aid or help forward the end and objects aimed at, is not only galling to the pride, but simply heart-rending. In these operations I am so 'fine drawn' as regards the margin I have to allow for untoward events, that any serious repulse would be most inconvenient if not dangerous. The number of my troops is uncomfortably approaching the danger point. When therefore I am left a whole week without news of what is going on, or what had taken place after a hard fought fight such as that on the 17th instant, the tension on all vital parts of the bodily system becomes almost intolerable.

It is all owing to Stewart having been wounded. I went to see the three companies of Rl. Irish parade before marching off & said a few words to them. They are magnificent-looking men, wiry and strong, not a fat man in the Battalion. It has been blowing hard all day and the dust in camp has been very unpleasant.

Thursday 29th January

Sent for Evelyn Wood & told him he was to be my Chief of the Staff which has pleased him very much. Received a telegram from Hartington[193] in the middle of the night of a very complimentary character to all concerned, and announcing that the Queen had promoted Stewart to be Maj. General. This, I had yesterday, (in a private cypher telegram to Hartington) urged him to do. Ordered a post to be established to run daily between this & *Gakdul*. Buller started at noon for the desert—may God go with him. My earnest and parting request to him was, to do all in his power to avoid being shot.[194]

News from Earle dated this morning.[195] He is detained at a rapid just above *Amri* Island which he reports will take him 3 days to get his column over. He says strong force from *Berber* expected tomorrow or next day at *Birti*, so perhaps enemy will fight there after all—I sincerely hope so, & that God may bless us with a real & substantial victory. That would clear the horizon all round, and perhaps under Earle's further progress very easy to &

even beyond *Berber*. If we are to have a fight, the nearer to this it takes place the better for every reason.

The telegraph is very well worked here by Webber. Yesterday there was very naturally a great deal done by it, as some of the messages were very long that went to the newspapers. The work done amounted to 16833 words sent from here—310 transmitted through here & 1485 words received. That sent over a single wire for about 1400 miles is very creditable. Drs.' reports received this morning refer hopefully to Stewart: they say the bullet has not injured the intestines. I earnestly hope he may live to fight many a battle yet. . . .

Friday 30th January

It has been blowing hard from the North for the last two days & nights, with now & then partial lulls. This morning when I got up at sunrise, very cold. I remark that in the medical reports the Doctors refer to the wounded after both actions having suffered severely from cold during the night. . . .

I am today preparing the following plot to sew distrust in the Mahdi's camp. I have written a letter in French to Mr. Pain the Frenchman in his camp who is supposed to be a good deal in his secrets. This letter refers to previous imaginary correspondence and to a monied agreement between him & me with a view to the Shieks whose names he is supposed to have sent me in last imaginary letter to me & I beg of him to assure them that I shall keep my promises to them. I remind them to be sure and make the signal agreed upon when I move to attack the Mahdi to prevent all possibility of my soldiers killing them. I wind up my letter by asking Pain whether he wished to be paid here, in *Cairo* or in *Paris*. I tell him of the heaps of dead left by the enemy in both the recent actions, that I hope soon to shake hands with him in *Khartoum* & end by saying I enclose proclamations in Arabic for his friends the Sheiks whose names he had sent me—(I don't repeat them naturally). The proclamation in Arabic is magnificent & is addressed to all the Sheiks who are friends of the Frenchman Pain. It winds up by offering $10,000 to those who brought Mahamed Ahmed into my Camp. I shall take care this reaches the Mahdi's camp & it will cause that imposter not only to doubt this villainous Frenchman, but it will make him uneasy as to the fidelity of his own entourage.

The stern wheel paddler which has been named the *Lotus* is now safely above the *Hannek* cataract: she was put together at *Semneh*. She has therefore been a great success: as she draws very little water, she will be most useful on this *Abu Fatmeh-Korti* reach which is about 200 miles long.

Our losses in camels from killed in action & died during the recent operations near *Matammeh* amount to fully 250. I shall have to buy some more which is provoking, as I am afraid it may interfere with my hiring market. We have now about 320 hired camels working between this & *Gakdul*, & I expect 100 from Saleh today or tomorrow. The natives give their camels no grain on this journey; they graze them every day & allow them to feed as they march along which they do slowly. They only do 20 miles a day so they take five days in going to *Gakdul*. Earle is seriously delayed at a cataract about 8 or 9 miles from *Birti*. It is reported to [be] very bad and some days will be required to pass his forces over it.

Saturday 31st January

Four companies of the Rl. Irish marched this morning for *Gakdul* which place they are to reach in 7 days. More camels coming in daily for conveyance of stores to *Gakdul*. Today Talbot's Convoy was to reach *Gabut*. I hope he has done so without any fighting. I want to do all I can to avoid frittering away my little army in skirmishes & to keep them for big occasions. News from Earle up to yesterday evening.[196] The water immediately in front of him very bad, so that there is little chance of his being able to attack the enemy at *Birti* before Tuesday 3rd instant. Butler had reconnoitred that place & found it occupied. A runaway soldier reports the numbers there very large—about 15,000—of whom he says only 300 have rifles with 30 rounds a man. They have the gun which Stewart spiked before he was murdered. Mohamed el Kheir, Emir of *Berber* had written to Abdul Magidwad Kalik who is in command at *Birti* telling him we had occupied *Matammeh* & sent steamers into Gordon laden with grain. That we were too strong for the *Birti* force & he had better fall back on *Abu Ahmed* &c.

I most sincerely hope he may not do so, but that we may be able to strike a heavy blow at *Birti*. If we can do so, I shall endeavour to open negotiations for the surrender of *Berber*.

February 1885

Sunday 1st February

A very cold morning. We had church parade at 7 a.m. which was too early owing to the cold as it is bad for the men to stand about so long on parade with empty stomachs when they are chilly: especially when idiotic Commanding Officers parade their men one full hour before the church service begins. The last company of the Rl. Irish started this morning on foot for *Gakdul*. Rode in the evening with Evelyn Wood to look at the sick camels we have out grazing.

Monday 2nd February 1885

News from Earle's column is that *Birti* is deserted and we have occupied it:[197] enemy retreating towards *Abu Ahmed* via *Shukuk* Pass. Hassein, the stoker of Stewart's steamer, had escaped to Earle's camp. Two uncles of Suleiman Wady el Gamr have come & asked for peace. Unless this means there is to be no fighting until *Khartoum* is reached, I am sorry the enemy have retreated or dispersed. But please God we shall have no more bloodshed until the day when I can attack the Mahdi to deliver *Khartoum* from that villainous false prophet.

Tuesday—3rd February

Saleh is sending 250 camels. The first installment [*sic*] to arrive here tomorrow. Northerly wind quite cold. If we could only have three months more of this climate. Another telegram[198] from Hartington urging upon my consideration the advisability of occupying the *Hamdab* and *Tambuk* wells near *Suakim,* and asking for my opinion. They seem to be anxious to force me to say that active operations against Osman Digma would be a great help to me. This I don't think and will not therefore say. From the first whenever the question has been mooted I have always replied, 'By all means crush Osman Digma, it will go far towards settling the country. It is merely a question of selecting the right commanders and of finding the necessary troops. I regard it however as a proposal to indulge in an expensive luxury, for to send back sufficient troops from *Berber* to *Suakim* when I have squared matters with the Mahdi, has always been part of the programme I have laid out for myself here.' My answer today is very much the same, but in answer to a fresh subject started in telegram, I have said that the defeat of Osman Digma would be useful in enabling me to use the Berber–Suakim route for the *Khartoum* refugees &c. &c.

I have urged the necessity of taking one squadron from each of three selected Regts. at home, one to be armed with lances, & Col. Croppy Ewart[199] to command Cavry. Regt. thus collected. Greaves[200] to be given local rank of Lt. Genl. to command all. It would be necessary to give him this rank as Fremantle[201] is his senior as a Maj. Genl., thanks to his having served all his life in *London* in the Guards, although Greaves is a much older soldier. Fremantle may be a Napoleon for all I know: he is an ardent soldier & a very charming fellow, but as he has never been tried, it would be madness to entrust him with command when we have a man available whose nerve and fighting qualities have been already tested.

Wednesday—4th February 1885

[Marginal note: Koomassee taken 1874.]

In the two fights of the 17th and 19th Janry. our losses were in killed 13 Officers & 98 N.C.O.'s & men; and in wounded 18 Officers and 175 N.C.Offrs. & men. Practically this reduces my fighting strength by 275 men. As far as I have been able to gather from the returns I have called for, there were drowned coming up the river in our whalers, one officer and eleven privates and five voyageurs. Forty boats were abandoned but many of these were subsequently repaired and are now in use. I should imagine that about 20 whalers were hopeless wrecks. Of those abandoned the Cornwall L.I. are responsible for 16. The West Kent only left two behind. In all, seven Battalions came up river to *Korti* in whalers, and one, the Sussex, in Native craft. I regard this as most satisfactory. I am publishing a General Order today announcing that the Rl. Irish Regt. has won the £100 which I gave from my own meagre purse as a prize to the Battn. which came up in the best time. I shall try and have my G.O. telegraphed home to amuse Mrs. Ouida and the 'Generals of the Old School'. This foolish woman, anxious for notoriety, seems to forget that it is *possible* I may know my own trade a little better than the female writer of immoral novels. If she had only condescended to make enquiries, she would have found that money has often been offered by British Generals to their men as an inducement to them to undertake hazardous enterprizes. My money reward was nothing more than a boat-racing prize, and I know it was fully understood and appreciated by those for whom it was meant. I am now anxiously looking out for the news of Talbot's convoy having safely reached *Gabut* & of Wilson having returned from *Khartoum*. I hope Wilson may himself be the bearer of this news.

The Yarrow boat arrived here yesterday evening. She has been a great success. If the Government had ordered a dozen last April and sent them out here with all speed what sums of money would have been saved which now go into Mr. Cook's pocket. I inspected the camels of the Lt. Camel Regt. yesterday evening & I was sorry to find so many of them unfit for work. I sent McCalmont off this morning to *Abu Gus* to buy a few camels if he could pick up any there that were suitable.

At 7 p.m. just as I was going to dinner I received letters from *Gabut* to the 1st and from Buller at *Gakdul* to the 3rd inst. I was certainly knocked out of tune by the dreadful intelligence that *Khartoum* was taken by Mahdi's troops on 26th January & that Gordon's fate was uncertain but he was said to have been killed. I earnestly pray he may have been killed, for to him death was always looked forward to as the beginning of a glorious and new life, whereas if he be alive he may be kept for years in prison by this cruel monster Mahomed Ahmed. Sir C. Wilson who started on 24th Janry. with two steamers for *Khartoum* reached *Tuti* Island on the 28th January where they were received by heavy fire &

obliged to put back—one steamer was wrecked on 29th Janry. & the other having safely passed the Shabluka cataract was wrecked on 31st inst. on an island about 4 miles above a position occupied by enemy and between 30 & 60 miles above *Gabut*. Wilson had landed his party safely on Island, & Stewart-Wortley [Stuart-Wortley?] had dropped down river in a small boat & brought the news to *Gabut*.202 A steamer had gone to bring Wilson off the Island. I fear the treachery of native pilots & crew, but still as natives take some time in forming decisions I trust that Wilson & party are now safe at *Gabut*. If not, their being made prisoners will complicate matters extremely. Just as I may say my hand was ready to take hold of the prize, it has thus, by the decree of an inscrutable but wise Providence, been snatched from my grasp. If the traitors who admitted the Mahdi's troops into the city had but waited another few days, the arrival of Wilson at *Khartoum* would I believe have burst the whole seige up. The moral effect of English soldiers having reached the place, & brought in provisions, no matter how little, would have given such heart to the defenders & so depressed the besiegers, that the Mahdi's game would have been up. God has however willed it otherwise for His own divine reasons, & we must bow our heads accordingly, & say 'Thy will be done.' I sent off an express to Buller about 10.30 p.m.203 desiring him not to undertake the offensive operations he contemplated, as he had written to me saying he meant to take *Matammeh* at all costs. He wrote under the assumption that I would still push forward to *Khartoum* apparently failing to see how the fall of that place has altered everything. I have no longer any 'mission' to accomplish, and I am sure the British Govt. would not think of a campaign for the conquest of the Soudan or for 'smashing up' the Mahdi. But even if the Govt. were prepared to embark in such an operation, the season is so late, that it would be a very hazardous undertaking. I told Buller that I hoped to hear from home in 24 hours, as I had asked for instructions, but I presumed that the course we should follow would be to concentrate all our Force on the *Merawi–Abu Gus* line of river, from whence we had clear navigation to *Abu Fatmeh*, & there for the present to await events. In the meantime all our wounded must be withdrawn from *Gabut* and *Abu Klea*, to *Gakdul*. I telegraphed all this news at length to Lord Hartington and asked for instructions.204

What a business there will be in England over the news! I told him I was keeping back all press telegrams & would do so, until I heard from him. If anything can kill old Gladstone this news ought to, for he cannot, self-illusionist though he be, disguise from himself the fact that he is directly responsible for the fall of *Khartoum* & all the bloodshed it entails: that it was owing to his influence, active measures for the relief of Gordon were not undertaken in time. Whilst Gordon was starving, this arrogant Minister who poses as a great Statesman, but without any just claim to be considered one, was discussing to himself whether Gordon was 'hemmed in' or 'surrounded' and no one could persuade him that *Khartoum* was besieged or Gordon in any danger. Never were the destinies of any great nation committed to a more incompetent pilot. And yet a pack of fools & theoretical vestrymen contrive to worship him with an almost idolatrous reverence. What an ending to all our labour, and all our bright hopes, is this!!

Thursday—5th February 1885

Up writing a little after 4 a.m. I determined upon sending off the Lt. Camel Regt. to *Gakdul* to assist, if necessary in saving Wilson & his party, or if they be safe, as I have every reason to hope, to help in withdrawing altogether from *Gabut*. I sent messenger last night to Earle ordering him to halt where he is.[295] Duplicate goes to him this morning. Sent another officer off this morning to Buller at *Gakdul* with instructions,[206] Am sending into the Mahdi's camp to try & ascertain Gordon's fate. It is quite possible the Mahdi may not kill him. Indeed quite possible he might give him up, as a holy man like Gordon is very much respected and feared by Mahomedans.

I expected to have had 250 camels here yesterday from Saleh: I know they reached *Debbeh* two or three days ago, and the first instalment of 150 left that place *en route* for this. The news from *Khartoum* has evidently reached that worthy trimmer & he has stopped them in consequence. This is the first indication we have had of how the fall of *Khartoum* is likely to affect our position. At present we could not maintain ourselves at *Matammeh* if unassisted by the Sowarrab and Hawawir tribes, and it is very possible they may now follow Saleh's example. Had telegrams[207] from Baring saying that the Fall of *Khartoum* was rumored in Soudan & then spread in *Cairo,* so he has officially announced it. I am glad the 'leakage' has been at home not here, for although the rumor is in camp, I have not announced it and shall not do so until tomorrow or next day. Heard from Sir R. Thompson that Ministers were out of town—they are so always when wanted—& that Cabinet would not meet until tomorrow early. He asked me a question from Northbrook, whether my line of communications were in danger. I am down in my luck. What a 'facer' this news is to us all, for never was there a little Army embued with a higher spirit or more determined to push on, every man seeming to work as if the result depended upon his own individual exertions.

They have done all they could, & when brought into contact with the enemy they fought like heroes. It is not their fault they were not here two months ago, nor is it mine: that fault lies at Mr. Gladstone's door, shared by that great self-important lump of flesh Sir W. Harcourt[208] & perhaps one or two others of this curiously-composed Cabinet that has for years been steering the National ship upon every rock they could discover.

Friday 6th February

.... It is a most curious fact that none of the natives near here have yet even had a rumor of *Khartoum* being taken. We have had the two chief men of the Hawawir in camp today to receive dresses & swords of honor & they when asked said they had heard nothing of it & did not believe it, as had it been true, they said, the news would have spread all over the land like wildfire.

One of the men employed in the Intelligence Department was at the *Gabra* wells on the 31st Janry. where large collections of cattle & of old men & women & children of the Jualin and Hassineeahs were collected, and no rumor of the fall of *Khartoum* had then reached that place. This is very curious.

About 9.30 p.m. I received the decision of the home Govt.[209] and of all the surprises I have had, it has been the greatest. They have actually picked up enough courage to tell me to protect from the Mahdi the Districts 'now undisturbed'. They don't wish any retrograde movements & are prepared to support me in every possible way, by sending troops to *Suakim* &c. &c., adding they did not wish to prevent me from going to *Berber*, if I thought such an operation desirable. I have replied[210] that I require some more explicit declaration of their policy. Do they mean us eventually to destroy the Mahdi's power? If not, any advance upon *Berber*, which I think they wish me to attempt, would be merely undertaken for party purposes to keep Mr. Gladstone in office. In fact the Cabinet today have realized that nothing could save them except a spirited policy, and their telegram to me is the result. It smells far more of the Caucus than patriotism. 'Let all your soldiers,' they say, 'grill for the summer in the Soudan, let many of them be killed & wounded, we care not, so long as the country will recognize that we have at last roused ourselves & adopted a spirited policy.' This seems to be their reasoning. They do not seem to realize how the fall of *Khartoum* has completely changed the military position. The Mahdi has now a large Army at his disposal, and the reports I have had from *Gabut*—given I presume on the authority of Kasm el Moose—say that with the capture of *Khartoum* 15000 rifles & 15 camel guns with plenty of ammunition fell into the Mahdi's hands. He is quickly becoming a great Military Power. When surrounding *Khartoum* he suffered from sickness amongst his troops, wanted money and had very little food. Now the prestige of his success will cause the tribes to join him. He will be regarded as irresistable.

The Govt. intends us to remain in the Soudan all the summer— I fear our mortality will be great as British soldiers do not stand tropical heat well, and the dullness of their lives, reacting upon the want of any military enterprize or object to work for will break them down in spirit. An army forcing its way up the Nile against great difficulties for the purpose of relieving Gordon in *Khartoum* and hoping to have a real good stand-up fight with the Mahdi near that place is imbued with a very different spirit & sentiment from one doing nothing in camp for a long summer under a tropical sun.

No news yet as to the safety of Sir C. Wilson who causes me anxiety. What fresh cares seem to crop up every day! I did not get to bed until past midnight.

Saturday—7th February 1885

Sent off an officer at early dawn to *Gakdul* to tell Buller the news from England.[211] What I contemplate now is the capture of *Berber* by the combined forces of Buller & Earle & I think I shall go myself with Buller's column from *Matammeh*. I have told the Govt. to carry out their proposal to send force to *Suakim* for the purpose of crushing Osma[n] Digma. I begged of Hartington to send Greaves in command and as he is junior as a Maj. Genl. to Fremantle to give Greaves local rank as a Lt. General. I have recommended Croppy Stewart to command the Cavalry Regt.* to be sent there. The force† to do this could not well be at *Suakim* before the 21st March and could not have fought & disposed of Osman Digma until 1st of April at earliest, whereas *Berber*, please God, will be in our hands the first week in March.

I wrote to Buller again in the evening after I had had a fuller explanation of the Govt. Soudan policy[212] telling him to take *Matammeh* as he was so keen to do so. I hate to lose men on minor operations when I am engaged with an enemy so vastly superior in numbers, & especially when so far as we are here from all possible help. If the Mahdi were a wise General he would fight us every day, that is supposing his men would do so—and destroy us simply by attrition, as the butcher General Grant destroyed the Southern Army in Virginia.

The Mudir does not believe in our news from *Khartoum*. It is quite possible that the rumor that Gordon was shut up in the Catholic church which was strongly built may be correct. If so, it will force us to go to *Khartoum* and I don't think we are strong enough for the job under present conditions. Non-military people do not at a glance understand how altered are the conditions under which we should now have to advance upon *Khartoum* from those existing when the place held out. As long as Gordon with a considerable body of troops held *Khartoum* & *Omdurman*, the Mahdi could not concentrate any large force to oppose my advance without risking raising the siege & Gordon attacking all his positions round the city. In fact he dared not leave Gordon behind him to march forward to attack me. Such is the geographical position of *Khartoum* that a besieger must divide his force into three distinct divisions, each being divided from the two others by unfordable rivers. As long as *Khartoum* had not fallen I should therefore have been in a position to have attacked and beaten the Mahdi's Army in detail, being effectively assisted in doing so by Gordon's Artillery & steamers and all his best black troops. Now I should have none of this assistance & have to fight the whole of the Mahdi's army, not only six or eight times larger than mine, but with at least seven times as many guns as I have. I confess this is no pleasing prospect and if compelled to do so I

---

*Wolseley had later pencilled in 'Force' instead of 'Regt.'.
†Wolseley had later pencilled in 'little Army' instead of 'force'.

shall embark upon it with the greatest reluctance. To the soldier this is all very clear, but to the civilian mind no: men like Vernon Harcourt who are very plucky with other men's lives say, 'oh you have the force you calculated upon for the relief of *Khartoum*, go in and relieve Gordon.' Civilians seldom remember that an army has to be fed with provisions for the stomach, and with powder & shot for their guns.

Sunday 8th February

Divine service at 9 a.m. Sent off an express to Buller[213] with duplicate of yesterday's orders desiring him to clear enemy out of *Matammeh*. Mudir does not believe that *Khartoum* has been taken & no native here has heard the news except from us. God grant such may be the case, but I cannot allow my mind to rest on such good hopes.

Monday 9th February

In the morning busy in getting off my post for England.[214] It is most unfortunate that my letter-bag from home did not come today with the home mail that left *London* on the 16th Janry.: it was by accident left at *Abu Fatmeh* with the heavy bags of Newspapers. I shall not get it now for several days.

All day occupied in calculations for the capture of *Berber*. Having to deal with two columns makes the problem difficult so as to enable both to combine in front of that place about same time.

Late in the evening just before sundown I started with Swaine for a short walk before dinner but had not gone more than a few hundred yards when I heard Arthur running after me & calling out. When he reached us he gave us the cheering news that Sir C. Wilson had just ridden into camp.[215] Thank God he & his party are safe. Charley Beresford behaved splendidly,[216] having had a round shot through his boiler, had to anchor under fire to repair the damage. Wilson scouts the idea that *Khartoum* is still held by Gordon: from the crowds of the Mahdi's people on Tuti Island & on the spit of land at junction of two Niles—which is in fact part of city limits—it is he says impossible that Gordon still holds out. He believes the story that Gordon was killed the day the Mahdi's troops were treacherously admitted into the city, & he is certain that Gordon will never allow himself to be taken alive. He brings with him the last part of Gordon's journal from 5th November up to 14th Decbr. & several letters from Gordon to me & others.[217]

Tuesday—10th Febry.

The first detachmts. (3 companies) of West Kent started for *Gabat* via *Gakdul* this afternoon. They marched and had only hired camels with them. Read Gordon's letters & a good deal of his journal. Oh what sad, melancholy and yet most interesting reading! We so nearly saved him. He says in the last few pages[218] if only a steamer were to arrive with 100 English soldiers the effect would be the relief of the place: if he had or could have only told me this I would have strained a point and risked the attempt. But why think of it now—too late, too late: Mr. Gladstone's imbecility to blame. Gordon's death, if he be dead, & the fall of *Khartoum* lies at Mr. Gladstone's door: but I suppose that won't affect him much, for has he not passed a new *Franchise Bill*!!! ??? And yet this is the man entrusted by the country with its destinies. May God help England, but it would seem that He had turned his back upon it when he allows men of Mr. Gladstone's calibre and character to rule it.[219]

Wednesday 11th Febry.

For some days past I have remarked that Swaine was not himself. He has completely changed, & this morning he told George that he had broken down. Poor fellow, I pity him with all my heart. I am sending him home & he leaves at once. He will be of great use to the Govt. in letting them know what this country is like, and as he knows nearly all that I know, will give them more information than it is possible to communicate in writing. Have today informed the Govt.[220] of what strength of force is required for the autumn campaign. Yesterday had a telegram saying H.R.H. proposed Stephenson, Alison[221] & Graham[222] to command troops to operate against Osman Digma with Greaves Chief of Staff. Asking what I thought: my answer was that of combinations proposed, Graham & Greaves would be best.

Sir C. Wilson's nerves seem to have gone so completely from his experience of real war that I told him today I meant to leave him here when I left as I wished him to take care of the Mudir. I don't *think* he was very sorry and I shall be glad to be rid of him.

He is so melancholy that he gives one the blues to look at him and he is enough to demoralize any little army he is associated with. I wish I could have sent him with Swaine this afternoon. I can understand a man in a responsible position like myself breaking down, for this sort of a war cut off from all possible help is trying to those who have to be responsible to England for its success, but why a subordinate whose only stake is his own wretched life should lose his nerve, is beyond all comprehension. May the Lord God who made me never punish me by sending fear into my heart. And yet the Duke of Cambridge with his great square fat bottom to his fire in the Horse Guards will tell you that one man is as good as another & talk about war as if it were the child's play that His Royal mind glories in, of moving troops about in a mechanical fashion in Hyde Park. The stern realities of war, as they appear to man when surrounded by a savage enemy seven or eight times more numerous than you are, are serious even to the bravest; for the more experience you have of war, the more you realize how many men have no nerve & that in such battles as these we must fight here, each and all of our lives depends [more] upon the courage of others, than upon ourselves.

I read a good deal of poor Gordon's journal. I read it to get all the information I can from it before I send it home. Otherwise I should not do so, it is such a very depressing occupation to me under present circumstances. He says that Stewart took the greatest possible trouble to find out all particulars regarding the fate of Hicks' Army & had recorded all the particulars in his diary—perhaps we may get it when we take *Berber* where all Stewart's papers are said to be. Gordon says[223] 10000 soldiers including 2000 cavalry, 4000 camp followers & 7000 camels perished in two days from thirst: 17000 rifles, 1,000,000 rds. S.A.A., 7 Krupp, 6 Nordenfeldts, and 29 Mountain Guns with 500 rds. each were captured. '(Perhaps 300 men were spared out of this host)' 8 Englishmen & 8 Germans were killed & according to all accounts they were so exhausted that they were unable to move.

In the evening after dinner telegram[224] from Brackenbury announcing his successful fight of yesterday in which however, alas, poor Earle was killed. I fancy the enemy were not numerous but occupied a very strong position amongst rocks with their backs to the river. Eyre comdg. South Staffordshire killed. Our other losses were trifling, but they all mean so many men less for our final coup, & these Arabs can afford to lose 10 for every one Englishman either killed or wounded.

Thursday 12th February

Wilson firmly believes the Mudir is playing us false. I cannot believe it for I am sure he is wise enough to see that if we left the country, he could not hold out a month in *Dongola*. He must see that our success is his, & our destruction would be his also. However I have requested Baring to send up Prince Hassein as a sort of Special Commissioner from the Khedive with power over all Mudirs & I propose to keep him with the Mudir to watch him & see that he runs straight.

Buller left *Gakdul* on Sunday 8th inst. & should reach *Gobat* either this evening with all the Rl. Irish or tomorrow. I don't expect him to attack *Matammeh* therefore until Sunday 15th although he might possibly do so the day before.[225] I don't like attacking these mud towns. You cannot hurt them by artillery, and they are very easily loop-holed and defended. I have calculated upon losing 200 in taking it. It is most curious that we have no native report as yet of the fall of *Khartoum*: it is, Wilson thinks, most suspicious, and indicates treachery.

Each day brings with it anxieties. Today a letter from Brackenbury saying that 30 percent of his biscuit was unfit for human food owing to the bad packing cases in which it had been sent from England. This will delay his advance on *Berber*, so I do not believe it is possible for him to leave *Abu Ahmed* before 26th February.[226] I have had to send fresh instructions to Buller accordingly.[227] It is a most difficult matter to work two columns each independent of the other as regards inter-communication so that both should combine for the attack on *Berber*; one is about 180° S.E. of this & the other about the same distance, or rather will be when it reaches *Abu Ahmed* in a N.E. direction from *Korti*.

Friday 13th February

Out riding in the early morning as usual. Grove[228] has not yet got into my ways & is not therefore such a good Military Secretary as Swaine was. Now I hear the other Swaine wants to go home. He has fearfully bad varicose veins & is really quite unfit for active service. I fancy also want of nerve runs in the veins of the family as a failing they cannot get over. Had a telegram from Hartington in answer to mine upon the subject of my going forward beyond the reach of the telegraph from which I gather they don't want me to leave this. However I have all next week to make plans now that bad commissariat arrangements at home delay the advance on *Berber* so long. Also a very secret telegram[229] asking me whom I considered should receive a dormant commission in the event of my turning up my toes. I shall answer tomorrow, Buller certainly, next Greaves, next Wood. Graham is a good fighting man but has not enough brains to command in Chief. A letter was found near the position held by the enemy on the 10th instant from the Emir of *Berber* announcing the fall of *Khartoum* & death of Gordon on the 26th January.[230] The missing bag with my letter of the 16th Janry. from home reached me today. The letters were sad reading as they were all couched in terms believing I should have been in direct communication with Gordon by the time I received them. Alas, how the position is different!! My heart sinks as I think of what our prospects were six weeks ago and what they are now. If the Mahdi was a skillful [*sic*] General & had 5000 good men how he might make me smart [?sweat?] now, for my position is a dangerous one.

Saturday 14th February

A violent dust storm blowing all last night. A messenger from *Khartoum* has reached *Debbeh* bringing the news that *Khartoum* was taken 26th Janry. The Mudir now believes the news, although Saleh telegraphs to him from *Debbeh* that some Sheiks of his tribe, the Kabbabish, had just reached him having left *Omdurman* nine days ago, everything being as usual there, the Mahdi's power steadily declining. I heard from Buller the night of 10th or very early morning of 11th instant from *Gabat*.[231] He had made all arrangements to bring away all the wounded & sick from that place on the 12th and meant to take *Matammeh* as soon as possible. Told Wood he must go to *Gobat* with fresh instructions to Buller. He knows. . . . [one full line crossed out] exactly how we stand as regards supplies & camels, and if Buller can push on to *Berber* will be able personally to conduct the withdrawal of all the garrisons from the desert to this place.[232] He is my last available General, but Dormer will be here in a few days.

Sunday 15th February

A man who was—he says—a cavass in *Khartoum* when it was taken has come in. He saw Gordon shot: also saw our two steamers reach Tuti Island. He says there was no talk of surrender the evening before *Khartoum* was treacherously surrendered. They had provisions enough to have held out a long time. He is so circumstantial in his statements that I am inclined to believe him. The nights are still *very* cold. Whenever I have to get up during the night or very early morning to write, I put on a heavy great coat over my flannel sleeping clothes, and am cold even then. The days are however warmer than before. We have strong northerly winds at night which blow clouds of dust into our tents. In the morning the sky is sometimes covered with stormy clouds that in any other country would mean rain. Prince Hassein is coming here as Commissioner under the Khedive and to represent H.H. *au près de moi* but to be distinctly under my orders in all things. I hope he may be of use in exercising as a Mahommedan & as a Prince direct influence over the Mudir. I am now very badly off for camels, and all my energies must now be directed to purchasing as many as I can even up to 1000. Church parade at 9 a.m. Had a gallop in the desert in the evening. Wood starts tomorrow morning for *Gakdul* and *Gobat*. I am on tenterhooks for news of what Buller has done at *Matammeh*. Oh what a campaign of anxieties is this!

Monday 16th February

English Post left. Wood started about 7 a.m. It blew hard last night & most of the day also, and we were enveloped in clouds of dust until sundown.

I had a parade at 4.30 p.m. & turned out every man I could to make a show, as the Mudir had an idea we were weak. He attended the parade on horseback and was astonished to find we had so many men here. Unfortunately it was so dusty there were not as many natives present as I should have liked. However the demonstration was good and has had the effect I aimed at, although the number on parade was only [blank space].

I am now in great straits for want of camels to purchase: sometime ago, I could obtain plenty to buy and none to hire—now the case is reversed. The tribes find they can make so much money by hiring that they don't care to sell any but their bad camels. Sheik

Saleh still pretends he does not credit the fall of *Khartoum*. If Buller took *Matammeh* on Saturday I ought to know of it here next Wednesday the 18th instant. I calculate upon his losing 200 killed & wounded, but if God is merciful to me perhaps our loss may be very small. An easy capture of the place would be of inestimable advantage to us at this juncture. In God is my trust.

Tuesday 17th February

Bitterly cold at daybreak. Went out a little before 7 a.m. and had a pleasant gallop until 9 a.m. Even up to 10 a.m. the wind in the shade was extremely cold. We have strong winds always with the new moon here. I have been anxious all day as I thought it possible I might hear from Buller today that he had taken *Matammeh*, and a native rumor has been current that he took the place but with heavy loss & that he had been wounded. Just as I was going to sit down to dinner at 7 p.m. letters arrived from *Goubat* from Buller dated 12th instant in which he drew a melancholy description of the position in which he found himself, his steamers worn out, his camels so weak as to be nearly useless, whilst if he dismounted his Camel Regt. to carry provisions on their camels, the men's boots were so worn they [would] not last to *Berber*. The Mahdi had already sent large reinforcements of men, guns and ammunition to *Matammeh* and had left *Khartoum* himself on the 9th instant for that place (I don't believe a word of this report about the Mahdi having started for *Matammeh*). Under these circumstances, & having regard to my instructions to him dated 5th Febry., he meant to evacuate *Goubat* forthwith and retire on *Abu Klea* and *Gakdul*. I am glad of this on the whole, for I have for the last fortnight felt myself to be in an essentially false position with my force split up into two portions and have had many anxious hours in consequence. Of course I hate the notion of falling back from *Goubat*, but as long as I remain there unable to advance and fight the Mahdi I am in an essentially false position & the sooner I get out of it the better. I thought Buller would look upon the capture of *Matammeh* in somewhat more serious light when he came to look at it. I have seen many of these mud villages taken in India where, although the enemy was a poor fellow compared to the Soudanese soldier, we always lost heavily in such attacks. The General of the old school will rub his hands when he hears I have fallen back and I shall be denounced for all the fighting which has led to no result. It was undertaken in order to save Gordon & solely for that purpose: it was always risky to move across this Bayuda desert, but as long as the Mahdi was fully occupied at *Khartoum* I could afford to run a risk in such a cause and for such a prize as the relief of Gordon. With *Khartoum* in the Mahdi's hands my present force is totally inadequate to meet him except under very advantageous circumstances. I hope I make myself clear to your non-military mind. I may still be able to take *Berber*, but if so it must be done by an advance of all my spare troops up the Nile valley. I shall therefore halt Brackenbury when he reaches *Abu Ahmed* & will bring back Buller to *Merawi* from whence he may be able to reach *Abu Ahmed* in time to advance on *Berber* before the really hot season begins.

I have telegraphed this home in a secret despatch to Hartington.[233] It will kill the Govt. I think: I am sorry for Hartington but I have no mercy on that most ignorant of *soi-disant* Statesmen, Mr. Gladstone. He is responsible for Gordon's death and all the bloodshed and horrors attendant upon the fall of Khartoum. For myself I already feel a weight off my mind for which I am grateful to God, and I shall feel another man when I have all the troops now in the desert concentrated in this neighbourhood.

How one month has dissipated all my high hopes! all my visions of fighting a well-contested engagement outside of *Khartoum* and of my riding into that city that same evening and of congratulating my old friend Gordon upon his heroic & magnificent defence of that place, all, all dashed to the ground, and in their place I feel myself obliged to retreat! What a horrible word! and to retreat before a rabble such as that the Mahdi commands! It is a heavy blow to sustain, a heavy punishment to have inflicted upon me. And yet I know it is all for the best. God has something better in store for England or for me which we should not have secured had all gone on as my calculations, based upon Gordon's assurances that he could hold out, led me to hope if not to expect. God's will be done, but it nearly breaks my heart. In my endeavor to save Gordon when Mr. Gladstone had postponed the attempt in the base and silly manner he did, I have lost poor Stewart very badly wounded, possibly never to serve in the field again, and many other gallant [men?] all sacrificed to Mr. Gladstone's hopeless incapacity as a Minister and as a ruler over our affairs.

Wednesday 18th February

Sent off special messenger—an officer[234]—to *Gakdul* with fresh instructions to Wood & Buller, approving of the latter's determination to withdraw from *Goubat*, and desiring him to fall back upon *Merawi* to 'refit' so that if it became possible a little later on, he might follow Brackenbury to *Abu Ahmed* for an advance on *Berber*. If I cannot take *Berber* until the Autumn, I shall leave a garrison of 1000 men in *Abu Ahmed* and collect large quantity of supplies there during the summer to be my advanced depot when I advance in September or October on *Berber*. George is a great comfort to me, as he is a very good Staff officer and is most hard-working and careful. If I determine upon an advance on *Berber* now, Buller might overtake Brackenbury by pushing across the desert from *Birti* to the cataract near *Abu Egli*, which is the route Ismael Pasha followed when he invaded the Soudan to conquer it for Egypt. Letters in the evening from Buller dated *Abu Klea* 15th inst. saying he had evacuated *Goubat* the day before.[235] We have now great difficulty in purchasing good camels, as the natives prefer to hire their good camels & sell us the useless ones only.

Thursday—19th February

Dormer and Grenfell arrived. Zohrab by my orders told the Mudir that we had evacuated *Gakdal*. He is in despair. He cannot realize the position at all & insists that if we had taken *Matammeh* we should have had all the country with us &c. &c. Zohrab evidently agrees—neither of them know what war is when made with troops who can't stand the sun and require pounds of food every day. Hartington has most foolishly entered into a contract for the construction of a Rl.Rd. from *Suakim* to *Berber* on the 4' 8" gauge—(the English standard). Such a line can never be constructed before end of year, whereas a narrow gauge one might. I suppose this is again the advice of Sir Andrew Clarke, R.E. In a telegram[236] to Hartington today I expressed myself strongly on this subject. I fear I shall not be able to arrange for the capture of *Berber* before hot weather sets in as I could not leave with Garrison of that place after I had taken it enough supplies to warrant me in leaving any garrison there at all.

After dinner a letter reached me from Regy Talbot announcing to me in most feeling terms the death of poor Stewart. I feel as if I had lost my right arm in this business & I cannot hope to see his like again. He was out & out the best man I had about me and to all his military acquirements and qualities he added the rare advantage of being a universal favorite and of being the very pleasantest official to do business with. It is at moments like this that a loathing comes over me for war, that science and art in the study and practice of which I have spent my whole life & to which I have devoted all my energies and whatever brain power God has gifted me with. This valuable life is another holocaust on the altar of Mr. Gladstone's self-opinionated ignorance. There are hundreds of men who could rule England better than this overrated talker, but I only know of two or three men fit to fill the void in the list of Generals which my friend Stewart's death has made. So-called statesmen of the Gladstone type can be picked up by the dozen in the debating societies of England but the combination of qualities required to make a leader like Stewart is rarely to be found in any country, even in countries with large standing armies.

Friday 20th February

Oh my child I am half broken-hearted with this campaign. All day long have disagreeable telegrams been coming in. Buller has had the enemy firing into his camp at *Abu Klea* & has lost two men & had had 16 wounded when he wrote on 17th inst. and doubtless has lost many more since then.[237] He has no transport to move his men, so he has to wait until Wood can send him camels.[238] Wood was to send him some today: they cannot reach him until 23rd & he cannot get back to *Gakdul* until 27th instant. Things go from bad to worse, so I have determined to carry out my original proposal to the Government, viz. to concentrate my troops between *Abu Dom* (opposite *Merawi*) and *Abu Gus,* holding the river also from that place via *Dongola* to *Abu Fatmeh*.[239] I have sent express messengers to Brackenbury telling him this, and have informed the Government.[240] Our camels in the desert are so poor & weak they can scarcely carry even light loads, and there is an apparent unwillingness on the part of the Sheiks here today to send out laden camels to *Gakdul*. God help us. But I write this in low spirits & take a gloomy view of things whilst this fit is on me, but I sing & whistle more loudly than usual in my tent so that all near me should think I was light of heart. I am now examining localities for summer camps, as this site has become too foul from use and it is essential we should encamp where the desert comes down to the river. That fellow Webber R.E. begged to see me today and had the coolness to tell me that the education of his children demanded his presence at home. I said he ought to have thought of that before he came out here and that he could only leave this by leaving the Army. I am sorry to see an English Gentleman behave in this way. Primrose has gone into hospital so I have put Dormer in command of this camp for the present. All will I know come right in the end, but in the meantime all the anxiety falls on me. Besides our troops will be a little down in their luck. The prospect of living under tents in the desert during a Soudan Summer is by no means cheery. As long as fighting is ahead our men are all there and as keen as mustard, but a very dull life in the desert under a Soudan Summer is not calculated to make them jolly. They must all feel they have fought hard and all to no purpose. A triumphant enemy who is afraid to fight them follows them up with skirmishes & so insults them.

Saturday 21st Febry.

Rode down the river this morning below *Ambukol* about $1\frac{1}{2}$ miles to look out for a good desert camping ground and found a site which I think will do very well for a moveable Brigade although I sent Sir C. Wilson there last evening & he came back & reported there was no desert on the river in the *Ambukol* neighbourhood. I am having a sketch made of it. Put up a solitary quail—saw some packs of sand grouse, some gulls in the river and some 'Did you do it' plover on the banks during my ride.

    Food for our camels is becoming a great difficulty since the dourra has been cut. I am afraid we shall have much trouble to keep them alive during the summer. Am establishing a water post at 12 mile hill which I shall keep supplied from here with water by means of all the horses I have in camp, both of the Egyptian Cavalry & the 19th Hussars. About 250 soldiers and sailors belonging to the steamers that were at *Matammeh* with some of their Officers reached camp today. Two Circassian officers whom Zohrab Bey knows very well and says are very good soldiers came to see me. Both were quite certain that it would not under any circumstances have been possible for us to have saved Gordon:

that the villains who betrayed him were so implicated & compromised in treason that they feared if the English relieved *Khartoum* Gordon would have them hung [*sic*] as traitors. They said that to several people Gordon has incautiously said, 'Wait until the English arrive! I shall then deal with those who have been disloyal'—that it was our arrival at *Goubat* that made these traitors surrender the place as they were afraid we should reach *Khartoum* & relieve it before they could save themselves. It seems this opinion is largely shared by many of the officers who knew what was going on in *Khartoum*.

How difficult it is to arrive at truth in dealing with Easterns. Both these men said Kashm el Moose was a coward & that many times they had to drag him from his cabin when under a heavy fire; this is the man I have just made a pasha! for his services. These officers tell me I shall have no difficulty in obtaining the services of any number of black soldiers who will gladly leave the Mahdi & join me—I should be very glad to raise a few thousands of such soldiers & I shall do my best to obtain them.

Sunday 22d February

Church parade at 9 a.m. Our little clergyman preached a sermon that he had preached to us already before. This is too bad, especially as it was a poor, weak affair.

There is so much difficulty in getting Buller's troops back from *Abu Klea*, that I am kept in an anxious condition. The fact is Buller did not take proper military precautions on arriving at *Abu Klea* for the protection of his camp. If he had occupied the heights which overlooked his position with a few small posts the enemy could not have harassed him with a distant rifle fire as they did. Buller writes me letters filled with arrant nonsense about marching on *Berber* when he knows our camels cannot enable him to come creditably out of *Abu Klea*.[241] I have however now sent Wood positive orders to vacate the desert posts which are very difficult to keep up and occasion me no end of anxiety. They were established to support the advance across the desert which I made against all my military convictions and solely with a view to saving Gordon if I found him in extremes when my party with Wilson in his steamers reached *Khartoum*. As soon as I found *Khartoum* had fallen, I kept them up hoping at first against hope I might be able to take *Berber*, but as soon as I abandoned all hope of being able to do so the sooner these desert posts could reach me here the better.

English post arrived. I had no heart to write letters in answer but I had to write one to the Queen & to the Duke of Cambridge. My letters contained only platitudes and old news. It is bitter reading this perusal of home letters that were written before the news of *Khartoum* having fallen had reached England. The congratulations with which my letters are filled are like the apples of the Dead Sea: they are indeed gall and wormwood and add to the bitterness of my cup.

Monday, 23d February

Busy all the morning getting my English post off. The weather has suddenly become much hotter: the sun more powerful. Read Gordon's diary all day, a sad employment, but I must read it for the information it contains. A letter from Brackenbury dated 18th instant.[242] I am anxious about my letter of recall reaching him before he goes beyond the spot where Stewart was murdered for I have a horror of retiring before an eastern enemy; they are always more or less easy to tackle when you go at them boldly but they are unpleasant to retreat before. I have told Brack. to get hold of the Sherkook pass before he begins to move his main body.

Tuesday 24th Febry.

Gordon says in Vol. III of his journal at date of 6–10–84 'The appearance of one British Soldier or Officer here settles the question of relief vis-a-vis the towns people for then they know, I have not told them lies.'[243]

At several places in his Journal he speaks very contemptuously of Artillery—under date of 24–9–84 he says—'I can say I owe three defeats in this country to having Artillery with me which delayed our march, & it was the Artillery with Hicks which in my opinion did for him.'[244] Sent off another copy of my instructions to Brackenbury by special messenger from *Abu Dom* and have ordered Rundle at *Korosko* to send one through that desert to him. These Ababdehs show rather an indecision of purpose since the fall of *Khartoum* for the cure of which I must now look to a victory by Graham over Osman Digma. Had a grand function in the evening with the Mudir when I presented him with the Commission signed by the Queen for his Knighthood as K.C.M.G. He wore a most gorgeous uniform as a Pasha with epaulettes & aiguillet[te]s &c. Sheik Saleh was present looking cunning and cruel as usual. I have telegraphed[245] to Baring saying that I think it would be better to make me Governor-General of the Soudan, as all my acts & proclamations would have much greater weight if emanating from the Governor-Genl., than simply from the General in command of H.M.'s Army: besides making me Governor-General would emphasize the inauguration of a new policy. I believe the approaching Soudan war to be a hideous mistake, the outcome of Mr. Gladstone's foolish policy in Egypt, beginning with that wicked, cruel and senseless bombardment of *Alexandria*. As a soldier I was very glad to go to Egypt in 1882 and simply as a soldier nothing could suit me better than this coming autumn campaign in the Soudan, but as an Englishman fully alive to our military weakness, to the almost impossibility of even carrying on the routine duties of peace with our existing Army establishments, I look upon this coming campaign with dislike. The civilian gentlemen who rule from Downing St. are prepared to rush into any war when by doing so they can retain office, and they do it with a light heart on account of their ignorance, but any soldier who knows our Army as I do can only view a serious war with dread, and this war in the Soudan is likely to be the most serious war we have undertaken since the idiotic cabinet of 1854 declared war against Russia. What makes me take this view is that I cannot foresee where this coming war is to end. If the Mahdi be wise he will retreat before we can tackle him seriously: we shall have spent ten millions & done nothing & when we begin to withdraw we shall very likely have a pack of yelping curs at our heels taking long shots at our retreating troops. The prospect is not a pleasing one to me. The relief of *Khartoum* was a definite, well-defined objective, and when it fell I confess if I had been at home I should have recommended the Cabinet to have withdrawn this Army to *Wady Halfa*. Indeed I think even now that would be the wisest course. I would tomorrow willingly say to France either consent to our terms as regards the debt &c. or take over the Govt. of the Country yourselves and send your troops there to relieve ours. As I have over and over told our Authorities, the Cape of Good Hope is a much more important place to us than Egypt. I argued this out with Northbrook last year, but he would not have my arguments. If you want to control the Suez Canal—the control of which I don't care much about if we hold the Cape strongly—you can do so from Cyprus. Make Famagusta a strong port, also Simondstown & clear out of the Soudan & of Egypt as soon as we can. I am sure this is our true policy having regard to the incompetence of our Army owing to its small numbers, and to the fact that we no longer rule any sea not even the English Channel much less the Mediterranean. Radicalism has reduced us to a second-rate power & we either accept the fact or have the courage to put our Army & Navy on a proper footing. This latter Mr. Chamberlain and all other screwmakers & carpet-makers from Birmingham will never consent to. Our effacement as a first-rate power is therefore a necessary and inevitable sequence. These are what the Tories would call unpatriotic sentiments. They look upon England as if [it?] were still the England that Pitt made it, proud of itself and self-confident. Faith had not died out in the Nation. There was a belief then in God and in the power and future destiny of England. Now there is no faith except in money & universal suffrage.

Wednesday 25th February

.... Telegram from Brackenbury dated 21st instant from *Hebeh* the scene of poor Stewart's murder. He had crossed all his force from the left to the right bank of that place, and was to advance towards *Abu Ahmed*—40 miles off—on 22nd (Sunday last).[246] I am afraid there is no chance of his receiving my telegrams of 20th instant before he reaches that place. Perhaps it will be all for the best: my trust is in God: I do my best, I use my judgement to the best of my ability, the rest is in God's hands.

Nothing could have been better than my scheme for the relief of Gordon & of *Khartoum* & yet it failed utterly by about 48 hours. For that 48 hours [word overwritten] Mr. Gladstone is solely at least entirely responsible, and yet I read in Reuter's telegrams that he answers the motion for a vote of censure by appealing to the House for a vote of confidence!! Was there ever such brazen impudence! In the history of England of my day, this loss of time by an ignorant Minister is more certain to leave its mark heavily upon our Army, our resources and out national debt than any event that has occurred since I have been a soldier. Convoy of [? space left] sick and [? space left] wounded arrived in the afternoon at 5 p.m. The weather becoming steadily hotter day by day. Thank heavens I have finished all Gordon's journals today. They are intensely interesting: occasionally the human side of my hero comes out in a little egotism; and he repeats himself continually. But he is not an inspired writer. He was a mortal. And yet if God ever granted the gift of inspiration in our day to men, I know of no one more suited from the purity of his life, his intense faith in God and in Christ, and from what I may call his close communion at all hours of his daily life with his God, to have received such a commission from the Almighty. He trusted in God & yet God allowed him to be murdered, and all his labor & pain, all his self-sacrifice & devotion to duty to go for nought. Until just towards the end of his journal that has come into our possession—14th Decbr. last—he seemed to have always been confident he would be relieved. This is a lesson to me, when I say trust in God and feel He will not forsake me in my difficulties. My faith tells me this, but so it seems to have told Gordon & yet he died just as his safety was almost secured to him. God's wrongs are not as ours and are to us inscrutable. Abraham is commended all through the scripture because of his extreme faith in God which induced him to draw his knife to slay his son when ordered by the Almighty to do so. But then in his case, God, having proved and tested his faith, rewarded him for his faith and spared his son. In Gordon's case, the aid so near at hand was prevented from reaching him & he was murdered.

Thursday 26th February

Much warmer today. I dread to think of the ordeal our men have before them. We have no knowledge of how the heat of summer may affect them. This makes me intensely anxious. Oh how I long for the Autumn. May God preserve their health during the coming summer. A note at midnight to say that Buller had sent in Kasm-el-Moose to *Gakdul* which place he reached on 25th instant with a message from Buller to say that all his column would be at *Gakdul* today. My mind is now quite at ease on that score. I have sent messengers to Brackenbury across the *Korosko* desert telling him to come back to *Merawi* for the summer. I expect he reached *Abu Ahmed* yesterday if there was no fighting, but today if the enemy attempted to defend it. I have asked to be made Governor-General of the Soudan, but I suppose old Granville will funk taking even that step. Attached to Gordon's journal are many letters & papers of various sorts, amongst them a long epistle from Mahmond Ahmed (the Mahdi) telling Gordon of Stewart's murder and describing all the cypher books and papers that were taken in Stewart's baggage. From them he learnt how much corn there was in the Stores and the number of rounds of ammunition Gordon had still in his magazine. How foolish of Gordon to have given all this information in clear. He should have above all things left his cypher books & sent out all his information in cypher. I learn from the Pasha who had command of the steamers at *Goubat*, that no powder was made in *Khartoum*, but that there was a limited quantity in store there. None & no percussion caps had been sent there from Egypt for the last three years, and as they had no machinery for pressing the used cartridge cases before refilling them, many of these when refilled would not fit into the chamber of the rifle. We know already that a large number of their cartridges won't explode. If you visit a spot where the enemy have fired much, you will find not only the empty cartridge cases, but also numbers of filled ones on the cap of which you can see the mark of the striker showing they had been tried but would not go off.

Friday 27th February 1885

. . . . Had a telegram at last from *Abu Dom* containing Brackenbury's message[247] from a camp about 16 miles above where poor Stewart was murdered in which he acknowledges receipt of my orders of 20th inst. desiring him to fall back on *Merawi*. Thank God, for I had almost given up the hope of stopping him before he engaged the enemy at *Abu Ahmed*, and any lives lost there would have been thrown away since I have resolved upon not holding that place during the summer. I shall now be able to concentrate my troops where I can afford to laugh at the Mahdi and all his following. God has been merciful to me in this matter. The Mudir says that by an expenditure of £30,000 he can secure the Mahdi. I have told him I will pay that amount whenever the Mahdi is brought a prisoner into my camp. He says he will produce him here in 40 days—nous verrons—I don't however believe a word of it. It would be the best spent £30,000 ever expended by this Govt. if I could catch this villain and send him to keep Arabi company in prison. News is that Buller and all his column have reached *Gakdul*: he was to leave for *Korti* this morning, so we may have him here tomorrow night.

I am so grieved for poor Valentine Baker:[248] he had just lost his eldest daughter, and he now telegraphs to say his wife is dead. She was the best of wives to him, and heaven knows she had many trials to put up with on his account. The Mudir's troops near *Dugehyet* have had a skirmish with some Hassineahs and seem to have had the worst of it.

Saturday 28th February

.... Letter from Buller in which he acknowledges the justice of the 'pot' I gave him in one of my letters[249] where I pointed out the 'stuff' he was writing to me about a forward movement to *Berber* when he said his men had no boots and his camels were unable to carry, in fact when he knows full well that the move was entirely beyond our powers.

March 1885

Sunday 1st March

Divine service as usual. English post in early—sad reading the papers: what stuff they contain! It is really curious that men should be found capable of writing the nonsense that has been written about our doings here. It is not that non-military writers jumble up strategy & tactics, not having any conception of what these words mean. I am astonished to see letters and articles from men about our movements in which the movement of 5000 men here or there is referred to as if the Soudan had no deserts and was as well provided with roads and railways as Belgium & as rich in farm produce as Yorkshire. Men discuss the march of a force from *Suakim* to *Berber* as they would of marching from *Aldershot* to *Plymouth*. Camels are referred to as if they were as plentiful as rabbits are in Richmond Park, as if they required no food and never required rest and never died. I feel certain that all the force we employ this coming autumn will have to come to *Berber* by the Nile route, for I don't believe in the Suakim–Berber railway having any direct influence upon our military operations. Its construction will have a strong indirect bearing upon the Soudan question, for it will show the people we mean to stay here at least for some time.

Buller arrived; the sun had made him more ugly than usual —as argumentative as ever—he is right and everyone else is wrong.

I had a review of all the rag-tag and . . . bob-tail that were in

Gordon's four steamers—I never saw such a lot of men—a large proportion of them of the lowest type, many, very little above the monkey in brain development. Gordon does not speak of them in complimentary terms in his journal. I was told on good authority, that when going to *Khartoum* the other day in one of the two steamers that took Wilson's party, a child began to cry and make a noise: one of these scarcely-human creatures standing by took it up and threw it overboard. I made them a speech through an interpreter and told them we meant to stay here if necessary for a hundred years, but we meant to go to *Khartoum* and destroy the Mahdi's power there. I told them that any promises made to them by Gordon would be religiously carried out by me &c. &c. Much hotter today.

Monday 2nd March

.... This has been the hottest day we have had yet. Out riding in the evening one felt a regular hot current of air on one's face. Brackenbury's column ought to be at *Merawi* and Wood here, with everyone from *Gakdul* about the 10th or 11th instant.

Tuesday 3rd March

Deliciously cool about 4 & 5 a.m. yet during the day the heat was very great. We had the first touch of the Kamseen wind which was as if from a furnace. Kashm el Moose arrived—an amiable old man, very black. I made him a pasha which has pleased him very much. In nearing *Korti* about midnight, he fired off some of his rifles. Captn. [J.C.K.] Fox 19th Hussars was at that hour on his way out to our first water post, his English servant alone with him. As they ... neared 12 mile hill where this post is, he saw firing and heard shouting: thinking the post was attacked he came back here in all haste, reported this to the Chief of the Staff who told him to mount his detachment (about 70 troopers) and start off for the post supposed to be attacked. You can imagine the jeers with which they were received when they scouted cautiously up to 12 mile hill about daybreak....

Wednesday 4th March

Rode with Buller to inspect a village above this as a quarter for troops. I should prefer putting my men into well-built villages to housing them in straw huts provided the villages were fairly clean & surrounded with desert on three sides, the fourth being the river. There is a difference of opinion on this subject amongst the doctors: my experience is the doctors are humbugs and almost always wrong. They take up a fad, and ride it to death until some other doctor starts a new theory, when it is universally adopted by the profession although diametrically opposite to the theory upon which they had been previously acting. Letters from Wood of 2nd inst., & from Brackenbury of 1st inst. The former hoped to clear out of *Gakdul* today & the latter to be at *Abu Dom* on the 6th instant. . . . A curious theory seems to be very generally believed amongst the enemy as regards Stewart's fight at *Abu Klea*. They assert that we opened our square to let them in & then closed in on them killing everyone who entered the trap. I am glad to say that all who did get in, left their bodies there, so the result bears out this Arab theory.

I received yesterday from Hartington[250] a question which had been asked him in Parliament & desiring me to answer at once. It was a silly question about Buller filling in the wells at *Abu Klea* before he retired from that post. I shall not reply until asked again & then I shall refuse to answer & say that I appeal to the good sense of the House of Commons (very little of it to spare in that assemblage) and of the English people (who are mostly fools) to protect me against questions which can or could only be answered with authority to the injury of this army &c. &c. I shall be curious to learn the result of my appeal. 69 sick and wounded arrived here today, they are the last to come in from the desert column.

I shall soon begin my plans for the Autumn: they will be based on the hope that I may be able to move forward with a column from *Hamdab* on the 15th Septr. . . .

Thursday 5th March

Brackenbury reached *Merawi* today—all doing well. The last three days have been extremely hot, making me rejoice more and more that I did [not?] move upon *Berber*. The men coming in from *Gakdul* will feel this heat extremely. The convoy of sick & wounded that arrived yesterday buried seven coming here which I attribute entirely to this great heat which has suddenly jumped upon us. I rode at 6 a.m. this morning about 7 miles down the river & decided upon a site at *Tani* for Dormer's Brigade to encamp on. . . . We have not heard lately from *Khartoum*. Dormer & a company of the Essex go there (to *Tani*) tomorrow, to begin laying out the camp and collecting hutting materials. The flies are beginning to be again a horrible torment and the hot weather seems to have brought out scorpions in some numbers. I can foresee an unusually disagreeable summer.

Friday 6th March 1885

. . . . Some very disingenuous telegrams yesterday about my extension of Halfa Railway in which I recognize Andrew Clarke's style. I have refused to give detailed information asked for but have said that unless extension asked for is carried out, autumn campaign cannot take place.

This has been a diabolical day; clouds of dust with high wind so that water party could not find 12 mile hill.

Saturday 7th March 1885

. . . . The Naval Brigade & the Artilly. with reserve Ammunitn. arrived from *Gakdul*. Great amusement in camp at Mr. Gladstone's answer in the House when questioned about our doings with Russia; he said his policy would be 'a national one'. We have come to a pretty pass, when it becomes necessary for the Cabinet to assure us that it will act on national lines.

Russia evidently imagines we are so hopelessly committed to a big business here that she can afford to invade Affghanistan and do what she likes on our Indian frontiers. How small the Duke of Argyle [*sic*] and all that silly lot who poohpoohed Rawlinson[251] and all the Military Party for their believe [belief?] that Russia had designs either on Affghanistan or India: no terms were too abusive to be heaped on the heads of the unfortunate soldier who pointed out the danger, & to obtain the sobriquet of a 'Russiaphobist' was to be regarded as an idiot by the *Daily News*, the Duke of Argyle [*sic*], and all that lot who consider every man a fool who differs from them. I wish I could see my way out of this Soudan business quickly, for with our small military resources I don't like the idea of having us tied down to military operations at this great distance from the sea-board, the duration or magnitude or extent of which I am unable to estimate. I wrote home by last post to Brett, pointing this out, and I hope he may show my letter to Hartington. What I recommend is coming to terms with Turkey and paying the Sultan well to take over this Soudan. It is not a noble policy, but a nation that has lost its military spirit and forsaken Empire for the Caucus & party politics, with an inferior Navy and an Army that is ridiculous in numbers cannot afford to be proud. We must soon give up reminding the world of military and naval achievements in the past, for I know of nothing more ridiculous than a weak, timid people living upon its ancient renown. Who has not turned from the cowardly & ignoble modern Greek who swaggered about Salamis or Thermopalae? And so the world will soon begin to laugh at us when we refer to the destruction of the Spanish Armada, Blenheim, Trafalgar & to Waterloo. No nation can exist in power & obtain the respect of others which strives to live on the virtues of its people in past generations in order to shirk the responsibilities of the present. The game is too well known and won't pass current.

Sunday—8th March

Talbot and the Heavies arrived. They have lost 100 men killed and wounded during this short campaign.[252] I shall send them down to the neighbourhood of *Fatmeh* or rather *Hannek* to refit. I hear the men are done up, morally and physically. This is however only Buller's story and I take his statements on such subjects with some reserve. I am to see them on parade tomorrow. Brackenbury with his Nile Column arrived: he has become a little consequential since he has assumed the role of a commander.[253] His men are very fit. I went to see his wounded in the evening: all doing well except one poor fellow who had his leg off. Inspected the Naval Brigade & Canadian Voyageurs—made a speech to each. Gave a silver cigarette case to Mr. Benbow as a present from myself to mark my high appreciation of the valuable services he rendered when he mended the steamer's boiler under fire. He seemed highly pleased. Today has been pleasant and by no means overpoweringly hot. The Mudir started in his steamer for *Merawi*.

Divine Service in the morning. English post of 13th ultimo arrived in forenoon. South Staffordshires went down to its new encampment about 7 miles from this, where hutting has been already begun. The place where the camp is to be is named *Tani*.

Monday 9th March

The Guards and Light Camel Regt. arrived. I inspected the Cornwall Lt. Infy. & Gordon Highlanders: Brack. in command of the parade and in his glory. He is an excellent officer & now on the high road to advancement. Indeed unless he be shot in the Autumn the hatred of H.R.H. cannot keep him back any longer: I shall have him made a Majr.-Genl. whether H.R.H. likes it or not....

Tuesday 10th March

Inspected the Light and Heavy Cavalry Camel Regts. at 7 a.m. Their turn out was very good. It blew hard last night, and we have had a great deal of dust during the day. The Hd. Qtrs. of the Sussex Regts, arrived & the Heavies left in boats in the evening for their summer quarters near *Hannek* cataract. At 8 p.m. a sing song in Essex Regt. camp.

Wednesday 11th March

Baring telegraphs[254] that Egyptian war minister expects a rising at *Dongola* shortly—I don't....

In my morning ride into the desert I met the Hd. Quarters & wing of Rl. Irish and the remaining two guns R.A. By degrees I am getting in Wood's force, but it comes in slowly. Inspected the Guards' Camel Regt. It looked very well on parade. They start tomorrow for *Dongola*. George started for *Abu Gus* which he is to command for the summer.

News from home very warlike: in fact we seem to be all but at war with Russia. Nearly all our Newspaper Correspondents have now left: on the whole they have been a good lot this time and we have been on very good terms with them.

Poor Major Gough who was wounded in the head at *Abu Klea* has never been the same since although he has returned to duty and insisted on assuming command of his Regt. Buller had a turn-up with him when he was in desert, & now Wood has suspended him from duty & sent him in here. I wrote him as nice a letter as I could under the circumstances saying the public service must come first before all other considerations: as these two General officers had so reported to me I must send him home, as it was evident that since his wound, he was not in a fit state to have command of a Regt. . . . Poor fellow, I am extremely sorry for him. I shall send him home on a medical certificate.

Yesterday I wound up a telegram [255] to Baring—through whom I correspond to the Foreign Office—in these words, 'Please tell Ld. Granville I cannot wait any longer: I must issue proclamation & will do so on my own responsibility if I do not receive answer to this by 14th instant.' I think this tone & style of language will make old Pussy Cat 'Sit-Up': I don't suppose his diplomatic ears ever heard such dictation before, but then he has not had to deal much with soldiers before. How long will the country be satisfied to allow their foreign affairs to be in such weak, old and palsied hands.

Mildmay Wilson[256] of the Scots Gds. dined with me, and as I know him to be a good sensible man with plenty of nerve & pluck, I gently drew him out on the subject of the delay in sending the steamers to *Khartoum*, It seems there were about four hours lost in moving the square forward to the river. The camels were laden several times & every preparation made for marching upon the Nile, but as often were counter-orders issued.

Kasm el Moose with 4 steamers arrived at *Goubat* about 9 a.m. on 21st Jany. & the two steamers might have started that afternoon for *Khartoum*: instead of doing so they did not start until 8 a.m. on the 24th Janry. and then only went a few miles (about 13) when they halted for the night to take in wood although they had plenty on board.

Sir Charles Wilson is clearly responsible for all those delays, but poor devil he had lost any nerve he ever possessed: *Abu Klea* did for him in that respect: he must never again be employed on active service: the Irish Survey is better suited to men of his mettle. It is too dreadful though to think of the fearful consequences that have resulted from his unfitness. He could have reached *Khartoum* quite easily on the 25th Janry. & had he done so, Gordon would still—in all human probability—be still alive.

Great God, it is too dreadful to dwell upon the hairbreadth by which we failed to save Gordon & *Khartoum*. I still think if Stewart had not been wounded, we should have saved *Khartoum*. Is it then to be wondered at that I hate the sight of Sir C. Wilson? I have asked that he may be recalled as wanted for his Survey, and when he goes, I hope I may never see him again. He is one of those nervous, weak, unlucky creatures that I hate having near me on active service: yet he is clever.[257]

In looking back now, I feel the greatest strain I have ever had on my nervous system was the interval of seven days between the date when I received the news of *Abu Klea* and that of the fight on the 19th Janry. (the 21st & 28th Janry.) I have led three storming parties, and have had many a bad quarter of an hour of intense suspense since I have been a General but all this is nothing when compared to those seven days. This was all Sir C. Wilson's fault; he ought to [have?] sent me news on morning of 20th Janry.

To me now, if I were to judge of all this by any very finite reason I should bemoan my bad luck and be miserable over it. I do denounce Gladstone for all that has occurred, but yet I feel as certain as I can be of anything that all this is ordered for the best. It may be the beginning of the waking up of England, and it may oblige us to assume such responsibilities that the old National spirit which made us great, may be reproduced. There is no price too dear to pay for such a boon. Let us suffer, so that men & women may learn that the English people have a grander destiny than that of acquiring riches in order that we may live, steeped to the lips in luxury & effeminate living. It is only a great war with all its ups & downs that can make men of us again.

Tuesday 12th March

Stanley Clarke, who is quite useless as a soldier, asked to have a few minutes' conversation with me. I was in my tub, having come in from my morning ride, when he presented himself. Told him to wait a few minutes, which gave me time to think of what I should say for I guessed he wanted to go home. Of course this was it, a great deal of bosh about his position about H.R.H. My blood began to boil and I could not formulate an answer as I had intended. I am most anxious to get rid of him as he is quite useless. I blurted out 'of course you know that any man who now goes home shall never serve under me again.' Then I remembered how advantageous it would be to the Army to get rid of him, so I told him to write to the Prince on the subject. The result will be that I shall get rid of him, and I shall never have to suffer him again as an officer under my command. He is worse than useless.

A telegram from Baring saying that Zebehr's sons have left *Cairo* and gone no one knows where. Another just in to say the rumor was a mistake. The father is however at *Alexandria* and may bolt at any moment. I have again today[258] urged his arrest & the arrest of all his family. Granville wants explanations—what is it we accuse him of &c. &c.—my answer is 'war cannot be carried on in this shilly-shally way & on these Rosewater principles.' I feel that I shall yet have a row with Granville & Co. before I have done with them. I am at this moment master of the position & will for the nonce at least have my own way. I am afraid that inaction for five or six months of summer will however reduce my power—I can do nothing to tickle the English people in that time, and consequently with the usual fickleness and unreasoning impatience of the mob, they will get tired of me and of my preparations.

The Guards' Camel Regt. left at 4 p.m. for *Dongola*.

In the evening a telegram from Baring transmitting one from Granville saying that military necessities required Zebehr's arrest: that he was to be put on board a Man-of-War and kept there until further orders. This means that all the responsibility of the arrest is to fall on me. I don't mind—rather like it.

A warm day.

Wood is at last at *Hawayet*. I find that since the 1st of this month I have sent him out over 900 camels, and yet he is not satisfied. He is a very puzzle-headed fellow in all arrangements connected with movement of troops.

Friday 13th March

Rode to Dormer's camp about $6\frac{1}{2}$ miles down the river from my camp and inspected the South Stafford & the four guns of Egyptian Battery. Buller was with me and as we rode along we discussed the price of Native labor. He dilated upon how *he* found upon arriving at *Korti*, that Stewart had mismanaged the matter & how *he* had put it right. Really the vanity of men like Buller & Wood and a host of other good men is quite curious: also the extreme jealousy one of the other. Buller has always evinced the most extreme jealousy of Stewart: now Stewart was much the better man of the two all round, although Buller has some excellent military qualities. Buller never loses a chance of crabbing Stewart's ability and making out that he was constantly wrong.

I received a '*most confidential*' telegram[259] from Hartington explaining that the position with Russia in Affghanistan is so critical that it is not at present expedient to issue my proclamation or to make me Governor-General of Soudan. It goes on to ask my views as to how the present security of my force & power of ultimately advancing on *Khartoum* would be affected if Graham's force were sent on to India before or after defeat of Osman Digma. I am sending home a long answer that will cost as a cypher telegram a long price, protesting against such a course. I point out the absurdity of contemplating a war with Russia when the question of removing or retaining about 5000 soldiers at *Suakim* becomes a matter of serious national importance. If we are to have a war with Russia I have recommended a bold national policy of carrying on both wars at the same time, to call out the Reserve &c. &c. But my sincere and heart-felt advice is to pay the Sultan well to send an Army of 30,000 men here at once, & he may be inclined to agree as the destruction of Mahmond Ahmed is more important for him than for all the other reigning houses put together.

Saturday 14th March

My telegram was not got off until midnight but it will be in time for today's Cabinet. I told them Graham's force *must* crush Osman Digma: that my position here 1400 miles from the sea would be a dangerous one if the people for a moment thought I was not strong and that I did not intend to destroy the Mahdi in the autumn. . . . [One line inked over.] The withdrawal of Graham's force might oblige me to fall back on *Dongola* and *Hannek*.

During my early ride this morning met the remaining companies of Rl. Irish and the Hd. Qtrs. of the West Kent. I expect Wood with the Mounted Infry. and remaining odds & end[s] of posts in desert here tomorrow.

The news from home looks as if Russia would settle the Affghan business for the time being, getting something out of us however for her 'moderation'. It will do us as a Nation good and open the eyes of silly men like the Duke of Argyle, Grant Duff[260] and all that set who have hitherto believed in Russia and pooh-poohed the soldiers who warned the nation that she was making every military preparation for giving us trouble in India. . . .

Evelyn Wood turned up in the evening looking very well.[261] I am sorry to say Wardrop is not at all well. This camp is becoming very foul with smells of dead camels. We have had Col. White[262] of the Essex Regt. as Commandt. here & a more useless man it would be difficult to imagine. The two Lt.-Colonels of the Cornwall L.I. are both useless & I have requested officially that the Commd. of the Battn. may be given to an officer from [sentence not finished. .]

I have for some time urged the arrest of Zebehr, but Granville has asked for proof of guilt &c. &c. Baring has behaved very well in the support he has always given on these points. A few days ago I telegraphed, the time had arrived when this arrest could not be any longer postponed: at last it has come to pass for he was arrested today & put on board an English man-of-war: arrest was made quite quietly. I hope some interesting papers may be found in his house. As soon as Osman Digma has been disposed of, I hope to make several other arrests. It is only by these sudden arrests & search for papers we can really do much here. When we advance in the autumn it may be necessary to hang a few head men.

I have been out of wine in my mess for the last two months: lime juice and water and whiskey and water being our only drink —no one misses the wine.

Sunday 15th March 1885

Divine service at 7 a.m. I go as a matter of form, but it is painful to see a beautiful liturgy made such a dead uninteresting form of. These clergymen we get in the army seem to have no tact, no idea of human nature and to think that all they have to do is to read over the morning service and preach the first nonesense [*sic*] that comes into their heads: today the sermon was about St. John in *Patnos*, nine-tenths of the listeners knowing nothing and caring less about St. John and his doings and having no idea of what *Patnos* is or was or where it is.

The English post of the 20th Febry. arrived at 11 a.m. The conduct of that old rascal Gladstone going to see a burlesque when the sad news from here had reached him, shows him in his true light. Surely the greatest punishment God can inflict on a nation is to make it believe a lie or to have faith in a lying ruler like Gladstone. We are being severely punished for believing in him. But the nation deserves punishment for believing in such charlatans.

Wardrop returned not at all well but I hope a few days' rest may set him up again.

Monday—16th March

As I see in the papers that the Egyptian war fund is again being opened I telegraphed in our private cypher to Loo telling her to subscribe £100 in her own name. English post left. Mounted Infry. marched in clearing out everything from the desert. At last my little army is, thank God, concentrated on the Nile and ready for any number of Mahdis now.[263]

The messenger who arrived here yesterday from *Omdurman* says Mahmond Ahmed is still there but that he is in trouble in *Khordofan* and especially at *Obeid* to which place he had been sending off troops. Natives as a rule do not much mind flies, but this messenger seemed more struck with the vast quantities of flies round the rebel camp than by anything else about it. If you wished a drink of water, you were obliged to drink out of the nozzle of your water bottle. Food was very dear, and large numbers were ill, many had died. Poor Gordon's head was in a tree. I am sending this man back with a companion either to buy or to steal it: I think I shall get it.

Inspected the Rl. Irish & the West Kent in the evening, also the Battery of screw guns. These two Battalions marched past as well as I have ever seen any march past at Aldershot. I always tell the men the same, it was not their fault that we were not into *Khartoum* in time to save Gordon. That old crocodile Gladstone in making his statement about Egypt, never said one nice thing about the exertions made by the Army that has struggled so hard to make up for his folly and want of statesmanship.

This infernal Mudir is giving me trouble again: it is difficult to make him out. He was received with all honor at *Abu Dom* by Butler and yet is very insolent in his letters to Butler & will not give him the supplies he wants for his camels or the materials he requires for the men's huts.[264] He is the vainest fanatic I have ever had to deal with. I shall now threaten him with the withdrawal of my troops from *Abu Dom*: this will frighten him for he knows he could not keep his own troops in that neighbourhood if we withdraw.

A private telegram from Swaine through the War Office advising me in arranging for the summer quarters of my troops to take into consideration the likelihood of a change of policy on the part of the Govt. I have always regarded this as *very* possible indeed, almost probable....

Tuesday 17th March—St. Patrick's Day

Fortunately there is no intoxicating drink to be had in camp, or we should have all the Rl. Irish drunk this evening. Telegram from Baring asking for my opinion on Ld. Granville's proposal to declare all the Slaves in the Soudan free!! What idiots there are in high places. A telegram[265] from Hartington saying my despatch in which I describe Wilson's proceedings when en route from *Goubat* to *Khartoum* & back casts a slur upon Sir C. Wilson & that he cannot publish it until Wilson has had a chance of rebutting the slur. The fact is, I pass no comment whatever upon Wilson, but my despatch shows up the Govt. very strongly & the Cabinet does not therefore wish it published. I have replied, I did not see how despatch blamed Wilson & that I wished it published in justice to myself & to those under my command. Several of my recent despatches will be disagreeable reading to Govt. and I must have them published in vindication of my reputation as a General and of this Army the men of which have done all that men could do to carry out my plans. I foresee some trouble with Hartington on this score.

The Prince of Wales telegraphs that Clarke must remain here as his return home would be misinterpreted. I cannot sanction this, as he is unfit for command, & his application to go home at such a time as this shows he is entirely deficient and wanting in all soldierlike instincts or feelings. All he came here for was that he wanted to obtain an English medal or decoration as he had a number of foreign ones which he had not the cheek to wear as he had never obtained any in his own country. He did not hesitate to say this to several [. . . ?]. I had been casting about in my mind for some time for some excuse to get rid of him, when blessed moment he came & asked to go home to his beloved Marlborough House. Having thus got him on the hip I am not likely to lose the advantage I have gained.

What a clever old rascal Gladstone is to give the Gordon family £20,000. He hopes thus to influence them about the publication of Gordon's diary. Gordon's diary is one great denunciation of Gladstone and all his works and if published at length wd. be very damaging to the Govt. Hence this liberality on the part of this 'Great, original Machiavelli': he thinks he has squared the family—*for his time*, after that he has no care for anything.

Inspected the Sussex Regt. & the Mounted Infantry in the evening. A horrible day of hot wind and clouds of dust.

Wednesday 18th March

Started on a camel at 5.30 a.m. for *Abu Dom* (opposite *Merawi*) taking with me Buller & his A.D.C. Lord something FitzGerald, Zohrab Bey & Arthur. Seven hours very pleasant going over the desert brought us to our destination. Butler who commands at *Abu Dom* came out to meet me.[266] He is quite happy having to create a station, hut his troops, & being in command has restored his equanimity. He is doing very well. Of course there is the usual 'Didn't I tell you so?' No prophetic almanack editor ever professed such powers of prediction as to future events as Butler does. Butler however never gives anyone the benefit of his predictions until after the events have occurred, but he evidently thinks he has published them years or at least months before. He is really a good fellow with all his inaccuracy of statement and other failings for which Irishmen are well-known but with all the quick vivid imagination and all those pleasant sympathies with his fellow man, all the quickness and wit and other good qualities for which Paddy is celebrated. He has Paddy's faults in an ordinary degree, but he has all his good qualities, talents & virtues to overflowing; in fact he is gifted far above the ordinary Irishman & that means that the Englishman & the Scotchman are stupid and uninteresting mortals when placed beside him. He makes me very angry at times, but I always like him: his faults are more amusing & less objectionable than the virtues of many men.

The camp here is on the desert which comes down directly to the river: it is very healthy. There is a very nice little mud fort with flanking towers close to the river, recently built by the Mudir's orders. Butler is constructing mud huts for his men.[267] I saw the Black Watch and the other troops that form Butler's force in the evening on parade. All looked healthy and well turned out.

The Mudir is at *Dugayet* where he is collecting a large force of all his odds and ends to begin some campaign, where I know not. On the road today I overtook several parties of armed men all en route to join him. It blew hard from the north all day, and travelling was in consequence very pleasant.

Thursday 19th January [March ?]

Started on a camel at 5.30 a.m. for *Korti*. Had a little breakfast before we left. Reached my camp in eight hours, the camels being a little tired. I make the distance to be 30 miles, good. My face and especially my nose burnt very sore by reflected heat from the desert for the sun never touched them. Last night it blew extremely hard, and this morning when I woke—I had slept in my clothes & boots—I had to put on an overcoat. At *Merawi*—opposite *Abu Dom*—is a curious hill that has been scarped towards the river and temples cut into it. Round the base of this rock once stood the great city of *Meroe* ruled over by Queen Candyce when the Romans attacked and utterly destroyed it. There are many ruins I am told there, avenues of Sphinxes, temples &c. There are also several pyramids, but of different proportions from those in Egypt, these being much taller in proportion to their base. I had not time to cross the river to explore the place as I should like to have done. I advised Butler to apply to the British Museum to ask for funds to make excavations: he would do the work well, & the occupation would add to his local interests. He has constructed a little square redoubt on high ground near his camp to command the ground around; when working at the redoubt it was found the site had been that of a temple: in fact the counterscarp on one face of the work is the wall of the temple.

The river has fallen so low that our steam pinnaces have now to be worked between *Hannek* & *Merawi* in three or four stages, there being three barriers over which they cannot pass with safety.

I enjoyed my two days' outing very much: it was so pleasant being away from our camp and in the bright clear desert. The desert of sand such as that around *Ismaillia* and behind *Dongola* and at many other points where there is no vegetation, no trees, nothing but sand and burnt rocks is dismal and dreary and fatiguing to the eye, but when it is hard and fairly level, good going for camels with plenty of bushes and trees and tufts of grass to be seen at intervals, it is very fascinating to me. One seems to inhale vigor and youth and health; its solemn stillness is curious and affects me agreeably. In a forest one can never be quite certain of being alone; the very trees seem to watch you and listen if you sing or speak aloud, but in the desert you realize the complete solitude until it becomes almost something that had length and breadth, that was almost tangible. These Arabs who for centuries have lived in it could if they liked settle down in houses along the Nile, but the desert has a charm for them, dirty filthy creatures as they are.

Friday 20th March 1885

Had a pleasant ride in the desert in the morning. Primrose and a number of others left in the 'Lotus' for England—Colonel Clarke amongst others. I had an unpleasant interview with him yesterday, which I believe I felt more than he did. I told him he did not come up to the mark & must therefore go home. I think he does not care in the least as long as he gets home. He is no soldier & I was a fool to have brought him out at all. . . .

The robber whom we have had prisoner since poor Stewart's first march into the desert was released today being well paid for having acted as a guide upon several occasions. In going away I promised him $40,000 if he would make Mahmond Ahmed prisoner and bring him to me. He said that with his friends—he is an Hassineah—he would try to do so. I don't believe in their [*sic*] being any chance of getting hold of this villainous false prophet by any such means but Major Turner[268] who now is my best Intelligence Officer thinks the chances are good, so I make these promises to please him.

This infernal Mudir is giving me trouble again. I have done all a man can do to make him work cordially with me, but it is of no use. He telegraphs to me now that he wishes to resign his appointment and bring numerous charges against Colonel Butler & other Commandants of stations. I have told him in reply that I am astonished and pained by his telegram, the contents of which I will discuss with him when he reaches *Dongola*.

Saturday 21st March

Deliciously cool night & cold morning: two blankets over me at daybreak. Graham had a skirmish yesterday[269] & lost a few men. He sends me a telegram today enumerating all the branches of the service & saying they are all heroes. He is beginning too soon with this 'butter' and will leave himself nothing to say by and by when he has had a tough, stand-up fight.

Sunday 22nd March 1885

Another fight in the *Suakim* neighbourhood.²⁷⁰ In the first one where Graham himself was present there seems to have been considerable confusion & greater loss of life than there should have been. Graham telegraphs today saying that Croppy Ewart is responsible for the loss owing to the very bad way in which he handled his cavalry. The fact is that cavalry charges except when the enemy is broken & running away are a mistake with these Arabs.

In today's fight McNiell was commanding, and although it seems to have taken place without about six miles of *Suakim*, he seems to have been surprised when making his yeriba & to have lost heavily especially in transport. This is not a good beginning. Graham has requested me to withhold the rank of Brigr. General from Ewart which I had telegraphed he might confer upon him.

English post in. I find that the by-no-manner-of-means wise man Northbrook when speaking in the House of Lords described Sir C. Wilson as my 'Political' officer. A more misleading statement it would be difficult to imagine. I am writing to Lord Hartington by this post about this matter....²⁷¹

Monday 23rd March 1885

Busy writing all the morning for the English post which closed here at noon. McNiell's loss yesterday was about 150.²⁷² He seems to have been entirely surprised which is not creditable to him. I telegraphed today to Graham desiring him to use his Cavalry when columns move & to scout the country round them in all directions.

The Merawi Vakeel—the little Circassian—arrived here yesterday in the Mudir's steamer with a message from that worthy to the effect that the position below the Dugayet cataract was a very bad one & that if my troops would not support him in the event of his being attacked his people must fall back. I have told him to do so, but to hold *Tangaeri* and also place a small post somewhere about halfway between that place and *Korti*. To hold *Debbeh* with at least 400 soldiers. I shall continue to have troubles & difficulties with this Mudir fellow until I can speak to him with the authority of Governor-General. I have begged him to send raiding parties into the desert to pounce on the Hassaneeah cattle &c., but it is impossible to say what any of these fellows will do, you can never count upon their obeying any order given to them by anyone who does not mean to kill them if they fail to obey.[273]

I have today had the most corroborative evidence of what I had previously ascertained regarding the details of poor Gordon's death. One of the messengers who took in a letter from me to Gordon in returning with an answer was caught and put in chains at *Omdurman*. There he remained until early in January when he contrived to escape into *Khartoum*. There he again saw Gordon & told him all that had befallen him. Gordon said never mind, the English will soon be here and you can then go back in safety to your family. On the 17th January Gordon made a great sortie to the South and inflicted great loss on the enemy, having about 200 killed on his side. When the enemy were admitted into *Khartoum* all the inhabitants were in bed. The scoundrel of a Pasha who betrayed the place was killed by the Mahdi's orders. Gordon was killed at the door of his palace: he was shot but then pierced with many spears. He saw Gordon's head cut off & taken to the Mahdi. All the Turks & Shaggeahs surrendered and having given up their arms were at once killed. The Soudanese soldiers were taken as prisoners to the Mahdi. The townspeople were nearly starving when the place was betrayed. Dhourra was selling at about [blank space] the Ardeb*, and meat could scarcely be had at any price. He managed to cross the Blue Nile and when waiting there to find an Arab who would hire him a camel he saw our two steamers come up the river firing on the rebels & being fired at by them.

There is a rumor today from a very unreliable source that the Mahdi has been killed.

I inspected the 19th Hussars in the evening. They turned out in a most creditable manner....

Evelyn Baring begins to be in a funk about the preservation of peace in lower Egypt: the fact is, for economical reasons, he has reduced the Army & the police to such an extent that he is not now able to dispense with the attenuated Army for police duties. I cannot dispense with the Army on my line of communications or with its assistance in extending the Rl.Road to *Firket* and I shall wash my hands of all responsibility as to the success of the autumn campaign if this be forced on me. He proposes to supply me with civil laborers for Railway works: my answer is that even if

---

*A unit of dry measure used in Egypt and Moslem countries varying from $\frac{1}{2}$ peck to $7\frac{1}{2}$ bushels.

liberally furnished it would not be equivalent to labor provided by Battalions of well-fed stout Egyptian soldiers well-disciplined & working under their own officers. That completion of railway extension in time fixed up, depends upon having Egyptian Army & that Autumn campaign cannot be attempted without that railway. I found only one Battn. in Egypt upon my arrival last Autumn. I now propose to have two there: I can do no more & these are my last words. Baker has the power to obtain as many men as he wants by conscription and he must do this. Baring has been very good in supporting me all through but he is inconsiderate on this point. Graham telegraphs, McNiell killed 1000 of the enemy yesterday.

Tuesday 24th March 1885

The camp very busy preparing for our move. At about 12.30 p.m. I embarked in a 'whaler' (in which I now write this) with Zohrab & Grove, the rest of my belongings going in a nugger and in other whalers. My whaler is towed by my little toy steam pinnace. Stopped at *Tani* to see how Dormer was getting on. His huts are all of mud walls and are in a forward state. Bivouaced for the night on the right bank, where the bright yellow sand of the desert came down to the river. . . .

If this war of ours in the Soudan does nothing else it will affect the ideas of the people, and may possibly alter their manners & customs a little. If the railway is made from *Suakim* to *Berber*, the iron-horse if it were nothing else, would undoubtedly introduce new ideas. Some of the arts of civilization must follow the railway no matter how wild or uncivilized be the people through whose territory it is pushed.

Wednesday 25th March

Started at 5.30 a.m. The river so low that we ran aground several times. Reached *Debbeh* about 10.30 a.m. The fort there is held by the Mudir's Bashi Bazouks—a rare looking lot of rascals. We have about 100 of details in a little detached work. These are to rejoin their Regts. at once, a company of the Egyptian Army taking their place. This company had just arrived when I landed. They would fire a salute for me out of their one gun and when ramming home for the second shot, the charge ignited blowing several fingers off the hand of the gunner. The vents of all these guns are in a wretched state, so that it is difficult to serve it. This is the second or third time they have had accidents when firing salutes with this same gun. Gordon described the vents of his guns being in a terrible condition and as the Mahdi takes less care of his guns, has fired them more frequently, let us hope he may have endless accidents with them. I found Lt. Col. Donills[274] of the Gordon Highlanders in command, Lanyon[275] being here awaiting Wood's arrival. He asked me what his position was to be & I told him: once or twice in the course of our conversation he reminded me that he was senior Colonel in Egypt, and said he had not yet learnt what his position was to be &c. &c. If he is not satisfied with what he can get, he must go home again. He was bitter & ironical about Sir C. Warren,[276] who, having served under him during some operations he conducted from the Diamond fields into some country never heard of before & against tribes whose existence is only known to a select few who have been to the Diamond Diggings, now refers to these operations as having been carried out by himself.

I breakfasted at *Debbeh* & then went on to *Kurot*, where Brackenbury's moveable column is encamped. It is about 3 miles below *Debbeh*. I rode about & looked at the position which has been well selected. Then on to *Abu Gusnee* where George is Commandant. I like this position least of all I have seen. We bivouaced for the night on the right bank on a clean sandy spot about half-way between *Abu Gusnee* & old *Dongola*. The Officer Comdg. the Bashi Bazouks at *Debbeh* was open-mouthed in his abuse of the Mudir, saying we should never get on as long as he was in power here, & that he wants to stay up the river so as not to be at *Dongola* to receive Prince Hassan. . . .

Thursday 26th March

I am disappointed with the beginning that Graham has made. His losses have been inordinate and out of proportion to what he has done: his chief feat has been, as far as I can gather, in shooting his own transport animals when McNiell was surprised, for surprised he certainly was. . . .

Friday 27th March 1885

Started at 5.30 a.m. . . . Reached *Dongola* about 8.30 a.m. long before I was expected so I avoided all Guards of Honor and official receptions. To me they are horrible at any time, but at this particular time they would be worse than a mockery. I left this place in December in high hope. I return having failed to realize those hopes, the man I went out to save having been killed: in other words I return having failed to accomplish what I started to execute and all honors and receptions would therefore be very much out of place. In the eyes of the Natives, the Mahdi has beaten us. It is but natural they should judge by results and think this. If we had beaten the Mahdi of course we should not have come back, but would have gone on to *Khartoum*. That we did not go onto *Khartoum* was simply because the siege and capture of *Khartoum* had not entered into the Government policy when this army was sent to Soudan, and no preparation was therefore made either as regards the strength or composition or armament of this Army for any such serious operation as the Siege of *Khartoum*. When I left England, the Govt. would not listen to my proposal of 'smashing the Mahdi' which is now their only policy.

Found the English post of 6th instant awaiting me when I reached my old quarters in Ali Goot's Garden. Had a most interesting letter from Goshen and an ordinary one from Hartington. Both say the war is unpopular at home & the latter says it is only Mr. Gladstone's personal influence over the Liberal party that carries it along to consent to our operations. I know well how radicalism & Mr. Gladstone's preaching has debased the spirit of the English people, and they will not any longer submit to the pressure on their resources of a war for any but the most self-evident object. Any such coalition as that made against Napoleon at the beginning of the century would now be impossible for us. I quite foresee the difficulty the Cabinet will have in carrying through this campaign for the Tories will ally themselves with the radicals in opposing the war, and I should have long since abandoned all idea of our Autumn campaign if it were not that I can foresee how impossible it will be to preserve peace & quiet in Egypt unless the Mahdi is well smashed up. Gordon never said any truer or wiser thing than that it would be quite as easy to keep the cholera out of Egypt as the Mahdi by means of garrisons on the frontier. We are in Egypt, and we cannot get out of it, and our presence there imposes on us the necessity of defending it and maintaining order there, and this we cannot do unless we can dispose of Mahmond Ahmed. The policy announced by the Govt. is 'to crush the Mahdi's power at *Khartoum*'. This I extracted out of them at the point of the bayonet when they had lost their head on the fall of *Khartoum*. If we go to *Khartoum*, public opinion will insist upon our staying there long enough to establish an orderly and fairly strong Government there. In the meantime the Cabinet do not wish to have their hands tied by any such announcement as those I made at *Korti* to Kasm el Moose's soldiers, that we intended to remain here 100 years if it [was] necessary in order to re-establish order in *Khartoum*. The Cabinet don't therefore like the tone of my proposed proclamation which Baring approved of. What a thing it is to serve a lot of party politicians! My Tory friends say 'Resign my dear fellow if you don't have your own way,' but would that be a patriotic course to adopt? I don't think so in the present instance. Had I been Evelyn Wood I should have resigned everything, aye, even my commission in the Army, before I had consented to the arrangement with the Boers, which he carried out to prevent General Roberts from superceding him, but I have not yet been asked to do anything which I think is derogatory to England. By the line of policy they adopt, my difficulties are greatly increased, but everything in public life is one of compromise. As long as they give me what I ask for on military grounds, I must not dictate to them the manner in which they are to manipulate party warfare at home. If they ask me to do anything which I believe to be derogatory to the honor of England or of H.M.Army, I shall certainly resign, but I must not cry until I am hurt. . . .

I have no good or well substantiated news of a recent date from the Mahdi's camp. It is quite certain that a man named Seyid el Makki (from *Debbeh*)* has started a sort of opposition Mahdi on his own account in Kordofan. This may be the germ of a new movement that will hekp us considerably. Unless the Turk be brought in here as I recommend, we must go to *Khartoum* in the Autumn.

Reuter's telegram announces despatch of an Army under Roberts up the Bolan. I am glad the Govermt. has at last pulled itself together to show a little pluck: it may save us from war with Russia & if it does not, it is much better to fight Russia now than to fight her ten years hence whence her power of the Turcoman

* [Marginal note: This el Makki belongs to the Khatomia sect: he is a well known Fakir in his own district & has the reputation of being a very holy man.]

would be more consolidated and railways constructed from the Caspian to Serakhs. I should like to see Affghanistan before I die, but I am getting old, and when I have settled the 'Mahdi', I shall enjoy rest & quiet and books & peace and green fields in some rural part of England, far away from all the worry as well as the humbug of life. Today has been indeed trying.

Saturday 28th March

Telegram[277] from Hartington saying that it would be better if I were at *Cairo* than at *Dongola* and that my presence might be required at *Suakim* where things were not going on satisfactorily. Replied quite ready to start at once for *Suakim* if he thought it desirable I should do so, but that if my presence would do any good the sooner I went the better: I therefore asked for an early answer....

Sunday 29th March

Hartington tells me to go to *Cairo* & the *Suakim* point can be settled when I get there. I shall start tomorrow evening if possible. I don't like leaving this Army just at this moment, but still I feel I could be of use at *Suakim*.

Reuter's telegram tells me of great naval preparations in England, & that a fleet is to be equipped for the Baltic at once. Alas, poor deluded England! led astray by that foolish parody of a statesman, Mr. Gladstone. She is now about to be plunged into war all round when she has neither an Army or a Navy fit for war. But retorts Mr. Chamberlain & his trading friends, 'if we have no Army, it is your fault because we pay fourteen million a year to support it.'

First of all, as it happens, we soldiers contribute as much towards the revenue of the country as any other class of the community: we have no immunity from taxation and we pay towards the maintenance of the Army even when we are in colonies where no one else pays income tax, or when we are in distant & barbarous regions such as this far-off Soudan. And secondly this argument is childish. The fourteen millions a year are spent upon the support of an armed police to do the police duties of the country at home & abroad. The strength of our Army is only just maintained at a figure to enable it to maintain order at home and in our foreign possessions. No margin is provided to enable the country to equip a force for the field in the event of a war in Europe. In a military sense we are quite helpless when war is forced upon us. We have neither the trained soldiers nor the equipment nor the warlike material to enable us to undertake military operations against a European enemy. Each successive Govt. is told this by its military advisers but the party politician treats these warnings with contempt. I hope if war is forced upon us now the people in their anger may lynch the coward Harcourt, hang the plucky Gladstone and throw Dilke[278] and Chamberlain into the River. As for men of the Northbrook calibre, merely tar, feather and kick them with the contempt they deserve.

Monday 30th March

Telegram from Hobart saying Loo proposed starting for *Cairo* next Friday. Of course I shall be only too delighted to see her, but then I may be only a day there and it is a long journey in the heat of April for a very bad sailor to make. England fitting out merchantmen as fast cruisers. France, I am glad to see, has had a serious defeat in China. She is sending out large reinforcements & has asked for £8,000,000 to carry on the war.

The Mudir arrived about 3 p.m. A little afterwards I received a telm. from Baring in reply to one I sent him saying the Khedive had telegraphed to the Mudir desiring him to proceed at once to *Cairo*. I started from my Hd.Qtrs. a little after 5 p.m. and walked down to the boat waiting to take me over the river via the Mudirieh. There I met the Mudir, whose eyes told me he had received his orders & was taken aback by them. On crossing the river I found everything in great confusion, the arrangements made for my journey not being all that could be desired. I am not well served in my As.D.C. since Wardrop left me. I got off about 6.30 p.m. Full moon but to my horror & astonishment it rose as if it were a new moon, being very nearly totally eclipsed. However by 8 o'clock we had a brilliant moon. The desert between *Dongola* & *Fatmeh* is a dead level of hard sand; very good going for camels. What I suffered trying to keep myself awake lest I should tumble from my camel. Fricke rode his donkey which carried him well. It was a lovely night & our guide was the head of all the camel men in this province.

Tuesday 31st March

Reached *Abu Fatmeh* at 5.30 a.m.: distance from *Dongola* by desert route about 35 miles. We halted for an hour a little before daybreak. Found Maurice, who is [in] command, looking very well. Telegram to say Loo leaves next Friday for *Cairo*. She will be there some days before me. Also telegram from her warning me that I shall be pressed when at *Cairo* to agree to policy of retreat & that Govt. will endeavor to make me responsible for it. Khedive sends a yacht to *Assuan* for me & has placed Kasr el Noose palace again at my disposal. Inspected the Hospl. which is in excellent order—about 9 offrs. and 120 of all other ranks. Maurice has this place very fairly tidy—quite wonderful for a man so untidy and erattic [*sic*] as he is. We had intended starting about 5 p.m. but decided to put off our departure in hopes of getting our letters as I heard from Buller that by an unfortunate mistake my mail bag had not been de[t]ained at *Sal* as ordered. It came on to blow very hard at sundown and quickly developed into a violent storm the heaviest I think we have yet had. Fricke and some of our baggage camels carrying bedding & food had started early in the afternoon so they came in for the full benefit of it. The storm was so great that we did not get off until half an hour after midnight. It blew pretty fresh even then, rendering blue goggles very necessary. Received a cypher telegram from Loo giving me a warning from an illustrious person that when I reached *Cairo* the policy of retreat was to be discussed & the Govt. who wished to adopt it were anxious to put the responsibility on me. It was hoped I would not be a consenting party to any such unworthy policy.

April 1885

Wednesday 1st March. [April?]

Reached *Kaibar* at 5.30 a.m. where we found Fricke's party. Col. Trotter[279] of the Egyptian Army in command of the troops here. We pushed on without halting to *Doulgo* & reached it at 9.30 a.m. There we halted for the day under a straw shelter in the village and read our letters from home up to 13th inst. having met the postman en route & taken my bag from him. We left *Doulgo* at 4.30 p.m. and reached *Absarat* at 7.20 p.m., where we put up in an empty Hospital straw hut.

Judging from my letters, war with Russia seems inevitable. We are not ready either by land or by sea for any war, but we never shall be, and a serious war may enable or force the Nation to wake up from this dream of wishy-washy but debasing radicalism and once more take its position as a first-rate power in Europe. War purifies a degraded Nation and thanks to Mr. Gladstone's teaching we have become degraded and grovel[l]ing in spirit & aspirations. We had so much power to do good & to teach the people manliness, courage, honesty & self-respect, but in order to gratify his vanity, he has sought for and obtained general popularity by pandering to every selfish & ignoble feeling, to a greed for gain & a desire to seize upon & enjoy the property of others.

Thursday 2nd March [April?]

Childers showed me a letter from his father in which he said the discussion in the Cabinet after the small majority on the Vote of Censure ended in a vote as to resignation of Govt.—Ministers to stay in by casting vote only. It appears there was near being a split in Cabinet as to whether Graham's operations should be entirely under me or independent of me. If he had been made independent, I should have resigned.

There is a small rest hospital here, with a doctor in charge. The perfume of the thorny acacia—the scent tree as it is called here—is quite delicious now at many places along the river: indeed at places it is rather overpowering: the blossom here is invariably yellow. In the Transvaal there were I think varieties of color.

We started at 4.30 p.m. to cross the 40 miles of desert included in the great bend made here by the river. Our guide is Abu Bakr. I have mentioned him before. He is I believe one of those most engaged in carrying on the correspondence between Mahmond Ahmed & his friends & relations living near *Dongola*. It was he who brought the summons from the false prophet to the Mudir calling on him to join him. He is I think the nicest native I have yet met in this part of the world.

We started from *Absarat* at 4.30 p.m., our baggage having gone on in the middle of the day. We went a good pace at least 5 miles an hour over very bad ground for the first six miles, & overtook our baggage at 6.45 p.m. just as it had halted, it being then too dark to go any further. We had something to eat & slept until 9.15 p.m. when the moon rose & we all started again, travelling until 3.30 a.m. when, being near *Magraker* & not wishing to arrive until people were about, we halted & slept until 5.30 a.m. & then rode into *Magreker* reaching that place at 6.15 a.m. . . .

Friday 3rd April

Put up in a native house which was clean & nice. Started again when the moon rose at 10.15 p.m. & reached *Akasha* at 4.45 a.m. [Saturday 4th April] where I lodged in the tent of Col. Wynne[280] of the Egyptian Army. In all these night marches, the North Star is in our immediate front and the Southern Cross directly behind us but not high above the horizon. The nights in the desert are truly delightful. This one was so cold towards morning that I could not sleep towards daybreak & yet I had on a substantial silk jersey, a flannel shirt, a serge uniform patrol jacket, a karkee cotton patrol jacket over it, & over all, a very warm closely-fitting military great coat. As long as we have such nights, we stand any amount of heat during the day. It is generally said there is little or no twylight in tropical countries: this is certainly not the case here, for a good hour or more after sunset there is a very pleasant light, with a long after-glow before the night regularly sets in.

I calculated that just about the time I was starting last night, Loo was getting into a Rl.Rd. carriage at Charing X on her way to *Cairo* which place she will reach three days before I do. Yesterday being idle I ran through a number of papers that reached me by the last post. They contain some articles written in a spirit very hostile to me. Of course I must expect this: I came here to save Gordon & to relieve *Khartoum* & I have done neither, and I cannot expect the fools who compose society or who write for newspapers to have any standard of excellence except success. Besides I have very many bitter enemies some of whom—Hamley for example, although no soldiers, can wield a pen with considerable force. However, although I don't think I am peculiarly thick-skinned, all such criticism runs off me as water 'does off a duck's back'. I know I did my best, and I verily believe no one could have done better. No one knows, or at the time knew better—indeed it is doubtful if anyone knew as well as I did—the risks I incurred in sending a small force across the desert to *Matammeh* for the purpose of pushing forward at all hazards to *Khartoum*, if it was found that by so doing Gordon could alone be saved.

I laugh to myself as I fancy the ponderous & pompous sentences in which our would-be English Jomini[281] would have denounced me if I had not made some more than ordinary effort to save poor Gordon's life. I made the effort & intended to have accompanied the little column myself that was to march on *Khartoum*, if Sir C. Wilson brought me back word that by so doing Gordon could alone be saved: so now poor Hamley has to content himself with falling back upon the rules of strategy which he knows to perfection in theory, but cannot practice before an enemy, like so many other theorists on war. He denounces me for violating those rules, and he certainly has theory on his side, but every practical soldier who knows war in the field as well as on paper would have cried shame on me, if I had not made a supreme effort, no matter what the risk incurred might have been—to preserve the life of the ever memorable Gordon.

Besides what theorists like Sir E. Hamley always forget is, that war has ever been (and must ever be where directed by a practical leader of men) a close, minute & very delicate calculation of chances. I have no intention of recapitulating what were the chances I calculated upon for the success of my plan—the geographical position of *Khartoum*, the composition & condition of the Mahdi's Army, my command of the river by Gordon's steamers & my power of crossing and recrossing it at pleasure, an advantage debarred the Mahdi and lastly the magnificent quality of my troops, but I am sure that if all the information I possessed at the end of last year were communicated to any impartial but practical soldier they would agree with me that my project, although hazardous, had many prominent elements of success about it, & that if all the pros & cons were carefully weighed & balanced it would be admitted that there could be little doubt that the column of between two & three thousand men for this venture* would most certainly, under good leadership—not under men of Genl. Hamley's stamp—have reached *Khartoum* in safety, and then have been able, assisted by Gordon's Black Troops— not Fellaheen—to attack the Mahdi & destroy him. If thought advisable, it would have been possible to have awaited in *Khartoum* the arrival of Earle's column before attacking Mahmond Ahmed in the neighbourhood of *Omdurman*.

It must be remembered that my intention was to have awaited at *Matammeh* the arrival of Earle's column if Gordon said he could hold out a few weeks longer. Indeed if he had said so, I meant to have moved down the river from *Matammeh* a strong Brigade to cooperate with Earle in the attack on *Berber*.

I had always believed that the arrival of steamers with red-coats on board at *Khartoum* would have so altered Gordon's position at that place, that he would have been in no immediate danger and could then have easily held out until I had taken *Berber* and was able to advance on *Khartoum* with my little army concentrated in one column. Gordon's diary shows how entirely he concurred with me in this opinion.

In fact, I thank God that I made this attempt to save my comrade's life: in looking back at the last four months, this is to me the pleasantest feature upon which my mind can rest of all the many events they brought forth. I feel now that Gordon is dead & *Khartoum* in the enemy's hands, I should never have forgiven my-

*[Marginal note: column intended to save Gordon. Heavy Camel Regt., Light Camel Regt., Guards Camel Regt., Mounted Infry., Sussex Regt., West Kent, Rl. Irish.]

self if I had not made a great effort to save him, even although in making the attempt I should violate every one of those rules which theorists of the Hamley type can never rise superior to. Although I failed, I am most grateful to God that he allowed me to make the effort I did to save the life of my friend Gordon, the life of one of the two only heroes I ever knew.

Saturday 4th April 1885

This *Akasha* is a very holy place in Mussleman estimation as the tomb of the Saint of that name, the friend of the Prophet. I believe he personally saw more and knew more of Mahmomed than any other of his followers. His tomb here is a very ordinary affair like that to be seen in many places over the bodies of Sheikhs or holy men, but no good Mahomedan will pass it without entering to say his prayers and leaving some small gift offering to the Sheik in possession. It may be local prejudice, but here they tell you this spot comes next to *Mecca* in Mussleman estimation.

I left *Akasha* at 5 p.m., Grenfell, the new Sirdar, having arrived during the afternoon. He is to go on with me to *Cairo*, as Baring wishes him to be present when we discuss with Nubar the future of the Egyptian Army. Baring & Nubar want me to spare more men from the Egyptian Army to augment the civil police: I say no, I want everyone to work on my railways & protect my line of communications, and if this proposal be carried out, I shall not be able to carry out my autumn campaign. I have offered one more Egyptian Battn. and put my foot down saying this was my last word on the subject.

From Wynn[e]'s camp at *Akasha* to the 'Rail Head' is about 31 miles. The sick & wounded coming down country have in this condition of Nile to be taken by land over the desert between those two points. Two 'Rest camps' have been formed, at distances from *Akasha* of 9 & 19 miles, so each convoy of sick makes the distance in three short marches, the worst cases being carried on stretchers by Egyptian soldiers. This organization is well done by the Medical Offrs., Dr. [G. E.] Will in charge.

I started at 5 p.m. and did not reach the first rest camp until about 7.15 p.m. There we halted until the moon rose, having a good sleep in a hospital marquee. I have been out of sorts internally all day, so this rest was pleasant as the jogging of a camel is not pleasant when the bowels are out of order.

Under weigh again at 11.15 p.m. & reached the *Ambigole* wells station at about 1.30 a.m.

Sunday 5th April

Dr. Will, who accompanied me during our night march, gave me a good tin full of arrowroot & Tarragona wine, which set me up. We left the wells at 2.15 a.m. and reached the Rail-Head at 4.50 a.m. having travelled mostly over the new line of railway extension. The embankments & cuttings are mostly done & ready for the rails, the first installment of which are now coming up to *Halfa*. At Rail-End I saw Major Scott R.E.[282] who is constructing the line & with him examined the plans & sections of the extension. I feel confident it will be in working order to *Akasha* by middle of July, unless authorities at home fail to supply us with the rails & rolling stock as promised.

I had to wait until 9.15 a.m. at Rail Head for Fricke & the other servants as their guide had taken them astray & lost two horses during the night. Started in special train at 9.45 a.m. and reached *Halfa* (50 miles) at 1.15 p.m. The line is now in good working order, the new carriages good & comfortable. Found Prince Hassan & a number of officers &c. awaiting arrival of train. Col. Duncan R.A. the Commandant in full force. Went on board the diabeah I lived in when here last October in which Col. Duncan now lives. Prince Hassan dined with us. He is a gentlemanly man but I do not quite like his countenance. He is living on board one of our steamers which is inconvenient. I told him he had better go back to *Cairo* & that he could rejoin me in the autumn. I do not however intend at present that he should do so. A Prince, even this sort of Prince, is a millstone round one's neck: few of them care to toil and still fewer know how to spin, but all of them wish to have a surrounding equal to that of Soloman in all his glory. Now that Mustapha Yagha Pasha—*the* Mudir par excellence—has left *Dongola* never to return there as long as I rule anywhere in the Soudan, my object in having Pe. Hassan with me falls to the ground. The ex-Mudir has started for *Cairo* with all his family. He must now feel that he has overleaped his mark, and made a fool of himself. If he had cordially & honestly thrown in his lot with me he might have been a big man, but he thought I was in his power & could not do without him. Today has been very hot here, not a breath of wind even to shake the lazy tired-looking Egyptian flag that flies from this diabeyah. English post of 20th March reached me at Rail End. Strong party at home against our Autumn campaign here.

Waddy Halfa—Monday 6th April 1885

Had a delicious night's rest. We have been travelling now for six nights, so had to snatch our sleep as best we could, but never having it in comfort. A quiet, clean cabin, with one's boots & clothes off made last night really enjoyable. It blew a violent gale all the afternoon & the diabeeah bumped so heavily that I felt inclined to be sea-sick & thought at times she would go to pieces. Visited the hospital in the evening: 200 beds well organized & maintained doing great credit to all the medical officers concerned. There are several points where I see great improvement in our Army since 1882, but in no department is it so marked as in the Medical. There are now six sisters working here and they complain they have not enough work to do. There are now in hospital here 7 Offrs. (two wounded) & 79 of other ranks of whom 13 are wounded, 9 with dysentry, 8 enteric fever & 5 with diarrhoea. In going & returning from the hospital the clouds of dust rendered life almost unbearable. Went to the telegraph office & had a talk with Sir C. Wilson over the wire on Arab matters, and the effect which our giving up the Soudan would have upon the riverain population north of *Assuan*.

Dined with Prince Hassan on board the steamer on which he came here. He is a dull host, and does not on this slight acquaintance strike me as a man of intelligence or any deep thought: but he is eastern, and may hide his light under a bushel.

Tuesday 7th April

Embarked in the stern-wheeler, the *Water-Lilly* at 5 a.m. before it was clearly light & started in a few minutes downstream, our faces towards the North. We passed *Abu Simball* about 9 a.m. This *Water Lilly* & her sister vessell [sic] the *Lotus* have been and continue to be invaluable to us. This rock temple of *Abu Simball* does not impress me: perhaps if I went inside I might feel awestruck. The only monument that really impressed me in Egypt has been the Sphinx.

Reached *Korosko* at 4 p.m. Lt. Col. St. Leger,[283] Cameron

Highldrs., Commdg. the Station. The Garrison consists of Cameron Highlandrs. 18 offrs. & 467 of all other ranks & a few gunners of the Egyptian Artilly. Out of 484 N.C.Offrs. & Rk. & F. (English) there are 24 in hospital. This I think will be the hottest station in the Soudan where our troops are located. I landed and inspected the huts that are being built for the men: they are of kutcher brick. Found fault with the Commandant for the inordinate number of guards on duty. Started again in about half an hour, telling the four Sheikhs with whom Rundell [sic] works here that I hoped soon to see them again when on my way back to *Dongola*. It has been a deliciously cool day: indeed quite cold at times. I had a great coat on until about noon.

Wednesday 8th April

Off again at first streak of daylight, and reached *Assuan* or rather *Shelal* at head of Cataract about 1 p.m. Found Henderson [284] awaiting me on the beach. It did not take long to transfer ourselves & baggage into a steamer below the cataract, getting over the intervening distance by rail. The garrison here consists of the I/Yorkshire (606)—279 men of 2/Essex, 31 R.A. odds & ends making a total of 43 offrs. & 976 men of other ranks (British) and of 209 of other ranks Egyptian Army.

We started again about 3.30 p.m. & at 4.15 p.m. met the Khedive's Yacht, the *Zeirt-el-Bahrein* (the lustre of the two Seas) which he had kindly sent to meet me & bring me down to *Assiut*. We anchored a little after sundown.

During the day we passed numbers of boats of all sorts laden with stores for the Army: we looked at them & thought of the English tax payer who has to pay for all this. I pity myself and those who urged Mr. Gladstone to prepare for the relief of *Khartoum* early last spring, but as for the main body of the English taxpayer I have *no* pity for him: he has in his utter folly set up for himself the most contemptible of idols, the G.O.M., and he persists in believing in him; let him therefore pay for this folly: possibly it be a warning to future generations. If God punishes men in the world, and if *we* are any judges of right & wrong, he will send down this old hypocrite in shame to his grave & with the outcries of the nation he has misgoverned ringing in his ears, as he dies despised & hated by every good Englishman. Poor Primrose died this morning.

Thursday 9th April

.... A lovely day: halted for a few minutes at *Edfu*, to send some telegrams & stopped over half an hour at *Esneh* to coal: there the Mudir paid me a visit: he wears patent leather boots & speaks French—must therefore be a villain. Moored alongside right bank for night at sundown about 20 miles south of *Keneh*.

I cannot shake off this horrid diarrhoea, which has stuck to me since starting from *Korti*.

Friday 10th April

Under weigh at 5.20 a.m. Reached *Keneh* at 6.45 a.m. Stopped to coal & left again at 8.15. Spenser sent me a letter from his father in which he distinctly said that at any moment, orders might be sent here ordering us all to India. It is therefore quite evident that if Russia does not come to terms, we shall scuttle out of the Soudan & leave the Mahdi in possession. Reached *Solag* about 5 p.m. where we took in some coal. There I had a telegram saying Loo had reached *Cairo* yesterday evening.

We moored to the Rt. bank for the night about 12 miles below *Sohag*. A lovely day—Climate delicious. I feel a great difference between the climate here and that at *Dongola* or *Korti*.

Saturday 11th April 1885

Under weigh at 5.15 a.m. We are frequently touching ground: indeed the navigation of the Nile below *Halfa* at this season is very difficult and precarious. The river will fall a little still which fact makes me tremble for the extension of my Sarras Railway, and on it everything depends as regards our Autumn Campaign. Reached *Assiut* about 11.30 a.m. Found Colonel Loyd in command. Started in special train about noon & reached Bulak Station near *Cairo* about 10 p.m. having picked up Loo & Frances[285] at [blank space] to which place they had come out from *Cairo* to meet me. Drove to the Kasr el Noose which the Khedive had placed at my disposal.

Sunday 12th April 1885

Put on a white shirt and smart clothes which felt curious after the flannel and serge garments I have lived in since September last. Paid the Khedive a visit which he returned in the afternoon. Baring came to see me: he says the Govt. are only too anxious to find some excuse for *not* going on with Soudan campaign. The Bosphore Egyptienne has been suppressed by Nubah and the French party here are white with rage, and vow vengeance....

Monday 13th April

Went with Loo & Frances to the Bazaar—very interesting to both of them. The French Agent here—Barrere, the low communard, is absent—called on Nubah and demanded the immediate restoration of the Bosphore & the dismissal of the police officers—one of whom is English—who carried out its suppression. Nubar refused and with that brutal and ungentlemanlike rudeness for which the French are so well known, this consular agent having expressed some threats turned on his heel and left, without even saying goodbye. Nubar's position is a strong one: he says he has done nothing illegal, and if the French think otherwise, the courts of law are open to them. The Khedive has become frightened at all this, and wishes to give in, but if this were done, we had better clear out of the country, as our influence & prestige would be at an end forever amongst every class of Egyptian. It is unfortunate this position was not taken up a year ago, for coming at this moment, the complication is unfortunate when war with Russia is in the air.

Tuesday 14th April

Loo, Frances, Spenser Childers, Zohrab & myself started about 6 a.m. for the Pyramids, where we had a pleasant breakfast, and 'did the sights'. On our return I found a telegram[286] from Hartington, 'Secret & Confidential' informing me that Imperial interests might necessitate withdrawal of all troops from Soudan and the concentration in Egypt of all those now up the Nile. That I was to prepare in secret for carrying out this concentration.

What a blow to all my hopes, and what a policy to adopt! I have asked what is to be the frontier to be held, recommending—if a purely defensive position is to be taken up—to hold *Korosko* & *Wady Halfa* as outposts and *Assuan* with the bulk of force.

Wednesday 15th April

Sent another 'Secret and confidential' telegram[287] to Hartington, urging Govt. in strongest possible terms not to withdraw from the province of Dongola & giving forcable [*sic*] reasons for my advice. But nothing will avail. The old imposter Gladstone is afraid of the radicals who are dead against all forward policy in Egypt, so he is only too anxious to avail himself of the excuse of a threatened war with Russia—which he never means to embark in, if he can, by no matter what surrender of national honor, possibly avoid it. This dodge of heading telegrams 'secret & confidential' and giving them no number & signing then, not 'War Secretary', but Hartington is done to avoid having ever to produce them & to avoid having to send them to the Queen to see. My heart is low when I allow my thoughts to dwell on the position of England, dragged down as he has been by Mr. Gladstone and the obedient pack who do his bidding. Riches and the greed for money & the luxury of all classes cause us to think only of the moment & of our own ease & comfort: no one works now 'for the State'. Gladstone has taught the uneducated classes to mock at National honor or National renown. But please God his day of punishment is at hand. May he be torn limb from limb by the people he has deceived.

Loo & I dined with Ben Stephenson at a great official party given in our honor.

Thursday 16th April

English post in: letter (private) from Hartington informing me that Govt. were determined to get out of the Soudan campaign & were casting about for some good excuse to do so. What a lot they are. They have no policy for abroad except to do nothing: they never do anything until public opinion forces them & then, as in the Khartoum business, they move too late. A telegram from Ponsonby at Aix-les-Bains where the Queen is, asking me for an answer to the Queen's letter which Loo brought me. Replied, answer sent by post 14th instant: he has none of the cyphers I have and I could not telegraph my views on the Soudan in clear. I added however, 'I strongly urged forward policy as most befitting our honor & our interests.' I forget the exact words. I went round the hospital in the Citadel which is in perfect order. Loo & I dined with Khedive. I hate to look him or any of his Ministers in the face: indeed I blush with shame as I catch the eye of a street donkey-boy: how they with all despise us when they learn that we are to retreat before the Mahdi. Nubah and the Khedive would be glad to see the Turk at *Suakim* and in *Khartoum*.

Friday 17th April 1885

Telegram from Hartington[288] in answer to two of mine asking if I were to begin to scuttle, saying nothing must be done until the Queen's approval to their foreign policy had been obtained, so in the meantime I am sending up the Nile tons & tons weight of rails, provisions & various stores. This accounts for the telegram I received from Ponsonby yesterday....

Saturday 18th April

The news from home seems to point to the continuance of peace. I don't think Russia will go to war because I don't think her arrangements for it are yet perfect, & she is poor, and can see that with the Affghans on our side, if Turkey would join us, she must go to the wall and lose territory as well as reputation. If we were ruled by a Statesman, our course would be as follows: Keep this Russian question open for another year and during that time push forward your Railway to *Kandahar* and if the Amir would allow it to *Girishk* and even to *Farah* on the Farah Road. Enter at once into the closest alliance with the Amir and with the Sultan. Supply the former with 30,000 Martini Henry's & ten million rounds for them. Help him freely with officers to teach his men their use: give him Engineers to improve the defences of *Herat*. Induce the Sultan by subsidies to take over *Suakim* & the Soudan. Discuss with him plans of campaign against Russia & dangle before him the hope of getting back *Kars* & *Batoum*, possibly more territory towards *Tiflis*.

This done let us march in October on *Berber* & *Khartoum*, destroying Mahmond Ahmed's strength; establish the Turk there; bring our Army back to *Cairo* next February, perhaps via *Suakim*. Collect an army of 20,000 British at *Quetta* before hot weather of 1886 sets in; and in the summer of that year bring matters to a crisis with Russia whether she will or not. We must fight her sooner or later on this Affghan question and the sooner we do so the better, for every year her position on the Tejend & Murgh-Ab

Rivers will become stronger. The creatures however who pass for Statesmen in England only think of the moment. 'A stitch in time etc.' is not in accordance with their principles. They are always prepared to purchase peace whilst in office at any price entirely regardless of what is to come ten years or even five years or even one year hence. They don't believe they can purchase peace even for a year too dearly. It is the conduct of the reckless profligate who is prepared to purchase momentary enjoyment at any price, squandering his fortune and ruining his future prospects for the pleasure and ease of the day. This principle, or rather I should say unprincipled system, applied to the foreign policy of any State, is the policy of the Vestrymen of the Gladstone & Harcourt level when they borrow or are but the clothes of the Statesman. . . .

The feeling seems to be gaining ground here, that we shall have no autumn campaign in the Soudan. There can be no doubt that Mahmond Ahmed is by no means as strongly seated or established in power as he would like. He has had to send large numbers of Kordofan to quell the rebellion against him there. He has now called in all his troops from *Matammeh* & outlying stations. He is still at *Omdurman*, but his head man Abdullah is in the palace in *Khartoum*. *Sennar* & *Kassala* still hold out. Osman Digma has written to Mahmond el Kheir at *Berber* that the English having defeated his troops are now advancing on *Berber* & that there is no use in resisting them: that all his men have dispersed & left him. . . .

Sunday 19th April

. . . . Now is the moment for us to show a bold front all round. If we don't do so we shall be in a bad way. It is difficult to believe in any courageous policy emanating from our present Cabinet. If Gladstone gives in, were I in Baring's place I would resign forthwith: his face here would then indeed be blackened in the eyes of all men here. . . .

It is strange I can get no orders from home. We are still pushing forward all our preparations for an autumn campaign, which Hartington in a private letter tells me is *not* to take place: that the Govt. were casting about for a good excuse to get out of any such undertaking.

I presume it was expected the Russian difficulty would have supplied that excuse, but now that war with that power is not to come off *at present*, they are at a loss for an excuse for their intended change of front. They cannot certainly obtain from my telegrams any assistance in their cowardly policy.

Graham has been sending columns out in all directions, but has not found the enemy. Osman Digma's army has broken up, and he is evidently without any following. I wish we could find good summer quarters in the hills for our troops.

Monday 20th April 1885

Graham occupied *Tambouk* yesterday—no enemy seen. Rl.Rd. is now a few miles beyond *Handoub*. Not a line or message from Hartington for two days, but a telgm. today from 'Chief' informing me that Maps & Papers I had asked for about Caucasus, were on their way to me, but if I had *left for home before they arrived here,* they were to be sent back &c. I have determined to send Spenser Childers home by this week's mail to explain my views on Soudan matters to his father and the Cabinet. News from England as regards Russia more warlike....

Tuesday 21st April

Telegram 'Secret & Confidential' from Hartington[289] received early in the morning telling me that today Govt, would explain in Houses of Parliament their Soudan policy, which would be withdrawal of Graham's force except such portions of it as will be required for protection of *Suakin* and the railway which it is intended to push on to *Tambouk*, or some other place in the neighbourhood, the suspension of Suakin–Berber Rl.Rd., the suspension of all action up the Nile against the Mahdi, the withdrawal of all our troops from Province of Dongola & their concentration, so as to be available for national requirements, the defence of southern frontier of Egypt by having a strong Brigade at *Assuan* and outposts at *Korosko* & *Wady Halfa,* with armed steamers manned by Rl. Navy on reach *Assuan–Wady Halfa*.

Of all the miserably foolish policies this is the worst. I have protested against it with all earnestness, but party exigencies make it necessary. The whole thing means concession to radical opinion. In the morning I begged of them not to tell the world & the Mahdi what they would & would not do: that in war it was foolish to take the enemy into your confidence. But the statement must be made I presume to satisfy the party 'below the gangway'. I have pointed out that to withdraw from the Province of Dongola will be not only to hand it over to the Mahdi & to Anarchy, but to lose the loyalty of the Ababdees and other great frontier tribes who regard the possession of that Province as signifying which is the stronger side. This withdrawal policy will in the end cost us dear indeed. I have still a glimmering hope, they may not withdraw the troops for some months, & that in the meantime, circumstances may become too strong for the Govt. at home, and force them to reconsider their position. A horrible suspicion comes over me, that the Cabinet purposely magnify the danger of a war with Russia in order to trump up a plausible excuse for their change of Sudan policy. Bismarck said when Odo Russell was thrown over by the Govt. (Mr. Gladstone's) in 1870–71, on the question of the Black Sea treaty, that he wondered how any gentleman could serve such a Government. I have long realized the truth of that statement.

I am glad to say that Baring's views as to the folly of withdrawing from the Province of Dongola entirely agree with mine. I have written a despatch to Lord Hartington dated 16th inst. in which I condemn the Govt. proposals in the strongest terms, & point out the serious dangers they will expose us to. . . .

Wednesday 22nd April

Reuter's telegram has of course informed all the world that we don't mean to fight in the Autumn. It had evidently staggered those in the front, for first comes a telegram from Wood begging Reuter's News might not be disseminated in his neighbourhood & then one from Buller saying he had ordered Wood to arrest the Sheikh of the Hawawir tribe and wished to arrest Saleh also. . . .

Thursday 23rd April

. . . . The news from home is very warlike, but I cannot even now believe in war. It is a real treason to begin a war with a great power like Russia when we have absolutely no army to place in the field. However there is this to be said. We are ruled by such dishonest and such silly men that we shall never be in any way better prepared than we are now & we must fight Russia about this Affghan business sooner or later. If the war be postponed for a few years Russia will have her Railway to *Seraks* and we shall be in no better or at least very little better condition for war than at present when all England is united on the question and the loyalty of the Indian princes is so pronounced.

How I wish that England had been ruled for the last five years by some real statesman instead of the scarecrow vestryman Mr. Gladstone decked out in a Statesman's uniform. Had Ld. Beaconsfield been in Downing St. we should never have committed the follies we have perpetrated in Egypt, but what can be expected from an administration whose policy is based on cant & cowardice.

Friday 24th April

.... A telegram[290] from Hartington saying I am to go to *Suakim* as soon as a ship can be placed at my disposal. I cannot get any definite instructions out of him about concentrating the troops now on the Upper Nile: I am afraid he wants me to act and then to make out that I am responsible for the movement. I have telegraphed today saying I intend going to *Suakim* & hope to be back here again on 12th May. To report upon matters there & to receive orders from home as to the evacuation of *Suakim* by the 14th May. That all the troops to leave should be on board ship by 1st June on which date the *Abu Dom* detachment should begin to move down stream & that all the Force now in the advanced position on the Nile should be concentrated at *Dongola* & *Abu Fatmeh* by 1st July. I then proceed to raise the question of withdrawing the civil Government and handing over the whole of the Dongola Province to the Mahdi & to anarchy. I saw Baring on this point, & he telegraphed to the fossilized Granville for instructions: but we shall get none. The more this withdrawal is studied the more difficult it seems to become. Assuming that we are not to have an Autumn Campaign, it is a cruel absurdity that our silly Cabinet did not in the *first* instance order me to concentrate & fall back at once when they ascertained that Gordon was dead. They made a great splash to save their places. What a set of men to serve?

Saturday 25th April 1885

Inspected the 2nd Sussex Regt. and the Depot of Regts. up the Nile at 7 a.m. in the Kasr-el-Nil Barracks. The Sussex turned out remarkably well. In one more year it will be a splendid Battn. Had a little fever in the evening & felt rather wretched. A horse Mr. Rousell lent me to ride had one of his eyes bitten out last night by one of the orderlies' horses who got loose—I have now to buy him for £40. Rec'd orders to communicate with transport officers at Suez who will provide a ship to take me to *Suakim*.

Sunday 26th April

.... I cannot obtain any positive orders from Hartington as to when I am to begin withdrawing the troops, & I cannot leave for *Suakim* until this is settled. There seems to be a desire to make me take the initiative on all these points, so that if any growl in Parliament should be heard as to the precipitancy of our retreat, or as to the tardiness of our beginning to move, the blame may be thrown on me. I am not however this time to be caught in that trap.

Monday 27th April

The news from Europe says, the Russian question is to be referred to Arbitration. No answer yet from Hartington so I don't see much chance of getting off tomorrow. I spent most of the day in bed with an irrepressible diarrhoea, but had to get up to dine with Mr. & Mrs. Rousell. The party was for me & I could not avoid it, but oh, such a party for a man lately come back from long residence in the wilds of the Soudan & heartily sick & tired of thinking & talking of Egypt. About a dozen pashas!!! Not a woman to talk to, & Mrs. Rousell very kind but a bore, and poor me unable to eat anything and to sip only a little weak brandy & water.

Tuesday 28th April

Telegram from Hartington[291] authorizing me to begin my movement from *Abu Dom* at once. Until Cabinet meets today he cannot answer my other questions. Called on Baring who had had no answer from Granville. Told him I was then on my way to telegraph office to have a talk over the wire with Buller & order him to begin evacuation. Also that I had authorized Buller to seize all the near relatives of the Mahdi in the Dongola Province to keep them as hostages for the White sisters now in his camp. I then went to telegraph office & talked for two hours over wire with Buller giving him general outline of the plan for carrying out this truly foolish retrograde movement. Reuter says war with Russia now inevitable. Baring saw Nubar, & told him we meant to concentrate at *Dongola* & to withdraw all troops & civil employees from all points south of *Dongola*. Nubar consulted the Khedive and both are in a state of consternation as to the effect this move will have on people in Egypt.

Wednesday 29th April

Went a little after 10 a.m. to say good bye to the Khedive, found him much perturbed about withdrawal from *Dongola* & the ultimatum he had received on the sanitary question from France, Austria, Germany & Russia. I presume this sanitary business is simply put forward to annoy us. I sympathized with the poor man who said he had now been Khedive for five years & had only two months of quiet—and it is peace & quiet he desires most. Poor Egypt, he said, the outside powers seemed determined she should have no peace. Saw Baring for a few minutes: the Bosphore business is settled: there has been a compromise & we have had to give way on a point where if we had had a strong Govt, and any friends in Europe there would have been no concession. But our only friend is Italy: Mr. Gladstone with that want of Statesmanship which has always been his chief characteristic has so managed our national affairs that the friends we had under Lord Beaconsfield have been snubbed and converted into actual enemies, & the only Power he attempted to be in close alliance with, France, because, She being a Republic, that connection pleased the Radicals, has turned against us with a bitterness purely French. Hartington telegraphs[292] I may keep troops for the present at *Dongola*, as concentration will take some time. Granville telegraphs to Baring that eventually no troops will be left at *Dongola* & asks if we could not set up some Native Govt. at *Dongola*!!!! What an old Goose!! Until the Mahdi be disposed of, no settled Govt. can be established there, for as soon as we leave, his emissaries will step in & anarchy will be rampant. Had a very interesting letter dated 18th instant from the Queen. Poor Lady, she is nigh broken-hearted at having her Kingdom made ducks & drakes of by the Gladstone Company. I have been feverish and very diarrohatic all night, & feel as if I had no backbone and that any bone I did possess had been bruised if not broken.

Started at 11.30 a.m. by train for Suez. Visited the graveyard at *Tel-el-Kebir*, & reached my ship about 7.15 p.m. The ship is *The Queen* of the National Line: over 4000 tons burthen (2730 tons register), her Captain's name is Cochrane. We put to sea by moonlight at 8.30 p.m.

Thursday 30th April. Lat. 27°36'N. Long. 34°–E.

Buller in a letter received yesterday tells me that Brackenbury is simply detested by everyone in his camp: so much so, as to be injurious to the interests of the public service. I have been seedy all day and cannot shake off this horrid diarrhoea. During the greater part of the day, the African & the Asiatic coasts were both very plainly visible.

What barren lands! not a bush, or other green thing to be seen; burnt up rocks & sand. The Sinai Peninsula could not have appeared as any chosen or promised land to a people fresh from the luxuriant cultivation of the Nile Valley: a more repellant-looking land it is difficult to conceive. The sea was the deepest blue, with curling waves in the early morning, the wind being behind us. The air has been perfection, but perhaps a little too hot towards evening. I wrote a long letter to the Queen. Idled away the day very pleasantly reading Hayard's Article on Lord Melbourne, and could almost imagine I heard him talk as I read his dictatorial and knock-me-down sentences, each being as much a challenge as the coat-tail of the proverbial Irishman; a defiance to anyone who would dare to question his infallibility on any subject about which he condescended to be oracular. Beato, the photographer whom I remember in the Crimea & whom I knew well during the Indian Mutiny & China war is on board, as amusing as ever, his attempts to speak English—which he understands very well—being as ludicrous as formerly. He has made & lost many fortunes since I last [saw] him, & now for the spell returned to his former trade, that of photography.

May 1885

Friday 1st May 1885. Lat. 23°37′N., Long. 36°23′E. noon.

Still suffering from simple diarrhoea which compels me to live on slops. Read the little new red book on Addison by Mr. Courthope, whoever he may be. Pleasant reading: how one Knight of the Pen loves to discourse upon a predecessor. Like the newspaper correspondents being extremely proud of St. Leger Herbert because he was a gentleman, as brave as a lion, and admitted to the intimacy of the best in the Army, not because he was a buffoon and professional jester like Billy Russell, but because he was socially their equal. In the same way the literary host is proud of one who left such a mark upon the literature of his time as Addison did because socially he was a long way above the ordinary litterary [*sic*] hack: of course he was ready to undertake a job for a fee as any lawyer was and ever will be to undertake a case regardless of its own intrinsic merits or its infamy. Thus Addison wrote the campaign for an arranged fee, which was some Government office. Swift's pen was wielded to his eternal disgrace for a fee he always hoped for but only obtained a small moiety of: he wanted to be a Bishop and he wrote for first one party, then for the other, believing he should have his promised honorarium, but instead of an English Bishopric he was only made an Irish Dean! How he cursed because the pay was not good enougn. Never did a man more infamously sell his talents, and neither before nor since has such a wit, such a genius, put his talents up to auction.

Today as yesterday has been calm. The African coast in sight all day.

Saturday 2nd May

A lovely morning on deck at 6 a.m. Reached *Suakim* & anchored in the very narrow and confined harbor at 4 p.m. We lost the best part of two hours when near the place by a vessel ahead of us (No. 89) having run on a reef and hoisted signals of distress. We had to bear down upon her and then found her hard & fast, although any land-lubber could plainly see for some miles off the reef she ran on. The distance from Suez to *Suakim* is 728 miles. It is very difficult navigation entering the harbor & turning a great long ship like this in it. I am delighted to find there is no enteric fever with this force. This is proof conclusive that enteric has its origins in bad water: here all water is distilled! Graham, Greaves, Fremantle & many other friends came off to see me. Very hot & steamy: men healthy but bowell [*sic*] complaints common.

The Govt. must make up its mind to do one of two things, embark the troops leaving only a small garrison to hold the place, or keep the troops here & prosecute the campaign & the railway. Whilst they are looking about for a policy & hoping something will turn up, our men are grilling. As long as they felt they were taking part in a campaign all well and good, they would work hard and endure even excessive heat with good spirits, but now that every donkey-boy in *Suakin* has been told we are going to 'hook it', our men take no further interest in the affair and if not sent away will suffer severely in health.

The Reuter of today asserts that the Czar has proposed to leave his dispute with us to the arbitration of the King of Denmark & that we have accepted. The old story with Mr. Gladstone. We bluster and swagger and sing Rule Britannia to a select audience, but we take precious care to avail ourself of the first excuse for not fighting: any loophole, no matter how small or how unworthy of a great people, is eagerly seized as a way to crawl ignominiously out of any danger or difficulty, leaving it to the special pleading of such cowardly lawyers as Sir Wm. Harcourt, & to the hair-splitting casuistry of Mr. Gladstone, to his eloquence in words & his perversion of facts under the guise of honesty to persuade our poor, ignorant people that a noble policy had been adopted and stuck to whilst he signs away unblushingly our rights under the excuse that he does so in conformity with the decision of the arbitrators we had agreed to.

I should like to know if the Govt. mean to insist upon Russian troops withdrawing from *Penj-Deh*, before he will consent to arbitration? The whole position ante-bellum should be re-assumed before an arbitration had been accepted. We have had enough of arbitration; everyone hates us so cordially, that every arbitration is given against us. We know what we want as a nation, & that we must have, & it is only a cowardly Government who prefers ignominy to fighting, that would resort to arbitration under such circumstances. In fact it is only resorted to in order to disguise the baseness & cowardice of our Ministers.

Sunday—3rd May

I am weak & wretched, and very angry because I cannot shake off this diarrohea [*sic*]. . . . I returned the Commodore's visit in the morning and the Governor General's—(Chermside) in the evening. Chermside spent several hours with me. He is painfully circumspect, so diplomatic that one has to *corkscrew* any opinion out of him. However, I learnt that he did not think much of Graham or of the way in which operations had been conducted here lately. He declares that from the first all truest and most reliable information has been . . . supplied to Graham by the Intelligence Department. That Graham had never consulted him in any way. I am afraid I must give Graham up as incorrigibly stupid. I shall not take him on service any more. Greaves is open-mouthed against him, but so he would be against any man placed over him in a position that he thought he ought to have had. Greaves must have command of a Division and never anything more: he wants discretion & command of temper for an independent command.

Monday 4th May

. . . . I am very much amused by the attempt Lord Granville made to get an opinion that might possibly agree with that held by the Govt. regarding withdrawal from the Upper Nile. A message to Baring came from that worn-out old official asking him to obtain the views of Wilson & Kitchener, one a Colonel the other a Captain on the Staff of the Army I command. This is another effort that is being made to try and invest Wilson with the duties of a political officer, which I would sooner resign than permit. However I said I would telegraph to Buller & desire him to obtain the views of those two officers & to send them forward with his own. Called in to bless, they have cursed the evacuation policy in louder terms than I ever did, and Baring has in consequence advised Nubar not to order the evacuation of *Merawi* by the Civil employees for the present and the subject will be discussed today by the Cabinet. Such a Govt. to serve! Mr. Gladstone has I presume purchased the silence of the Radicals on the £11,000,000 vote by promising them to abandon the Soudan & withdraw our troops: now everyone here, myself, Baring, Buller, Wilson & all to whom they have appealed for opinions tell them that to withdraw our troops will be madness.[293] However, with one who clings to power as Mr. Gladstone does, it is quite certain he will throw over the interests of his country in the interests of his wretched party. I had a long letter from Hartington in which he never once mentioned Russia!

Tuesday 5th May

Still seedy & very weak: did not stir all day: wrote letters on deck.

Wednesday 6th May

Received a telegram[294] from Hartington saying he would tomorrow answer my proposals about Garrison to be kept here. I presume there will be a Cabinet today to settle the Upper Nile policy.

I am much better today. Landed at 3 p.m. & went by rail to *Otao*, 18 miles where I found the 15th Sikhs just returned from their long night march. Graham had gone out from *Suakim* about midnight with Mounted Infantry. & Camel Corps and a force had marched in the same direction from *Otao*. The information upon which this movement was made turned out to be very sound and the result was very satisfactory, about 2000 goats & sheep were taken & some 50 of the enemy killed.

I saw the 15th Sikhs on parade without arms. They are a splendid body of men. The Native officers seemed mostly fine old warriors. One young & very good looking fellow had an Arab sword, which I remarked. It was then explained to me that in McNiell's action of the 22nd March he had killed some of the enemy with his sword, but that in cleaving one fellow in two he broke his Regulation Sword. I told [him] I would present him with a new sword which seemed to please him very much.

I then inspected the Battalion of the Coldstream and a dirtier and more unsoldierlike set of raggamuffins I never saw on parade: the men were filthily dirty, large numbers of them had no hand guards on the barrels of their rifles, many of the men had no puggaries & altogether they seemed in a very unsatisfactory state. I then returned to *Handoub,* where McNiell commands, and inspected his force which consisted of the 1st Berkshire, 1st Shropshire, the Australian Battery, 5th Lancers & 21st Hussars (one squadron of each). They were all beautifully turned out, the two Infantry Battns. presenting a marked contrast with the slovenliness and unsoldierlike appearance of the Coldstream.

In coming home, when passing through the piles of stores of all sorts, railway, hutting, medical, commissariat, &c. &c., I thought of poor silly John Bull who continues to trust Mr. Gladstone who has uselessly imposed all this cost upon him. How he can believe in a minister who lands a large force here to construct a railway 250 miles in extent and who stops the work when 18 miles have been laid. If Mr. Gladstone were a statesman he would have a policy, based upon a careful study of what the future had most probably in store for England in Egypt, but he cannot have one, first from that incapacity which prevents him from forming any opinion worth having upon the foreign relations of our country, from that peculiarity of intellect which, so able in the management of party politics, is utterly incapable of managing the great affairs of a great nation, but chiefly because he has not the wisdom or the courage to adopt any line of conduct and stick to it. He wants place & power, & when it is a question between losing those spoils, or changing the lines upon which he was acting & to which he had pledged himself, he goes right about face as quickly as 'Jim Crow' does. He is to me the most contemptible charlatan of our day. But the English people have not yet found him out. They still allow him to squander their hard-earned savings in abortive undertakings countermanded as soon as they have begun & only continued long enough to have incurred almost all the cost which their completion would have entailed.

Thursday 7th May

Busy all the morning writing letters for the English post which left at noon: Hartington had promised to let me have answers to all my questions today, but he telegraphed[295] instead that I should receive my instructions tomorrow. . . . The *Jumna* was to have left this at daybreak, but I asked the Commodore to detain her, for it seems absurd to let her go empty to Bombay, if we are in a few days to send away the bulk of the troops now here. In the evening I went over the *Ganges*, which is quite perfect in all her fittings as a Hospital ship. She can put up 140 patients in berths, a small number I think for such a large ship (4000 tons & about 2600 tons register). I am sure that as a rule no steamer should be taken up as a Hospital ship: the machinery takes up too much space and cramps & hampers up the decks which should be clear fore & aft for the sick. The Navy ought always to keep some old sailing ships or some old Screw Liners, with the engines removed, ready to be converted into Hospital Ships in time of war. Then if I could I should like to have small ships for the officers alone, for when they are on board the same ship all the good accommodation is monopolized for the Officers. I went from the *Ganges* to the point of land upon which it is proposed to erect the hospital for the British portion of the Garrison to be left behind here, & also to quarter one half of the English Battn. remaining behind. . . .

Friday 8th May

Was on shore at 6 a.m. and went out by rail to the Hd.Qtrs. Camp where we found horses waiting for us. I then inspected all the troops now here. The Grenadiers were clean & well turned out: a great contrast to the Coldstream. The Native troops were beautifully turned out, clean & soldierlike. What a detestable climate this is: it resembles that of Cape Coast Castle without being deadly. I turned out—I had slept on deck—at daybreak & even then,—the coldest moment of the 24 hours, it was hot, sweltering & muggy—all one's body bathed in unwholesome perspiration, making one feel limp and powerless. Of this I am certain, Englishmen could not march on foot in this climate at this season of the year. . . . A telegram from the Queen saying she wants to see McNiell's report upon his action of the 22nd March. Landed in the evening and inspected the Base Hospital in II Redoubt. Found it in good order.

Saturday 9th May

Landed at 6 a.m. and rode round all the position it is proposed by me to hold, coming back through the Bazaars of the town....

At last received telegram[296] from Hartington announcing policy. Of course it is unwise, coming from such a Cabinet it could not be otherwise, but some of its suggestions are such that no schoolboy even would have dreamt of them. The troops from the Upper Nile are to be withdrawn as soon as I can do so with most convenience to the civil employees to be brought away & with best regard to the health of the troops. Buller says the sooner this is begun the better, but that the little Vakeel wants 15 days start, before we begin: he wants 5 weeks, but that he cannot have. So there is an end to all our hopes of seeing *Khartoum* and of ever reaping any fruits from the successful fight we have had or any return for all the blood we have lost or the diabolical hard work we have endured. Only three months ago, this Government determined upon destroying the Mahdi's power at *Khartoum*, and went to an enormous expense in the purchase of steam boats of various sorts & sizes, & consented to the extension of the Wady Halfa railway with a view to an autumn campaign on the Upper Nile. Now their policy is, cost what it may, to scuttle out of the Soudan.

As regards this place, they won't have my proposal to abandon the Rl.Rd. They order me to arrange for holding it during the summer; ask what troops in addition to the garrison I had proposed for the occupation of a restricted extent of territory—round which I went this morning—I considered would be required to hold railway at *Otao*; whether I could find some suitable place in the hills as a military station, and lastly whether I could not manage to pay native tribes to protect railway. I sent off for Chermside, Graham, Greaves & the *P.M.O.* to answer various questions on matters referred to either directly or indirectly in this silly telegram. I wrote out the substance of my answer, in which I denounced these proposals made by Hartington. I do not believe the Govt. will dare to carry them out in the face of my protest....

Scarcely a night passes without the enemy cutting down some of the telegraph poles. Osman Digma is reported to have gone away further into the hills & to be about 50 miles from this now, at the same time there are indications that he is regaining strength and reputation, & the number of his followers increasing.

Sunday 10th May

Landed about 5.15 a.m. & cantered over to the water forts where I found a squadron of the 9th Bengal Cavalry & one of the Mounted Infantry awaiting my arrival. We then started for the scene of McNiell's fight of 22nd March. The country & the bush is much more open than I expected to find it. The sight round the Yeribah is disgusting with half-buried men & half-burnt camels. There is and can be no doubt McNiell was surprised: he had one squadron of Cavalry—not nearly enough for the force & number of animals he had with him—and it ought to have been pushed forward at least a couple of miles whereas I believe it merely formed a line of groups of 4 men at about 1000 yards in advance of the Yeribah. The best proof that he was surprised is that when attacked many of his men were at a distance from their arms & accoutrements which they had most improperly been allowed to take off whilst employed in cutting brush for the protection of the Yeribah. Graham should not have sent such a mass of camels into a thick and very thorny bush until a strong post had been established ahead, and indeed I think he would have acted much wiser if he had ordered McNiell more to his left where the country is much more open. He certainly ought to have sent all his available cavalry with the column to have protected it from surprise during the march. Bad luck seems to have followed McNiell and indeed I may say all this Force from the first. All the spies had warned Graham that the enemy meant to attack on the first opportunity our men whilst they were engaged in making a Yeribah, and he ought consequently to have sent out a larger force less encumbered with transport animals. I believe there were about 1100 Camels and 400 Mules besides some carts. . . .

There is to be a sort of vote of censure in the House of Commons tomorrow evening: I most sincerely hope Gladstone may be turned out but I am afraid there is no such luck in store for England. . . .

Monday 11th May

Went out in a large steam launch to the outer harbor where there are 28 ships lying mostly laden with Railway material for which transports the country pays a large sum. English post of 1st instant arrived about 11 a.m. It is a certainty we shall now have an arbitration about *Penj-Deh*—that means of course, that old Gladstone has arranged to run away. A very hot and disagreeable day. Oh such a climate to keep British soldiers in!

Tuesday 12th May

Landed and started at 5 a.m. by train for *Otao*, from which place I rode on to *Tambouk* with a small Mounted Infantry escort. Inspected the Battn. of the Scots Guards that is there. It looked well and in workmanlike condition. As I rode along I thought of poor Herbert Stewart who last year gave me such a good description of this country & of the ground round *Tambouk*. I went ashore in the evening & dined at Head Qtrs. Mess—bad dinner. An extremely hot & unpleasant day.

Wednesday 13th May

Piping hot and as disagreeable as any climate can be: but if I feel this sitting in light clothes on board ship, what do our poor men feel this climate to be, when grilling in their hot tents, with barely enough water to wash their bodies. How I wish every British soldier could be withdrawn from this filthy place. Remained on board all day, but went ashore in the evening & strolled through the Bazaars. The woodwork of the windows is very pretty and evinces considerable taste. Saw some fairly nice silver bracelets being hawked about, but I did not buy any as most absurd prices were asked for them. The officers of the Guards have run up the price of everything here. I saw any quantity of spears that had evidently been made here yesterday.

Thursday 14th May

English post left at noon. In the morning rec'd a telegram[297] saying that under the circumstances represented in my telegram of 10th inst., my former proposals for reduction of force and withdrawing from the *Otao* & *Hamdoub* & taking up railway, are approved. No Govt. (for party reasons) could have dared to decide otherwise in the teeth of my telegram of 10th inst. In the evening I had another message ordering Guards home at once. A spy in from Osman

Digma's camp says he is still in his old place near *Tamanib* and has about 1000 followers with him: the number increasing, as he has announced that we are the victims of a cruel malady which will destroy us. Mr. Brewster[298] who is the central figure of the Intelligence Dept. here, dined with me. He said he believed that during last year & this year together we had *killed* at least 10,000 of the enemy in this neighbourhood. No wonder the Natives declare they have an everlasting blood feud with the 'white helmets' as they call us.

I saw Chermside and desired him if possible to enter into some agreement with the 'Friendlies' for the protection of the Rl.Rd. on the following terms. We give them over the fortified posts we have constructed at *Otao* and *Hamdoub*: to give them a small amount of Arms & ammunition & from £1500 to £2000 worth of grain a month for the next five months. We should run a daily along the line as they protected it from injury.

I believe myself that an armour-plated train with from 15 to 100 soldiers and a Construction Detachment and two Gatlings on board, ought, with very little help from the 'Friendlies' posted in *Hamdoub* and *Otao*, to be able to keep the Line open. I don't relish the idea of trying this, but of course the Govt. would like beyond measure to avoid having to announce that the Railway we so recently put down, was now to be taken up again. They would like to be able to tell '*the House*' that the Friendlies had undertaken to protect it, even although in their hearts they might feel certain the agreement entered into was not worth the paper on which it was written. I think it unlikely the Friendlies will accept my offer, but if they accept, I am quite satisfied they will not attempt to hold the Line if Osman Digma moves against them. However if they will accept & that even for a month, the Line is kept open, it will help the Govt. This may be dishonest, but party politics and dishonesty are united with the closest bonds, and if I want to help the party in power in this matter, I must stoop to party tricks.

Friday 15th May

Telegraphed my congratulations to Middleton & his troops in Manitobah.[299] I saw Capt. Constable R.E.[300] on board: he has had ten years' experience on the Rajpootana (Metre Gauge) Rl.Rd. He described this line here as the worst he had ever seen: not even the sidings on a contractors line are usually so bad. Instead of about 2000 sleepers per mile, there are not he says more than about 1200. The rails are laid level instead of with the usual cant inwards of about 1 in 20, & consequently all the wheels have very little bearing on the rails. The fish plates are not fitted to the rails: the engines cannot drag up more than seven carriages, & yet the gradients are nor more than 1 in 100. Altogether a more pitiable attempt to construct a railway, or a more wretched railway when constructed, it would be difficult to conceive.

The Grenadier Gds. embarked in *Jumna*—Scots Gds. will do so tomorrow & Coldstream in *Deccan*. Graham & Staff in latter Ship also.

Inspected New South Wales contingent at 6.15 p.m. & made them a 'neat & appropriate' speech with a good deal of 'Rule Britannia' in it. Wrote my farewell order in breaking up the Soudan Army.[301] Dined with Sir A. Young[302] on board his Yacht. Had a telegram[303] from Stephenson in answer to question I put to him as to what should in future be our force in Egypt: I told him to confer with Baring. They say, that in danger of the troubles we may expect as a consequence upon our policy of retreat from *Dongola*, there must be in Egypt, in addition to garrison on frontier, at and beyond *Assuan*, one Regt. of Cavly., one Horse Artillery & two garrison Batteries and $8\frac{1}{2}$ Battns. of Infantry.

Consequently, by our policy of retreat, and of handing over the Province of Dongola to the Mahdi & to anarchy, we shall gain one field Battery (that now at *Cairo*) one & a half Battalions of Infy. and shall require to be augmented by one Regt. of Cavalry.

Saturday 16th May

Sent off copy of Stephenson's telegram and a strong argument from myself[304] to War Secretary on folly of proposed retreat from *Dongola*, asking 'is it too late even now to reconsider policy of retreat?' The Brigade of Guards embarked: also Graham & Fremantle. All accounts say that Mahmond Ahmed is on his last legs, even the Baggara tribes are deserting him. Went ashore in the evening to see Chermside.

Sunday 17th May 1885

The *Jumna* & *Deccan* steamed out of harbor at 6 a.m. with the

Brigade of Guards on board. There are six condensing ships here of an aggregate tonnage (gross of 12191 tons): Working full power they can distil 860 tons daily, but usually they only make when using all boilers only 687 tons: they can carry 3835 tons of drinking water: the average daily consumption has been about 400 tons. The present stock in hand is about 4700 tons. There are six Tank vessels of an aggregate gross tonnage of 1957 tons and they can carry 1277 tons of distilled water. . . .

Telegram from Baring saying Buller has been ordered to move all Egyptian soldiers & civil employees from Province of Dongola to *Wady Halfa*, all idea of setting up a Govt. there having been abandoned!! I don't think this is wise, & it certainly is most undignified. . . .

I telegraphed to Hartington saying that for military & political reasons I had determined not to take up railway even if friendly Tribes refuse to accept my offer about protecting it. Brewster & Capt. Molyneux[305] of the Intelligence Department came on board by appointment. The Tribes are to give their final answer tomorrow, and as I shall not know it until late in the afternoon I have postponed my departure until Tuesday.

Monday 18th May

Inspected the Indian Contingent at 6.30 a.m. *The Queen* hauled in alongside No. 4 pier & took in some mules to go back with us to Suez as Stephenson says he wants 1000 mules for transport work in Egypt. The remainder I send to India. I am still in great hopes of being able to sell all the spare camels here to a contractor. Went to see McNiell on board the *Belimba*, & told him he was to return to Egypt with me & so go home by mail to England. He is better today, but still far from well.

This harbor is extremely foul and stinking. Greaves maintains that much of the enteric fever comes from having the drinking water distilled or rather I should say condensed from what he calls the 'sewage' of the harbor. He is very amusing: talking this morning of the egotism of dear Graham's dull & very badly-put-together despatches, he said, 'I was once telling Lord Airey[306] some anecdote of myself or my own performances when Airey said, 'Greaves, your memoirs will be very interesting whenever they are published.' Greaves said 'I was bridling up with pride at Lord Airey's estimation of my career and of my doings when he added, 'However my dear Greaves you may have some difficulty in finding a printer that will have sufficient type for the vast number of personal pronouns of the first number.' I sank into my boots at this, said Greaves with a loud laugh as loud as when he convulses himself with delight when he makes a good joke. It is a good trait that he can laugh quite as loudly at himself as he can at anyone else. He is quite happy now that he has got rid of Graham.

At 5 p.m. Mr. Brewster & Captn. Molyneux came to see me; they had been to *Otao* & interviewed the Amara Sheiks there to receive their final [answer]. They all cried at hearing we were about to bolt, but declined our offers: they said they were not strong enough to hold *Otao* & *Hamdoub*. They were told my offer did not continue, having been declined, it would hold good no longer. So there ends my attempt to carry out the wish of the Govt. to arrange with some tribes for the protection of the Railway during the summer. The Officers Commdg. at *Otao* & *Hamdoub* reported their men could not any longer be employed in protecting the parties working on the Rl.Rd. I fully concurred, for I feel that in such a climate to expose British soldiers all day to the sun would be to kill them. I have therefore ordered all further work on the Rl.Rd. to cease. At Brigdr. Hudson's[307] request, I have ordered one squadron of 9th Bengal Cavalry to be retained here.

I dined with Chermside. Post from England arrived at noon. I hear the Cabinet is a most unhappy family; Gladstone very anxious to resign: the radicals Chamberlain & Dilke extremely angry that the new taxation to cover the vote of credit does not hit property more: these two demaguoges [*sic*] denounce the increased taxation of beer and spirits. If Gladstone goes, there will be a split between the Whigs & the Radicals.

I hear Brett is in disgrace about some papers in connection with Russia; I am not sorry, for I think him a most uppish Gentleman that did Hartington no good: I am glad he is no longer connected in any way with the War Office. . . .

Tuesday 19th May 1885

. . . . The Indian Govt. won't buy any of our railway plant. They ought to be forced to buy *all* our rails at a reduced price—so it is all to be landed at *Suakim*. Captain Fellows R.N.[308] the Transport Officer assured me it would take about *seven months* to land it. A nice demurrage we shall have to pay: well, according to this calculation the rails &c. for the first 100 miles only of the line could not have been stacked ashore until the middle of December!! A nice look out for me this would have been, if the advance up the Nile had been continued next Autumn and I had in any way depended upon the construction of the Berber–Suakin Railway as a factor in my military calculations. Had a telegram from Sir R. Thompson saying Spenser Childers left for *Cairo* this Friday: this does not look as if it were meant to bring me home soon. Perhaps the Govt. do not relish the idea of having an accusing angel in England whilst the Session lasts; perhaps they have lost all confidence in me & that Hartington finds Alison is more useful to him than I used to be. I had a note yesterday from Sir C. Wilson begging of me to relieve him from his present painful position, as he felt he could not with any conscience carry out the new policy of the Govt., having for some months back over & over again repeated to the people with whom he had dealings, that we positively meant to advance on *Khartoum* this coming autumn. He goes on to say that if he were not entirely dependent upon the Army for a living, he would like to resign his commission. I fully enter into his feelings, & have over and over again debated within myself which was the truly patriotic course to follow; whether to resign, saying I could not in decency or in honor or with any self-respect carry out the new policy which the Govt. had adopted in direct opposition to that which it has previously determined upon; or whether I should put my own personal feelings in my pocket, and carry out the policy deliberately adopted by the Govt. which the English people placed in power, & of which they evinced their approval by keeping them there. When last in *Cairo* I wrote out the telegram resigning my position here & debated in my mind for one night whether I should or should not send it. It is needless to add I did not send it, for here I am still engaged in carrying out a policy that I regard as foolish, criminal and derogatory to the nation whose honor is my honor. I know of no more difficult question to solve than that of at what point it becomes the duty of a man in my present position to resign. If I were to follow the bent of my own inclinations I should have resigned the day Hartington telegraphed to me that the Govt. had resolved to withdraw all our troops from the Soudan. At noon Lat. 20°–09′ N; Long. 37°–32′ E: Run since starting 66 miles.

Wednesday 20th May

. . . . I have had some talk with McNiell regarding the late operations near *Suakin*. He says the Staff sent out were horribly bad. Graham was not equal to the task; he can fight a Brigade, but he can organize nothing. His plans were bad: they were badly designed, and misfortune overtook all he attempted. The expedition he sent McNiell on, was very badly conceived in every way & from every point of view. Lat. 24°29′ N. Long. 36°E. Run 274 miles.

Thursday 21st May 1885

Lat. 28°.05′ N: Long: 33°.25′ E. Run 262 miles: Noon: distance from Suez 124 miles: the total distance from *Suakin* to Suez is 726 miles (nautical). . . .

. . . . I read with the greatest interest and admiration Lord Salisbury's speech at *Hackney* on I think the 6th instant. Its statements of fact are undeniable & its arguments are unanswerable. This present Govt. has always declared itself to be most anxious to get rid of its Egyptian responsibilities, but in giving up the Province of Dongola to the Mahdi, they rivet the links of the chain that binds us to Egypt. Unless the Mahdi dies soon I see no end to our occupation of the Delta, & even if he were to disappear, some one else of the same Kidney would start up & keep the sentiment . . . alive. Of course Mr. Gladstone may succeed in calling in *all* the European Powers to assist in holding Egypt or he may denationalize not only the Canal but also Egypt itself.

Anchored at Suez, outside harbor at 11.30 p.m.

Friday 22nd May

Entered the harbor about 6.30 a.m. . . . . Left Suez by the ordinary daily train at 9.15 a.m. & reached *Cairo* at 4.30 p.m. Drove to *Kasr el Noussa*.

Found that by orders from home the Guards Brigade had been ordered to *Alexandria* to await orders & I am warned not to sell any camels without obtaining special permission. I suppose there is some temporary hitch in the Russian negociations, but it is quite certain that we mean to give way on all points. Spenser Childers met me at Rl.Rd. Station having reached *Cairo* last night. From what he tells me, it is evident Govt. must dissolve on Irish

Crimes Act, the Cabinet being divided thus, all my noble Lords insist on a new Bill, whilst the simple Rt. Honbles. are against its renewal. Lord Spenser[309] would resign if it be not renewed, so it is an impass[e]. I suppose Hartington would attempt to form a new Govt., but I presume the radicals would not join him & without those vermin, I am sure he could not carry on long. I telegraphed home asking if I was now to go home as I did not see I could be of any further use here. I hope I may be given the *Iris* to take me to Venice. In what a different position I am returning home from that in which I went home in 1882. And yet I deserved success more in 1885 than in '82. Forty-eight hours too late at *Khartoum* has made all the difference!!

Saturday 23rd May

Baring called on me early & we went together to see the Khedive & Nubar Pasha. Baring is open-mouthed against the Govt. & especially Mr. Gladstone: if a red-hot radical feels so strongly against the old impostor, men like me may be excused for despising him & looking upon him as a curse of England. We discussed a proposal of Buller's for the creation of a ridiculous Govt. at *Dongola* which was to cost money & to entail handing over to the men entrusted with the formation of this Govt. a quantity of arms & ammunition. I am most anxious to go through the form of setting up some Govt. to assume charge as we clear out, even although I know in my heart that any such Govt. will be essentially and entirely hollow, and will disappear the instant that a couple of hundred of the Mahdi's dervishes reach *Dongola*. But I think it is so shamefully scandalous to run away carrying with us all the civil employees of the present Govt. and handing over what according to Eastern notions is a fairly governed Province, that for the credit of our name I should like to see some administration created to replace us, even although it be merely a bogus one.

However we can pay too heavily for this sham Government, and I think that Buller's proposal would cause us to do so. The result of our conference was a telegram to Buller telling him so. Paid Prince Hassan a visit in the evening. Everyone here in despair at our retreat from the Upper Nile. . . .

Saturday 24th May: The Queen's birthday

I had a nice telegram from Her Majesty yesterday asking how I was. I telegraphed to Her this morning thanking Her for it & saying I hoped She would live long over a people proud of their strength and jealous of their national honor, or something to that effect. In the evening I had the following answer. 'Most grateful for kind telegram & congratulations. I pray to be always able to do my best for the happiness & honor of my dear country. What are your movements? The Queen'.

I had an answer from Hartington[310] about my going home: says although there is no serious hitch with Russia, whilst Guards are detained here I must stay for at least this week. The only possibility of troops being required anywhere is in India. Whether he means by that the possibility of my having to go there or not, does not appear. I am told on good authority, the idea of the Govt. in the event of war, was to send me with all the troops that could be collected to *Riga* to raise the Poles. If given a sufficient force this would be an operation entirely after my own heart, but I fear it would be one entirely beyond the military strength of England, as our nation is now constituted. Such a policy would bring the Germans & the Austrians on our backs, sooner or later, & without having studied the operation it would seem to be one of great risk, lest before we could get at the Poles our Army near *Riga* should be crushed by numbers. To be successful in any such great undertaking, a very different form of Govt. from our present one would be necessary. In democracies like our's, it has always been found necessary to create a Dictator in times of great national danger. Mr. Lincoln was, by the good sense of the American people, allowed to assume to himself all the powers of a Dictator during the North & South War. The notion that any great war could be carried on by a Cabinet constituted as ours is at present is simply childish.

Greaves telegraphs that as our troops moved out of *Hamdoub*, a few shots were fired from a distance at them. Buller's estimate as to dates are—*Abu Dom* to be evacuated 26th May. Brackenbury is to command the rear Guard, which should clear out of *Dongola* the 21st June: he Buller intended leaving that place on the 15th June, and he hoped everyone and everything would be cleared out of *Abu Fatmeh* by the 10th July. Telegraphed today to Wood[311] offering him the command of the troops at *Assouan* & on the frontier. He will be furious, for his vanity is such that he thinks he should be commander in Chief everywhere. If he refuses it, I have recommended Grenfell for the post. . . .

Monday 25th May 1885

An armour plated train ran out along the line towards *Hamdoub* & found the Line cut in two places and about half a mile on our side of that place removed bodily, sleepers & all. Rec'd. orders to send all the plant now on board ships to England. Guards to disembark at *Alexandria*. Armed steamers up the Nile to be manned by soldiers in future. The Cabinet has saved its existence for the moment by agreeing to renew the Irish Crimes Act for one year: they will thus tide over the electors in November without a break up which everyone thought so imminent. . . .

Tuesday 26th May

In the afternoon rode to the *Bulak* arsenal and saw one of our stern-wheel steamers launched most successfully. Dined with Zohrab. Admiralty have demanded all the Officers & men of Rl. Navy now up the Nile: it appears they have so whittled away the number of Lieutenants on the establishment that now they cannot find enough good men of that rank for their iron-clads. There is a significant expression in the 'Reuter' of today which points to the return here of Ismail vice Tewfik to be pensioned off. . . .

Wednesday 27th May

. . . . A report from *Dongola* that the Mahdi was sending Hussein Pasha Khalifa to *Cairo* to treat: I don't believe it unless he is in his last extremity. Went to see Lady Baring off in the evening. Station crowded with idlers who are glad to have an excuse to go anywhere or do anything. Large number of officers and others started also for England. . . .

Thursday 28th May

. . . . English post arrived. This detention of troops is on account of a serious hitch in the Russian negotiations. The Czar, who knows full well that Mr. Gladstone would sooner surrender the Isle of Wight than fight for it, is naturally determined to get what he wants. He says he will fight for what HE wants, so of course poor England will be made by her nefarious rulers to eat humble pie and apologize. Every Englishman should now carry about with him printed in several languages an abject apology saying 'my dear friend have pity on me, don't kick me, I beg your pardon —I was in the wrong: I apologize.' The paper should bear the Gladstone arms, that is, supposing that family of traders ever had any.

Tani was evacuated today....

Friday 29th May

Went to see the Howling Dervishes: I am glad I have seen them for no one can ever worry to go and see them again. Rode in the evening to see Stephenson who is better. George arrived looking well: he returns to India.

Saturday 30th May

I have now plenty of idle time on hands, so I am working at a new edition of the Soldier's Pocket book, which always interests & amuses me. I no longer feel any interest in keeping this diary....

June 1885

Monday 1st June

Had a long ride through old *Cairo* where I visited the oldest Mosque here—of course it was mostly in ruins. Evelyn Wood arrived looking very much pulled down from constant diarrohoea [*sic*].[312] Dined at the club with Genl. & Mrs. Davis:[313] he is a good rollicking but very foolish Irishman & she is a very nice little woman. Telegram from Loo saying she is at *Milan* & will stay there until she hears from me. Also one from Hartington saying I might sell the camels at *Suakim* & he would soon tell me as to my own movements. However the Guards are still to remain at *Alexandria*. . . .

Wednesday 3rd June

Rode through the tombs of the Khalifs and over the Mahattan heights. With Rev. Vandyke as interpreter had a long conversation with an old Egyptian soldier of the 5th Regt. who was in *Khartoum* when it fell. He saw Gordon's head on a short spear in the Omdurman camp & often saw people go up to it & pluck hair from the head and beard and say to him, 'ah you were one of Gordon's soldiers: see his head.'

Thursday 4th June 1885

My birthday and my wedding day. 52 years old & 18 years

married!! I cannot realize that I am so old & that I should now take care of my digestion & not jump about lest I should sprain my ankle or break some of my bones now become brittle from age. I never expected to have lived so long but then I expected to have done something more in the world before the time came for my final departure from this world of meanness and lying & cowardice and cant. God's ways are inscrutable: why he should take away from England a man like Herbert Stewart in the prime of life and of his usefullness [*sic*] to the state, and leave us that hoary bearded old sinful & untruthful humbug Mr. Gladstone is beyond our understanding. He has some good reason for humbling us and humiliating us as a nation, & Mr. Gladstone is the fiend selected for this awful work....

Saturday 6th June

Cairo—Arrived here at 5.15 a.m. Found the English mail of 29th ultimo awaiting me. Amongst my letters, one from Lord Spencer, saying the Queen has through Mr. Gladstone approved of his recommendation that he should offer me the vacant Ribbon of St. Patrick &c. &c. Of course this is a great honor, for it is a decoration generally given to Irish peers only. I don't remember it having ever been given before for military services rendered. The distinction is I confess seriously marred by the introduction of Mr. Gladstone's name into the announcement. I should have valued it more highly, if his name had been omitted. This is to be my reward for work done here. Men cannot command success, but they can mortally and humanly speaking deserve it. My effort to relieve Gordon and the Khartoum garrison was a failure: an hour in such matters is as fatal as a month, & therefore I have no right whatever to any reward. And yet such is life that I don't expect ever to do anything better in the way of plans than that formed to save Gordon, designed to make up for the valuable time dawdled away through Mr. Gladstone's folly and ministerial incapacity. The conception from first to last was a most daring one, partaking of the romantic in many ways. Had it succeeded, it would have been I think the most memorable military event of the kind ever achieved. However it failed, and there is no use in crying over the few days, few hours indeed, by which it missed being a glorious success. I am to be a K.P! so I must be happy! When I read Ld. Spencer's letter I asked myself if I were gratified. That a man of

52 years of age who has already a bushel of medals and decorations should feel any new satisfaction and pride at having a new gewgaw conferred upon him, made me laugh as I put this question to myself, and I laughed all the more when I felt bound to admit that I did value this new toy, and was very much pleased at having it offered to me. Poor human nature! vanity, vanity, most truly is all nought but vanity in this world. Even my hero Gordon whom I revered when he lived and whose memory I shall always cherish, even he, great and glorious hero as he was, had his vanities. I knew him so well that I saw them crop up here & there, although he was unconscious of them. I, who was not worthy of being his servant may therefore be well excused for my innocent pleasure in having this new distinction conferred upon me. The difficulty with Russia continues, so the Guards remain for the present at *Alexandria* & as long as they remain I do so also. I feel that having been employed during my life in many various ways I am now converted into a *'demonstration'*. The Queen's birthday was kept today. All our troops paraded in the Abdin Square. I did not attend as I did not wish to come the Comdg. Officer over Stephenson who has behaved so well all through this Nile business & been so loyal to me who came here to supercede him.

I dined with him in the evening at an official 'banquet'. What a dull business it is having a meal with the 'Heads of Departments'. Thank Heavens their wives were not there. Reuter reported in the evening that the Amir of Affghanistan has been assassinated. If this be true it is the Russian 'counter' to our great Durbar.

Sunday 7th June

.... Up to this evening the refugees from the Dongola province number about ten thousand people, not counting those whom Buller describes as numerous who are floating down the river on their Shakiyehs. In fact we are leaving nearly a desert behind us for it would seem as if every man who had anything to lose is coming away.

Monday 8th June

Went to see the Khedive leave for *Alexandria* at 7 a.m. It now appears that *Kassala* fell about the 22 May and there was no massacre. . . . Reuter says the Russian business is arranged, the

Czar having made concessions. Of course he always makes concessions, for having settled in his own mind what [he] wants and means to have, he asks for a vast deal more, & pretends he will make war unless he gets all: is on the point of breaking off negociations: his diplomatists are very clever. They pretend they can make no further 'concessions!!!!!' Perhaps a third party is called in, but at any rate the business ends by the abandonment on their part of all the extra territory or advantages that had been demanded in the first instance in order to take them off at the last moment. Then the whole matter ends in paens of praise of the Czar's magnanimity & generosity by Gladstone, Bright, Chamberlain and all the Radical haters of England's greatness....

Tuesday 9th June

.... News from England that the Govt, yesterday only passed their budget by a majority of 12 & Reuter adds, Mr. Gladstone had announced that the Cabinet must consider their position. The telegram goes on to say it is believed the Ministry will resign. I never thought they would do so on previous divisions but now I think they will. Of course they can alter their budget, Mr. Childers resigning, but they can scarcely have the face to adopt this line. Party only is thought of—no one seems to remember there is an Empire behind all this talking machine of Parliament. If the Conservatives were to come in tomorrow I can't see how they could hold office for six months. If there is a change now, it will be the third time that my return to England has been celebrated by the defeat of the party that sent me out.

Since writing the above another 'Reuter' appeared explaining the previous telegram to be a mistake & announcing the Govt. had been *beaten* by 12, so at last the country has cast from it the most unworthy man who ever directed its affairs. May I never breath the same air with him again for he taints everything with cant, cowardice and untruth.

Telegram[314] from Hartington says, owing to defeat of Govt. he can send me no orders about myself or the Guards, so I shall be here for at least another week certainly.

Wednesday 10th June

Reuter announces the resignation of the Govt. & the adjournment of the House until Friday next. Rode in the desert with Greaves who arrived here yesterday, looking very well and jolly. Telegram announcing nomination to the vacant ribbon of St. Patk. Spenser tells me that his father told him in a letter received by the last post that in the Cabinet he had volunteered to alter his budget and remit the increased tax on beer, but that it was decided not to do so. This is the question on which the Govt. has fallen. I presume Chamberlain & Dilke have egged on the Radicals to vote against the Govt. because they wanted the increased revenue required to be drawn from the landowners & were also I imagine anxious to get out of office for the time: they don't relish the idea of belonging to a Govt. that will have to invent some scheme for paying the big bill which Mr. Gladstone's folly has imposed upon the nation. The refugees from *Dongola* are now over 11,000 souls....

Thursday 11th June

Dear old Billy Hewett[315] arrived. He is on his way home to take up the duty of a Lord of the Admiralty. He tells me the P. & O. ship he was on board was stopped at *Ismaillia*, the canal a little north of that having been blocked by a dredger sinking directly across it.... I am very glad this has occurred, although it causes considerable inconvenience, because it will show stupid men like Northbrook how easily this canal could be obstructed in time of war. It will also show us how long it will take to remove or rather dredge round such a simple obstruction as an unloaded dredger. I had an argument with Northbrook on this subject during our voyage in the *Iris* & told him I knew some places in the canal where by sinking a large ship filled with small stones, all navigation would be stopped for months. He knew nothing of the subject but pooh-poohed what I said in that vulgar & rude manner for which he is so notorious. I studied the subject very closely in 1882 when I prepared the plan of campaign to seize & to save *Cairo* from the fate which befell *Alexandria* mainly owing to the folly & ignorance of Northbrook. I knew something of my subject, Northbrook nothing, but I was not a Cabinet Minister and had never been a Viceroy of India, so because he was one & had been the other, he thought he could afford to be obstinate as well as rude....

Friday 12th June

The Queen who is still at Balmoral has sent for Ld. Salisbury. I wish that dear good Lady would go south at once. She is inconsiderate upon these points, having been badly educated upon them by Prince Albert.... Our camels at *Suakim* are dying at the rate of 25 per diem, and now a request has come to destroy 1500 as useless, and dangerous to the health of the rest....

Monday 15th June

.... An answer received from the Mahdi declining to give up his European prisoners whom he says are quite happy having all become Moslems & who do not wish to leave him. They all signed their names to the paper he sent. He says he is quite indifferent to the fate of those members of his family whom we have made prisoners & sent to *Halfa*.

Tuesday 16th June

Telegram from Sir R. Thompson in answer to one I sent him asking who was the new Secretary of St. for War, says nothing settled yet....

Thursday Waterloo Day

English post in: I am glad to find that several of my telegrams & despatches condemning the Govt. policy have been published and have had some effect. They will at least show the world that I have had the courage of my opinions....

Friday 19th June

Telegram from Thompson that if Conservatives form a Ministry *which* is certain, W. H. Smith[316] is to be War Minister. I wonder if he will persist in our reforms or give way to H.R.H., and go back. If the latter he will not be bored by having me as A.G.: I shall try doing nothing for some time....

Saturday 20th June

.... Some Egyptian soldiers escaped from *Berber* and have

reached *Dongola*. They say the rejoicings were great when the new of our retreat from the Dongola Province reached the rebels. I begin to feel very bored here, for I live in that uncertainty that it is difficult to settle down to any serious work, sleep excepted. News from England says Parliament adjourned until Tuesday next: that *pour parlers* are going on between the late Ministers & Ld. Salisbury's team, but that no official statement on the subject had yet been made. Telegram from the Queen saying she is very much pleased with the donkey I sent her. . . .

Tuesday 23rd June

It is at last arranged that Lord Salisbury does actually accept office, so I presume I shall hear something about my own movements before the end of the week. Just heard from John Hay that *Iris* is in dock at Malta, preparing for some trip such as that with me to *Venice*. I hope she may be sent here soon or else I shall have to go there by the mailsteamer. I shall be curious to know what line Mr. W. H. Smith will take up: I hope sincerely it may be one of progress. . . .

Thursday 25th June

A most flattering telegram to me from Lord Salisbury informing me they had today (24th) accepted the Seals & wished to express to me their entire confidence in me in the difficult task I was entrusted with, or words to that effect. How different from the party just retired, from whom I have not had a line of thanks. Of course Lord Spencer has given me the K.P., and perhaps that was intended to be a recognition from the Govt. collectively of the exertions I made to save *Khartoum*.

By this little *touch*, Salisbury has shown that he understands men & human nature, for the promptness & unexpectedness of his telegram has fetched me a good deal and would do so still more with most other men.

English post in. I had written to Thompson begging of him to get my despatch[317] on 'Selection in the Army' published: his answer just received: he says he spoke to Lord Hartington who said H.R.H. considered it such an attack upon him, that he could not publish it unless I omitted some sentences which in no way strengthened the argument. I intend replying that I approve of the paragraphs he refers to being omitted on condition it is then published. I am very anxious to see it in the newspapers before I return home, for I believe if published, it will inaugurate a new system for promotion to the rank of Lt. Colonel in the Army. . . .

Friday 26th June

The anniversary of the Khedive's accession. He has ordered about 4000 officials in *Cairo* to go to *Alexandria* to attend his levee today. All their expenses are paid, & I hear the cost will be about £10,000. So money is squandered on foolish objects in Eastern Courts. . . . Laid up with a bad eye—a serious matter for a poor devil who has only one that performs the recognized function of an eye. I remained in a dark room all day with my own thoughts and realised what a prison without books or writing materials must be. In the evening I dined with Charley Beresford in the public gardens. . . .

In the evening I had a telegram[318] from the War Secretary saying the Govt. wished for a full exposition of my views upon the position here and the best policy to adopt. Also one referring to that and saying I might send the Guards to Cyprus at once unless I wished to keep them here in consequence of any policy I wished to recommend in answer to previous message.

During the day, before receiving these two telegrams, I had one, asking me if troops still held *Dongola*, & if not how far north had troops reached in retreat. I was ordered to reply at once. All this is very startling and looks like a new departure: on the strength of these messages I have halted Brackenbury & his rear Guard at *Dongola*, although he has only one week's forage & provisions to the 18th July. *Fatmeh* would be clear of all stores & provisions, except what Rear Guard would require, by the 30th instant. How happy & grateful to God I shall be if, after all, I am allowed to put my foot on the neck of the Arch imposter, Mahmond Ahmed, before I return home. The idea is too delicious to dwell upon lest my disappointment should be correspondingly great.

Saturday 27th June

Rode in the morning to the Boulak station to meet the Black Watch on arrival. They left *Merawi* on the 26th so they have made the distance in 31 days. At lowest Nile this could only have been done in whalers. The men looked the picture of health, and of soldiers all over.

Despatched a long telegram to W. H. Smith in answer to him of yesterday, telling the Govt. emphatically that the true policy is to carry out the Autumn Campaign as originally contemplated and approved of. The only other alternative being to pay the Turk well to come in & take over the Soudan. Both my eyes bad—spent the day in a dark room rather gloomily.

Sunday 28th June

In the middle of the night had a telegram[319] from W. H. Smith saying Govt. wd. consider my telegram next Wednesday, but in the meantime to hold on to *Dongola* & report number of troops required to hold it apart from all question of Autumn Campaign towards *Khartoum*. He asks me the value of retaining *Dongola* in the event of no military operations taking place in the Autumn. I expected this, and felt that the retention of *Dongola* would be the Govt. program.

Charley Beresford had a telegram from his wife yesterday evening saying no decision would be come to about my return home for another fortnight. Telegram from Buller to whom I communicated in confidence the outline of Govt. proposal comes forward with 1000 objections; many of them have much weight, others are silly. The great difficulty is to find provisions for the men to be kept at *Dongola*, since the whole country has been so drained of all grain. The most difficult point will be to send away & replace the Kroomen whom we must keep on the river between rail end at *Fatmeh*.

Monday 29th June

Got off a long telegram[320] to W. H. Smith giving him details of troops required to hold *Dongola* & the advantages which its retention would secure. Also precis of what Buller says in opposition to our holding it. Remained in a dark room all day & my eyes feel much better.

Alas, we are to have that foolish man Bury[321] at the War Office as Under Secretary. The previous report was that Donoughmore was to have the place, & I wish it had been true. I suppose it is very narrow-minded, but I have always put down men who change from being Protestants to be Catholics as men of very small minds or at least minds entirely unsuited to practical life. I have known geese who thus changed—Denbigh,[322] Ripon,[323] Bury and many untitled fry, but all of whom the same mental calibre.

I would never employ a man on any important job who had so changed his faith. I can quite understand even extremely able men living and dying Roman Catholics having been reared by their mothers in that faith, and I am sure that God will accept them into his Kingdom as willingly as the most enlightened protestants but it is one of the thousand inscrutable actions of the Almighty that he should allow an honest man's mind to be so perverted & so blind to reason as to leave the simple faith of protestantism to take up with the priestcraft and humbug and deception of the Roman faith. A man educated as a protestant of any force of character could never surrender his will & reason to the keeping of another equally mortal human being & the man whose mind is so constituted as to allow him to do so is not of an order of intellect that should be entrusted with the conduct of any public affairs. How I should be ridiculed as a protestant bigot if I preached this view from the housetop; & yet I am sure I have no bigotry on the subject of religion and would just as soon have about me men who had been born Roman Catholics or born in the Greek Church as those who were born protestants. It is not on the score of faith that I object to employ men like Bury, it is because my own observation in life had taught me that men who have been born & educated in the free open enlightenment of low church protestantism, change in after life to popery, have minds of a nature, a chemistry, a character that unfits them for public life much less for any important role in the world's affairs.

Tuesday 30th June

English post left here at 8 a.m. That lunatic Mr. Gladstone has publicly announced his intention of again standing for Midlothian. I had hoped that God had delivered us from him. Why does he not die. Noble gallant men die or are killed in action and yet the Almighty allows this knave to live. I hear he now sits actually—not metaphorically—at Mrs. Langtrey's feet reading to her the 'Idylls of the King'. Telegram from Loo saying the Queen promises to see about my return. Message from Salisbury[324] that the Queen wished me to consider how McNiell could be best relieved from the unjust slur cast upon him. I shall write to the Queen by the next post on this matter. The less the subject is stirred up the better.

Charley Beresford gives me the following information about the passage of whale boats above the 2nd cataract that is interesting. Passed that cataract between 18th October & 6th December (both inclusive) 1884.

	Nos.
Whalers	
Western Channel	1
By train	26
Hauled through Bab	158
Portaged by Egyptn. Soldiers	587
Total	772
Gigs portaged	9
Whalers nos. 13 and 249 were wrecked in Bab	2
Grand Total	783

July 1885

Wednesday 1st July

Rode to the Boulak station to see the Guards Camel Regt. go through. Also the Gordon Highlanders. All were looking very well. I gave Col. Hammill[325] of the Gordon's a piece of my mind about the grumbling amongst his officers in which he set them an example. I told him none of his officers should have any rewards for the campaign. I thought he looked very guilty although he said he did not know who had written the lying letters that appeared in the *Standard*.

Thursday 2nd July

Telegram[326] dated yesterday evening from London after the Cabinet informs me that much as Govt. condemns the evacuation of *Dongola*, they do not mean under the circumstances to re-occupy it. They wish the Rl.Rd. held & leave it to me to decide what point shall be held south of *Halfa*. I replied the Rl. head, which is now *Akasha*, but I strongly urged railway extension to *Firket* as being above all the difficult cataracts, any forward movements that might be found hereafter necessary would be rendered easy by this extension. I have ordered Brackenbury to fall back at once to *Ahri* taking everybody & everything with him & on arrival there to hand over command of rear guard to whomever Grenfell shd. indicate & to come [up] country & return home. I have written to him saying I hope I shall be able to have him made a Major

General. I have ignored his wail about the insult he had received in being asked to serve under his junior Grenfell. Nowadays every man seems to think of himself only, starting with the notion that he is a Napoleon, and apparently entirely indifferent to the interests of the State. If in my carreer [*sic*] I had refused to serve under a Junior, I wonder where I should have been?* I always felt I should either be shot or else rise far above those whom favoritism pushed up the ladder whilst I was left to struggle up as best I could.

Mr. Smith's telegram ended by saying that H.M. Government would like to confer with me as soon as my duties have allowed me to leave. I have decided to go to *Venice* in H.M.S. *Iris*, Ld. John Hay had telegraphed that she would be ready at *Alexandria* on 7th instant, but a letter just received from her Captain says she will require to coal & clean up and will not be ready to start until evening of 9th. All this is so like the Navy—never inclined to help or be pleasant. With the exception of Billy Hewitt I have always found the Navy very civil when they want anything out of you, or hope to obtain promotion through a favourable report from you, but to help you individually when nothing can be got out of their friendly action never enters their head[s]: indeed they are determined not to help you unless obliged to do so by orders from home.

I expect Buller here on Saturday so I hope he will go home in *Iris* with me. Nubar Pasha is delighted at the news that we mean to hold *Akasha*. In conversation he told me that to hold the railway would go far towards neutralizing the bad effect our retreat had had on the popular mind here and amongst the Arab tribes. . . .

Friday 3rd July

. . . . A telegram[327] from War Secrety. saying the Govt. approve of my proposal to extend line to *Firket* on condition that Evelyn Baring concurs with me. This is the first time they have taken any notice of Baring or expressed any interest in what he thinks. I wrote & told him, sending copy of telegrams. He is evidently much hurt by their ignoring him, so he sends me back a rather shilly-shallow answer from which I could gather for certain. He objects to the Railway in toto: it can only be of use for a Soudan

---

*Wolseley never had occasion to serve under an officer junior to himself.

campaign to which he is strongly opposed &c. &c. He is at present opposed to everything—such is his humor. . . .

Saturday 4th July

Answered Baring's letter before I went out riding this morning & pointed out that he had not replied to my previous question. The Govt. had already settled the point on which he was inclined to argue, for they meant to hold the Rl. Road, & the question I had referred to him was where would be best for its terminus. He won't give any answer as he objects to the Rl.Rd. altogether. His arguments are weak.

Poor old Col Richardson[328] breakfasted with me and after the feast asked for a private interview. He then begged of me to find him employment when his time was up in his Battn. as would be the case on the 26th instant. I told him in as gentle & as roundabout a fashion as I could that I did not think he had any chance of further military employment, & therefore recommended him to accept his retirement. Poor old fellow he pressed me hard to help him, & I had not the courage to be brutal enough to tell him he could not be further employed, as he was entirely useless in every capacity. I told him when he referred to his services under me & to how hard he had striven to do his duty, that I had always found him a gentleman. What a sin to give such men the command of soldiers in action.

Mr Antoniades interviewed me—a good old fellow full of kindness & hospitality. He is however a dreadful bore, and his hospitality is like the plague. He belongs to a set of men to be found all over the East—few are however as good a fellow as he is. They don't read, & have a great deal of spare time on their hands. I presume they don't think much, and are intensely bored at being alone. Consequently they spend a considerable portion of their day in paying visits, and in gossiping. It never seems to occur to them that anyone should view life from a different standpoint, or wish for privacy and silence. I never should have temper to be an Eastern ruler, to be like poor Charley Gordon the Gov. General of an Eastern Country. All Eastern potentates may be said to live in public. If they write a letter it is dictated in open durbar: the idea that any public man, more especially any ruler or first minister should retire to read or write, alone, in the recesses of his own private appartment [*sic*], never enters into their philosophy.

The recognized principle is that you should always be accessible of approach. I could not lead such a life: it would [be] the weariness of very purgatory to me. I love to be alone & to commune with myself, and cannot imagine how any man can do much in this world who does not retire daily to take advice with himself and argue out in his brain the line of conduct he should pursue. By all means have your hours of pleasure, a boisterous pleasure if you will, having your dissipations, if they are necessary to you, see plenty of the world, transact the required business of the day with those whom it concerns, but then get away and commune with your heart as well as your brains, alone, and if possible in a noiseless quiet.

Went to the Boulak d'Akror station at 7 p.m. to meet Buller who looked very fit and delighted at the prospect of getting home next Tuesday. Most unfortunately the telegraph line continues down between *Assuan* & *Korosko* so I cannot communicate directly with Grenfell or Brackenbury. My telegram of the 2nd to the latter directing him to fall back was the last over the line before it was intercepted. Mine on the same subject to Grenfell failed to get through. I cannot settle either about Zohrab's promotion until the line is repaired to enable Grenfell to answer the Khedive on the subject. There is some court intrigue working against him that I cannot get to the bottom of. In the evening I received several telegrams that had been sent by steamer from *Korosko* to *Assuan*: one from Brackenbury informing me that his mounted troops were to leave *Dongola* today & that he with the Infantry and all the boats would leave that place tomorrow for *Fatmeh*: there he would stay perhaps until the 9th to see all stores, boats &c. &c. cleared out to the North. I dined with Stephenson: Baring was here; he goes home by the mail steamer on the 8th inst. Egerton having arrived this evening to act for him in his absence. Delightful weather: I still dine daily in cloth jacket, waistcoat & overalls: this tells its own tale in a country where there are no puckahs of any sort.

Sunday 5th July 1885

Rode at 5.30 a.m. Telegraph to *Dongola* re-opened. That place was completely evacuated this morning at 8 a.m. Brackenbury & the Infantry embarking in boats for *Abu Fatmeh*. The *Iris* arrived, but never reported 'herself' by telegraph as I had requested the Senior

Nl. Officer at *Alexandria* to do. Captain Rice[329] who commands her is a free and independent sort of fellow—what I should call an extremely bad form of man: very different in every way from Capt. Seymour[330] who commanded here when I went home in her in 1882. He is just the sort of swaggering snob who brings the Navy into bad repute with the Army and makes all soldiers hate going on board a man-of-war. Zohrab made a Pasha with military rank as Majr. Genl. I am very glad for I don't think there is any man who deserves a reward better than he does.

Monday 6th July

Paid visits to the Ministers to say adieu. Official hours here are from 7.30 a.m. till 1 or 1.30 p.m. I wish this was the rule in England. Received a very cool letter from Capt. Rice R.N. commonly known as 'Ground Rice' from having so often ran his ship ashore, which looking to our relative positions in the public service, & to the fact that he has been sent to *Alexandria* to carry me to *Venice*, amounts almost to an impertinence. He says it will be very inconvenient to him to start before Wednesday at earliest & hopes I will not come down before Tuesday evening. In his letter from Malta, he endeavoured to make me postpone my departure for several days evidently to suit his convenience. He never seems to think of *my* convenience. I at once wired to him that as Ld. John Hay informed me the *Iris* would be ready to sail early on Tuesday morning (7th July) I had made all my arrangements accordingly, and could not now alter them &c. &c. I left *Cairo* by the 6 p.m. train, Childers & Fitzgerald of the party, in the hope that at least the former would be allowed to accompany me, as the Senr. Navl. Offr. has stated in his telegram that all the Staff I had named could be accommodated.

On reaching *Alexandria* I went off at once to the Ras el Tia Palace to take leave of the Khedive. Buller and the others went on board the *Iris*. When I reached that ship I found that Childers had been told to clear out, so he must go home overland. Captn. Rice informed me he *would* start tomorrow about 8 a.m. We shall then lose at least four hours. What an ill-conditioned Jack in office!!. ...

I embarked in the *Iris* with very different feelings & hopes tonight from those which absorbed my mind in Sept. 1884 when I joined her at *Trieste*, on my way here. Those hopes were all doomed to disappointment. The plans I evolved from my brain when on board this ship & subsequently worked out, led to failure. We did not save poor Gordon. I had hoped to have got my troops & stores to *Korti* about a fortnight earlier than I did. All ranks worked like galley slaves to get them forward as quickly as possible, but to no avail. We had been sent out at least one month too late, and owing to the incompetence of Mr. Gladstone poor Gordon was sacrificed, and a host of the finest soldiers that ever wore the Queen's uniforms, now lie buried in the Soudan deserts. How awful is the responsibility of a man who dares to rule a country and who has not the knowledge required for such a position. And yet God does not seem to punish him for his presumption.

Tuesday 7th July

Did not get under weigh until after 8 a.m. Why I know not except it was done from simple 'cussed-ness'. I hear now he was absent from the ship all yesterday with some woman he fancies in *Alexandria*, so the convenience of myself and party was disregarded in order that he might have a 'good time' with some *female woman* here. The Khedive last night was very anxious I should carry away with me the conviction that he was entirely English in all his feelings & sympathies. Nubar was in waiting in the Palace, so I bid him good [bye], he saying he hoped to see me again soon in Egypt, which meant that a war with the Mahdi was certain sooner or later. We have had a head wind & the ship has been somewhat lively. Read Lord Malmesbury's memoirs all day when I did not sleep. I enjoy putting in a large stock of sleep at times: it seems to revive and rejuvenate one; and one can never have a better time for doing so than at sea where life is so intolerably dull and profitless. My brain has lain fallow all day, and the sleep and rest seems to have strengthened it. The Soudan & all its cares seem fading away from my memory like a dissolving view....

Thursday 9th July

Passed Zante, Ithica, Cepholonia &c. &c. and ran into the harbour of Corfu where the Mediterranean Squadron under Ld. John Hay was at anchor, as was also the whole Italian Navy. It was a pretty sight although the Italian ships—all built in England

—were hideous-looking monsters. Beresford tells me, the Italians here, *if* their ships were as well manned as ours are, could make short work of John Hay's squadron. This teaches one two lessons, increase our Fleet at *once* and at *all cost*; the second is, keep the Italians as our allies. We steamed directly through both Fleets, going so close to John Hay's flagship, the *Alexandre.* that we all but grazed her boom. The Italian ships looked dirty and untidy, & their crews like those to be seen in our merchantmen. A lovely day, going 13 knots ever since we left *Alexandria.*

Friday 10th July

Lovely day—not a drop of rain since we left Egypt. Passed the Island of Lissa where the Italian fleet was beaten by the Austrians in 1866. I believe the men on board the ships on both sides were in a blue funk and after a few rounds had been fired would no longer stand to their guns. I have always understood that when the action ended the few guns then firing were being served by the officers. In the afternoon our pace was eased down to 11 or 12 knots so as not to reach *Venice* before 8 a.m. tomorrow.

Saturday 11th July 1885

Fine morning. Steamed up to *Venice* through a long narrow channel and anchored or rather moored opposite the public gardens. The *Iris* could not turn there as the deep water is only 300 ft. wide & she is 330 ft. long. We breakfasted on board after we had moored (about 9 a.m.) and went to Mr. Cook's hotel, the Victoria. I spent the day going round curiosity shops. Paid Sir Henry and Lady Layard[331] a visit & went with them to see the glass mosaic manufacture. Left by train at 11.30 p.m. with one of Mr. Cook's best couriers.

Monday 13th July

Came by the St. Gothard tunnel & reached *London* today at 5 p.m. The horrid fashionable world came to meet me at the station & so ends my unsuccessful expedition for the relief of *Khartoum.*

W.

Bibliographical note

The available materials, original and secondary, for a study of the Khartoum Relief Expedition are voluminous. The official Cabinet and War Office papers can be found in the Public Record Office or War Office Library. Among the principal actors, political and military, in the Gordon drama, the private papers of Wolseley, Buller, Kitchener, Gladstone, Granville, Northbrook, Cromer and Gordon are deposited in the Public Record Office, the British Museum or India Office Library. The *Official History,* inadequate in many respects, notorious in its condemnation of Sir Charles Wilson and severely criticised on its belated publication in 1890, needs to be read in the light of Wilson's, Brackenbury's and Butler's own personal accounts. Further supplementary evidence should include accounts of the Nile Campaign contained in the numerous biographies and memoirs of those officers who stood less in the limelight, acted on the periphery of affairs or were too junior in rank to be of much significance; such as Beresford, Graham, Stephenson, Tulloch. Dundonald, Burnaby, Andrew Clarke and G. Sydenham Clarke. For detail and mood, one should also refer to the records of the war correspondents, Bennet Burleigh, Melton Prior, MacDonald and others.

Two of the most recent studies of British policy in the Soudan, making use of Mahdist archives, include Mekki Shibeika, *British Policy in the Sudan, 1882–1902* (1952) and A. B. Theobald, *The Mahdiya* (1951). The Canadian contribution has been ably dealt with by Col. C. P. Stacey in his *Records of the Nile Voyageurs, 1884–5*

(1959); while Julian Symonds's excellent book, *England's Pride*, provides the most readable and comprehensive treatment of the campaign as a whole.

My introduction has been drawn largely from Wolseley's own letters to his family, now in the Hove Free Library, supported by what I have found elsewhere relating to Wolseley in the Disraeli, Salisbury, Lytton, Cardwell, Northbrook, Cranbrook and Napier papers—to specify but a few of the collections consulted.

Notes

1 Reginald, Viscount Esher (1852–1930); Cheam, Eton and Cambridge; Private Secretary to Lord Hartington, 1878–85; Member of Royal Commission on South African War (1902); Chairman, War Office Reconstitution Committee (1904); Chairman, Committee to Reorganise Territorial Army (1906); Chairman, Committee on Organisation of Indian Army (1919); permanent member of C.I.D.; offered and refused Under-Secretaryship for Colonies (1899), Under-Secretaryship for War (1900), Governorship Cape Colony (1900), Secretary of State for War (1903), Viceroy of India (1908). See M. V. Brett (ed.), *Journals and Letters of Reginald, Viscount Esher,* London, Nicolson and Watson, 4 vols., 1934–38.
2 Spencer Compton, 8th Duke of Devonshire (1833–1908); Axminster and Cambridge; M.P. at 24, 1857; like Wolseley, unofficial observer of the American Civil War, August 1862–February 1863 where he visited both Northern and Southern Armies; U.S.S. War (1863–66); S.S. India (1880–82); S.S. War (1882–85). See B. Holland, *The Life of....*, London, Longmans, 2 vols., 1911.
3 General Sir Frederick Charles Arthur Stephenson (1821–1911); Crimea, 1854–6; China, 1857–60; Egypt, 1883–7. Commanded the troops on board the *Transit*—one of whom was Lt. Garnet Wolseley—ship-wrecked in the Straits of Banca, 10 July 1857, en route to China where he was to meet Gordon for the first time. Commanded Army of Occupation in Egypt before superceded by by Wolseley. See Sir F. C. A. Stephenson, *At Home and On the Battlefield: Letters from the Crimea, China and Egypt,* 1854–1888, etc...., London, Murray, 1918.
4 Major-General the Hon. J. C. Dormer.
5 The Treaty concluding the First Boer War.

6 George Leveson Gower, 2nd Earl Granville (1815–91); Eton and Christ Church; U.S. Foreign Affairs (1840–1); S.S. Foreign Affairs (1851–2); President of Council (1852–4); Duchy of Lancaster (1854–5); S.S. Colonies (1868–70). Technically responsible for Wolseley's Red River Expedition; S.S. Foreign Affairs (1870–4, 1880–5).

7 Thomas Baring, Earl of Northbrook (1826–1904); U.S. War (1868–72) when closely associated with Wolseley concerning Cardwell's reforms; Viceroy of India (1872–76); First Lord of Admiralty (1880–85).

8 Major-General (later General the Rt. Hon.) Sir Redvers Buller (1839–1909); Red River, Ashanti, Kaffir and Zulu Wars, Boer War, Egypt and Suakim; Quarter-Master General (1887–90); rival of Wolseley for Commander-in-Chiefship, 1895; A.G. (1890–97); C.-in-C., South Africa (1898–1900). See Col. C. H. Melville, *Life of* . . . . , London, Arnold, 2 vols., 1923; J. Symonds, *Buller's Last Campaign*, London, Hamish Hamilton, 1962.

9 Maj.-General W. Earle (1833–85); Military Secretary to Lord Northbrook (1872–6). Killed while commanding the River Column.

10 Louis Riel's headquarters and the objective of the Red River Expedition.

11 Maj.-General (later General the Rt. Hon.) Sir Henry Brackenbury (1837–1914); one of the foremost military administrators of his day; Instructor in Artillery, Woolwich (1862–4) resulting in two original research papers on 'Ancient Canon in Europe'; Fellow of Royal Archeological Institute and of Society of Antiquaries; published numerous articles on American Civil War, military reform and education (1861–6); Professor of Military History at Woolwich (1868–73); frequent special lecturer at R.U.S.I.; unofficial observer to the Franco–Prussian War, about which he compiled a history, subsequently suppressed; proposed with J. W. Hozier, 'Military History Review' which never materialised; Assistant Military Secretary to Wolseley in Ashanti, a 2 volume history of which campaign, totalling 795 pages, he wrote, revised and saw through the press in 6 weeks; Natal, Cyprus, and Zululand; Private Secretary to Lord Lytton (1879–80); -Military Attache, Paris (1881–2); Director of Military Intelligence (1886–92); Military Member of Supreme Council (1891–6); Member of Hartington Commission (1889–90); President of Ordnance Committee (1896–9); Director-General Ordnance (1899–1904). Commanded River Column upon Earle's death.

12 Brig.-General Sir Herbert Stewart; Military Consul in Asia Minor (1879–83); mortally wounded at Abu Klea.

13 Sir Ralph Thompson, Permanent U.S.S. for War.
14 Alfred Austen, poet laureate (1896–1913).
15 Unidentifiable.
16 Baroness Angela Georgina Burdett-Coutts (1814–1906); philanthropist and socialite. For her many charitable foundations, including endowment of schools and bishoprics, reform societies, R.S.P.C.C. and R.S.P.C.A., raised to the peerage in 1871. Administered Red Cross Hospitals during Russo-Turkish War. Entertained Gordon before he went to the Soudan in 1884.
17 Colonel Sir Cromer Ashburnham; Indian Mutiny, 2nd Afghan War, Boer War, and Egypt 1882.
18 General Sir Edmund Augustus Whitmore; Military Secretary to the Duke of Cambridge.
19 For Stephenson's reaction to his supercession, see Stephenson to his brother, Sir W. H. Stephenson, 22 September 1884, *At Home and On the Battlefield*, pp. 324–7. 'I have been loath to allude to the subject of Wolseley's appointment to the chief command in Egypt, for I naturally felt it very keenly, due so still, and probably ever shall, but I was anxious not to express myself upon the subject more than I could possibly help, but to keep my temper, submit, and put the best face on the matter I could. . . . The unexpected announcement that Wolseley was coming out, not merely to superintend the organising of the small boat scheme, but to take the chief command altogether, organise the force, appoint the staff, which was to be specially left in my hands, and command the expedition, was very startling.'
20 Admiral Lord John Hay; C.-in-C. Mediterranean. As temporary governor of Cyprus in 1878 before Wolseley's arrival, Hay had offended Wolseley by criticising the landing arrangements of his expedition. He had also reported adversely upon the practicability of the Nile scheme.
21 Commander T. F. Hammill, R.N.
22 Lt.-Colonel (later Lt.-General Sir) Leopold V. Swaine; A.D.C. to Wolseley (1878–9); Military Attache, Constantinople (1880–4); Military Secretary.
23 Wolseley's batman and butler.
24 Sir Evelyn Baring (later Lord Cromer), (1841–1917); A.D.C. to Sir Henry Storks, Ionian Islands, Malta and Jamaica (1858–64); Staff College, 1867; published *Staff College Essays* (1869), 'to show some of the officers of the Army that at all events *some* useful work is done at the Staff College, which it may reasonably be hoped will bring forth good fruit in time of war;' closely associated with Cardwell's reforms; Intelligence Branch (1870–72); Private Secretary to Lord Northbrook (1872–6) where attempted to reform Indian

Army; Intelligence Department (1876–80) where he wrote masterly appreciations on the Eastern Question, Defence of Constantinople and a Tigris-Euphrates Expedition; Financial Member of Supreme Council (1880–83); advocate of 'masterly inactivity,' opposed Afghan War and largely upon his advice, Ripon and Hartington withdrew from Kandahar in 1881; Northbrook had a high opinion of him as a strategist; Agent, Consul-General and Minister Plenipotentiary in Egypt, 1883–1907.

25 E. H. Egerton, Acting Consul-General.

26 Major F. M. Wardrop, 3 Dragoon Guards; A.D.C. to Wolseley; later Military Attache to Vienna.

27 Capt. (later Maj.-General) Andrew Gilbert Wauchope, Royal Highlanders; killed at Magersfontein, 1900.

28 Lt.-Colonel (later Maj.-General Sir) J. F. Maurice (1841–1912); son of F. D. Maurice, Christian Socialist and founder of the London Workingmen's College; won the Wellington Prize Essay (1872) both quoting and defeating Wolseley who applied for his services in Ashanti. Wolseley's lifelong friend, apologist and amanuensis. Controversial and eccentric military theorist and publicist; official military historian of the Egyptian and South African Wars; Professor of Military Art and History at the Staff College (1885–92).

29 Col. (later General Sir Richard) Harrison (1837–1930); Crimea, India, China, Zulu and Egyptian Wars; see his *Recollections of a Life in the British Army during the latter part of the Nineteenth Century*, London, Murray, 1908, p. 271; one of the most reliable and best-written military autobiographies of the nineteenth century.

30 Captain (later Admiral) Lord Charles William de la Poer Beresford (1846–1919); A.D.C., commanding Naval Brigade; took part in bombardment of Alexandria 1882; M.P. (1874–80, 1885–9, 1897–1900, 1910–16); 4th Naval Lord, 1886–8; C.-in-C. Mediterranean, 1905; C.-in-C. Channel, 1907–9; vindictive opponent of Fisher's naval reforms. See *The Memoirs of Admiral Lord Charles Beresford*, written by himself, London, Methuen, 1914, 2 vols., I, pp. 221–2.

31 Correspondent for the *Morning Post*, later killed at Abu Klea.

32 Battle of Tel-el-Kebir, Wolseley's masterpiece which resulted in a literary feud between himself, Hamley and G. S. Clarke over the part played by Hamley's 2nd Division.

33 François Certain Canrobert (1809–1895); Marshal of France; commanded 1st Division of French Army in the Crimea and on the death of St. Arnaud succeeded as C.-in-C.; after differences with Lord Raglan, resigned his command in 1855.

34 Frederick Augustus Thesiger (1827–1905); Crimean and Abyssinian

Wars; A.G. to Lord Napier in India (1869–74); commanded British Forces in South Africa, 1878–9.
35 Three days later, on 17 September, Gordon wrote in his journal: 'I have the strongest suspicion . . . that if you wanted to find Her Majesty's forces you would have to go to Shepheard's Hotel in Cairo.' See A. E. Hake (ed.), *The Journals of Major-General C. G. Gordon, C.B. at Kartoum*, London, Kegan Paul, 1885, p. 38.
36 Probably Col. J. S. Stewart.
37 Gordon maintained that, though perhaps necessary and inevitable, a forcible and arbitrary evacuation of the Khartoum garrison by a British expeditionary force before adequate securities against the Mahdi's reprisals had been provided, would create a core of resistance and treachery within Khartoum thereby further complicating the whole policy of withdrawal.
38 Col. C. E. Webber, Director of Telegraphs.
39 Lt. F. M. Beaumont, Staff Captain in charge of signallers.
40 Gordon to Baring, 17 September 1884, *PRO/WO/147/8*.
41 Same to same, 18 September 1884, *ibid*.
42 Col. (later Maj.-General) Sir Charles William Wilson (1836–1905); Cheltenham and University of Bonn; Secretary, North American Boundary Commission (1858–62); Ordnance Survey Palestine, Scotland and Sinai (1864–9); creator of the Intelligence Department (1869–76); Ordnance Survey Ireland (1876–9); Servian Boundary Commission (1878–9); Consul-General in Armenia (1879–82); Director of Military Education (1895–8); Chief of Intelligence. See Col. Sir Charles M. Watson, *The Life of. . . .* , London, Murray, 1909.
43 Maj. (later Maj.-General) A. G. Creagh; A.D.C., Wolseley's nephew.
44 Lt. (later Lt.-General) E. S. E. Childers; son of H. E. C. Childers, Chancellor of the Exchequer. A.D.C.
45 Lt. (later Maj.-General Sir) John Adye; Afghan, Egyptian, Soudan, Boer and Great Wars. Intensely loyal A.D.C. to Wolseley, 'the finest soldier I have known,' to whom he dedicated his memoirs, *Soldiers and Others I have known*, London, Jenkins, 1925.
46 Gordon appears the same day to have received similar intelligence; *Journals*, p. 68.
47 Wolseley to Gordon, 20 September 1884, *PRO/WO* 147/8.
48 Arthur Lawrence, Lord Haliburton (1832–1907); Nova Scotian; Director of Supplies and Transport (1877–85); Assistant U.S.S. of War (1891–5); Permanent U.S.S. of War (1895–7); Army Reformer. See J. B. Astly, *Lord Haliburton, A Memoir*, London, Briggs, 1909, pp. 46–70.
49 Kitchener to Wolseley, 21 September 1884, *PRO/WO* 147/8.
50 Wolseley to Kitchener, 22 September 1884, *ibid*.

51 The French Minister in Cairo.
52 Baring to Granville, 25 September 1884, *PRO/GD* 29/163.
53 Same to same, no. 891, 20 September 1884; no. 894, 21 September 1884, *PRO/FO* 78/3678.
54 On 19 September, Gordon had confided to his journal: 'Any expeditionary force that may come up comes up for the honour of England, and England will be grateful, and I can hang the yoke of Government on some one else, for the solution of the problem.' Cf. p. 58; Khedive's firman, 26 September 1884, encl. in Baring to Granville, no. 920, confdl, 29 September 1884, *PRO/FO* 78/3678.
55 Col. (later Lt.-General the Rt. Hon. Sir) William F. Butler (1838–1910); India, Red River, Ashanti, Natal, Zululand, Egypt and Soudan campaigns; Acting High Commissioner and General Commanding the Troops in South Africa, 1898–9. Prolific author, e.g. *The Great Lone Land*; *The Wild North Land*; *Akim Foo*; *Campaign of the Cataracts*. His *Autobiography* is probably the most brilliant of the 19th century, a classic equal to Robertson's *Soldiers and Statesmen*.
56 Baring to Granville, 25 September 1884, *PRO/GD* 29/163.
57 Lt.-Colonel F. T. Lloyd, Commanding at Assiut.
58 Gordon to Baring, 30 and 31 July 1884, encl. in Baring to Granville, no. 915, 28 September 1884, *PRO/FO* 78/3678.
59 Baring to Wolseley, 29 September 1884, *PRO/WO* 147/8.
60 James Fergusson (1808–86), prolific author of books on ancient architecture and stone monuments.
61 Col. (later Field-Marshal Lord) Francis Grenfell (1841–1924); Zulu and Egyptian campaigns; Sirdar of Egyptian Army (1885–92); see *Memoirs of Field-Marshal Lord Grenfell,* London, Hodder and Stoughton, 1925, p. 8. 'I was ordered to Assouan to superintend the transit of men and stores to Wady Halfa. As Assouan was to be my headquarters for an indefinite time, and there were no houses available, I hired a dahabeeh, the *Oonas*, and on it I spent the best part of the next two years.'
62 Captain F. R. Boardman, R.N., Senior Naval Officer.
63 Sir G. Arthur, *The Letters of Lord and Lady Wolseley,* 1870–1911, London, Heineman, 1922, pp. 122–4.
64 Rebel Zulu Chief whom Wolseley captured in 1879, thereby bringing to a close the Zulu War.
65 Maj. H. M. Rundle, Egyptian Army.
66 Capt. G. R. J. Shakespear, Bengal Staff Corps.
67 See also Wolseley to Lady Wolseley, 4 October 1884, *Letters,* p. 124.
68 Publisher of travel books.
69 Kitchener to Wolseley, 5 October 1884, *PRO/WO* 147/8.

70 Maj.-General (later Field-Marshal Sir) Henry Wylie Norman (1826–1904); Sikh War and Indian Mutiny; Assistant Military Secretary to the Duke of Cambridge, 1861; Secretary to the Government of India (1861–6); Military Member of Supreme Council (1870–77); Member of Home Council (1878–83); Governor of Jamaica (1883–8); Governor of Queensland (1888–96).
71 Sir Edgar Vincent (1857–1931), Eton and Coldstream Guards; Financial Adviser to the Egyptian Government, and Governor of the Imperial Ottoman Bank at Constantinople; M.P. (1899–1906); Chairman, Royal Commission on Imperial Trade; Ambassador to Berlin (1920–6); close friend of Streseman; instigated Locarno.
72 Maj.-General (later General Sir) E. B. Bulwer, Inspector-General of Recruiting.
73 Maj.-General J. H. F. Elkington, D.A.G. Auxiliary Forces.
74 Kitchener to Wolseley, 8 October 1884, PRO/WO 147/8.
75 Unidentified.
76 J. A. Cameron, Correspondent for the *Standard*.
77 Bennet Burleigh, Correspondent for the *Daily Telegraph* and *Central News*.
78 Unidentified.
79 Lt.-Colonel (later Maj.-General Sir) Thomas Fraser; foremost military engineering theorist in the British Army; see for instance Royal Engineer Prize Essays for 1875 and 1876 in *Professional Papers of the Royal Engineers*; deep student of the American Civil and Franco-Prussian Wars whose lessons he incorporated into the official military engineering textbooks; accompanied Colonel Home's Mission to Constantinople (1876–77); employed on various other secret missions throughout the Eastern Question, acting as Cabinet adviser concerning the Dardanelles defences; escaped from Majuba, 1881; later Inspector-General of Fortifications. See his *Recollections with Reflections*, London, Blackwood, 1914.
80 Lt.-Colonel F. Duncan, Egyptian Army.
81 See Gordon's opinion on the value of wire entanglements, *Journals*, p. 86: 'I think good wire entanglements, with mines, will defend any place, if one has anything like moderate troops behind the parapet. Wire entanglement ought to be twenty yards in depth, mixed with it the earth mines. No field artillery will neutralize their effects, and only a continuous bombardment of days will destroy them....'
82 Maj. (later General Sir) Herbert Chermside; Assistant Military Attache, Constantinople (1876–78); Military Consul, Asia Minor (1878–80); Egyptian Army (1880–84); Governor-General, Red Sea Littoral (1884–6); Military Attache, Constantinople (1889–96);

British Military Commissioner and Commander of British Troops, Crete (1897–9); commanded 3rd Division, South Africa, 1900; Governor of Queensland (1902–4).
83 Col. H. E. Colville, *History of the Sudan Campaign,* London, H.M.S.O., 1889, 2 vols., I, appdx. 29, pp. 240–3.
84 Maj. Wilberforce Clarke, R.E.; A.A.G., Railway Service.
85 General Sir Samuel Baker, explorer and traveller; brother of Valentine Baker Pasha and Maj.-General Sir T. D. Baker.
86 Lt.-General (later Field-Marshal) Sir Andrew Clarke (1824–1902); various civil and military functions in New Zealand and Australia (1846–57); Ashanti, 1863; Director of Engineering Works, Admiralty (1864–73); advocated purchase of the Suez Canal, 1870; Governor, Straits Settlement (1873–5); Public Works Department, India (1877–80); Inspector-General of Fortifications (1882–6); Agent-General, Victoria (1891–4, 1897–1902). With G. S. Clarke, strongly advocated the Suakim–Berber Railway as a means of permanently maintaining British influence in the Soudan.
87 The Rt. Hon. H. C. E. Childers (1827–96); Cheam, Oxford and Cambridge; First Lord of Admiralty (1868–71); Duchy of Lancaster (1871–4); S.S. War (1880–82); Chancellor of Exchequer (1882–85). See Lt.-Colonel S. Childers, *The Life and Correspondence of the Rt. Hon. H. C. E. Childers,* 1827–1896, London, Murray, 1901.
88 Butler, *Autobiography*, pp. 266–80.
89 Frank Lupton.
90 Frank Power, correspondent for *The Times* with Gordon in Khartoum. Gordon also had a low opinion of the felaheen as soldiery, castigating Wood's Army, as 'an useless expense.' See *Journals*, p. 139.
91 Baring to Wolseley, 21 October 1884, encl. in Baring to Granville, no. 974, 23 October 1884, PRO/FO 78/3679.
92 Wolseley to Baring, 22 October 1884, *ibid.*
93 See Melville, *Life of Buller,* II, p. 204: 'Wolseley allows me as much responsibility as I choose to accept. I think that I have the situation that really about suits me best, one, that is, involving all the responsibilities of execution without those of invention and preliminary organisation. I never have credited myself with much ability on the inventive side; all mine, if I have any, is one the executive side, and possibly if I have a strong point it is resource, which is a great help in execution.'
94 Baring to Wolseley, 23 October 1884, encl. in Baring to Granville, no. 974, 23 October 1884, PRO/FO 78/3679.
95 See Butler, *Autobiography*, p. 294.
96 *Ibid.*

97 See F. C. Denison, 'Diary of Canadian Contingent, Nile Expedition,' 26 October 1884; in C. P. Stacey (ed.), *Records of the Nile Voyageurs 1884–1885: The Canadian Voyageurs Contingent in the Gordon Relief Expedition*, Toronto, The Champlain Society, 1959, p. 107 ff.
98 Hartington to Wolseley, 27 October 1884, *PRO/WO* 147/8.
99 Wolseley to Hartington, s.d., *ibid*.
100 See Melville, *Life of Buller*, p. 203: 'There is just at present a great difference of opinion between me and Wood.'
101 Unidentified.
102 Surgeon-Major W. S. Pratt, on Wolseley's staff.
103 Lt. R. H. Maxwell, Camp Commandant and Provost Marshal.
104 Lt. R. A. J. Montgomerie, R.N.
105 Capt. R. S. R. Fetherstonhaugh, K.R.R.C.
106 Lt. Richard Poore, R.N.
107 Lt.-Colonel (later General Sir) J. Alleyne (1943–99); Red River, Zulu and Egyptian Wars; A.A.G., River Transport and in charge of boats for the River Column, under whom the Canadian voyageurs worked.
108 Maj.-General Sir H. H. Gough (1846–1909); see his *Old Memories*, London, Blackwood, 1909.
109 Rudolph C. Slatin Pasha; Colonel, Egyptian Army, formerly Governor and Commandant of troops in Darfur. See his *Fire and Sword in the Sudan: A Personal Narrative of Fighting and Serving the Dervishes*, 1879–85, London Arnold, 1897; Wolseley to Slatin, 7 November 1884, encl. in Baring to Granville, no. 1070, 25 November 1884, *PRO/FO* 78/3680.
110 See also Melville, *Life of Buller*, p. 207.
111 Cf. *Story of a Soldier's Life*, II, pp. 371–6.
112 Buller to Wolseley, 11 November 1884, *PRO/WO* 147/8.
113 Same to same, 12 November 1884, *ibid*.
114 Maj. C. T. Barrow, Scottish Rifles.
115 Col. K. G. Henderson, Commanding Assuan.
116 Unidentified.
117 Melville, *Life of Buller*, II, pp. 207–8; General Sir Henry Brackenbury, *Some Memories of My Spare Time*, London, Blackwood, 1909, p. 335.
118 Cf. Melville, *ibid*, p. 208.
119 Gordon, *Journals*, p. 273; Gordon to Wolseley, 4 November 1884, encl. in Baring to Granville, no. 1036, 15 November 1884, *PRO/FO* 78/3680; Wolseley to Gordon, 17 November 1884, encl. in Baring to Granville, no. 1119, 9 December 1884, *PRO/FO* 78/3681.
120 Col. C. S. Rowley, Grenadier Guards.

121 Small mounted machine-guns.
122 Buller to Wolseley, 24 November 1884, *PRO/WO* 147/8; Butler, *Autobiography*, p. 284.
123 Wolseley to Buller, s.d., *ibid*.
124 Capt. (later Colonel) W. W. C. Verner, D.A.A.G. (Intelligence); biographer of H.R.H. the Duke of Cambridge.
125 Wolseley to Buller, 27 November 1884, *PRO/WO* 147/8.
126 Col. H. B. P. Blundell, Grenadier Guards.
127 Col. H. H. D. Stracey, Scots Guards.
128 Lt.-Colonel Frederick Augustus Burnaby (1842–85), Royal Horse Guards; soldier, traveller and adventurer; author of sensational *Ride to Khiva* (1875) which earned the disapproval of the Duke of Cambridge; unofficial observer to the Russo–Turkish War; crossed the Channel in a balloon. Subject of at least three biographies. Wolseley had requested Burnaby's services, but had been refused by the Duke of Cambridge. On 27 September, Burnaby wrote to Wolseley concerning his application: 'By this time according to the papers you are on your way to Wadi Halfa, so I expect that my *friends* here have ignored your application for my services. There is a great row as usual in the clubs—and at the Guards' Club those who think themselves snubbed by having been passed over—wd hardly speak to their more fortunate brother officers—now en route to Egypt. Judging by the papers Gordon has nearly freed himself at Khartoum—& your detractors are already beginning to make light of your expedition. I have to preside at a large dinner in Leicester next week & mean to give it hot to these jealous enemies.' *WFP*.
129 Lt.-Colonel Wilfred Tolson, Royal Sussex Regiment.
130 Butler, *Autobiography*, pp. 282–285.
131 *Ibid*, pp. 285–7.
132 Butler to his wife, 12 January 1885, *ibid*, p. 295.
133 Buller to Wolseley, 5 December 1884, *PRO/WO* 147/8.
134 Charles Williams, correspondent for *Central News*; founder of *Evening News*.
135 Unidentified.
136 Unidentified.
137 Frederick Villiers, *Pictures of Many Wars*, London, 1902.
138 Melton Prior, *Campaigns of a War Correspondent*, London, Arnold, 1912.
139 Cf footnote no. 65.
140 Maj. the Hon. C. C. G. Byng.
141 Hartington to Wolseley, 15 December 1884, *PRO/WO* 147/8.
142 See Wilson, *From Korti to Khartum*, London, Blackwood, 1886, pp. xix–xx.

143 Wolseley to Gordon, 17 December 1884, *PRO/FO* 78/3683; Gordon's last journal entry is 14 December 1884.
144 Dr. William Russell, renowned war correspondent; founder-editor of *Army and Navy Gazette*.
145 See J. F. Maurice, 'Critics and Campaigns,' *Fortnightly Review*, V, July 1888, pp. 120–1.
146 Melville, *Life of Buller*, pp. 208–9: Brackenbury, *Memories*, p. 335.
146a Instructions to Earle, see *Official History*, II, pp. 81–2.
147 Lt.-Colonel (later Maj.-General Sir) Hugh McCalmont (1848–1924); Red River and Ashanti; Assistant Military Attache, Constantinople (1877–8); A.D.C. to Wolseley, Cyprus (1878–9); Zulu, Boer and Egyptian Wars; M.P. (1892–8). See C. E. Callwell (ed.), *The Memoirs of Major-General Sir Hugh McCalmont*, London, Hutchinson, 1924, pp. 232–3.
148 Col. (later General Sir) George B. Wolseley, Wolseley's brother.
149 Lt.-Colonel P. H. Eyre.
150 Vakil to Wolseley, 30 December 1884, encl. in Baring to Granville, no. 1, secret, 1 January 1885, *PRO/FO* 78/3799.
151 See Maj.-General H. Brackenbury, *The River Column: A Narrative of the Advance of the River Column of the Nile Expeditionary Force and its return down the Rapids*, London, Blackwood, 1885, pp. 9–12.
152 Wolseley to Mudir, 30 December 1884, *PRO/FO* 78/3799.
153 Maj.-General (later General) Sir Henry Ponsonby (1825–95); A.D.C. to successive Lords-Lt. of Ireland (1846–57); Crimea, Canada (1862–3); Private Secretary to Queen Victoria (1870–95). See A. Ponsonby, *Sir Henry Ponsonby, Queen Victoria's Private Secretary: His Life from his Letters*, London, MacMillan, 1942.
154 Wilson, *Korti to Khartum*, p. xxi; Wolseley to Baring, 31 December 1884, encl. in Baring to Granville, no. 1, secret, 1 January 1885, *PRO/FO* 78/3799.
155 Baring to Wolseley; Wolseley to Baring, 2 January 1885, encl. in Baring to Granville, no. 10, confdl, 2 January 1885, *PRO/FO* 78/3799; *Official History*, I, pp. 139–40.
156 See also Buller's comments, Melville, *Life of Buller*, pp. 209–10.
157 Wolseley to Baring, 3 January 1885, *PRO/FO* 78/3799.
158 Butler, *Autobiography*, p. 296.
159 Hartington to Baring, pte, 5 January 1885, encl. in Baring to Granville, no. 23, secret, 8 January 1885, *PRO/FO* 78/3799.
160 Douglas Mackinnon Baillie Hamilton, 12th Earl of Cochrane (1852–1935); Eton and 2nd Life Guards; commanded Life Guards (1895–9); fought in South Africa with distinction (1899–1900); G.O.C., Canadian Militia (1902–4) from which command he was removed by Laurier and Minto allegedly for attempting to subvert the political authority. Cochrane's account of his ride with the

Gakdul Despatches—which brought him immediate fame—disagrees with that of the *Official History* (I, p. 5) in placing the time of his arrival at 7 rather than 8 p.m. See Lt.-General, the Earl of Dundonald, *My Army Life*, London, Arnold, 1926, pp. 29–30. The war correspondent dining with Wolseley at the time was MacDonald; see *Too Late for Gordon and Khartoum*, London, Murray, 1887, p. 168.

161 See appendix 40, *Official History*, II, pp. 246–7.
162 Under command of Col. the Hon. E. E. T. Biscowen, with 24 officers, 401 other ranks, 9 horses and 10 camels.
163 Baring to Wolseley; Wolseley to Baring, 6 January 1885, encl. in Baring to Granville, no. 23, secret, 8 January 1885, PRO/FO 78/3799.
164 Col. Stanley de Astel Calvert Clarke, equerry to H.R.H., the Prince of Wales. See *Official History*, II, p. 6.
165 Wolseley to Hartington, 7 January 1885, PRO/WO 147/8.
166 Hartington to Wolseley, 8 January 1885; *Official History*, II, p. 142.
167 Wolseley to Hartington, s.d., *ibid*, pp. 144–5.
168 *Ibid*.
169 Wolseley's instructions to Stewart, 8 January 1885, *Official History*, II, pp. 6–8; to Sir Charles Wilson, *ibid*, pp. 8–9; also appdx. V, Wilson, *Korti to Khartoum*, pp. 303–33.
170 Instructions to Beresford, *Official History*, II, pp. 9–10.
171 Brett to Wolseley, 9 January 1885, PRO/WO 147/8.
172 Col. the Hon. E. Primrose, Grenadier Guards.
173 See Melville, *Life of Buller*, II, p. 215.
174 Hartington to Wolseley, 15 January 1885, PRO/WO 147/8.
175 Same to same; Wolseley to Hartington, s.d., *ibid*.
176 Wolseley was true to his word; see 1886 edition of the *Soldier's Pocket Book*.
177 See L. E. Henry, *Napoleon's War Maxims*, London, Gale and Polden, 1889, p. 17.
178 C.f. Wilson's journal, 12 January 1885; *Korti to Khartum*, pp. 13–14.
179 Stewart to Wolseley, 14 January 1885, *Official History*, II, pp. 10–11; also Stewart's Report, appdx. 41, *ibid*, pp. 247–8.
180 Melville, *Life of Buller*, II, p. 215.
181 Wilfred Scawen Blunt (1840–1922); traveller, politician and poet; extensive visits to Egypt, Turkey and India had disillusioned him with Britain's Imperial role; criticised the British occupation of Egypt. See his *Secret History of the English Occupation of Egypt: Being a Personal Narrative of Events*, New York, Knopf, 1922.
182 Earle to Wolseley, 20 January 1885, *Official History*, II, p. 86; Maj. J. C. H. Flood, 19 Hussars.
183 See *Official History*, II, pp. 85–6.

184 Stewart to Wolseley, 18 January 1885, *ibid*, appdx. 44, pp. 255–9; Melville, *Life of Buller*, II, pp. 216–7; Wilson, *Korti to Khartum*, pp. 22–41.
185 The casualties included Col. Burnaby, Lord Airlie and Lord St. Vincent.
186 The *Official History*, on the other hand, emphasised the difficulties likely to be encountered by Earle's column. The enemy force consisted of 1500 Dervishes, 1200 Monasirs and 300 Robatat and 'there was every reason to suppose that these men meant fighting. Their position was said to be a strong one, and behind them was the Shukuk Pass, a gorge which native evidence represented as capable of defence by a handful of determined men against an army.' II, p. 88.
187 *Ibid*, pp. 89–91.
188 *Ibid*, pp. 21–7. See also Wilson to Wolseley, 22 January 1885, encl. in Wolseley to Hartington, 29 January 1885, 'Despatch on Operations near Matemmeh,' appdx. 45, pp. 259–62. For an account of the night march and action at Matemmeh, upon which the *Official History* is largely based, see Wilson, *Korti to Khartum*, pp. 60–115. Pigott's departure had been delayed a day through lack of mounts, *ibid*, pp. 115–6.
189 For Buller's instructions, see Melville, *Life*, pp. 220–2; also PRO/WO 132/2.
190 *Ibid*, p. 218. Both Wolseley and Buller were pardonably excited but unduly critical of Wilson's handling of the action at Matemmeh. But see Wilson's own corrective account, *Korti to Khartum*, pp. 99–109; see also 'Supplementary Despatch from Col. Sir Charles Wilson to the Chief of Staff,' 14 March 1885, appdx. 45, *Official History*, II, pp. 262–6.
191 Wilson, *Korti to Khartum*, pp. 110–115; *Official History*, II, pp. 30–32.
192 *Official History*, II, p. 91.
193 Hartington to Wolseley, 28 January 1885, *ibid*, p. 32.
194 'Memorandum for Major-General Sir R. Buller,' 29 January 1885, *Buller Papers, PRO/WO* 132/2; see also Melville, *Life of Buller*, pp. 220–2.
195 Earle to Wolseley, 29 January 1885, PRO/WO 147/8.
196 *Ibid*; *Official History*, II, p. 92.
197 *Ibid*, pp. 93–4.
198 Hartington to Wolseley; Wolseley to Hartington, 2 February 1885, PRO/WO 147/8.
199 Col. H. P. Ewart; commanded Household Cavalry, Egypt, 1882.
200 Maj.-General Sir G. R. Greaves.
201 Maj.-General A. J. Lyon-Fremantle.

202 For Wilson's account, see *Korti to Khartum*, pp. 116–209; appdx. 46, *Official History*, II, pp. 33–34, 267–9; the Mahdi's letter regarding the fall of Khartoum may be found in the *Official History*, II, pp. 39–40; Wilson, *Korti to Khartoum*, appdx. 8, pp. 307–10. The official account of the fall of Khartoum, compiled by Kitchener, dated 18 August 1885, is found in appdx. 47, *Official History*, II, pp. 270–6. The officer was Lt. E. J. Montagu-Stuart-Wortley.

203 *Official History*, II, p. 53; Wolseley to Buller, 4 February 1885, *Buller Papers, PRO/WO* 132/2; Melville, *Life of Buller*, p. 224. The *Official History* states further that 'on the evening of the same day these orders were changed and Sir R. Buller was directed to go to Gubat'—but Wolseley's journal does not record this countermanding: indeed the opposite seems to have been the case; see entry 5 February 1885.

204 Wolseley to S.S.W., no. 44, 4 February 1885, *PRO/WO* 33/34, part II, p. 224; *Official History*, II, pp. 57–8.

205 Wolseley to Earle, 4 February 1885, *ibid*, p. 96.

206 Wolseley's instructions to Buller, 5 February 1885, *ibid*, pp. 53–55; Wolseley to Buller, pte, 5 February 1885, *Buller Papers, PRO/WO* 132/2; Melville, *Life of Buller*, pp. 225–6.

207 Baring to Wolseley, 5 February 1885, *PRO/WO* 147/8.

208 Sir William George Granville Venables Vernon Harcourt (1827–1904); statesman and reformer.

209 S.S.W. to Wolseley, no. 122, 6 February 1885, *PRO/WO* 33/34, part II, p. 227; *Official History*, II, p. 55; B. Holland, *The Life of Spencer Compton, 8th Duke of Devonshire*, London, Longmans, 1911, 2 vols., II, pp. 11–13.

210 Wolseley to S.S.W., no. 50, 6 February 1885, *ibid*; *Official History*, II, 58–9.

211 Wolseley to Buller, 6 February 1885 (midnight), *Buller Papers, PRO/WO* 132/2; Melville, *Life of Buller*, pp. 228–9.

212 Same to same, 7 February 1885, *ibid*; Melville, *ibid*, pp. 229–30; S.S.W. to Wolseley, no. 117, 7 February 1885, *PRO/WO* 33/34, part II, p. 229.

213 Same to same, 8 February 1885, *Buller Papers, ibid*; Melville, *ibid*, pp. 230–32; Wolseley to S.S.W., 8 February 1885, Holland, *op. cit.*, II, pp. 13–16.

214 Wolseley to Hartington, 9 February 1885, *Official History*, II, pp. 60–62; Hartington to Wolseley, 9 February 1885, Holland, *op. cit.*, II, p. 19.

215 Wilson, *Korti to Khartum*, pp. 273–4; Watson, *Life of Wilson*, p. 333.

216 For Beresford's account, see *Memoirs*, II, pp. 281–308.

217 See Book VI of Gordon's *Journals*, pp. 279–395.

218 *Ibid*, p. 394.

219 *Official History*, II, p. 62; Wolseley to Buller, 11 February 1885, *Buller Papers, PRO/WO* 132/2.
220 Wolseley to Hartington, 11 February 1885, *Official History*, II, pp. 146-7.
221 Lt.-General Sir Archibald Alison (1826-1907); son of the historian; Glasgow University; Crimea, Mutiny and Ashanti; received the thanks of Parliament and K.C.B.; commanded the Highland Brigade at Tel-el-Kebir, 1882 and the forces in Egypt, 1883; Head of the Intelligence Branch (1878-82); Military Member of India Council (1889-99).
222 Lt.-General Sir G. Graham (1831-1899); Crimea, China and Canada where he served on the Staff with Wolseley; Egypt, 1882 and Suakim (1884-5); see Col. R. H. Vetch, *Life, Letters and Diaries of Lt.-General Sir Gerald Graham,* London, Blackwood, 1901.
223 Gordon, *Journals,* p. 344.
224 'General Brackenbury's Report on Action at Kirkeban,' 10 February 1885, appdx. 48, *Official History,* II, pp. 277-9; Brackenbury, *River Column,* pp. 136-72.
225 On the same day, Buller was writing to Wolseley that, because of the great natural defensive strength of Matemmeh and its imminently probable reinforcement by 3-4000 fresh troops, the relative weakness of his own force and the collapse of his supply and transport system, he had decided to withdraw from Gubat to Abu Klea. *Official History,* II, pp. 56-7.
226 *Ibid,* pp. 112-3.
227 Wolseley to Buller, very pte, 12 February 1885, *Buller Papers, PRO/WO* 132/2; *ibid,* pp. 63-5.
228 Lt.-Colonel (later Lt.-General Sir) Coleridge Grove; Military Secretary to Wolseley.
229 Hartington to Wolseley, 13 February 1885, *PRO/WO* 147/8.
230 *Official History,* II, pp. 111-12.
231 This appears to refer to a letter, probably written on the night of 10 February but now untraceable, before Buller made his considered appreciation of 12 February.
232 *Official History,* II, p. 67; Wood, *Midshipman to Field Marshal,* II, p. 174.
233 Wolseley to Hartington, 17 February 1885, *PRO/WO* 147/8.
234 See footnote 26.
235 Buller to Wolseley, 15 February 1885, *Official History,* II, p. 68.
236 *Ibid,* pp. 68-9.
237 By 17 February, casualties numbered 3 killed and 27 wounded; *ibid,* p. 70.
238 See Minute by Wood, 20 February 1885, *ibid,* p. 71.

239 Wolseley to Buller, 20 and 21 February 1885, *Buller Papers*, PRO/WO 132/2; Melville, *Life of Buller*, pp. 246-7.
240 Wolseley to Brackenbury, 20 February 1885, *Official History*, II, pp. 122-3; Brackenbury to Wolseley, 24 February 1885, *ibid*, pp. 123-4.
241 Wolseley to Buller, 21 February 1885, *Buller Papers*, PRO/WO 132/2; Melville, *Life of Buller*, p. 247.
242 Brackenbury, *River Column*, p. 209.
243 Gordon, *Journals*, p. 156.
244 *Ibid*, p. 89.
245 Wolseley to Baring, 24 February 1885, PRO/WO 147/8.
246 *Official History*, II, pp. 120-1; Brackenbury, *River Column*, pp. 211-23.
247 *Ibid*, pp. 123-4; Brackenbury, *ibid*, pp. 246-51.
248 Valentine Baker Pasha (1827-87); Kaffir, Crimea and Mutiny campaigns; army reformer; shabbily dismissed from the Army, largely at the Queen's insistence, without pension or compensation for the purchase value of his commission, allegedly for molesting a young woman in a railway carriage; no court martial was held nor convicting evidence produced. Wrote best-selling alarmist work, *Clouds in the East* (1875) concerning Russian advances in Central Asia. Organised and commanded Turkish gendarmarie during Serbo-Turkish War 1876-7; commanded a Turkish brigade and organised defences of Constantinople during Russo-Turkish War, being created Pasha for his services. During Eastern Crisis, considered by Disraeli as a probable British Corps Commander in the event of war with Russia. Organised irregular forces in Asia Minor, Cyprus and Egypt (1880-84).
249 Buller to Wolseley, 17 February 1885; Wolseley to Buller, 21 February 1885, *Buller Papers*, PRO/WO 132/2; Melville, *Life of Buller*, p. 247.
250 Hartington to Wolseley, 3 March 1885, PRO/WO 147/8.
251 Maj.-General Sir Henry Rawlinson, strong advocate of Indian forward policy. Assyriologist and explorer; President of the Royal Geographical Society; Head of the Political and Secret Committee of the India Council; his publication of inflammatory *Russia and England in the East* (1875) censured by the Viceroy for disclosure of confidential documents.
252 Lt.-Colonel the Hon. R. A. J. Talbot, 1st Life Guards.
253 Brackenbury, *River Column*, p. 290.
254 Baring to Wolseley, 11 March 1885, PRO/FO 78/3812.
255 Wolseley to Baring, s.d., *ibid*.
256 Lt.-Colonel Mildmay W. Willson, Scots Guards.
257 Wilson sensed that he was being made the scapegoat for the failure

to reach Khartoum; see Wilson to his wife, 23 March 1885, Watson, *Life of Wilson*, pp. 341-2.
258 Wolseley to Baring, 12 March 1885, *PRO/FO* 78/3812.
259 Hartington to Wolseley, most confdl, 13 March 1885; Wolseley to Hartington, 14 March 1885, *PRO/WO* 147/8.
260 Sir Mount Stuart Elphinstone Grant Duff (1829-1906); statesman and author; U.S.S. India (1868-74); U.S.S. Colonies (1880); Governor of Madras (1881-6); *Notes from a Diary*, 14 vols., (1897-1905); President of Royal Geographical and Historical Societies.
261 Wood, *Midshipman to Field-Marshal*, II, p. 177.
262 Col. W. R. White, Essex Regiment.
263 Wolseley to Hartington, 16 March 1885, *Official History*, II, pp. 76-7.
264 Butler, *Campaign of Cataracts*, p. 181.
265 Hartington to Wolseley, 17 March 1885, *PRO/WO* 147/8.
266 Butler, *Campaign of Cataracts*, p. 185.
267 Butler, *Autobiography*, pp. 307-8.
268 Maj. (later Maj.-General Sir) Alfred E. Turner; D.A.A.G. (Intelligence); undistinguished career; see *Sixty Years of a Soldier's Life*, London, Methuen, 1912, pp. 85-114.
269 At Hashin; casualties were 10 officers and 80 other ranks killed, 30 officers and 360 other ranks wounded. Estimated strength enemy, 3000. *Official History*, II, pp. 197-200.
270 *Ibid*, pp. 200-208.
271 The following day, Wolseley asked Wilson for a report concerning his delay at Gubat before proceeding to Khartoum; this was produced by Wilson the same day—23 March (see Wilson to Wolseley, Watson, *Life of Wilson*, pp. 338-41; appdx. 46, *Official History*, II, pp. 267-9). But Wilson wrote to his wife: 'I see I am to be made the scapegoat for this failure. Even Lord Northbrook in his speech on the Vote of Censure assigns me a role which the Government distinctly refused to allow me to play. He tries to make me a political agent, whereas they insisted on making me a staff officer under Lord Wolseley. . . . You must not trouble about my not being praised by the Chief; I care nothing for it, but I did care very much when I found he had discredited the account I brought of the fall of Khartum and the death of Gordon.'
272 Maj.-General Sir J. C. McNiell; total British casualties, 149; camp followers, 176; camels, 501.
273 Cf. Butler, *Autiobiography*, p. 310.
274 Unidentified.
275 Col. O. T. Lanyon.
276 General Sir Charles Warren (1840-1927); archaeologist; reconnoitred for Palestine Exploration Fund in Jordan and Jerusalem

(1867–70); employed in Griqualand West (1876–7); commanded Diamond Fields Horse in Kaffir War (1877–8); commanded Bechuanaland Expedition (1884–5); Chief Commissioner London Metropolitan Police (1886–8); commanded 5th Division, South African War (1899–1900).

277 Hartington to Wolseley, 28 March 1885, War Office Library.
278 Sir Charles Dilke (1843–1911); politician, author, legalist and traveller; published *Greater Britain* (1868), an account of a world tour; radical M.P. for Chelsea (1868–86) of strong republican sentiments; prominent Parliamentary speaker on social, industrial, foreign and imperial problems.
279 Col. (later General Sir) Henry Trotter.
280 Col. A. S. Wynne.
281 General Sir E. B. Hamley (1824–93); novelist, military historian and theoretical strategist; Professor of Military History, Staff College (1859–65); Member of the Council of Military Education (1865–70); Commandant of the Staff College (1870–77); British Commissioner, Bulgarian, Armenian, Greek and Turkish Frontier Commissions (1879–82); commanded 2nd Division in decisive action at Tel-el-Kebir. Published *Operations of War* (1866); *National Defence* (1888); *The War in the Crimea* (1890); see A. I. Shand, *The Life of General Sir E. B. Hamley*, London, Blackwood, 2 vols., 1899.
282 Maj. D. A. Scott.
283 Unidentified.
284 See footnote 115.
285 His daughter, later the Viscountess Wolseley (1872–1933).
286 Hartington to Wolseley, secret and confdl, 14 April 1885, *War Office Library*.
287 Wolseley to Hartington, 14 and 15 April 1885, *ibid*.
288 Hartington to Wolseley, 17 April 1885, Holland, *op. cit.*, II, p. 33.
289 Same to same, secret and confdl, 21 April 1885, *ibid*; Wolseley to Hartington, secret, 21 April 1885, PRO/WO 32/265.
290 Same to same, 24 April 1885, *ibid*.
291 Same to same, 28 April 1885, *ibid*.
292 Same to same, 29 April 1885; Granville to Baring, pte, 28 April 1885, PRO/GD 29/201.
293 In *Life of Buller*, pp. 251–2, Melville cites a letter of Buller's purportedly disclaiming against Wolseley's policy and agreeing with the Government's evacuation policy. Melville is clearly wrong, for both Wolseley and Buller were agreed that it would be 'military madness, political suicide and sanitary murder' to evacuate the Soudan in mid-summer.
294 Hartington to Wolseley, 6 May 1885, PRO/WO 32/265; WO 147/8.

295 Same to same, 7 May 1885, *ibid.*
296 Same to same, 9 May 1885, *ibid.*
297 Same to same, 14 May 1885, *ibid.*
298 Maj. F. W. Brewster.
299 General Sir F. W. Middleton (1825-98); New Zealand War (1846-7); Mutiny; Staff in Canada (1867-70); Commandant of Sandhurst (1874-84); G.O.C., Canadian Militia (1884-90); cautious and ponderous in the planning and conduct of military operations, Middleton had been called upon to suppress Louis Riel's North-West Rebellion. The punitory campaign lasted barely three weeks and Riel, outnumbered if not outforced, surrendered on 15 May. For this signal triumph, Middleton received a knighthood and a Parliamentary grant of £20,000—not much less than Napier earned for Abyssinia, Wolseley for Ashanti or Roberts for Kandahar.
300 Capt. W. V. Constable.
301 See Graham's final despatch, appdx. 63, *Official History*, II, pp. 320-7.
302 Sir A. Young (1827-1915); sailor and Polar explorer.
303 Stephenson to Wolseley, 15 May 1885, *War Office Library*.
304 Wolseley to Hartington, 16 May 1885, *ibid.*
305 Capt. J. P. B. Molyneux.
306 General Richard, Lord Airey (1803-81); A.A.G. (1847-51); D.Q.M.G. (1851-3); Q.M.G., Crimean Expeditionary Force (1854-5), for which he was unjustly blamed but ultimately exonerated by a Military Commission; Q.M.G. (1855-65); Governor of Gibraltar (1865-70); A.G. (1870-6); died at Wolseley's home.
307 Brig. J. Hudson, Bengal Staff Corps.
308 Capt. T. Fellowes, R.N.
309 Lord Lt. of Ireland.
310 Hartington to Wolseley, 24 May 1885, *War Office Library*.
311 Wood declined the offer, which was subsequently accepted by Grenfell. Wood, *Midshipman to Field Marshal*, II, p. 181; Grenfell, *Memoirs*, pp. 90-113.
312 Wood, *ibid*, p. 181.
313 General Sir John Davis (1832-1901); Mutiny; Eastern Soudan and Suakim (1884-5).
314 Hartington to Wolseley, 9 June 1885, *PRO/WO* 33/44.
315 Admiral Sir William Hewitt.
316 William Henry Smith (later Lord Hambleden), (1825-91); initiator of railway bookstall, open-air advertising and circulating libraries; local government and philanthropy; Secretary to Treasury (1874-7); First Lord Admiralty (1877-80); S.S. War (1885, 1886); First Lord of Treasury and Leader of the Commons (1886-91); see Sir

H. M. Maxwell, *The Life and Times of W. H. Smith*; Viscount Chilston, *W. H. Smith*, London, Routledge, 1965.
317 See Maurice and Arthur, *Life of Lord Wolseley*, pp. 211–16.
318 S.S.W. to Wolseley, no. 321, 26 June 1885, *PRO/WO* 33/44, part II, p. 413; Wolseley to S.S.W., no. 324, s.d., *ibid*.
319 S.S.W. to Wolseley, no. 328, 27 June 1885, *ibid*, p. 415; Wolseley to S.S.W., no. 325, *ibid*, p. 414.
320 Wolseley to S.S.W., nos. 331 and 332, 29 June 1885, *ibid*, p. 415.
321 J. B. Bury (1861–1927); classical scholar and historian.
322 Unidentified.
323 Lord Ripon (1827–1909); Christian Socialist actively engaged in Volunteer movement; U.S.S. War, 1859; U.S. India, 1861; U.S.S. War (1861–3); S.S. War (1863–6); S.S. India, 1866; Lord President of Council (1868–73); Viceroy of India (1880–4); First Lord Admiralty, 1886; S.S. Colonies (1892–5); Lord Privy Seal and Liberal Leader in House of Lords (1905–8); adopted Roman Catholicism 7 September 1874.
324 Salisbury to Wolseley, 30 June 1885, *PRO/WO* 147/8.
325 Col. Denzil Hammill, commanded Gordon Highlanders, Egypt, 1882; El Teb and Tamai, 1884.
326 S.S.W. to Wolseley, no. 343, 1 July 1885, *PRO/WO* 33/44, part II, p. 419.
327 Same to same, 2 July 1885, *ibid*.
328 Unidentified.
329 Unidentified.
330 Capt. (later Admiral of the Fleet) Sir Edward Hobart Beauchamp Seymour (1840–1929); Crimea; China (1857–62); West Africa (1869–70); Egypt, 1882; C.-in-C. China (1894–97); commanded International Naval Brigade during Boxer Rebellion, 1900.
331 Sir Austen Henry Layard (1817–94); discoverer of Nineveh; witnessed Battle of Alma and gave evidence before Sebastopol Commission; visited India to study causes and effects of Mutiny; U.S. Foreign Affairs (1861–6); Ambassador to Madrid (1869–77); Ambassador to Constantinople (1877–80); negotiated Anglo-Turkish Convention, 1878; see Gordon Waterfield, *Layard of Nineveh*, London, 1964.

Index

Abdin Palace, Cairo, 13, 17
Abu Ahmed, 155, 156
Abu Dom, 171, 198, 199
Abu Fatmeh, 69, 73, 74, 182, 228, 235
Abu Klea, xxxvii; 149, 151, 160, 164, 165
Abu Kru, xxxvii, xxxix
Adye, Lt. John, 18, 19 47, 50, 74
Akasha, 184, 187
Alexandria, G. W. in, 236
'All Sir Garnet' (catchword), xiii
Alleyne, Lt.-Col. T., 58
Ambukol, G. W. hurries to, to influence local tribes, 72, 78, 82–3, 93
American Civil War, G. W.'s attitude to, xvii, 218
Angash, G. W. at, 30–1
Argyll, Duke of, G. W.'s opinion of, 161, 167
Army
 reform agitation and G. W., xviii; cost of maintenance of the, 180
Army and Navy Gazette, 'nonsense in', 95, 110
Ashanti campaign, G. W. and, xix, xxi
Ashburnham, Col. Sir Cromer, 11
Assuan, 26–7, 66, 190, 192
Austen, Alfred (poet laureate), 9

Baker, Gen. Sir Samuel, 42, 118, 176
Barère, Mr. (French Minister in Cairo), 19, 111, 192
Baring, Sir Evelyn (later Lord Cromer), 14, 18, 21, 32, 163, 164, 176
Barrow, Major C. T., 66, 83
Bashi Bazouks, 59, 87, 89, 123, 176
Berber, xxx–xxxi; Gordon's bombardment of, 30–1; G. W.'s preparations for attack on, xl–xlii; 111, 120, 124, 131, 137, 138, 143, 151–2
Beresford, Lord Charles, xxxvii; 15, 39, 48, 108, 140, 228; G. W.'s opinion of, 111
Birti, 128, 131, 132
Blundell, H. B. P., 73
Blunt, Wilfred Scawen, G. W.'s contempt for, 120
Boardman, Capt. F. R. (R.N.), 26
Boer War, xviii
Brackenbury, Maj.-Gen. Henry, xx–xxi, xli–xlii; 15, 61, 66, 73, 100, 142, 149, 154, 177; 'hated', 200; G. W.'s opinion of, 102, 162, 163; and the withdrawal, 218, 232
Brett, Reginald (Viscount Esher), 3, 73, 109, 112, 162, 214
Brewster, Major F. W., 211, 213, 214
Bright, John, G. W.'s opinion of, 65
Brindle, Father (Roman Catholic priest), 39, 94
Brown, John (of Queen Victoria's household), 117
Buller, Maj.-Gen. Sir Redvers, xx–xxi, xxxi, xxxv, xlii; 11, 32, 46, 49, 64, 65, 73; inefficiency over supplies, 67, 72;

261

friction with Butler, 75; in G. W.'s plans for advance, 100; ordered to Metammeh, 128, 140; in difficulties in Abu Klea, 146, 149, 151; 'my last available general', 144; at Goubat and Gakdul, 148, 156–7; 'extreme jealousy' of Stewart, 166; after Gordon's death, 139–40; G. W.'s opinion of, 112–13, 158, 166; and the withdrawal, 218, 229, 235

Burleigh, Bennet (*Daily Telegraph* and *Central News* correspondent), 34, 83, 95

Burnaby, Lt.-Col. Frederick A., xxxvii; 73, 112, 113; killed, 121, 122

Butler, Colonel W. F., xx–xxi; xxxi; 20, 47, 48; unfavourable reports from, 71; friction with Buller, 75; G. W.'s opinion of, 75–6, 171

Byng, Major the Hon. C. C. G., 86, 96

Cairo, G. W. in, 12–13, 17, 222–36

Cambridge, Duke of,
his distrust of G. W., xiv, xviii–xvix, xxii; G. W.'s opinion of, 6, 8, 40–1, 49, 61, 82; his ignorance of war, 117, 142; and death of Burnaby, 122; considers G. W.'s despatch as an attack, 227

Camel Corps
creation of the, xxxiv, xxxv; G. W.'s, guidance and plans for, 27, 41, 89–90, 96, 100; well trained under Gough, 60; on the march, and in action, 86, 121–2

Camels
boat-tracking experiments with, 16; G. W.'s poor opinion of, 37, 69; characteristics, speeds, etc., 69, 70; problems of their use, and shortages of, 44, 51–3, 55, 68, 115, 116, 119–20, 131, 132, 145, 149

Cameron, F. A. (*Standard* correspondent), 34, 83; killed, 128

Canada, G. W.'s service in, xvi–xvii

Canadian Voyageurs in Egypt, G. W. inspects the, 48–9, 162

Canrobert, François C., Marshal of France, 15

Cardwell, Edward, 1st Viscount, military reform programme of, xviii, xliv

Cataracts on the Nile, dangers and problems of, xxxiii, xxxv, xli, xlii; 12, 16, 33–6, 41, 47–9 *passim*, 50–1, 54, 126–7, 128

Censorship of military news, 34–5

Chamberlain, Joseph, G. W.'s opinion of, 65, 154, 180, 181, 225

Chelmsford, Lord, xx

Chermside, Major Herbert, 39, 80, 204, 211, 212

Childers, Lt. E.S.E., 18, 49, 55, 56, 80, 125, 126, 192, 216, 225

Clarke, Sir Andrew (Inspector General of Fortifications), xxix; G. W.'s poor opinion of, 42, 110, 117, 118, 148

Clarke, Col. George Sydenham, and the Staff System, xvix; feud with Hamley, xxiv; reports on bombardment of Alexandria, xxix–xxx; as one of 'new breed' of defence critics, xliv

Clarke, Col. Stanley, xxi; G. W.'s poor opinion of, 108, 113, 165, 173

Coal supplies and problems, 46, 57; Buller's inefficiency, 67

Cochrane, Douglas Hamilton, 12th Earl of, 107

Coinage and currency, Arabs' attitude to, 79, 124

Colburn, Jack (newspaper correspondent), 84, 113

Colley, Maj.-Gen. Sir George, xx; and high India post for G. W., xxii; G. W.'s opinion of, 76

Constable, Capt. W. V., 211

Cook, Thomas, & Son (travel agents), and the Nile Expedition, xxxiii, xxxiv; 21, 46; estimated cost of their services, 79; G. W. entertains the family, 80; and G. W.'s return home, 238

Creagh, Major Arthur G., 18, 65

Crimean War
G. W. loses sight of an eye in, xv; his ambition kindled by experiences in, xvi

Cypher-keys in messages between G. W. and Gordon, 67, 90, 156

Dale, 52, 58
Debbeh, 74, 81, 82, 87, 88, 119, 174, 176
Desert Column, xxxv, xxxvii, xli; 160
Desert marches, G. W. on, 50–2, 70, 118, 172–84

Dilke, Sir Charles, xliv; 225; G. W.'s opinion of, 181
Disease among the troops, 62, 63, 70, 71, 91
Disraeli, Benjamin, and the defence of India, xxi
Dongola, 44, 57–8, 59; G. W. impressed by good conditions in, 60–1; decline of the old town, 87; Guards' Camel Regt. leaves for, 166; withdrawal from, 200, 212 ff.; G. W. on the withdrawal, 217 ff.; complete evacuation of, 235
Dongola, the Mudir of, 8, 19, 44, 45; G. W. proposes him as ruling prince, 46; awarded K.C.M.G., 59, 153; appearance and character, 60–1; G. W.'s relations with, 57–8, 63–4, 82, 86, 106; G. W. rebukes him for impertinence to officers, 70; question of his succeeding Gordon, 71; his 'visions', 84–5; G. W.'s growing distrust of, 115, 118, 143, 169, 173–5; and Merawi, 162; at Dugayet, 171; sent to Cairo, 181, 188
Dormer, Maj.-Gen. the Hon. J. C., 3, 11, 12, 14, 148, 150, 161; and coal supplies, 67; at Tani, 176; G. W. on, 12
Dufferin, Lord, xlii–xliii

Eagar, Lt., suicide of, 73
Earle, Maj.-Gen. W.
in command of River Column, xxxv; 32; Wood and, 31; G. W.'s high opinion of, 6–7, 73, 74, 85; and Abu Ahmed, 98; in G. W.'s plans for advance, 100, 123, 125, 129; killed, 142
Egerton, E. H. (Acting Consul General), 14, 235
Egypt
G. W. on the army: 'disgraceful', 33; and on the fellaheen, 43; burial customs, 48; G. W. and the ruins, 22, 24, 172, 188, 192; G. W. on proposal for permanent British occupation, 96, 108
Esher, Viscount: see Brett, Reginald
Ewart, Col. H. P. ('Croppy'), 133, 139, 174
Eyre, Lt.-Col. P. H., 100, 142

Fellows, Capt. T. (R.N.), 214
Fox, Capt. J.C.K., 159
France
'jealousy and hatred' of England, 21; G. W.'s opinion of, 21–2, 192; strained relations with British in Egypt, 111, 200; war with China, 181: see also Napoleon
Franchise Bill, G. W. 'heartily sick of', 85
Fraser, Lt.-Col. Thomas, 35–6
Fremantle, Maj.-Gen. A.: see Lyon-Fremantle

Gakdul, 113, 116, 118, 130, 132, 134, 148, 149, 155–7, 160, 161
Game shooting on the expedition, 64, 68, 150
Gladstone, W. E.
his 'ransom for honours', xxiii; and the Egyptian problem, xxiv; attitude to need for Khartoum relief expedition, 7; agrees to G. W.'s going to Egypt, 7, 8; and the Penjdeh crisis, xliii; G. W.'s outbursts against, xxxix; 28, 72, 80–1, 101, 105, 136, 147, 149, 154, 169, 178, 180, 181, 183, 190, 193, 200, 203, 205, 206, 209, 217, 219, 220, 222, 230, 237; and Mrs. Langtry, 230; makes £20,000 grant to Gordon's family, 170; denounced in Gordon's diary, 170
Glover, Sir John, xx
Gordon, General Charles, xiv; Soudanese respect for, 29–30; daily routine during siege, 104; messages to Wolseley, xxxiv, xxxvi; 17, 18, 22, 103; messengers taken prisoner and letters found, 74–5, 114; his astuteness in dealing with Eastern ideas, 30; his journals, 152, 156; news of his death reaches Wolseley, and England, xxxviii; 134, 175; the aftermath, xl–xli; Wolseley's determination to retrieve the speared head, 169, 221; his dairy, 170; Gladstone's grant to the family, 170; Wolseley's opinion of, 23, 43–4, 155, 187
Gough, Maj.-Gen. Sir H. H.
and the Camel Corps, 60; and Mounted Infantry, 64, 72; wounded and sent home, 163–4

Graham, Lt.-Gen. Sir G., 141, 152, 173, 174, 177, 184, 203, 204, 205, 209, 213, 216
Grant, Sir Hope, G. W.'s admiration for, xv
Grant Duff, Sir Mount Stuart, 167
Granville, George Leveson Gower, 2nd Earl, 5; and full powers for G. W. in Soudan, 20, 155-6, 164, 166; proposes release of slaves, 170; on Dongola withdrawal, 200, 204
Great Gate, the (Egypt), 39, 41, 44
Greaves, Maj.-Gen. Sir G. R., 133, 141, 203, 204, 213-14, 225
Greeks, G. W.'s poor opinion of, 36, 102
Grenfell, Col. Francis, 26, 233, 235
Grove, Lt.-Col. Coleridge (Military Secretary to G. W.), 143, 176
Guards Corps, 68; 'the world could not produce finer soldiers', 72-3; G. W. inspects Camel Corps of, 79, 166

Haines, Sir Frederick, xxii
Haliburton, Lord, G. W. on supplies failures by, 18
Hamley, Sir Edward, xx; 185-6; feud with G. S. Clarke, xxiv
Hammill, Comdr. T. F. (R.N.), xxxi, xxxiii; and the Cataracts, 12; and the 'whalers', 47-8; G. W. rebukes, 232
Harcourt, Sir William Vernon, 137, 140, 203; G. W.'s opinion of, 181
Harrison, Col., 50, 66
Hartington, Lord, xxx-xxxi, xxxii; 5, 8, 109, 129, 166, 174, 180, 198, 199, 205 ff. *passim*; G. W.'s opinion of, 23
Hassan, Prince, 188, 189
Hassein (Hussein) Pasha Khalifa, 30, 71, 102, 145
Hassineyah tribe, 123, 137, 157
Hawawir tribe, 106, 115, 119, 120, 137
Hay, Vice-Admiral Lord John, xxxi; 12-13, 35, 236, 237
Henderson, Col. K. G., 66, 190
Herbert, St. Leger, 128, 202
Home, Col. Robert, xx
Hospital ships, supplies and equipment, 112, 115, 207

India, defence of, xxi, xlii
Indian Mutiny, G. W. and the, xv
Intelligence Department, G. W.'s dissatisfaction with, 30

Irish, G. W.'s opinion of the, 57
Irving, Henry (actor), G. W. on, 7
Italian fleet, G. W. on the, 238

Jakdul, xxxvi, xxxvii

Kaibar, 183
Kasm el Moose, 122, 138, 151, 159
Kassala, fall of, 223
Khartoum
taken by Mahdi's troops, 134; altered military situation after fall of, 139, 147; details of fall and the aftermath, 175: *see also* Gordon, General Charles
Khedive of Egypt
G. W. and, 12, 13, 16, 17, 20, 101, 190, 191, 193; hatred of Wilson, 44; alarmed by French attitude in Cairo, 192; and by British withdrawal from Dongola; 'English feelings' of, 237
Khor Moussa Pasha (Nile inlet), 44, 46
Kimberley, Lord (Secretary of State for India), xlii, xliii
Kitchener, Captain Herbert (later Earl), anxious for action, 19, 33; reports Gordon's attack on Berber, 30, 39; Mudir of Dongola 'impertinent' to, 70; sent to Debbeh to bring Sheik Saleh, 120, 122
Koomassee, 133
Korti, xxxii, xxxiv, xxxv, xlii; 89, 172

Langtry, Mrs., and Gladstone, 230
Lanyon, Col. O.T., 177
Layard, Sir Austen, 238
Lloyd, Lt.-Col. F. T., 20, 191
Lupton, Frank (Lupton Bey), 43
Lyon-Fremantle, Maj.-Gen. A. J., 133, 203
Lytton, Lord, and high India post for G. W., xxi

McNiell, Maj.-Gen. Sir John, xxx; 174, 176, 177, 206, 207, 209, 213, 216; Queen Victoria writes of 'unjust slur' on, 230-1
Mahdi, the, xxv, xxx ff. *passim*; G. W. underestimated power of, xxxiii, xxxix-xl, xlii; 'tells his beads' while

others fight, 58–9; G. W.'s peace offer to, 60; the price on his head, 71, 130, 156, 173; Gordon's messages fall into his hands, 74, 75, 114; G. W.'s plans for crushing, 141; and Government's policy for destruction of, 179; his relatives to be seized as hostages, 199; refuses to give up his 'happy prisoners', 226; reports of tribes deserting him after fall of Khartoum
Mahmoud Ahmed: *see* Mahdi
Mahomed el Kheir (Sowarrab Sheik), 89, 90–1, 93, 106, 124, 131
Maurice, Maj.-Gen. Sir J. F., 15, 48, 182
Maxwell, Lt. R. H. (Camp Commandant and Provost Marshal), 50, 125
Merawi, 156, 159, 160, 162, 173, 228
Metemmah, xxxvi; xxxvii, xli, 103, 108, 111, 118, 121, 124–5, 127–8
Molyneux, Capt. J. P. B., 213, 214
Montgomerie, Lt. R. A. J. (R.N.), 51, 89

Napoleon
G. W. on his Egyptian campaign, 27–8; on a country's strongest frontier, 118
Naval Brigade, 71, 111, 128, 161, 162
Navy, G. W. on the, 109, 219
Newspaper correspondents, G. W.'s views on, 83–4, 95–6, 110, 113–14, 163: *see also* entries for individual correspondents.
Norman, Maj.-Gen. Sir Henry, 32
North-West Frontier, problem of Russian influence on, xl, xlii; 161, 166–7, 179–80, 183, 223–4; G. W.'s policy for peaceful solution, 193–204 *passim*
Northbrook, Thomas Baring, Earl of, 5, 11, 14, 18, 19; on British naval supremacy, 21; G. W. and, 225

O'Neal (O'Neil), the Revd. Mr., 63, 94
Osman Digma, 89, 105, 109, 110, 121, 133, 138, 208–9, 210–11

Pall Mall Gazette, G. W. and the, 77, 110
Penjdeh crisis, xliii
Politicians
G. W. on 'cabinet without one manly instinct', 43; his contempt for, 80, 111: *see also* Bright, John; Chamberlain, Joseph; Gladstone, W. E.
Poore, Lt. Richard (R.N.), 56

Power, Frank (*Times* correspondent, on the fellaheen, 43
Pratt, Surg. Maj. W. S., 50, 55, 91; 'abject failure' in charge of mess, 73
Press, G. W. on the, 95, 158: *see also* Newspaper correspondents
Prior, Melton (*Illustrated* correspondent), 84

Red River Expedition (Canada, 1870) G. W. commands, xvii–xviii; comparisons with projected Nile expedition, xxxi, xxxii
Riaz Pasha, 16
River Column, the, xxxv, xli–xlii
Roberts, Gen. Frederick (later Earl), 179
Rowley, Col. C. S., 68, 72; G. W. thinks incompetent, 73
Rundle, Major H. M. (Egyptian Army), 29, 62, 85, 90, 124, 152, 190
Russell, Dr. William (Billy); war correspondent), 83, 95, 202
Russia and the North-West Frontier, xl; 161, 166–7, 179–80, 183, 223–4; G. W.'s policy for peaceful solution, 193–204 *passim*

St. James Gazette, G. W. and the, 77
Saleh, Sheik, 120, 122, 132, 146, 153
Salisbury, Lord, 216, 226, 227, 230
Scott, Major D. A., 188
Seyid el Makki (holy man), 179
Seymour, Capt. Sir Edward, 236
Shakespear, Capt. G. R. J. (Bengal staff Corps), 29
Shendy, 88, 98, 128
Shepheard's Hotel, Cairo, 16
Sint, G. W. at, 20–1
Slatin, Rudolph C., Pasha (Egyptian Army),
takes G. W.'s offer to Mahdi, 62–3; in chains in Mahdi's camp, 102
Smallpox among the troops, 63, 70, 71, 91
Smith, W. H. (bookstall initiator) becomes War Minister, 226, 229, 233
Soldier's Pocket Book, G. W. and the, 67, 117, 220
Soudan, the: British policy and G. W.'s plans to end campaign after Gordon's death, 194, 196 ff. *passim*, 203 ff. *passim*

Sowarreb tube, 89, 90–1, 93, 106, 115, 119, 120
Spies and spying, G. W. on, 97
Staff System: *see* Wolseley 'Ring'
Stephenson, Gen. Sir Frederick, xvi, xxx, xxxii; 11; opposes G. W.'s proposal to station ships at Alexandria, 49; and camel saddle supplies, 53; to operate against Osman Digma, 141; G. W. on, 4–5, 12
Stewart, Brig.-Gen. Sir Herbert, xxxv, xxxvi; 57, 58, 60, 65, 71, 72; appointed Brigadier-General, 75; in G. W.'s plans for advance, 82, 89, 100, 101, 108, 118–19; in 'a real big fight', 121, 123; G. W.'s anxiety for, 124; wounded, 127, 130; the Queen promotes, 129; Buller's denigration of, 166; killed at Abu Klea, xxxvii; G. W. on, 113, 149
Stewart, Col. J., 17; murdered, 31; doubts and rumours following his reported death, 33, 36, 38, 39, 44, 56, 58
Stracey, Col. H. H. D., 73
Suakim, 109, 117, 121, 174, 180, 198, 199; G. W. at, 203
Suakim-Berber railway, proposals for a, xxx, xxxi; 35, 110, 148, 158, 176, 215
Suez Canal, G. W. on control of, 154
Supply problems, xxxiv; 18, 37, 45, 46, 57, 67, 71–2, 90
Swaine, Lt.-Col. L. V., 13, 15, 141, 143

Talbot, Lt.-Col. the Hon. R. A. J., 148, 162
Tani, 161, 176
Tebelu, Gordon's wish to be succeeded by, 17
Tel-el-Kebir
G. W.'s victory at, xxiii; the Queen telegraphs to him on anniversary of, 15
Thompson, Sir Ralph (Permanent USS for War), 8, 215, 226
Tolson, Lt.-Col. Wilfred, 74, 88
Turkey and G. W.'s recommendation that it takes over the Soudan, 162, 194, 229
Turner, Major Alfred E., 173
Tuti Island, xxxviii; 134, 140, 145
'Twelve Mile Hill', 119, 125, 126, 159

Victoria, Queen, xiv, xviii–xix; agrees to relief expedition, 9; refuses creation of a General Staff, xxix; her messages to G. W., 116, 217–18, 230–1; and Gladstone, 116; 'I would die for her', 122; 'pleased with the donkey' from G. W., 227; her early opinion of G. W., xxii
Villiers, Frederick (*Graphic* correspondent), 84, 95
Vincent, Sir Edgar, 32

Wardrop, Major F. M., 14, 65, 70, 89
Warren, Gen. Sir Charles, 177
Wauchope, Maj.-Gen. A. G., 14
Wells, G. W.'s plan to seize the, 120, 133
West Africa, G. W. in, xviii
White, Col. W. R., 167
Whitmore, Gen. Sir Edmund, 11
Wild life, 43, 54, 55, 58, 63, 80, 88, 119
Wilkinson, Spenser, among 'new breed of defence critics', xliv
Will, Dr. G. E., 187, 188
Williams, Charles (correspondent for *Central News*; founder of *Evening News*), 83, 95
Wilson, Sir Charles, xx, xxxx, xxxvii, xxxviii; as the 'scapegoat' xxxix; and Stewart's murder, 56; and the Mudir's 'impertinence', 70; in Nile dash for Khartoum, 134–5; breaks down, 141–2, 164–5; 'I hate the sight of him', 164; 'slur' on, 170; Khedive's hatred of, 44.
Wolseley, Sir Garnet, birth, parentage, education, early career, xv–xvi; first independent command, xvi; Crimean War as inspiration, xvi; and Ashanti campaign, xix; in Natal, Cyprus, Zululand, xxi; failure of ambition to be given Indian command, xxii–xxiii; on his age, health and experiences, 42, 221–2; on effects of his Irish education and surroundings, 77; plans and preparations for expedition, xxxii; 14–15, 185–7; new plan following Gordon's death, 104–5; exhilarated by danger, 125; on civilians' lack of understanding of army's needs, 140, 153; opinion of camels, 37, 69; on use of cavalry against Arabs, 174; his belief in delegation of

work and responsibility, 46, 47; on democracy, 65, 110; on his lack of descriptive powers, 84; his opinion of Englishwomen, 39–40; on fools, 92–160; on strain of inactivity, 129; and jealousy and vanity among his officers, 74, 75, 119, 166; on his ponderous style of letter-writing, 84; and loyalty to the Monarchy, 117, 122; opinion of Ouida (novelist), 134; his peerage, xxiv; on qualifications for a commander, 97–8; as President for Society for Prevention of Bad Language, xiii; his contempt for flattery, 31; his religious faith, and views on the Church, 94, 105–6, 229–30; his relations with Royal Family, 122; gives up smoking 'as a punishment', 29; time as the 'greatest enemy', 119; ambitions for Governorship of Soudan, 155, 166; and the Wolseley 'Ring', xvi, xix–xxi; news of Gordon's death, 134, 175; reads Gordon's journal, 152, 156; new plan after Gordon's death, 104–5; broken failure of expedition, xl, xliii; his spirit of vengeance for death of Gordon, xxxix, xli; text of his General Order on the expedition, 76–7; returns home, 238.

For his opinion of his officers and other personalities, see under entries for individual officers, etc.

Wolseley, Col. George B., (G. W.'s brother), 100, 220

Wolseley 'Ring', the, xvi, xix–xxi, xliii, xliv

Wood, Sir Evelyn, xvi, xx–xxi; and the Nile Cataracts, 12; and Buller, 49; health troubles, 47, 114; and the Boers, 126, 179; becomes Chief of Staff, 129; ordered to vacate desert posts, 151; G. W. offers him command at Assouan, 218, 221; G. W.'s poor opinion of, 4, 14, 31–3, 85, 126, 166

Zebehr, proposal to arrest, 166, 168

Zohrab Bey, 50, 55, 57, 65, 71, 82, 84, 106, 107, 148, 171, 176, 192, 235, 236

3 1247 00367 4520